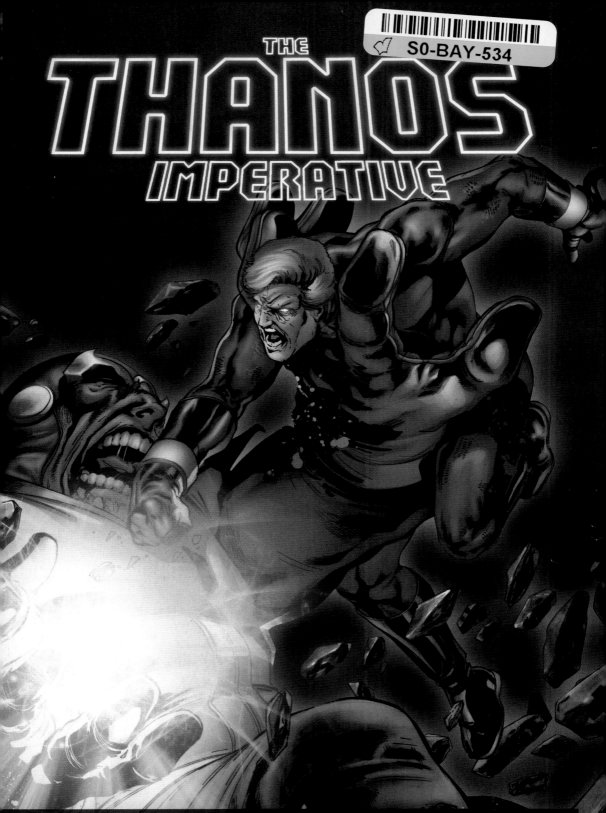

THE THANOS IMPERATIVE. Contains material originally published in magazine form as THE THANOS IMPERATIVE: IGNITION, THE THANOS IMPERATIVE #1-6 and THE THANOS IMPERATIVE: DEVASTATION. Second printing 2014. ISBN# 978-0-7851-4902-6. Published by MARVEL WORLDWIDE, INC., a subsidiary of MARVEL ENTERTAINMENT, LLC. OFFICE OF PUBLICATION: 135 West 50th Street, New York, NY 10020. Copyright © 2010 and 2011 Marvel Characters, Inc. All rights reserved. All characters featured in this issue and the distinctive names and likenesses thereof, and all related indicia are trademarks of Marvel Characters, Inc. No similarity between any of the names, characters, persons, and/or institutions in this magazine with those of any living or dead person or institution is intended, and any such similarity which may exist is purely coincidental. Printed in the U.S.A. ALAN FINE, EVP - Office of the President, Marvel Worldwide, Inc. and EVP & CMO Marvel Characters B.V.; DAN BUCKLEY, Publisher & President - Print, Animation & Digital Divisions; JOE QUESADA, Chief Creative Officer; TOM BREVOORT, SVP of Publishing; DAVID BOGART, SVP of Operations & Procurement, Publishing; C.B. CEBULSKI, SVP of Creator & Content Development; DAVID GABRIEL, SVP of Print & Digital Publishing Sales; JIM O'KEEFE, VP of Operations & Logistics; DAN CARR, Executive Director of Publishing Technology; SUSAN CRESPI, Editorial Operations Manager; ALEX MORALES, Publishing Operations Manager; STAN LEE, Chairman Emeritus. For information regarding advertising in Marvel Comics or on Marvel.com, please contact Niza Disla, Director of Marvel Partnerships, at ndisla@marvel.com. For Marvel subscription inquiries, please call 800-217-9158. Manufactured between 11/26/2013 and 12/29/2013 by QUAD/GRAPHICS, VERSAILLES, KY, USA.

10 9 8 7 6 5 4 3 2

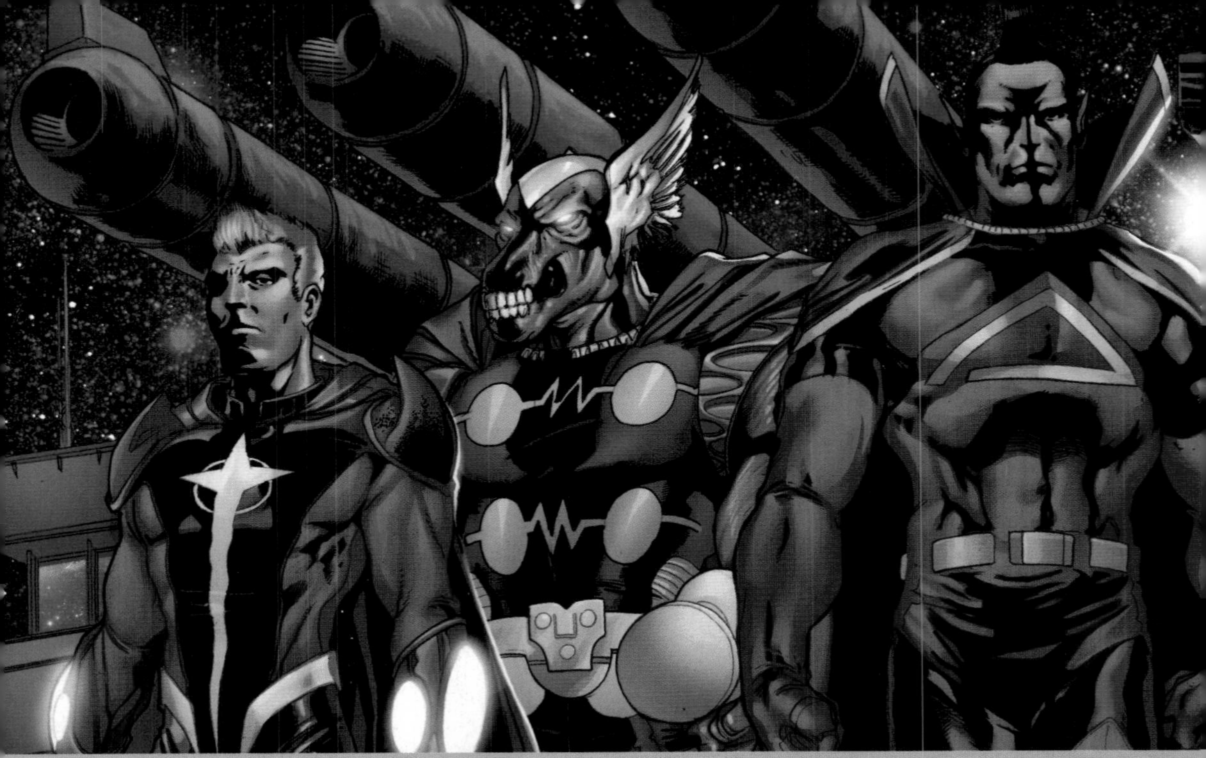

THE THANOS IMPERATIVE

WRITERS
DAN ABNETT & ANDY LANNING

THE THANOS IMPERATIVE: IGNITION

PENCILER
BRAD WALKER
INKER
ANDREW HENNESSY
COLORIST
WIL QUINTANA

THE THANOS IMPERATIVE

ARTIST
MIGUEL SEPULVEDA
COLORIST
JAY DAVID RAMOS WITH WIL QUINTANA

THE THANOS IMPERATIVE: DEVASTATION

ARTIST
MIGUEL SEPULVEDA
COLORIST
RAIN BEREDO

LETTERER
VC'S JOE CARAMAGNA
COVER ARTISTS
ALEKSI BRICLOT & ALEX GARNER
ASSISTANT EDITORS
RACHEL PINNELAS WITH JOHN DENNING
EDITOR
BILL ROSEMANN

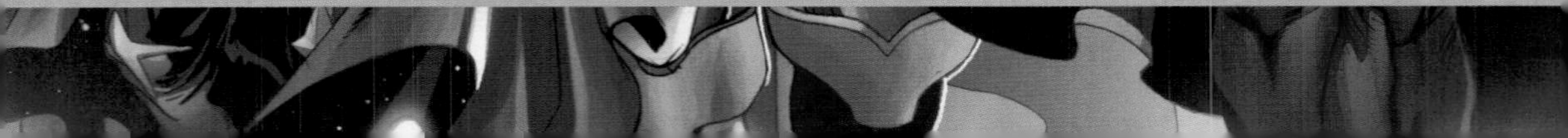

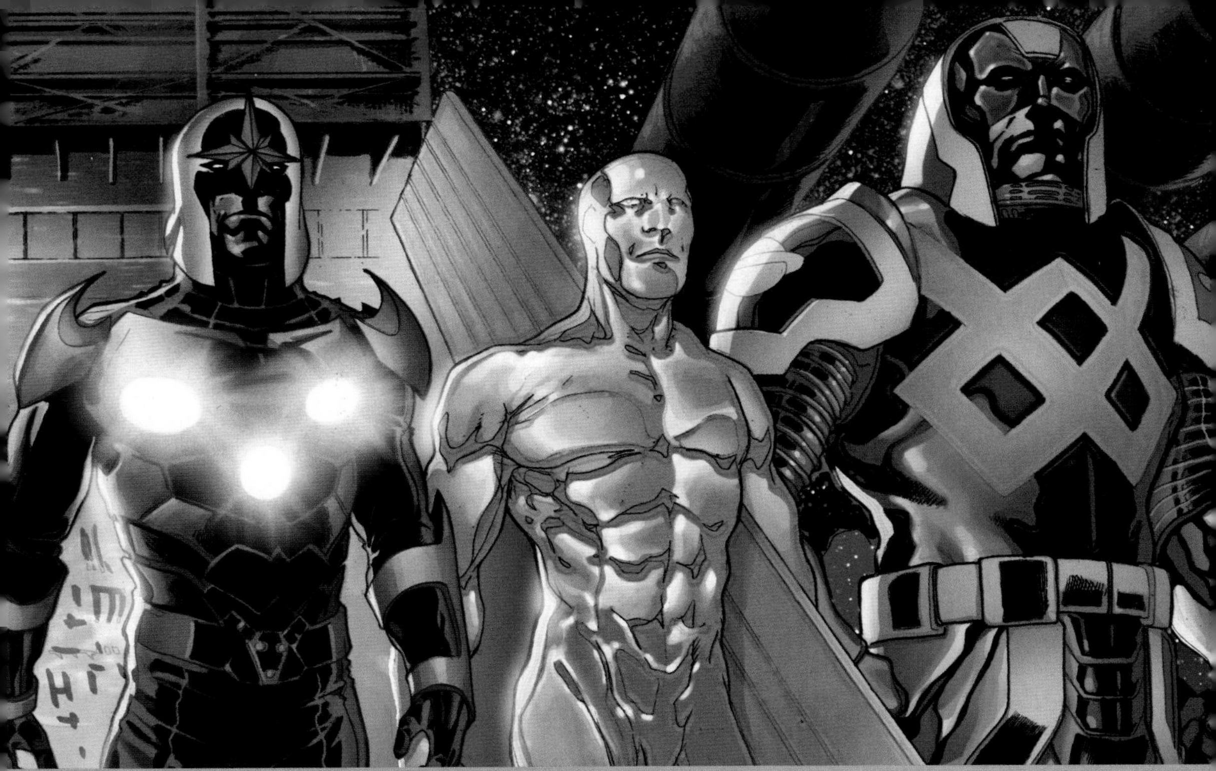

COLLECTION EDITOR
CORY LEVINE
ASSISTANT EDITORS
MATT MASDEU, ALEX STARBUCK & NELSON RIBEIRO
EDITORS, SPECIAL PROJECTS
JENNIFER GRÜNWALD & MARK D. BEAZLEY
SENIOR EDITOR, SPECIAL PROJECTS
JEFF YOUNGQUIST
SVP OF PRINT & DIGITAL PUBLISHING SALES
DAVID GABRIEL
BOOK DESIGN
ARLENE SO

EDITOR IN CHIEF
AXEL ALONSO
CHIEF CREATIVE OFFICER
JOE QUESADA
PUBLISHER
DAN BUCKLEY
EXECUTIVE PRODUCER
ALAN FINE

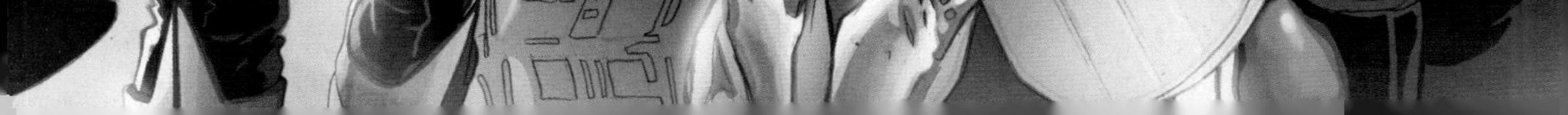

ALEKSI

THE THANOS IMPERATIVE

AFTER A SERIES OF FEROCIOUS INTERSTELLAR WARS, THE FABRIC OF TIME AND SPACE HAS BEEN WEAKENED, AND THE WALLS OF OUR UNIVERSE ITSELF HAVE BEGUN TO TEAR.

THE YOUNG EARTHMAN NAMED *RICHARD RIDER* IS THE LAST *NOVA*, AN EMPOWERED FORCE OF CHAMPIONS WHO ONCE PROTECTED THE GALAXY. RIDER HAS DISCOVERED THAT THE LARGEST TIME-SPACE TEAR, A VAST REGION KNOWN AS THE FAULT, IS A GATEWAY TO ANOTHER UNIVERSE, A HIDEOUS REFLECTION OF OUR OWN NICKNAMED THE CANCERVERSE.

ADAM MAGUS, THE INSANE CHARISMATIC LEADING THE UNIVERSAL CHURCH OF TRUTH, HAS HARNESSED THE CHURCH'S GREAT RESERVOIRS OF BELIEF ENERGY TO SPLIT THE FAULT AND USHER IN THE MALEVOLENT MANY ANGLED GODS OF THE CANCERVERSE.

PETER QUILL, A.K.A. *STAR-LORD*, IS THE LEADER OF A GROUP OF MISFIT ADVENTURERS KNOWN AS THE *GUARDIANS OF THE GALAXY.* HE KNOWS THAT THE CANCERVERSE IS A PLACE WHERE DEATH IS EXTINCT AND LIFE HAS TRIUMPHED. HE ALSO KNOWS THERE IS ONLY ONE THING THAT CAN STOP THAT DARK REALM'S INVADING FORCES...

...*THANOS*, THE MAD TITAN, AVATAR OF DEATH.

UNFORTUNATELY, THANOS IS DEAD.

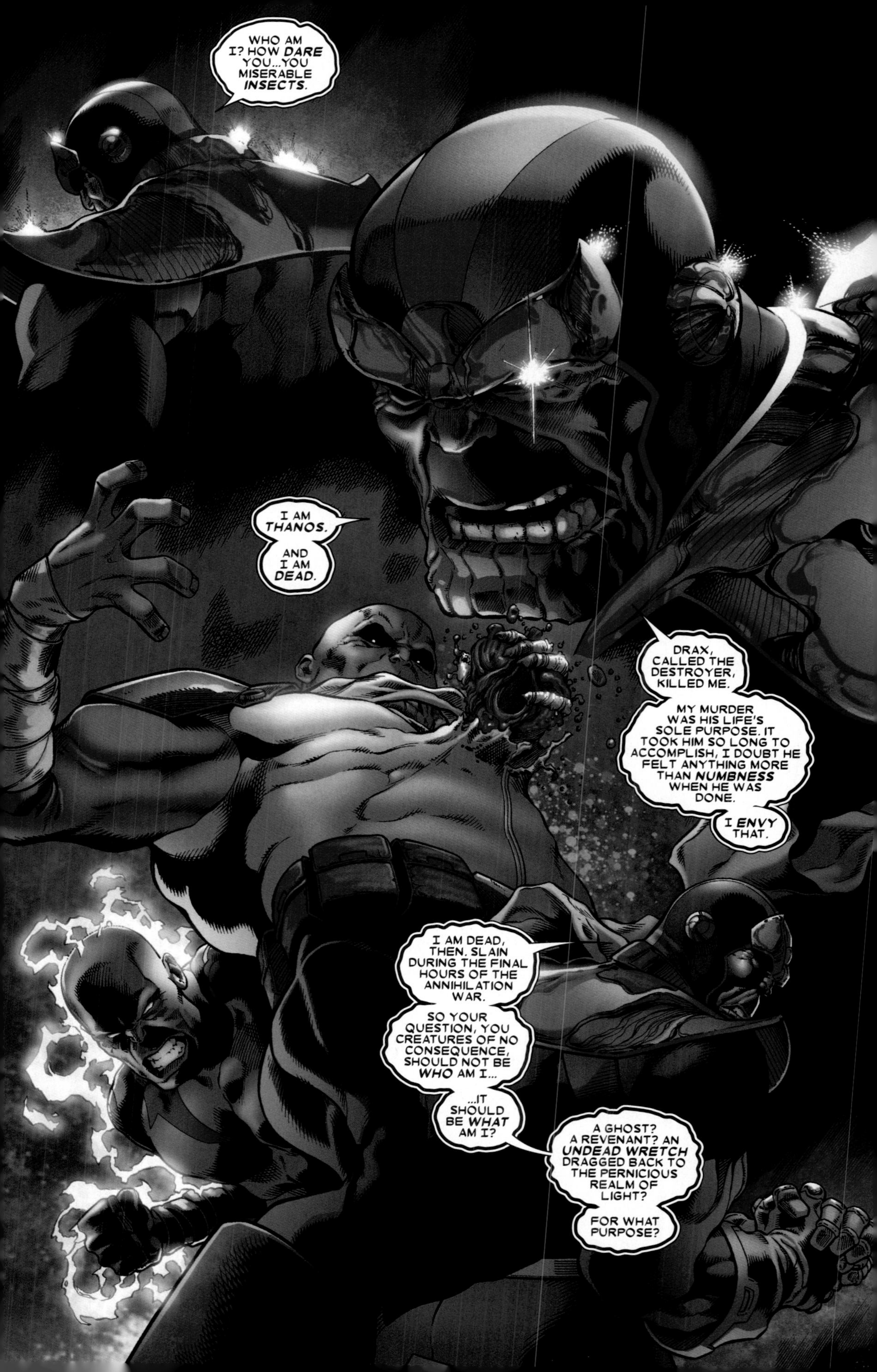
WHO AM I? HOW DARE YOU...YOU MISERABLE INSECTS.
I AM THANOS.
AND I AM DEAD.
DRAX, CALLED THE DESTROYER, KILLED ME.
MY MURDER WAS HIS LIFE'S SOLE PURPOSE. IT TOOK HIM SO LONG TO ACCOMPLISH, I DOUBT HE FELT ANYTHING MORE THAN NUMBNESS WHEN HE WAS DONE.
I ENVY THAT.
I AM DEAD, THEN. SLAIN DURING THE FINAL HOURS OF THE ANNIHILATION WAR.
SO YOUR QUESTION, YOU CREATURES OF NO CONSEQUENCE, SHOULD NOT BE WHO AM I...
...IT SHOULD BE WHAT AM I?
A GHOST? A REVENANT? AN UNDEAD WRETCH DRAGGED BACK TO THE PERNICIOUS REALM OF LIGHT?
FOR WHAT PURPOSE?

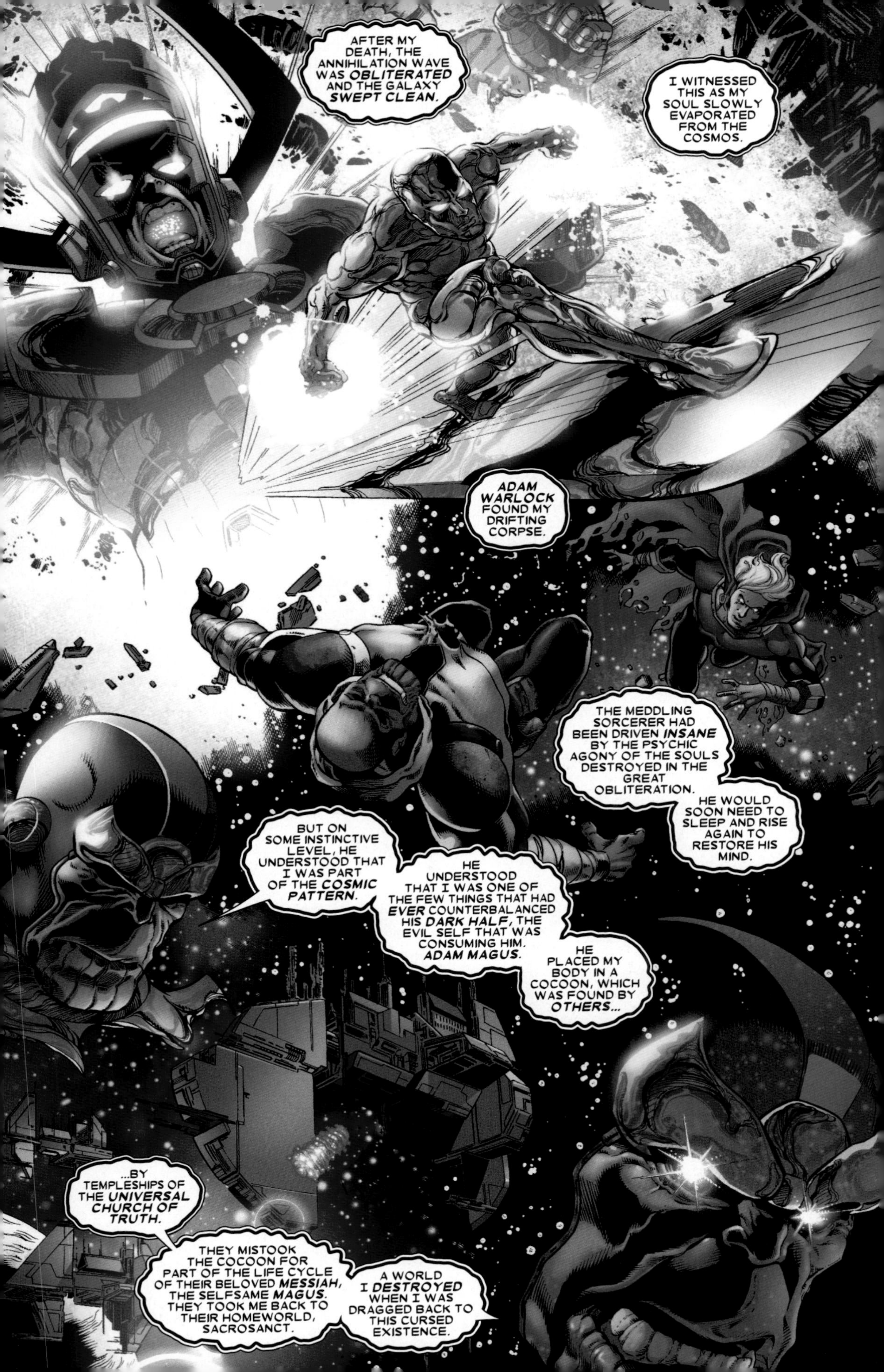
AFTER MY DEATH, THE ANNIHILATION WAVE WAS OBLITERATED AND THE GALAXY SWEPT CLEAN.
I WITNESSED THIS AS MY SOUL SLOWLY EVAPORATED FROM THE COSMOS.
ADAM WARLOCK FOUND MY DRIFTING CORPSE.
THE MEDDLING SORCERER HAD BEEN DRIVEN INSANE BY THE PSYCHIC AGONY OF THE SOULS DESTROYED IN THE GREAT OBLITERATION.
HE WOULD SOON NEED TO SLEEP AND RISE AGAIN TO RESTORE HIS MIND.
BUT ON SOME INSTINCTIVE LEVEL, HE UNDERSTOOD THAT I WAS PART OF THE COSMIC PATTERN.
HE UNDERSTOOD THAT I WAS ONE OF THE FEW THINGS THAT HAD EVER COUNTERBALANCED HIS DARK HALF, THE EVIL SELF THAT WAS CONSUMING HIM. ADAM MAGUS.
HE PLACED MY BODY IN A COCOON, WHICH WAS FOUND BY OTHERS...
...BY TEMPLESHIPS OF THE UNIVERSAL CHURCH OF TRUTH.
THEY MISTOOK THE COCOON FOR PART OF THE LIFE CYCLE OF THEIR BELOVED MESSIAH, THE SELFSAME MAGUS. THEY TOOK ME BACK TO THEIR HOMEWORLD, SACROSANCT.
A WORLD I DESTROYED WHEN I WAS DRAGGED BACK TO THIS CURSED EXISTENCE.

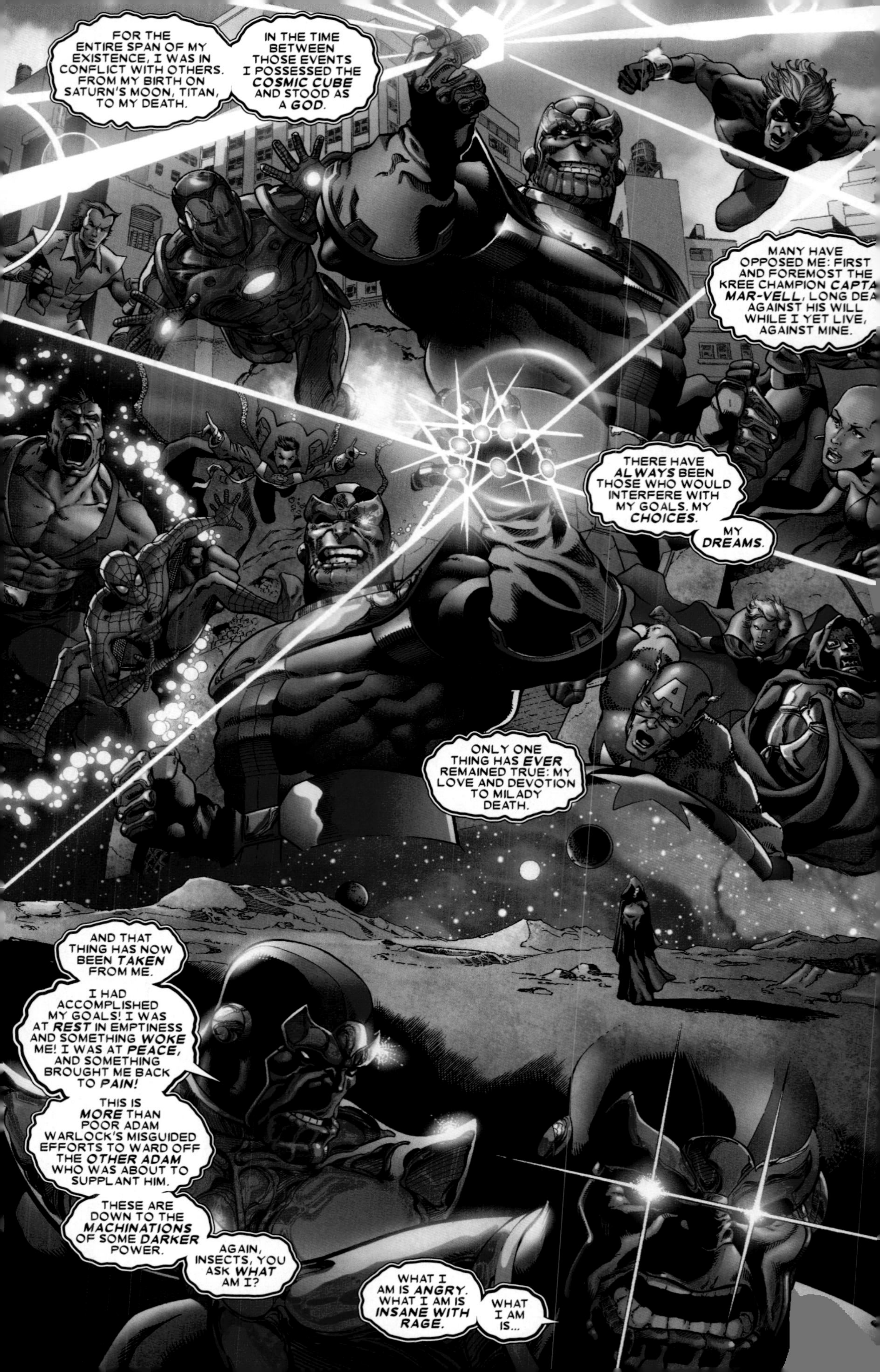

FOR THE ENTIRE SPAN OF MY EXISTENCE, I WAS IN CONFLICT WITH OTHERS. FROM MY BIRTH ON SATURN'S MOON, TITAN, TO MY DEATH.
IN THE TIME BETWEEN THOSE EVENTS I POSSESSED THE COSMIC CUBE AND STOOD AS A GOD.
MANY HAVE OPPOSED ME: FIRST AND FOREMOST THE KREE CHAMPION CAPTA MAR-VELL, LONG DEA AGAINST HIS WILL WHILE I YET LIVE, AGAINST MINE.
THERE HAVE ALWAYS BEEN THOSE WHO WOULD INTERFERE WITH MY GOALS. MY CHOICES.
MY DREAMS.
ONLY ONE THING HAS EVER REMAINED TRUE: MY LOVE AND DEVOTION TO MILADY DEATH.
AND THAT THING HAS NOW BEEN TAKEN FROM ME.
I HAD ACCOMPLISHED MY GOALS! I WAS AT REST IN EMPTINESS AND SOMETHING WOKE ME! I WAS AT PEACE, AND SOMETHING BROUGHT ME BACK TO PAIN!
THIS IS MORE THAN POOR ADAM WARLOCK'S MISGUIDED EFFORTS TO WARD OFF THE OTHER ADAM WHO WAS ABOUT TO SUPPLANT HIM.
THESE ARE DOWN TO THE MACHINATIONS OF SOME DARKER POWER.
AGAIN, INSECTS, YOU ASK WHAT AM I?
WHAT I AM IS ANGRY. WHAT I AM IS INSANE WITH RAGE.
WHAT I AM IS...

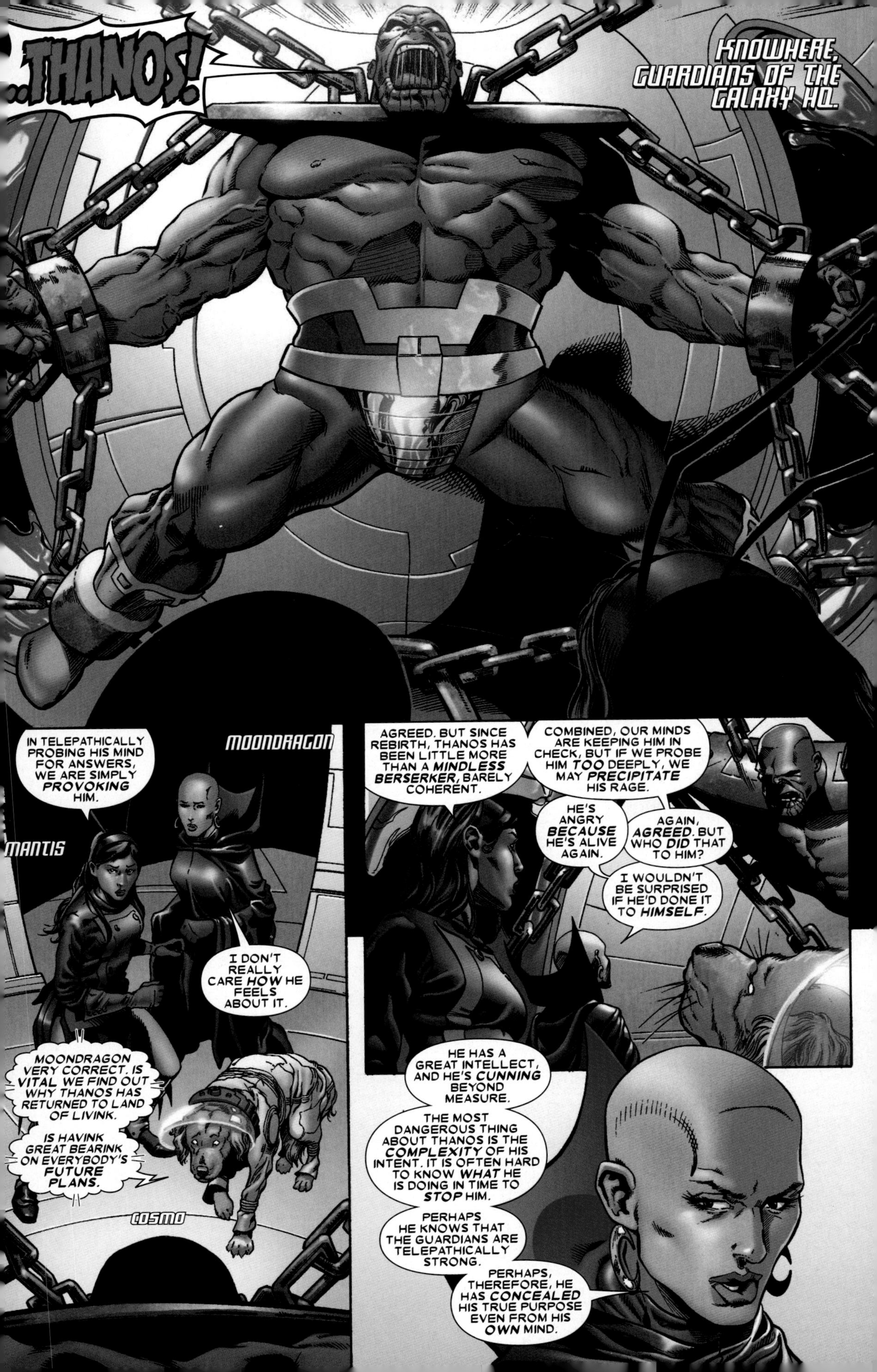
..THANOS!
KNOWHERE, GUARDIANS OF THE GALAXY HQ.
MOONDRAGON
MANTIS
IN TELEPATHICALLY PROBING HIS MIND FOR ANSWERS, WE ARE SIMPLY PROVOKING HIM.
I DON'T REALLY CARE HOW HE FEELS ABOUT IT.
MOONDRAGON VERY CORRECT. IS VITAL WE FIND OUT WHY THANOS HAS RETURNED TO LAND OF LIVINK.
IS HAVINK GREAT BEARINK ON EVERYBODY'S FUTURE PLANS.
COSMO
AGREED. BUT SINCE REBIRTH, THANOS HAS BEEN LITTLE MORE THAN A MINDLESS BERSERKER, BARELY COHERENT.
COMBINED, OUR MINDS ARE KEEPING HIM IN CHECK, BUT IF WE PROBE HIM TOO DEEPLY, WE MAY PRECIPITATE HIS RAGE.
HE'S ANGRY BECAUSE HE'S ALIVE AGAIN.
AGAIN, AGREED. BUT WHO DID THAT TO HIM?
I WOULDN'T BE SURPRISED IF HE'D DONE IT TO HIMSELF.
HE HAS A GREAT INTELLECT, AND HE'S CUNNING BEYOND MEASURE.
THE MOST DANGEROUS THING ABOUT THANOS IS THE COMPLEXITY OF HIS INTENT. IT IS OFTEN HARD TO KNOW WHAT HE IS DOING IN TIME TO STOP HIM.
PERHAPS HE KNOWS THAT THE GUARDIANS ARE TELEPATHICALLY STRONG.
PERHAPS, THEREFORE, HE HAS CONCEALED HIS TRUE PURPOSE EVEN FROM HIS OWN MIND.

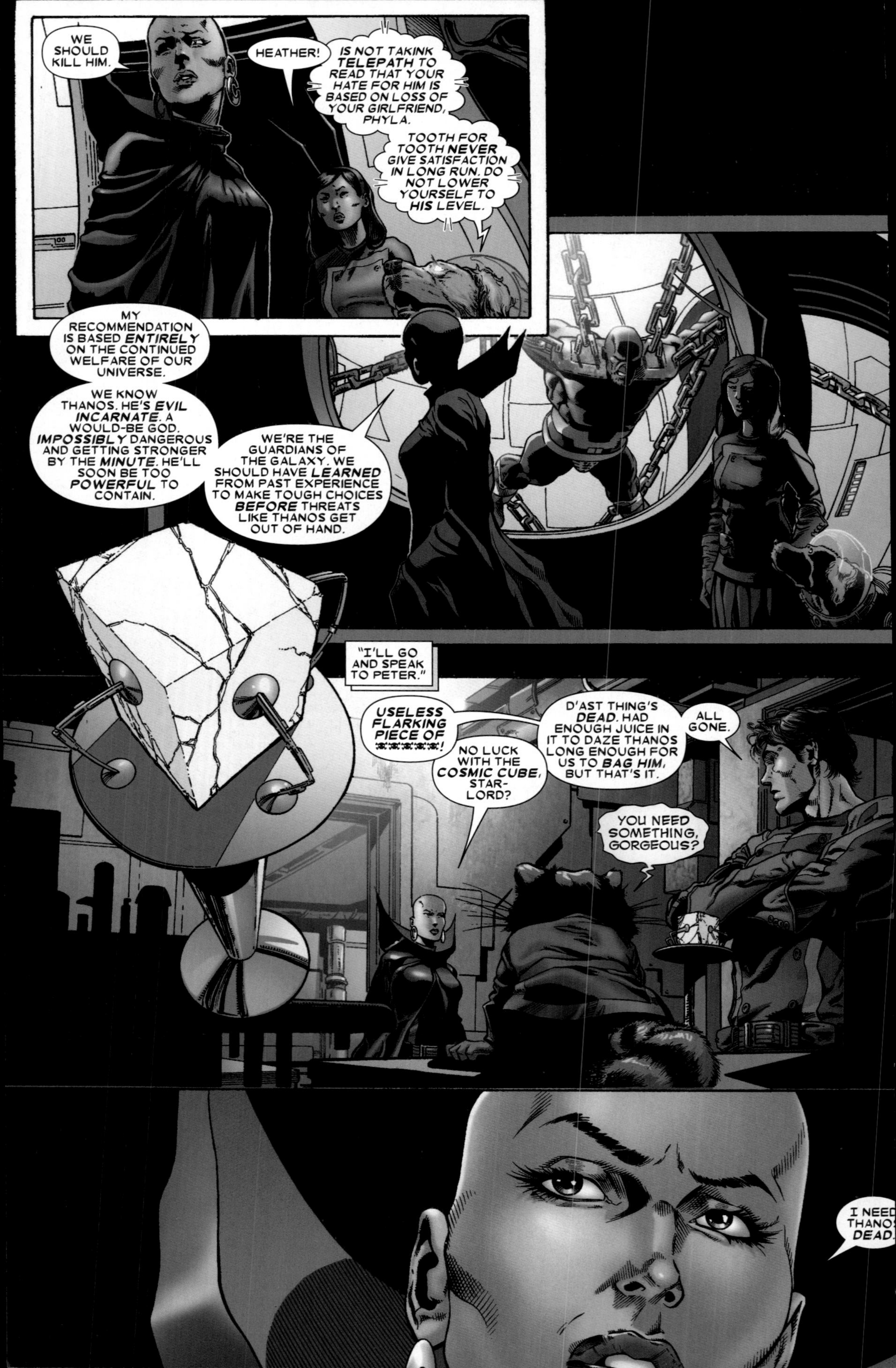
WE SHOULD KILL HIM.
HEATHER!
IS NOT TAKINK TELEPATH TO READ THAT YOUR HATE FOR HIM IS BASED ON LOSS OF YOUR GIRLFRIEND, PHYLA.
TOOTH FOR TOOTH NEVER GIVE SATISFACTION IN LONG RUN. DO NOT LOWER YOURSELF TO HIS LEVEL.
MY RECOMMENDATION IS BASED ENTIRELY ON THE CONTINUED WELFARE OF OUR UNIVERSE.
WE KNOW THANOS. HE'S EVIL INCARNATE. A WOULD-BE GOD. IMPOSSIBLY DANGEROUS AND GETTING STRONGER BY THE MINUTE. HE'LL SOON BE TOO POWERFUL TO CONTAIN.
WE'RE THE GUARDIANS OF THE GALAXY. WE SHOULD HAVE LEARNED FROM PAST EXPERIENCE TO MAKE TOUGH CHOICES BEFORE THREATS LIKE THANOS GET OUT OF HAND.
"I'LL GO AND SPEAK TO PETER."
USELESS FLARKING PIECE OF
NO LUCK WITH THE COSMIC CUBE, STAR-LORD?
D'AST THING'S DEAD. HAD ENOUGH JUICE IN IT TO DAZE THANOS LONG ENOUGH FOR US TO BAG HIM, BUT THAT'S IT.
ALL GONE.
YOU NEED SOMETHING, GORGEOUS?
I NEED THANOS DEAD.

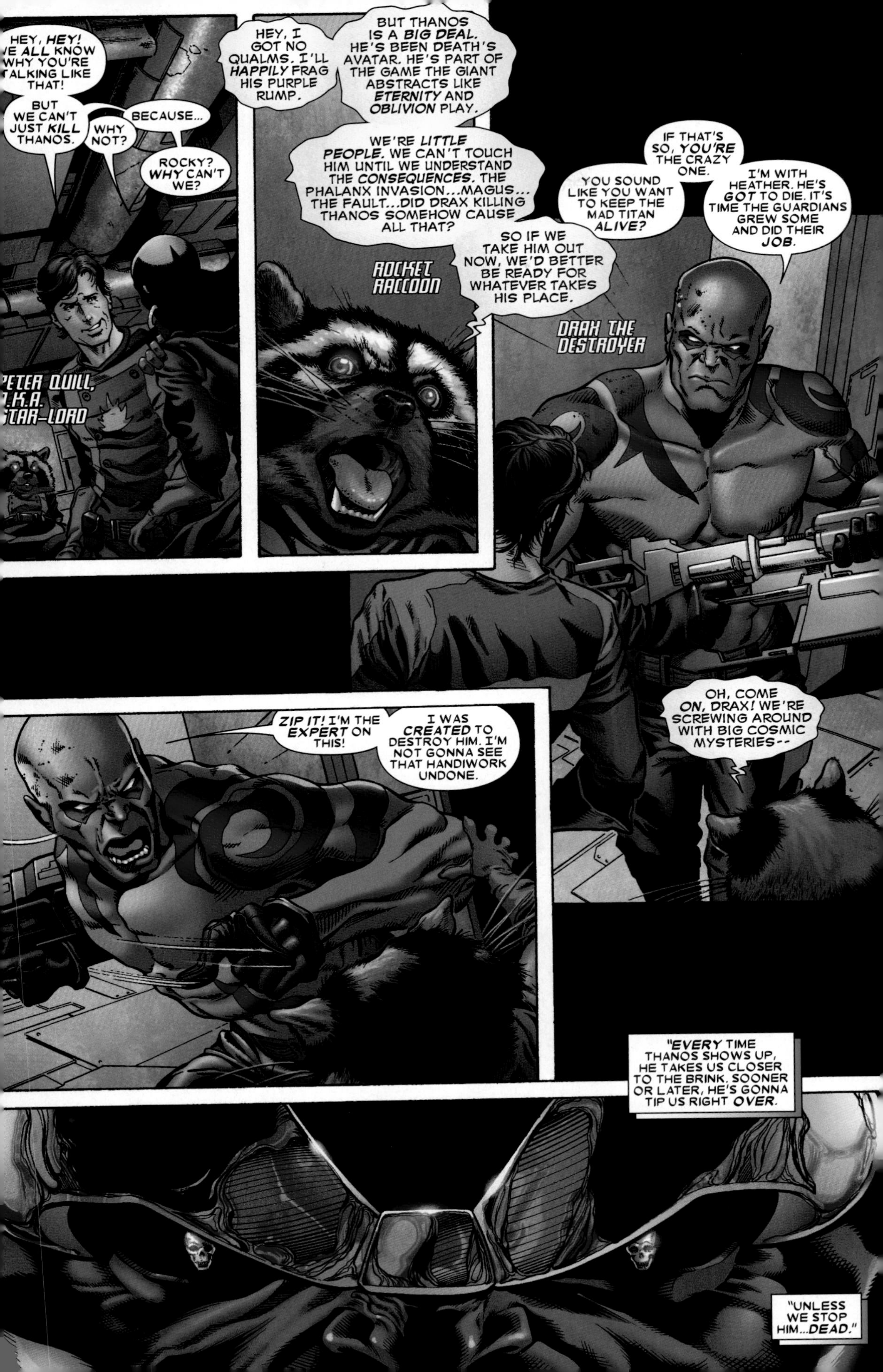
HEY, HEY! WE ALL KNOW WHY YOU'RE TALKING LIKE THAT!
BUT WE CAN'T JUST KILL THANOS.
WHY NOT?
BECAUSE...
ROCKY? WHY CAN'T WE?
PETER QUILL, A.K.A. STAR-LORD
HEY, I GOT NO QUALMS. I'LL HAPPILY FRAG HIS PURPLE RUMP.
BUT THANOS IS A BIG DEAL. HE'S BEEN DEATH'S AVATAR. HE'S PART OF THE GAME THE GIANT ABSTRACTS LIKE ETERNITY AND OBLIVION PLAY.
WE'RE LITTLE PEOPLE. WE CAN'T TOUCH HIM UNTIL WE UNDERSTAND THE CONSEQUENCES. THE PHALANX INVASION...MAGUS... THE FAULT...DID DRAX KILLING THANOS SOMEHOW CAUSE ALL THAT?
SO IF WE TAKE HIM OUT NOW, WE'D BETTER BE READY FOR WHATEVER TAKES HIS PLACE.
ROCKET RACCOON
YOU SOUND LIKE YOU WANT TO KEEP THE MAD TITAN ALIVE?
IF THAT'S SO, YOU'RE THE CRAZY ONE.
I'M WITH HEATHER. HE'S GOT TO DIE. IT'S TIME THE GUARDIANS GREW SOME AND DID THEIR JOB.
DRAX THE DESTROYER
OH, COME ON, DRAX! WE'RE SCREWING AROUND WITH BIG COSMIC MYSTERIES--
ZIP IT! I'M THE EXPERT ON THIS!
I WAS CREATED TO DESTROY HIM. I'M NOT GONNA SEE THAT HANDIWORK UNDONE.
"EVERY TIME THANOS SHOWS UP, HE TAKES US CLOSER TO THE BRINK. SOONER OR LATER, HE'S GONNA TIP US RIGHT OVER.
"UNLESS WE STOP HIM...DEAD."

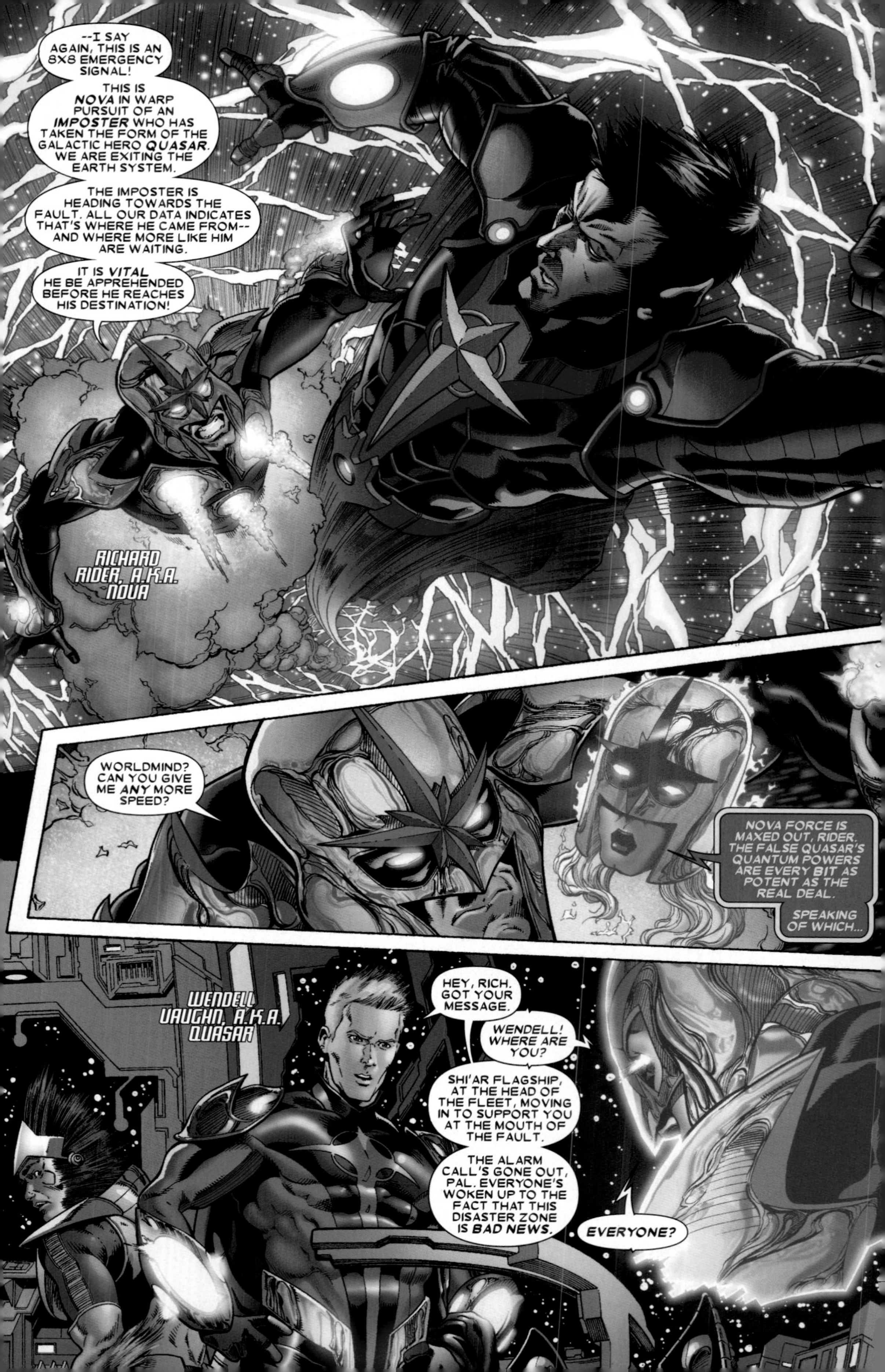
--I SAY AGAIN, THIS IS AN 8X8 EMERGENCY SIGNAL!
THIS IS NOVA IN WARP PURSUIT OF AN IMPOSTER WHO HAS TAKEN THE FORM OF THE GALACTIC HERO QUASAR. WE ARE EXITING THE EARTH SYSTEM.
THE IMPOSTER IS HEADING TOWARDS THE FAULT. ALL OUR DATA INDICATES THAT'S WHERE HE CAME FROM--AND WHERE MORE LIKE HIM ARE WAITING.
IT IS VITAL HE BE APPREHENDED BEFORE HE REACHES HIS DESTINATION!
RICHARD RIDER, A.K.A. NOVA
WORLDMIND? CAN YOU GIVE ME ANY MORE SPEED?
NOVA FORCE IS MAXED OUT, RIDER. THE FALSE QUASAR'S QUANTUM POWERS ARE EVERY BIT AS POTENT AS THE REAL DEAL.
SPEAKING OF WHICH...
WENDELL VAUGHN, A.K.A. QUASAR
HEY, RICH. GOT YOUR MESSAGE.
WENDELL! WHERE ARE YOU?
SHI'AR FLAGSHIP, AT THE HEAD OF THE FLEET, MOVING IN TO SUPPORT YOU AT THE MOUTH OF THE FAULT.
THE ALARM CALL'S GONE OUT, PAL. EVERYONE'S WOKEN UP TO THE FACT THAT THIS DISASTER ZONE IS BAD NEWS.
EVERYONE?

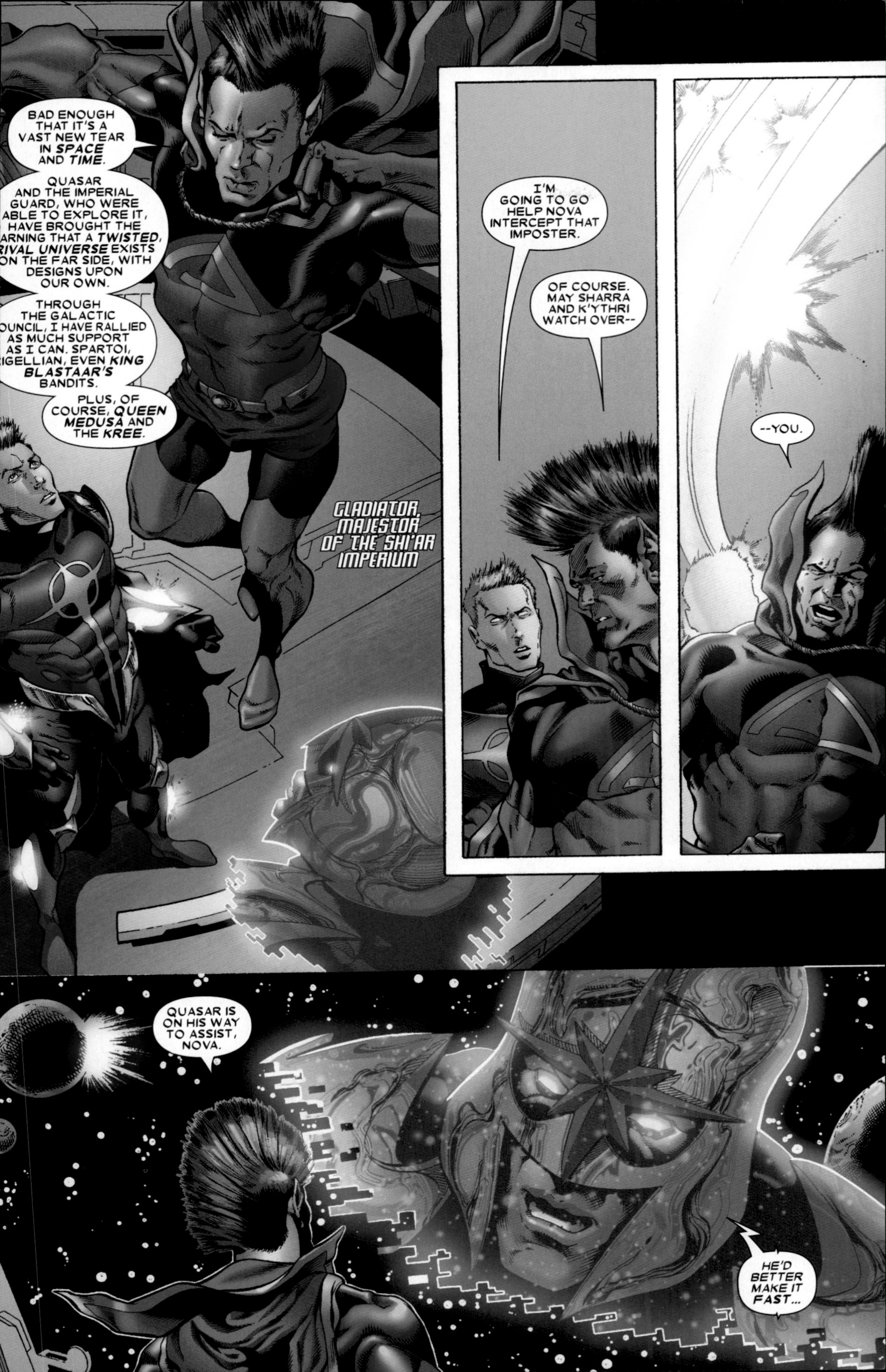
BAD ENOUGH THAT IT'S A VAST NEW TEAR IN SPACE AND TIME.
QUASAR AND THE IMPERIAL GUARD, WHO WERE ABLE TO EXPLORE IT, HAVE BROUGHT THE WARNING THAT A TWISTED, RIVAL UNIVERSE EXISTS ON THE FAR SIDE, WITH DESIGNS UPON OUR OWN.
THROUGH THE GALACTIC COUNCIL, I HAVE RALLIED AS MUCH SUPPORT AS I CAN. SPARTOI, RIGELLIAN, EVEN KING BLASTAAR'S BANDITS.
PLUS, OF COURSE, QUEEN MEDUSA AND THE KREE.
GLADIATOR, MAJESTOR OF THE SHI'AR IMPERIUM
I'M GOING TO GO HELP NOVA INTERCEPT THAT IMPOSTER.
OF COURSE. MAY SHARRA AND K'YTHRI WATCH OVER--
--YOU.
QUASAR IS ON HIS WAY TO ASSIST, NOVA.
HE'D BETTER MAKE IT FAST...

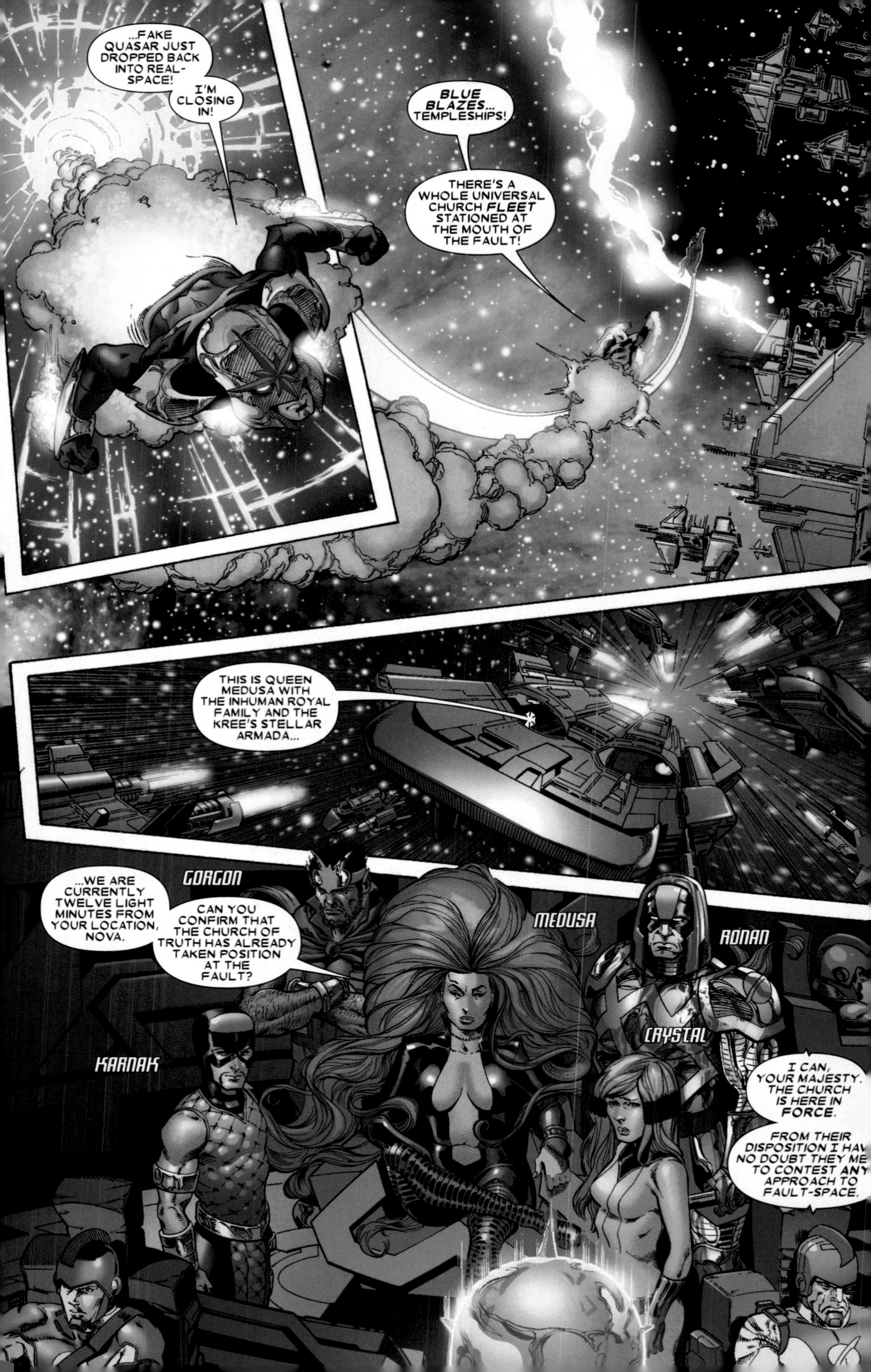
...FAKE QUASAR JUST DROPPED BACK INTO REAL-SPACE!
I'M CLOSING IN!
BLUE BLAZES... TEMPLESHIPS!
THERE'S A WHOLE UNIVERSAL CHURCH FLEET STATIONED AT THE MOUTH OF THE FAULT!
THIS IS QUEEN MEDUSA WITH THE INHUMAN ROYAL FAMILY AND THE KREE'S STELLAR ARMADA...
...WE ARE CURRENTLY TWELVE LIGHT MINUTES FROM YOUR LOCATION, NOVA.
CAN YOU CONFIRM THAT THE CHURCH OF TRUTH HAS ALREADY TAKEN POSITION AT THE FAULT?
GORGON
MEDUSA
RONAN
CRYSTAL
KARNAK
I CAN, YOUR MAJESTY. THE CHURCH IS HERE IN FORCE.
FROM THEIR DISPOSITION I HAV NO DOUBT THEY ME TO CONTEST ANY APPROACH TO FAULT-SPACE.

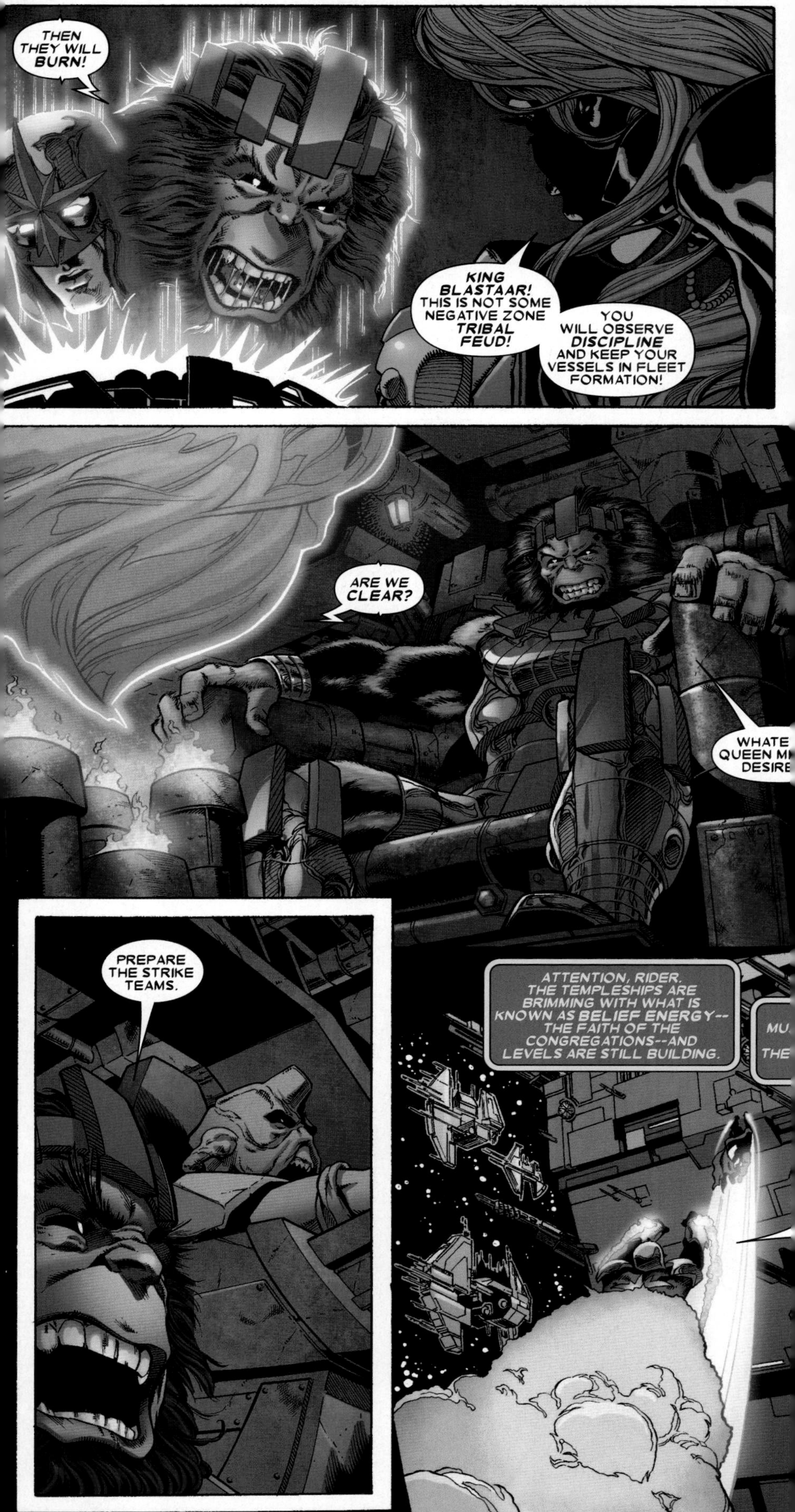
THEN THEY WILL BURN!
KING BLASTAAR! THIS IS NOT SOME NEGATIVE ZONE TRIBAL FEUD!
YOU WILL OBSERVE DISCIPLINE AND KEEP YOUR VESSELS IN FLEET FORMATION!
ARE WE CLEAR?
PREPARE THE STRIKE TEAMS.
ATTENTION, RIDER. THE TEMPLESHIPS ARE BRIMMING WITH WHAT IS KNOWN AS BELIEF ENERGY-- THE FAITH OF THE CONGREGATIONS--AND LEVELS ARE STILL BUILDING.

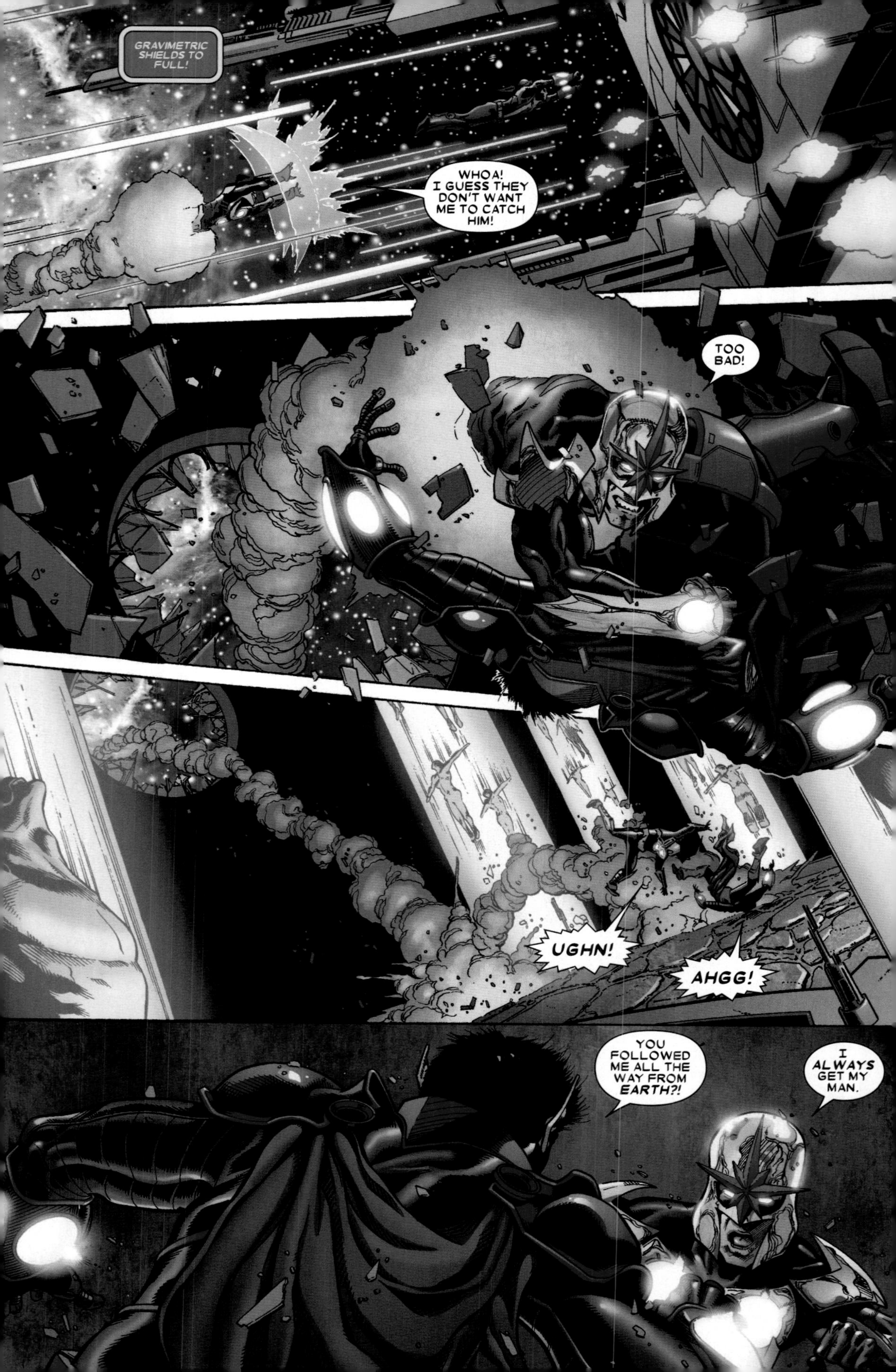
GRAVIMETRIC SHIELDS TO FULL!
WHOA! I GUESS THEY DON'T WANT ME TO CATCH HIM!
TOO BAD!
UGHN!
AHGG!
YOU FOLLOWED ME ALL THE WAY FROM EARTH?!
I ALWAYS GET MY MAN.

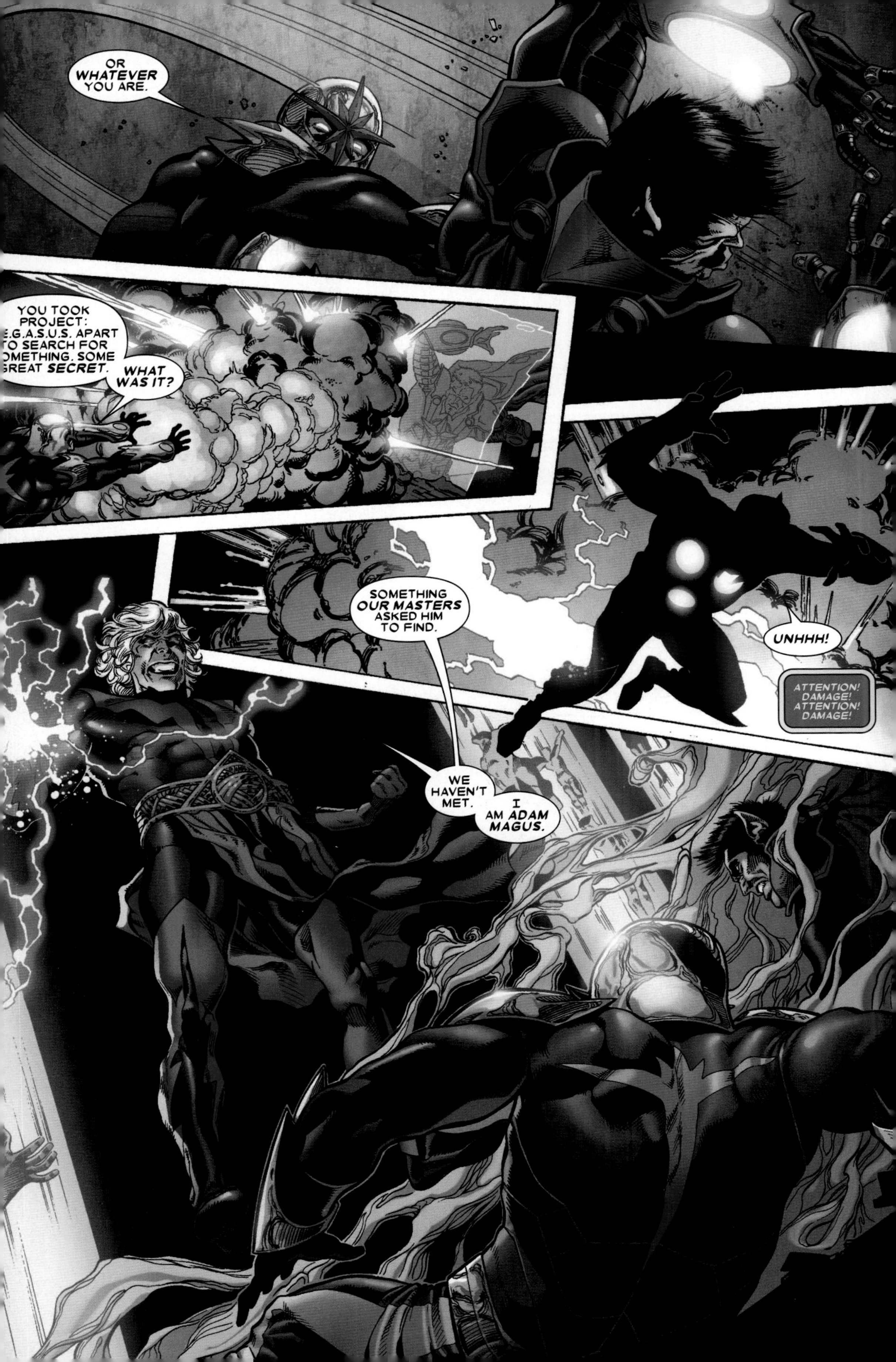
OR WHATEVER YOU ARE.
YOU TOOK PROJECT: P.E.G.A.S.U.S. APART TO SEARCH FOR SOMETHING. SOME GREAT SECRET.
WHAT WAS IT?
SOMETHING OUR MASTERS ASKED HIM TO FIND.
UNHHH!
ATTENTION! DAMAGE! ATTENTION! DAMAGE!
WE HAVEN'T MET.
I AM ADAM MAGUS.

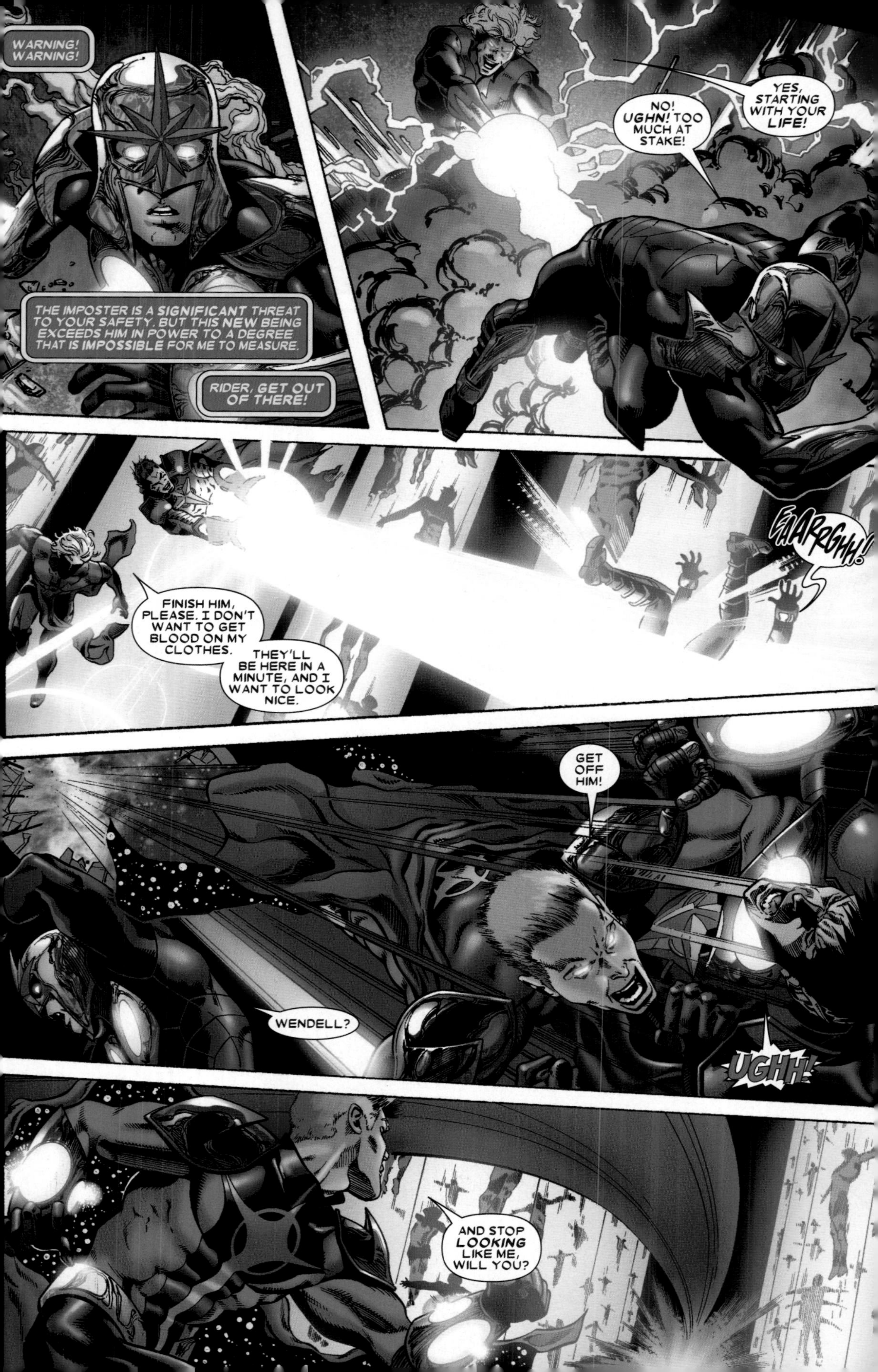
WARNING! WARNING!
THE IMPOSTER IS A SIGNIFICANT THREAT TO YOUR SAFETY. BUT THIS NEW BEING EXCEEDS HIM IN POWER TO A DEGREE THAT IS IMPOSSIBLE FOR ME TO MEASURE.
RIDER, GET OUT OF THERE!
NO! UGHN! TOO MUCH AT STAKE!
YES, STARTING WITH YOUR LIFE!
EAARRGHH!
FINISH HIM, PLEASE. I DON'T WANT TO GET BLOOD ON MY CLOTHES.
THEY'LL BE HERE IN A MINUTE, AND I WANT TO LOOK NICE.
GET OFF HIM!
WENDELL?
UGHH!
AND STOP LOOKING LIKE ME, WILL YOU?

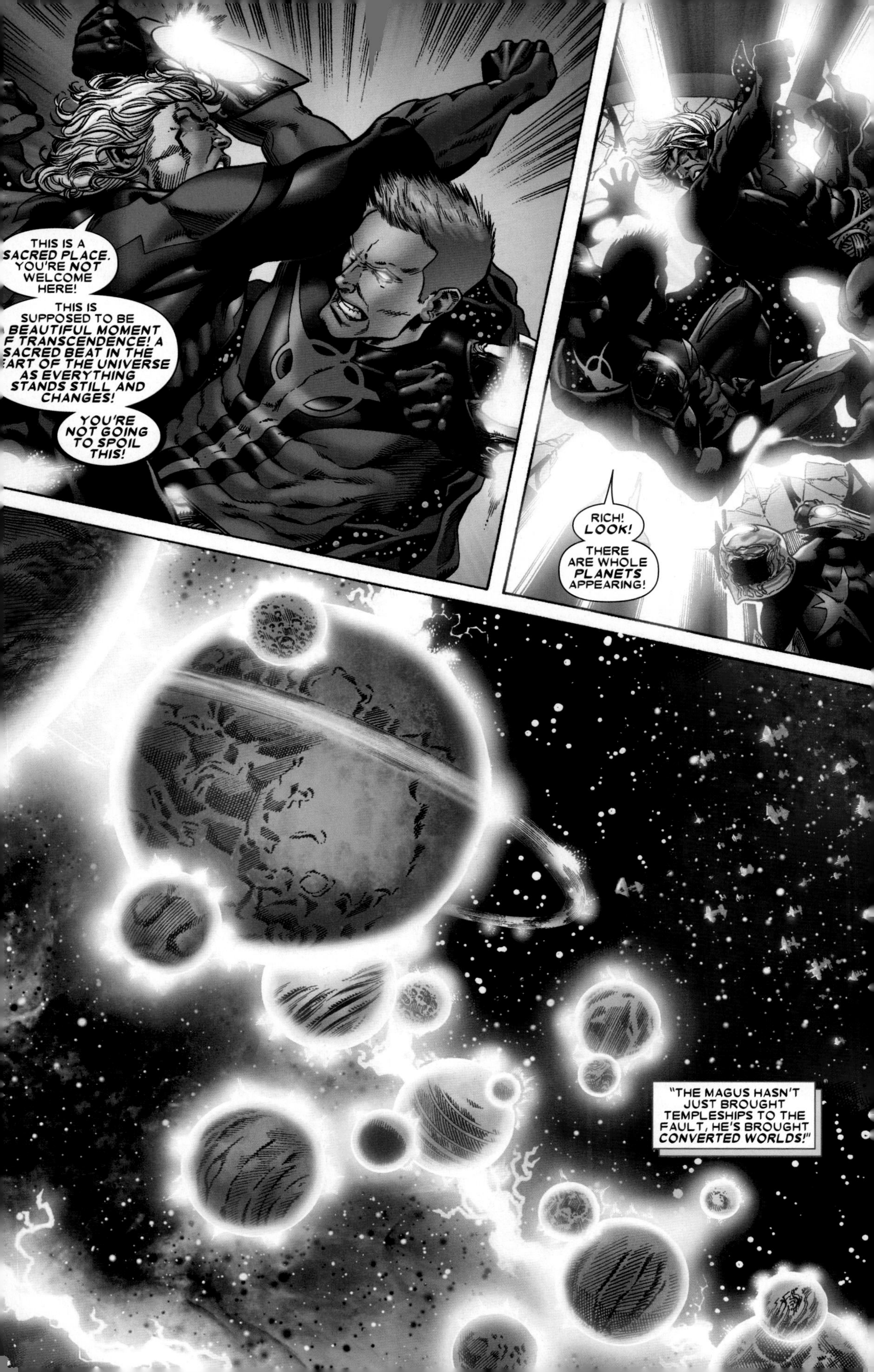
THIS IS A SACRED PLACE. YOU'RE NOT WELCOME HERE!
THIS IS SUPPOSED TO BE A BEAUTIFUL MOMENT OF TRANSCENDENCE! A SACRED BEAT IN THE HEART OF THE UNIVERSE AS EVERYTHING STANDS STILL AND CHANGES!
YOU'RE NOT GOING TO SPOIL THIS!
RICH! LOOK! THERE ARE WHOLE PLANETS APPEARING!
"THE MAGUS HASN'T JUST BROUGHT TEMPLESHIPS TO THE FAULT, HE'S BROUGHT CONVERTED WORLDS!"

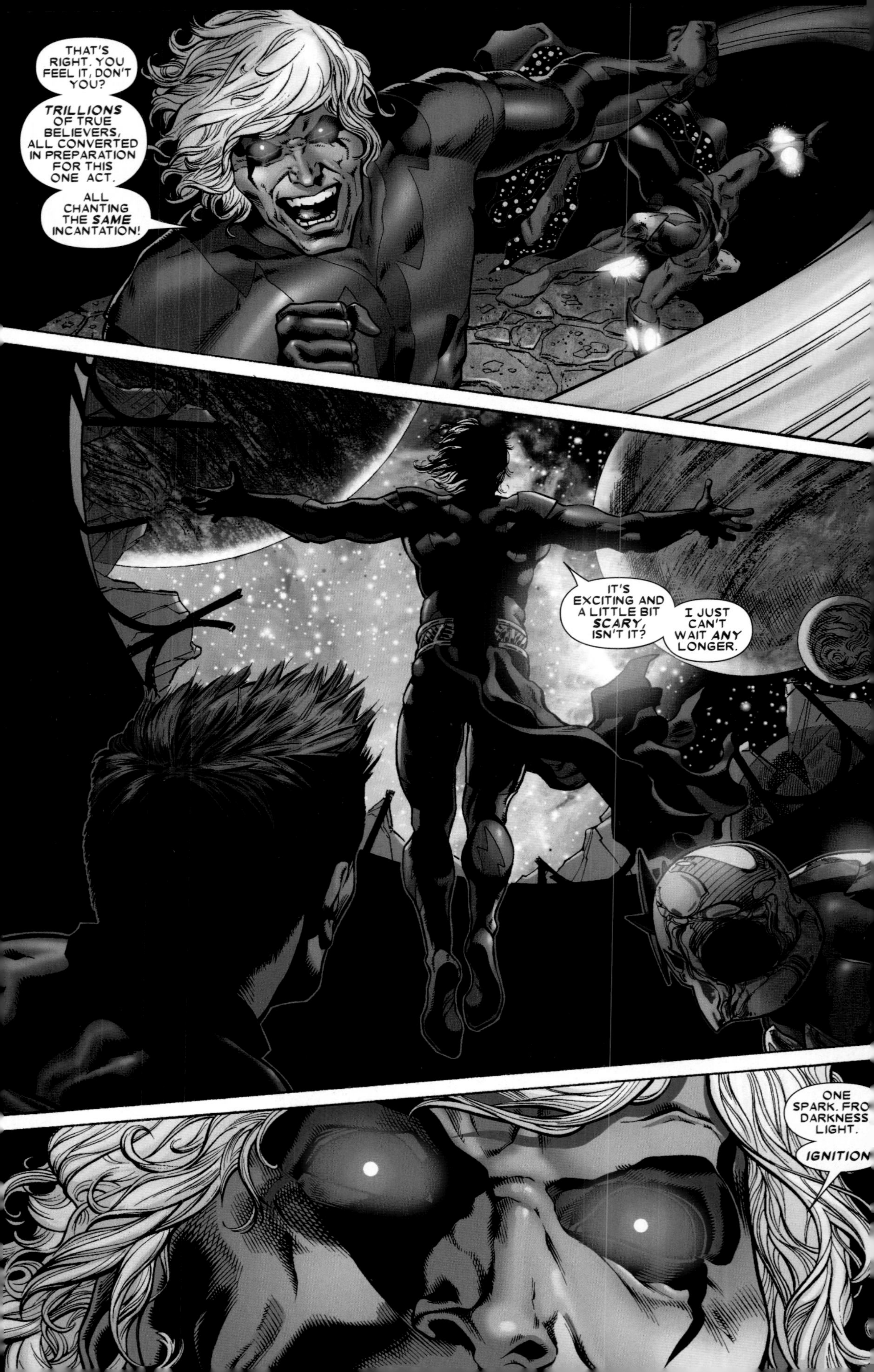
THAT'S RIGHT. YOU FEEL IT, DON'T YOU?
TRILLIONS OF TRUE BELIEVERS, ALL CONVERTED IN PREPARATION FOR THIS ONE ACT.
ALL CHANTING THE SAME INCANTATION!
IT'S EXCITING AND A LITTLE BIT SCARY, ISN'T IT?
I JUST CAN'T WAIT ANY LONGER.
ONE SPARK. FRO DARKNESS LIGHT.
IGNITION

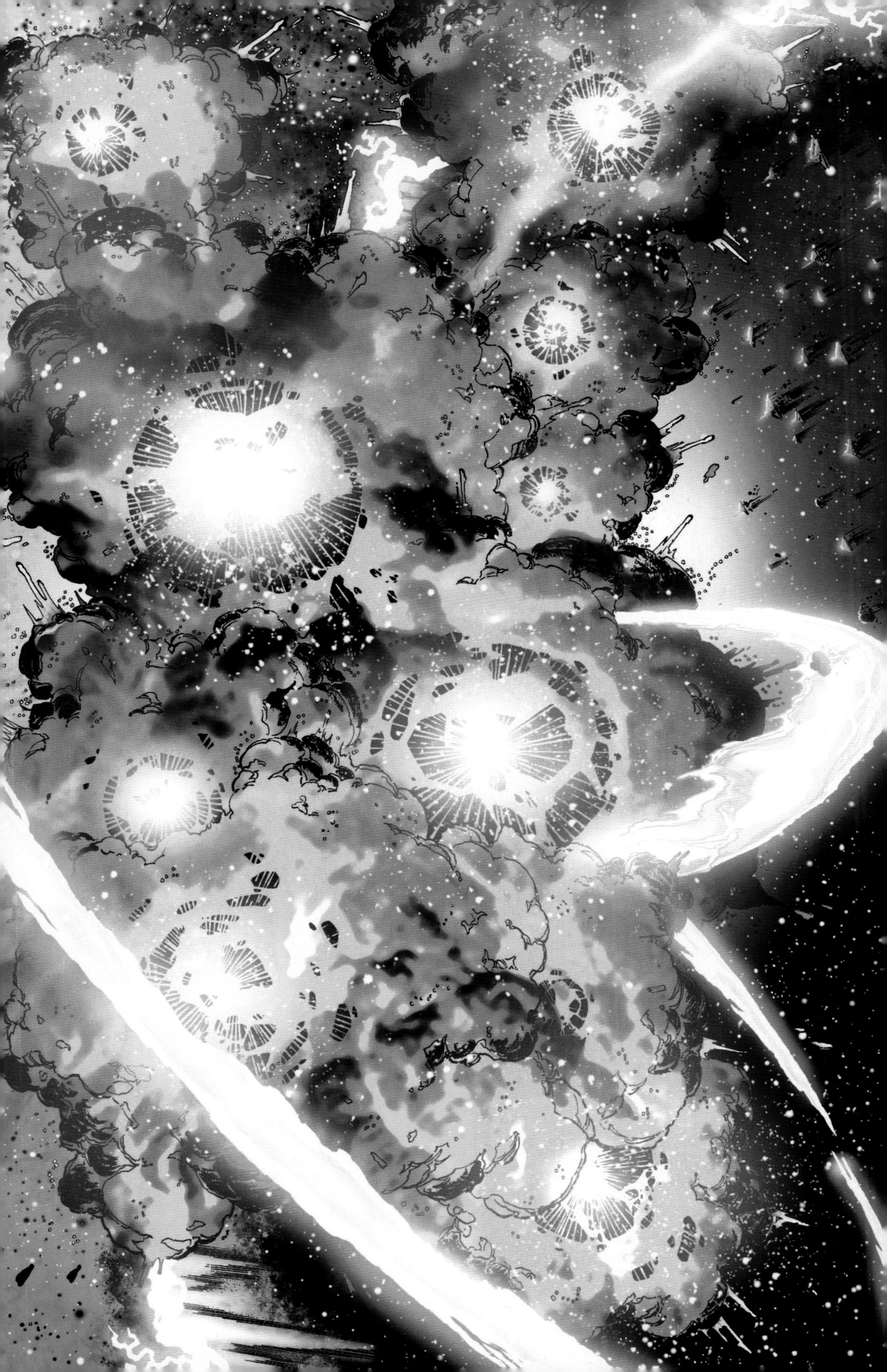

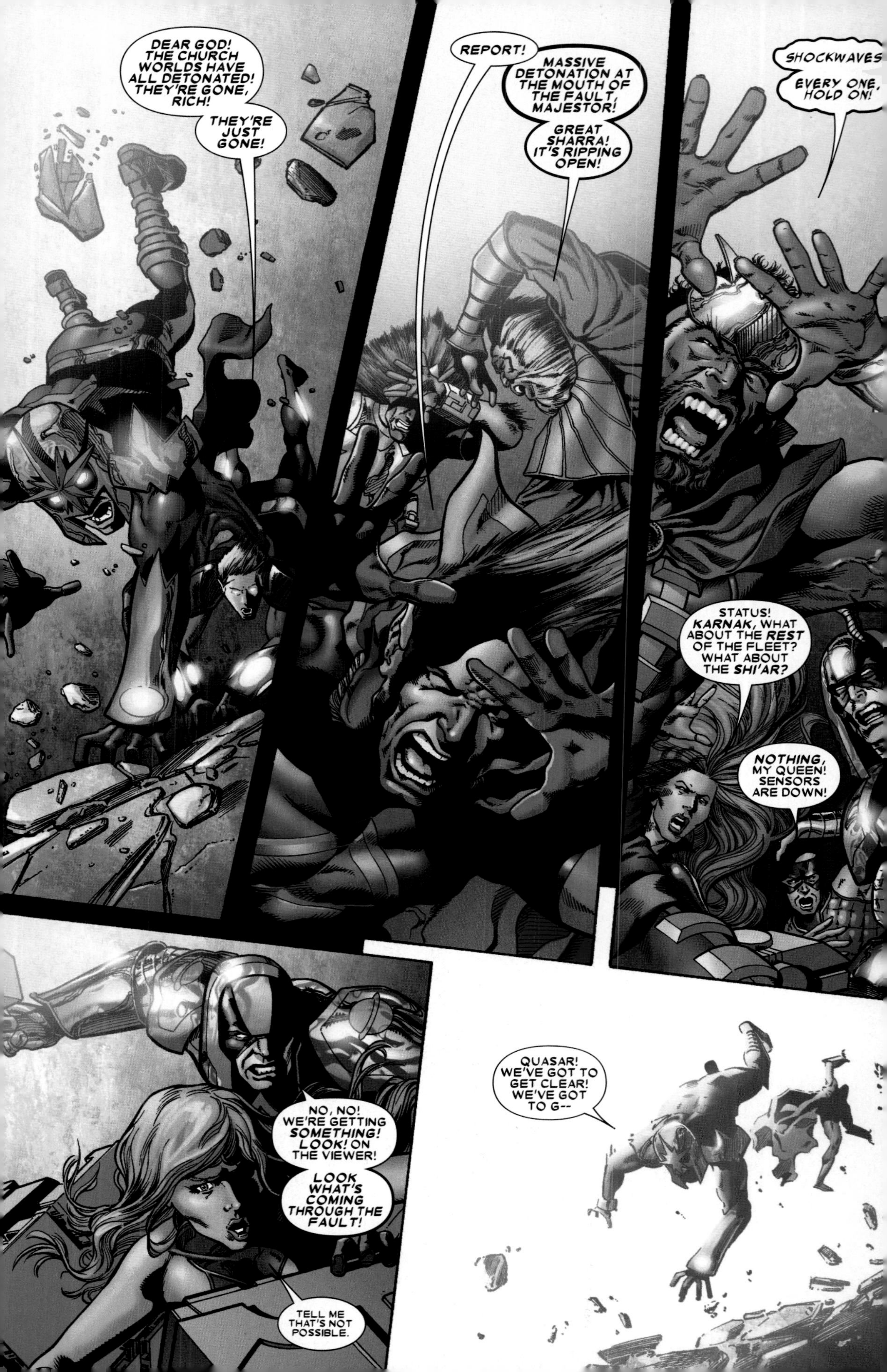
DEAR GOD! THE CHURCH WORLDS HAVE ALL DETONATED! THEY'RE GONE, RICH!
THEY'RE JUST GONE!
REPORT!
MASSIVE DETONATION AT THE MOUTH OF THE FAULT, MAJESTOR!
GREAT SHARRA! IT'S RIPPING OPEN!
SHOCKWAVES
EVERY ONE, HOLD ON!
STATUS! KARNAK, WHAT ABOUT THE REST OF THE FLEET? WHAT ABOUT THE SHI'AR?
NOTHING, MY QUEEN! SENSORS ARE DOWN!
NO, NO! WE'RE GETTING SOMETHING! LOOK! ON THE VIEWER!
LOOK WHAT'S COMING THROUGH THE FAULT!
TELL ME THAT'S NOT POSSIBLE.
QUASAR! WE'VE GOT TO GET CLEAR! WE'VE GOT TO G--

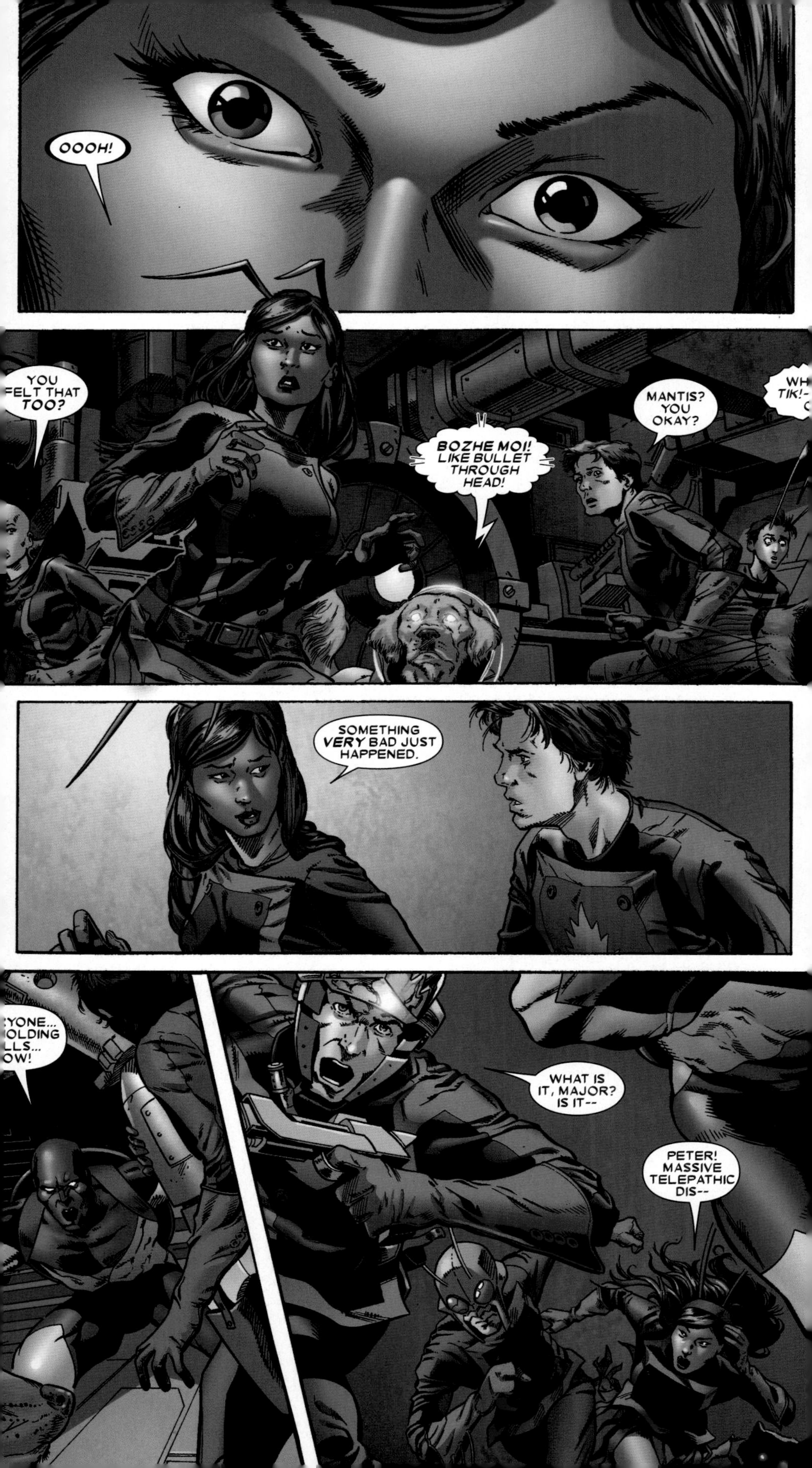
OOOH!
YOU FELT THAT TOO?
BOZHE MOI! LIKE BULLET THROUGH HEAD!
MANTIS? YOU OKAY?
SOMETHING VERY BAD JUST HAPPENED.
WHAT IS IT, MAJOR? IS IT--
PETER! MASSIVE TELEPATHIC DIS--

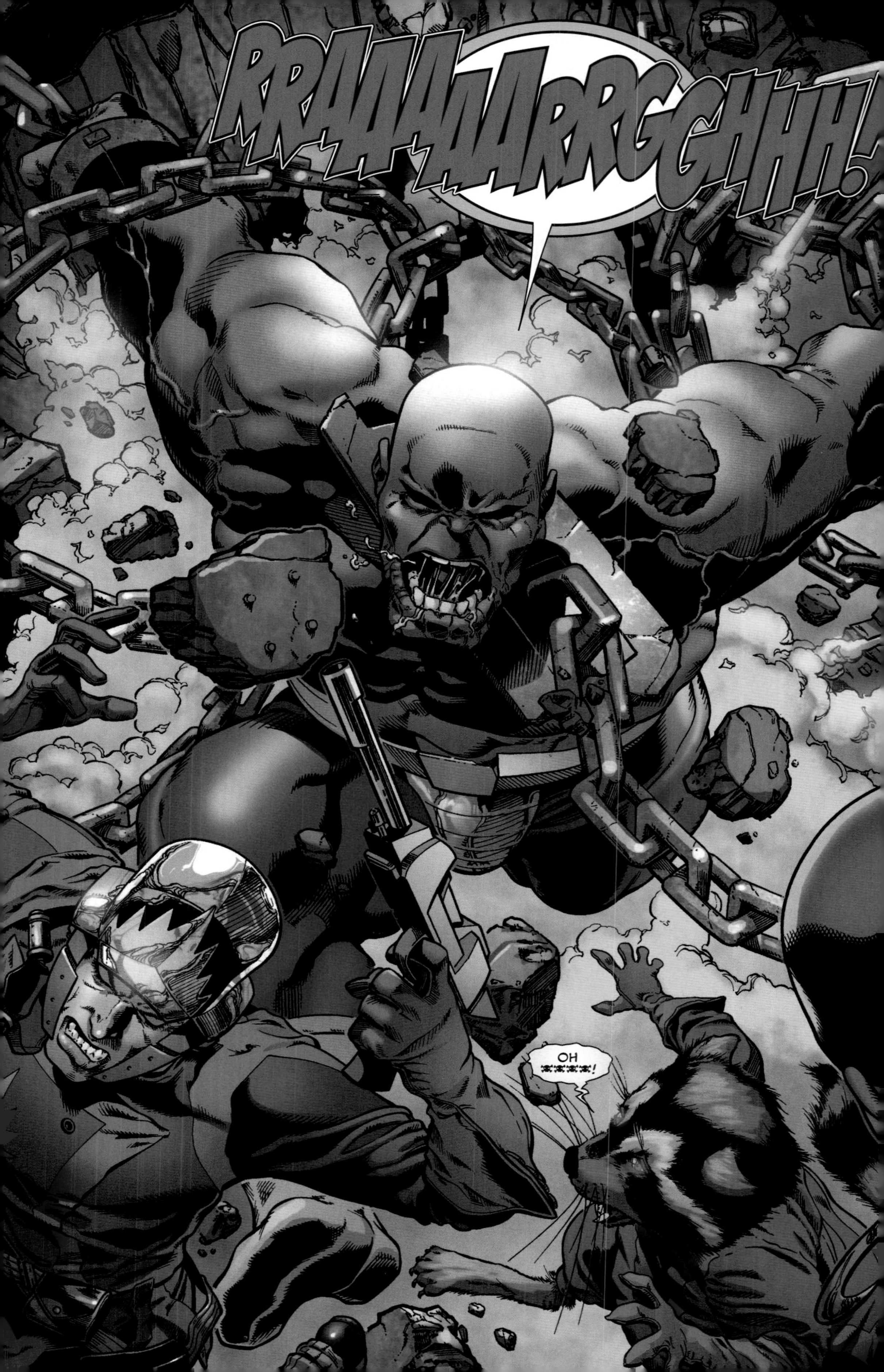
RRAAAAAARRGGHHH!
OH

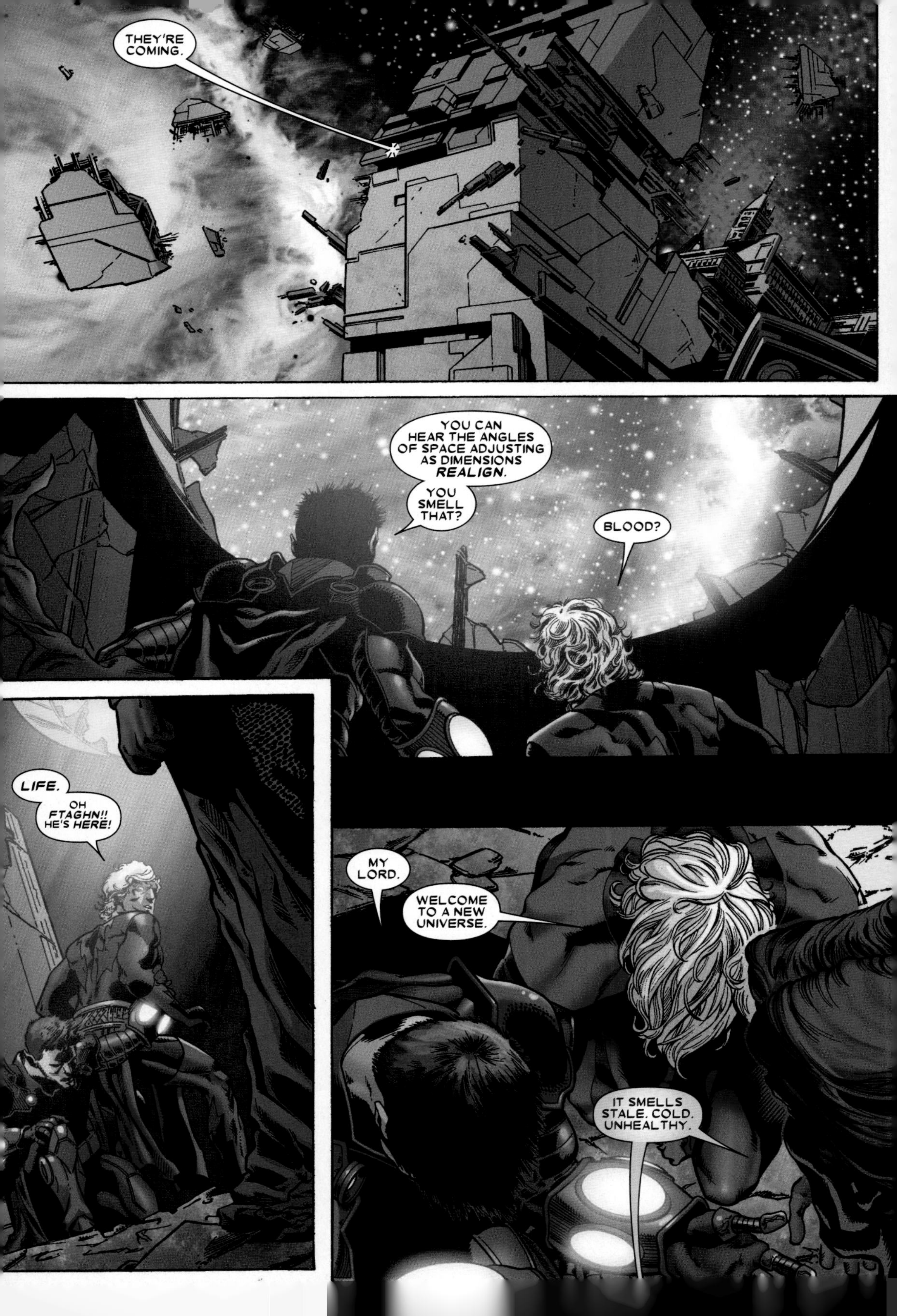
THEY'RE COMING.
YOU CAN HEAR THE ANGLES OF SPACE ADJUSTING AS DIMENSIONS *REALIGN*.
YOU SMELL THAT?
BLOOD?
LIFE.
OH *FTAGHN!!* HE'S *HERE!*
MY LORD.
WELCOME TO A NEW UNIVERSE.
IT SMELLS STALE. COLD. UNHEALTHY.

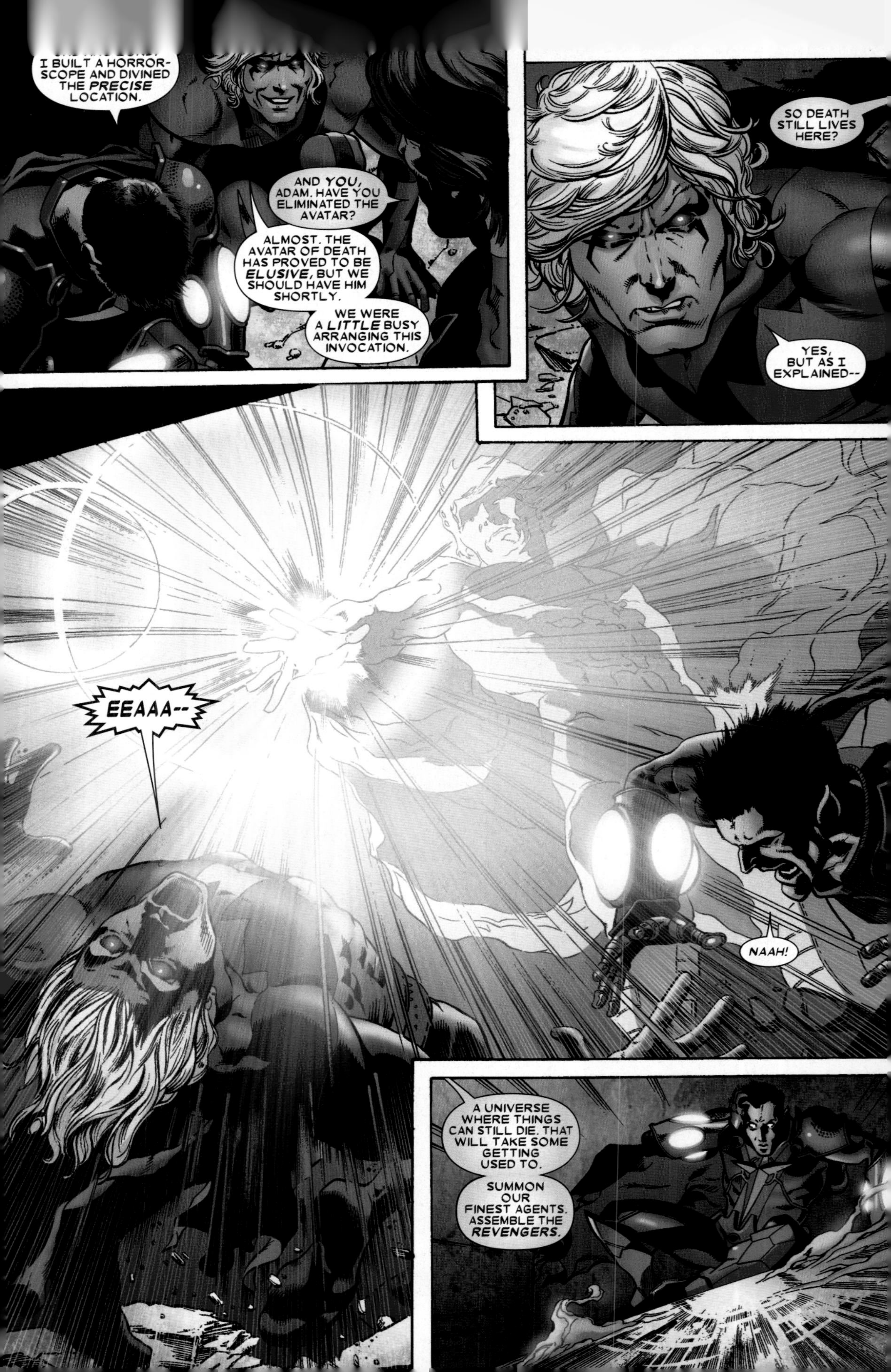
I BUILT A HORROR-SCOPE AND DIVINED THE PRECISE LOCATION.
AND YOU, ADAM. HAVE YOU ELIMINATED THE AVATAR?
ALMOST. THE AVATAR OF DEATH HAS PROVED TO BE ELUSIVE, BUT WE SHOULD HAVE HIM SHORTLY.
WE WERE A LITTLE BUSY ARRANGING THIS INVOCATION.
SO DEATH STILL LIVES HERE?
YES, BUT AS I EXPLAINED--
EEAAA--
NAAH!
A UNIVERSE WHERE THINGS CAN STILL DIE. THAT WILL TAKE SOME GETTING USED TO.
SUMMON OUR FINEST AGENTS. ASSEMBLE THE REVENGERS.

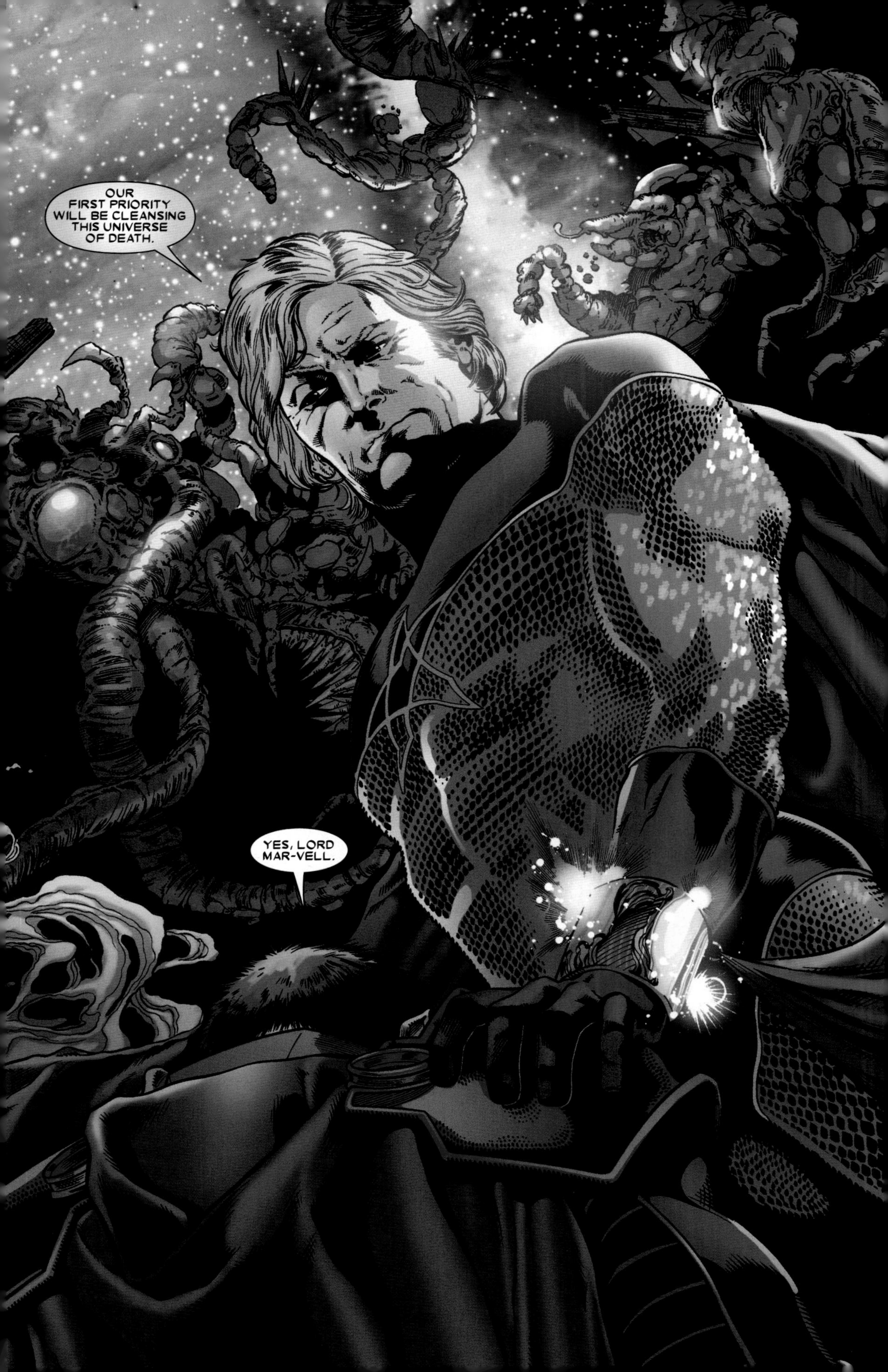
OUR FIRST PRIORITY WILL BE CLEANSING THIS UNIVERSE OF DEATH.
YES, LORD MAR-VELL.

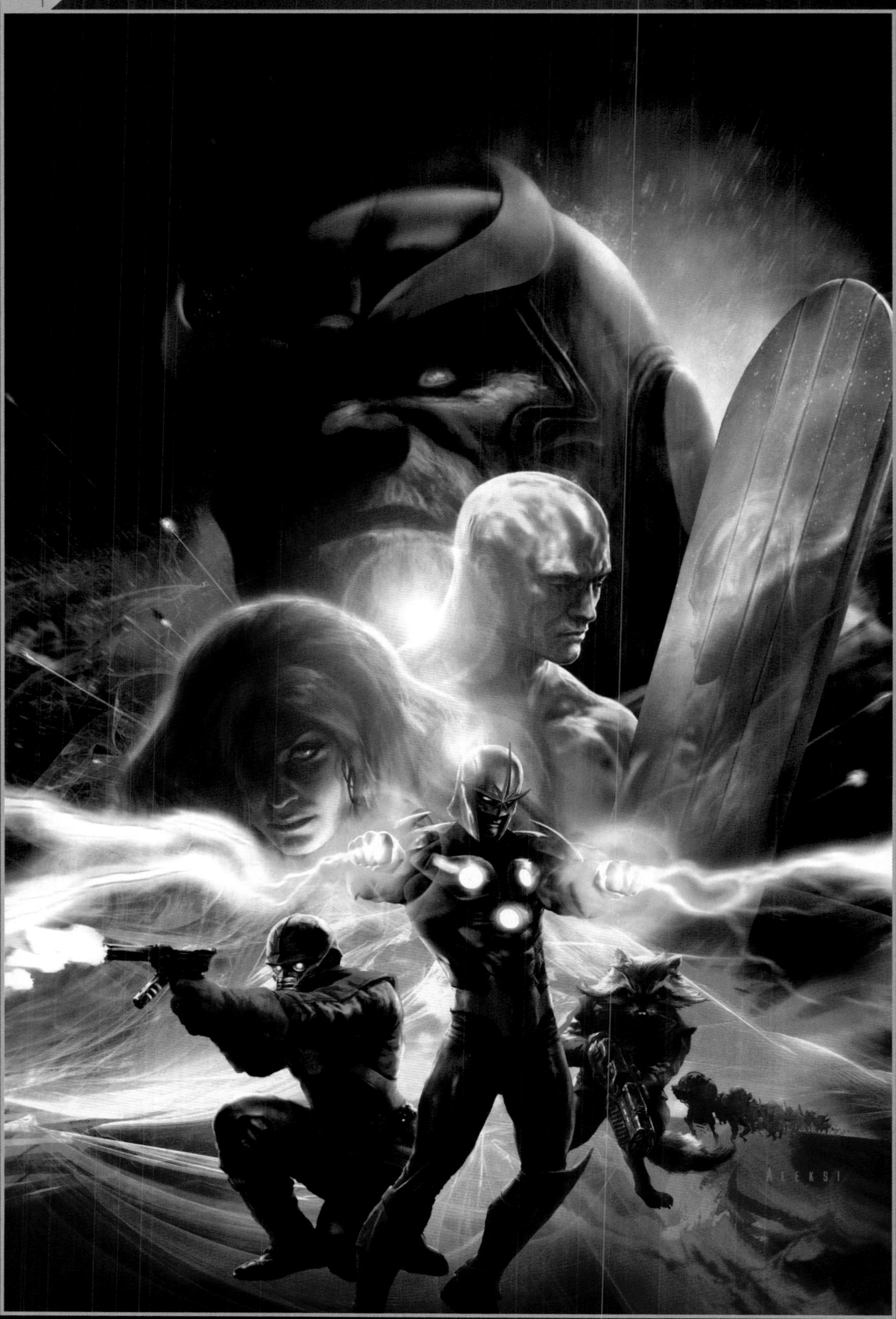
ALEKSI

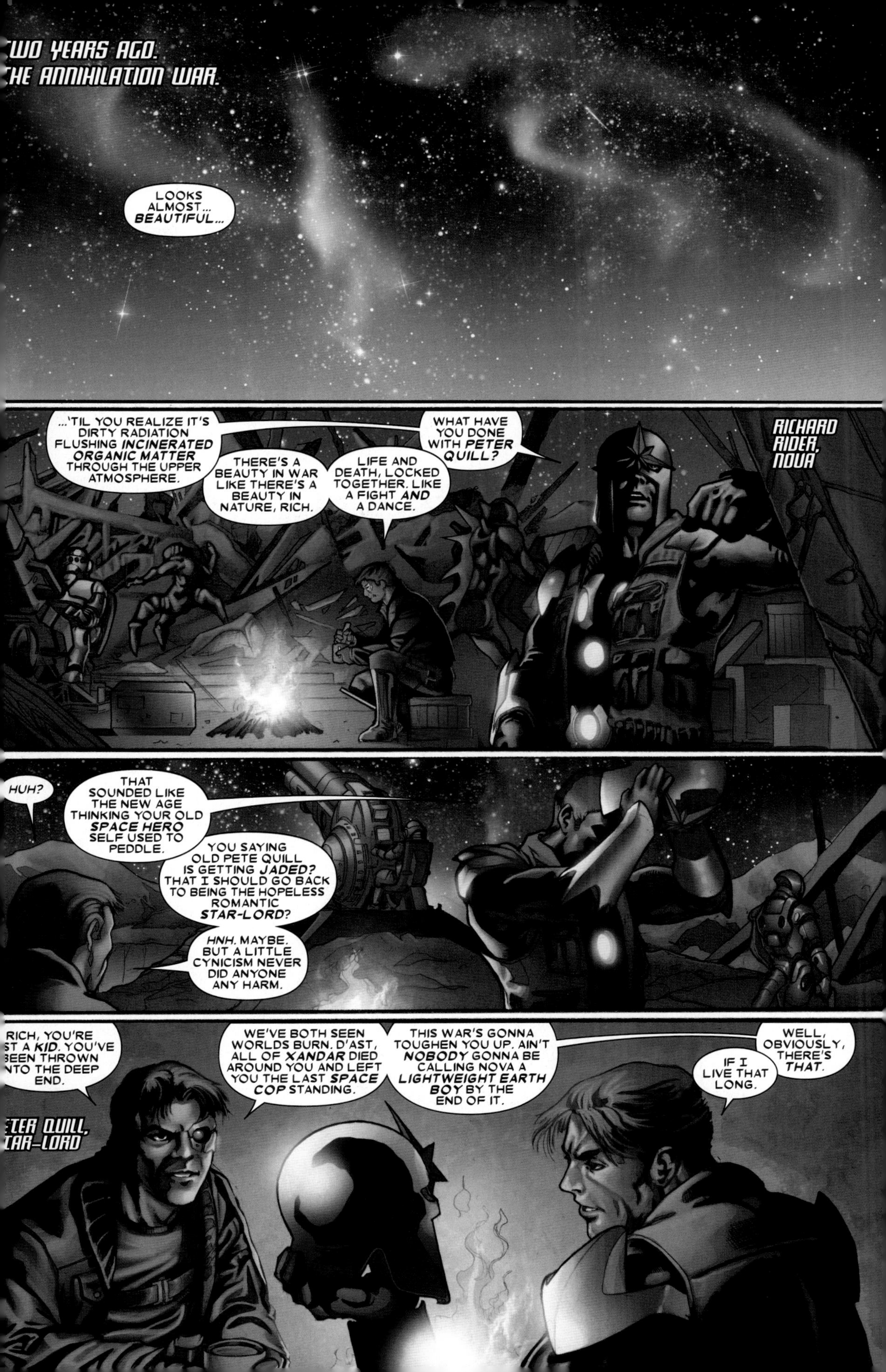
TWO YEARS AGO.
THE ANNIHILATION WAR.
LOOKS ALMOST... BEAUTIFUL...
...'TIL YOU REALIZE IT'S DIRTY RADIATION FLUSHING INCINERATED ORGANIC MATTER THROUGH THE UPPER ATMOSPHERE.
THERE'S A BEAUTY IN WAR LIKE THERE'S A BEAUTY IN NATURE, RICH.
LIFE AND DEATH, LOCKED TOGETHER. LIKE A FIGHT AND A DANCE.
WHAT HAVE YOU DONE WITH PETER QUILL?
RICHARD RIDER, NOVA
HUH?
THAT SOUNDED LIKE THE NEW AGE THINKING YOUR OLD SPACE HERO SELF USED TO PEDDLE.
YOU SAYING OLD PETE QUILL IS GETTING JADED? THAT I SHOULD GO BACK TO BEING THE HOPELESS ROMANTIC STAR-LORD?
HNH. MAYBE. BUT A LITTLE CYNICISM NEVER DID ANYONE ANY HARM.
RICH, YOU'RE JUST A KID. YOU'VE BEEN THROWN INTO THE DEEP END.
PETER QUILL, STAR-LORD
WE'VE BOTH SEEN WORLDS BURN. D'AST, ALL OF XANDAR DIED AROUND YOU AND LEFT YOU THE LAST SPACE COP STANDING.
THIS WAR'S GONNA TOUGHEN YOU UP. AIN'T NOBODY GONNA BE CALLING NOVA A LIGHTWEIGHT EARTH BOY BY THE END OF IT.
IF I LIVE THAT LONG.
WELL, OBVIOUSLY, THERE'S THAT.

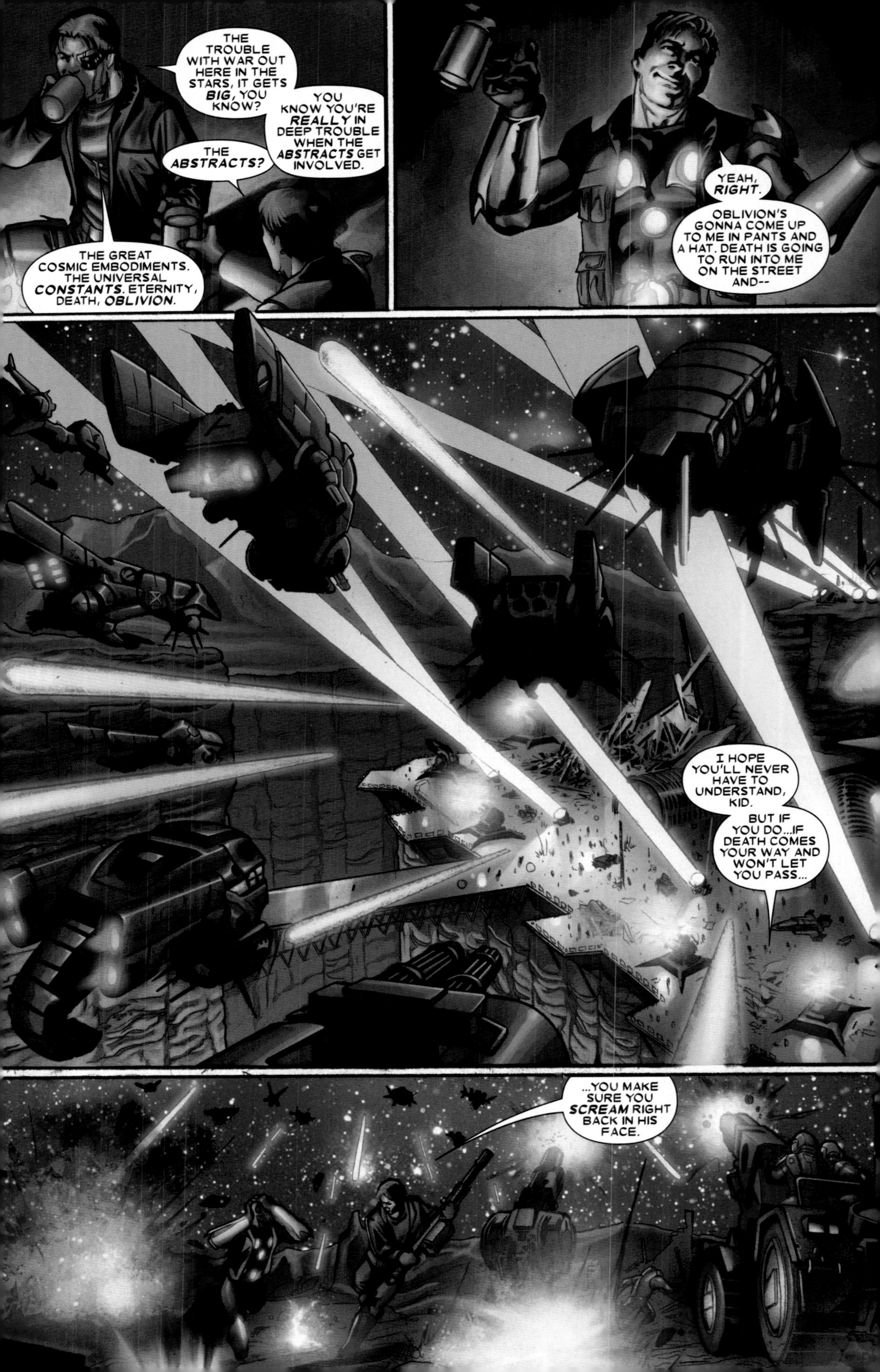
THE TROUBLE WITH WAR OUT HERE IN THE STARS, IT GETS BIG, YOU KNOW?
YOU KNOW YOU'RE REALLY IN DEEP TROUBLE WHEN THE ABSTRACTS GET INVOLVED.
THE ABSTRACTS?
THE GREAT COSMIC EMBODIMENTS. THE UNIVERSAL CONSTANTS. ETERNITY, DEATH, OBLIVION.
YEAH, RIGHT.
OBLIVION'S GONNA COME UP TO ME IN PANTS AND A HAT. DEATH IS GOING TO RUN INTO ME ON THE STREET AND--
I HOPE YOU'LL NEVER HAVE TO UNDERSTAND, KID.
BUT IF YOU DO...IF DEATH COMES YOUR WAY AND WON'T LET YOU PASS...
...YOU MAKE SURE YOU SCREAM RIGHT BACK IN HIS FACE.

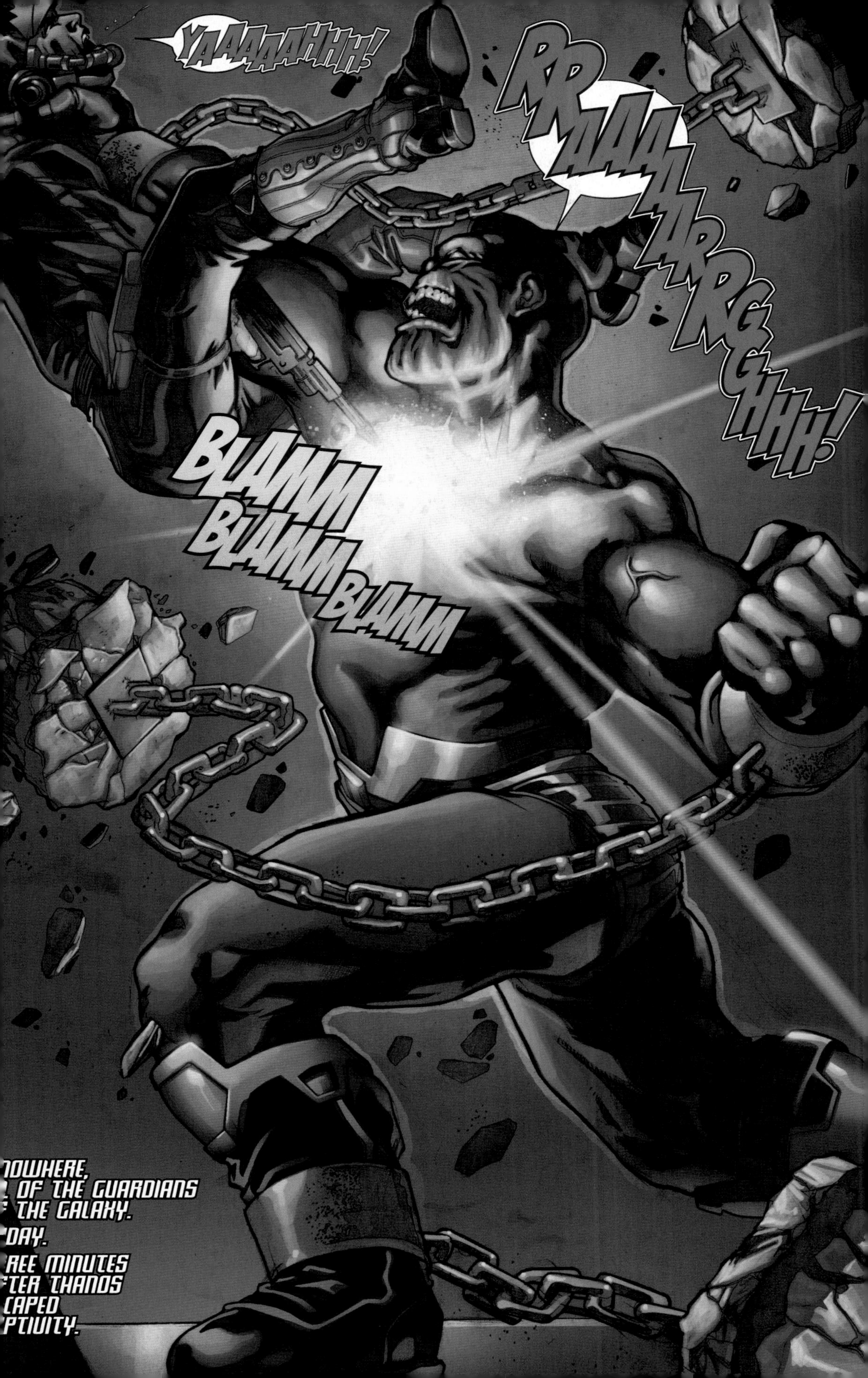
YAAAAAHHH!
RRAAAAARRGHHH!
BLAMM
BLAMM BLAMM BLAMM
OWHERE,
OF THE GUARDIANS
THE GALAXY.
DAY.
REE MINUTES
TER THANOS
CAPED
PTIVITY.

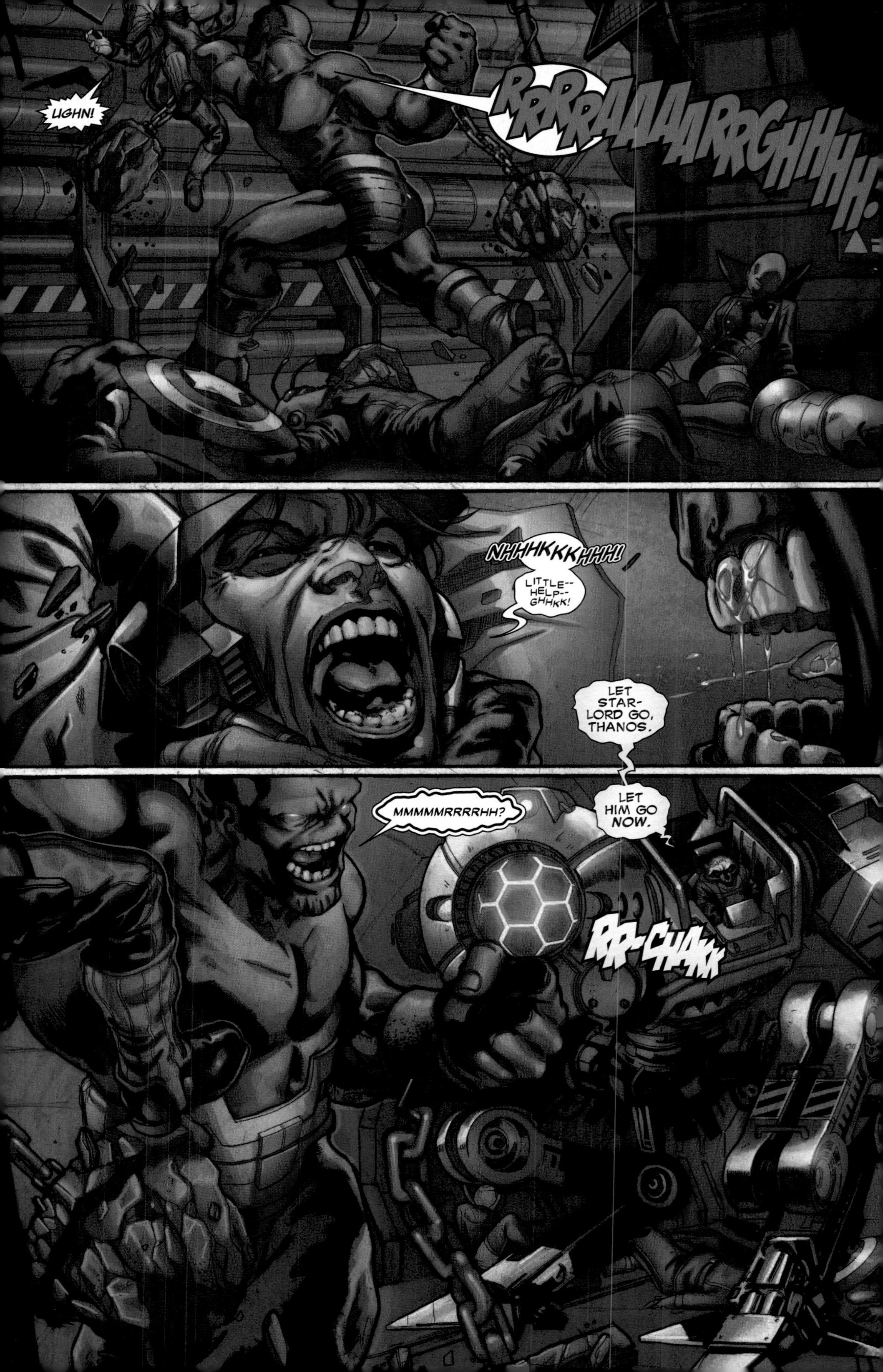
UGHN!
RRRRAAAAARRRGHHHH!
NHHHKKKHHH!
LITTLE-- HELP-- GHHKK!
LET STAR-LORD GO, THANOS.
LET HIM GO NOW.
MMMMMRRRRHH?
RR-CHAKK

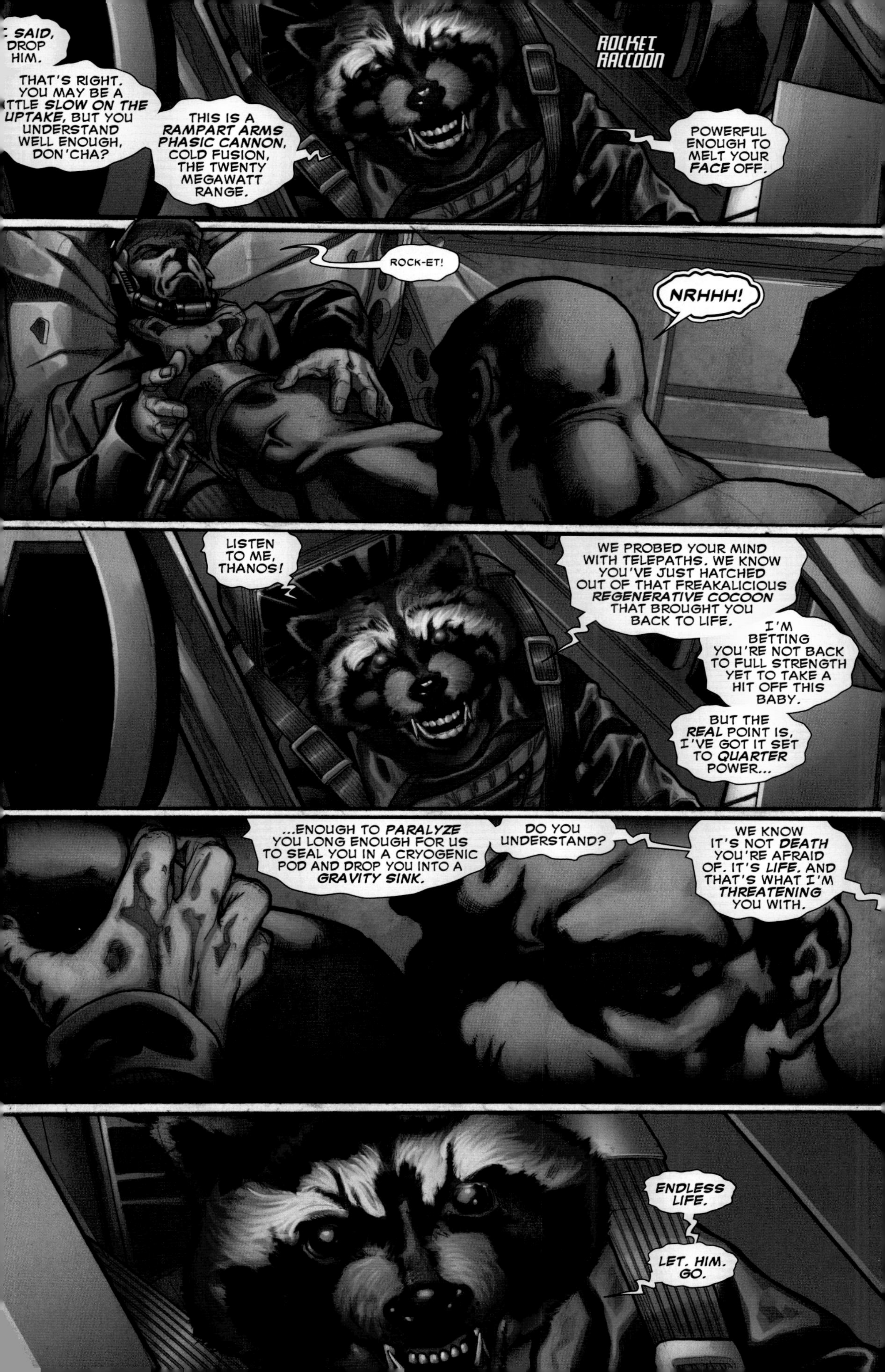

ROCKET RACCOON
SAID, DROP HIM.
THAT'S RIGHT. YOU MAY BE A TTLE SLOW ON THE UPTAKE, BUT YOU UNDERSTAND WELL ENOUGH, DON'CHA?
THIS IS A RAMPART ARMS PHASIC CANNON, COLD FUSION, THE TWENTY MEGAWATT RANGE.
POWERFUL ENOUGH TO MELT YOUR FACE OFF.
ROCK-ET!
NRHHH!
LISTEN TO ME, THANOS!
WE PROBED YOUR MIND WITH TELEPATHS. WE KNOW YOU'VE JUST HATCHED OUT OF THAT FREAKALICIOUS REGENERATIVE COCOON THAT BROUGHT YOU BACK TO LIFE.
I'M BETTING YOU'RE NOT BACK TO FULL STRENGTH YET TO TAKE A HIT OFF THIS BABY.
BUT THE REAL POINT IS, I'VE GOT IT SET TO QUARTER POWER...
...ENOUGH TO PARALYZE YOU LONG ENOUGH FOR US TO SEAL YOU IN A CRYOGENIC POD AND DROP YOU INTO A GRAVITY SINK.
DO YOU UNDERSTAND?
WE KNOW IT'S NOT DEATH YOU'RE AFRAID OF. IT'S LIFE. AND THAT'S WHAT I'M THREATENING YOU WITH.
ENDLESS LIFE.
LET. HIM. GO.

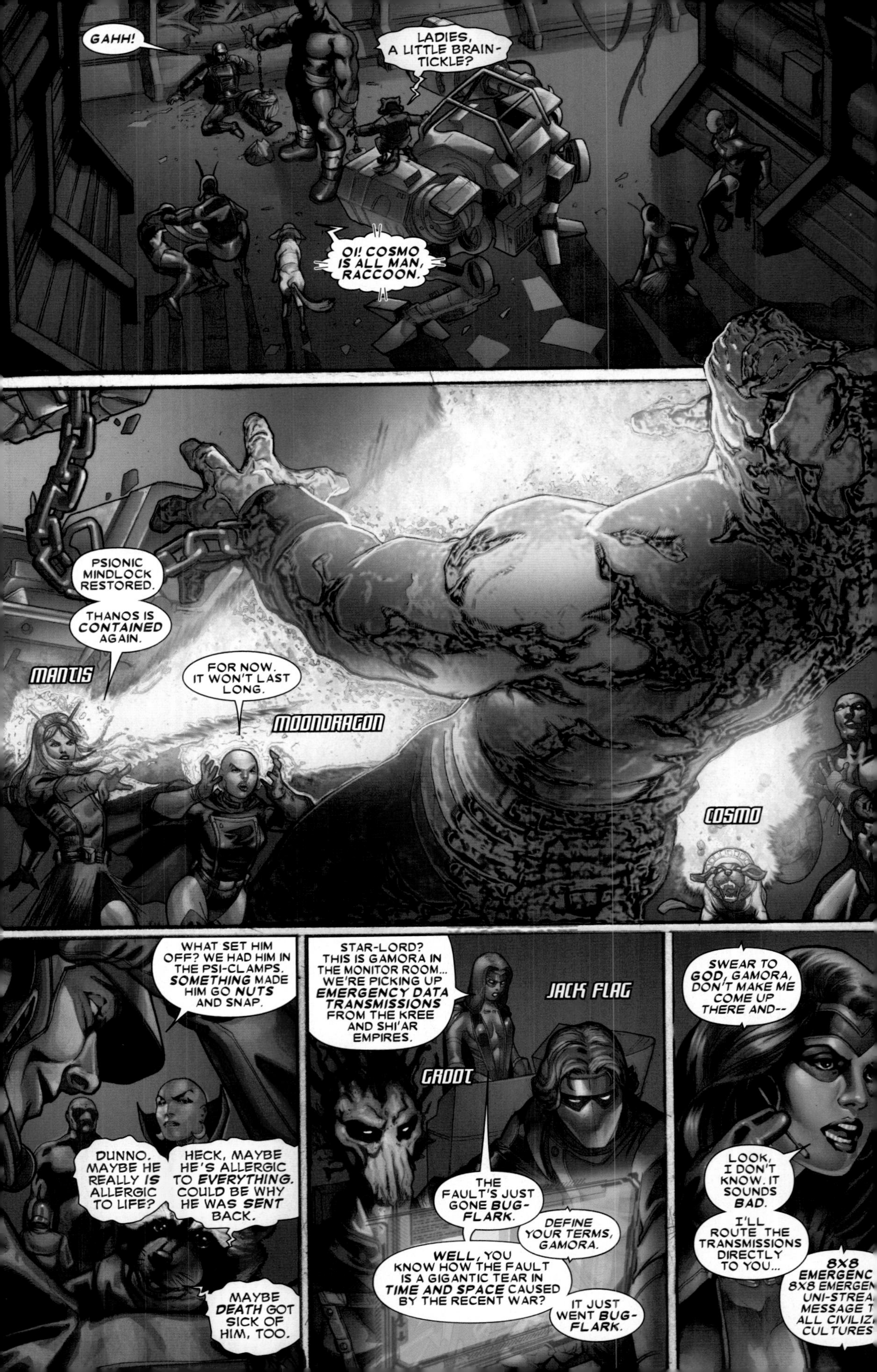
GAHH!
LADIES, A LITTLE BRAIN-TICKLE?
OI! COSMO IS ALL MAN, RACCOON.
PSIONIC MINDLOCK RESTORED.
THANOS IS CONTAINED AGAIN.
MANTIS
FOR NOW. IT WON'T LAST LONG.
MOONDRAGON
COSMO
WHAT SET HIM OFF? WE HAD HIM IN THE PSI-CLAMPS. SOMETHING MADE HIM GO NUTS AND SNAP.
DUNNO. MAYBE HE REALLY IS ALLERGIC TO LIFE?
HECK, MAYBE HE'S ALLERGIC TO EVERYTHING. COULD BE WHY HE WAS SENT BACK.
MAYBE DEATH GOT SICK OF HIM, TOO.
STAR-LORD? THIS IS GAMORA IN THE MONITOR ROOM... WE'RE PICKING UP EMERGENCY DATA TRANSMISSIONS FROM THE KREE AND SHI'AR EMPIRES.
JACK FLAG
GROOT
THE FAULT'S JUST GONE BUG-FLARK.
DEFINE YOUR TERMS, GAMORA.
WELL, YOU KNOW HOW THE FAULT IS A GIGANTIC TEAR IN TIME AND SPACE CAUSED BY THE RECENT WAR?
IT JUST WENT BUG-FLARK.
SWEAR TO GOD, GAMORA, DON'T MAKE ME COME UP THERE AND--
LOOK, I DON'T KNOW. IT SOUNDS BAD.
I'LL ROUTE THE TRANSMISSIONS DIRECTLY TO YOU...

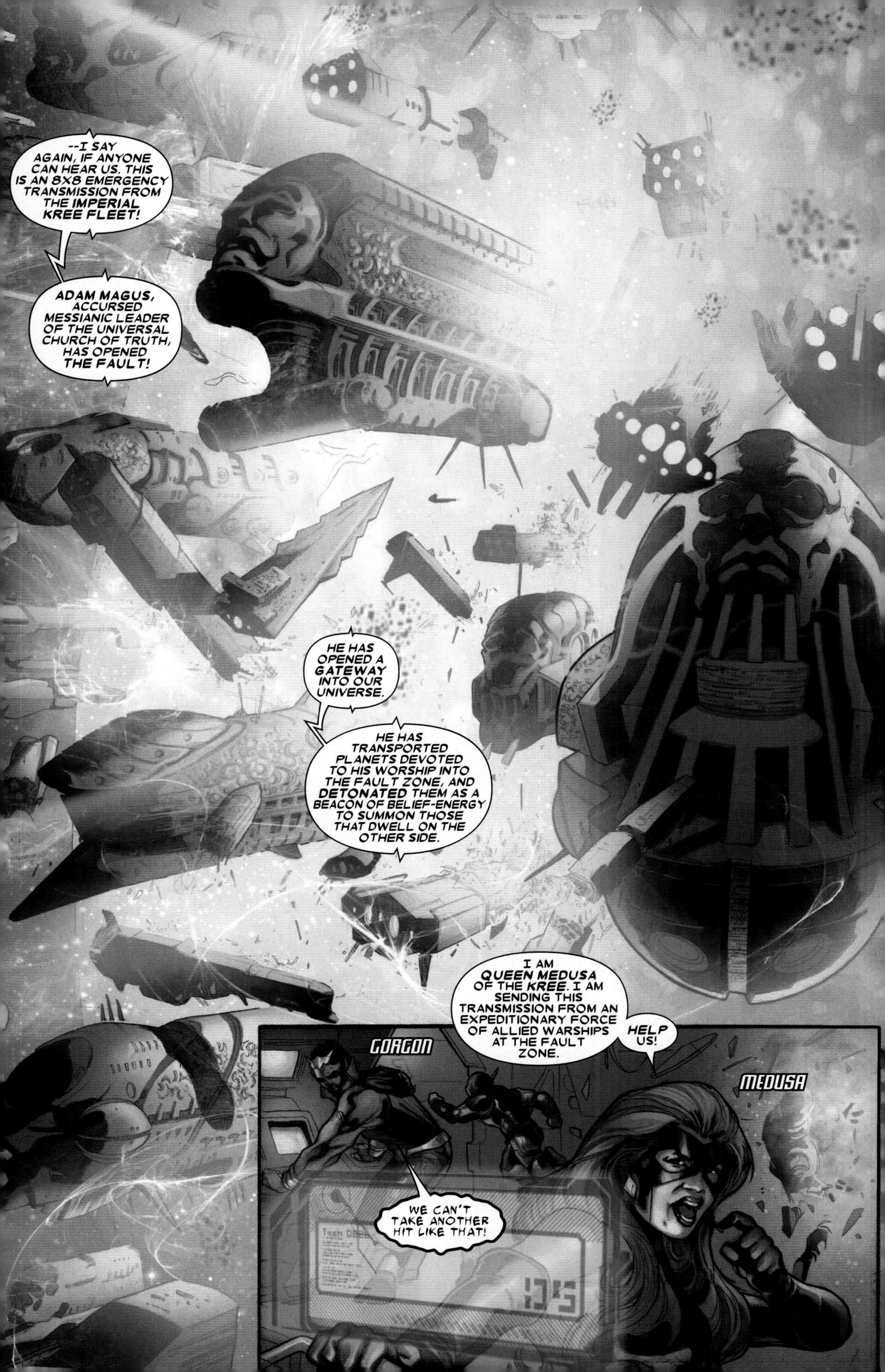
--I SAY AGAIN, IF ANYONE CAN HEAR US. THIS IS AN 8X8 EMERGENCY TRANSMISSION FROM THE IMPERIAL KREE FLEET!
ADAM MAGUS, ACCURSED MESSIANIC LEADER OF THE UNIVERSAL CHURCH OF TRUTH, HAS OPENED THE FAULT!
HE HAS OPENED A GATEWAY INTO OUR UNIVERSE.
HE HAS TRANSPORTED PLANETS DEVOTED TO HIS WORSHIP INTO THE FAULT ZONE, AND DETONATED THEM AS A BEACON OF BELIEF-ENERGY TO SUMMON THOSE THAT DWELL ON THE OTHER SIDE.
I AM QUEEN MEDUSA OF THE KREE. I AM SENDING THIS TRANSMISSION FROM AN EXPEDITIONARY FORCE OF ALLIED WARSHIPS AT THE FAULT ZONE.
HELP US!
GORGON
MEDUSA
WE CAN'T TAKE ANOTHER HIT LIKE THAT!

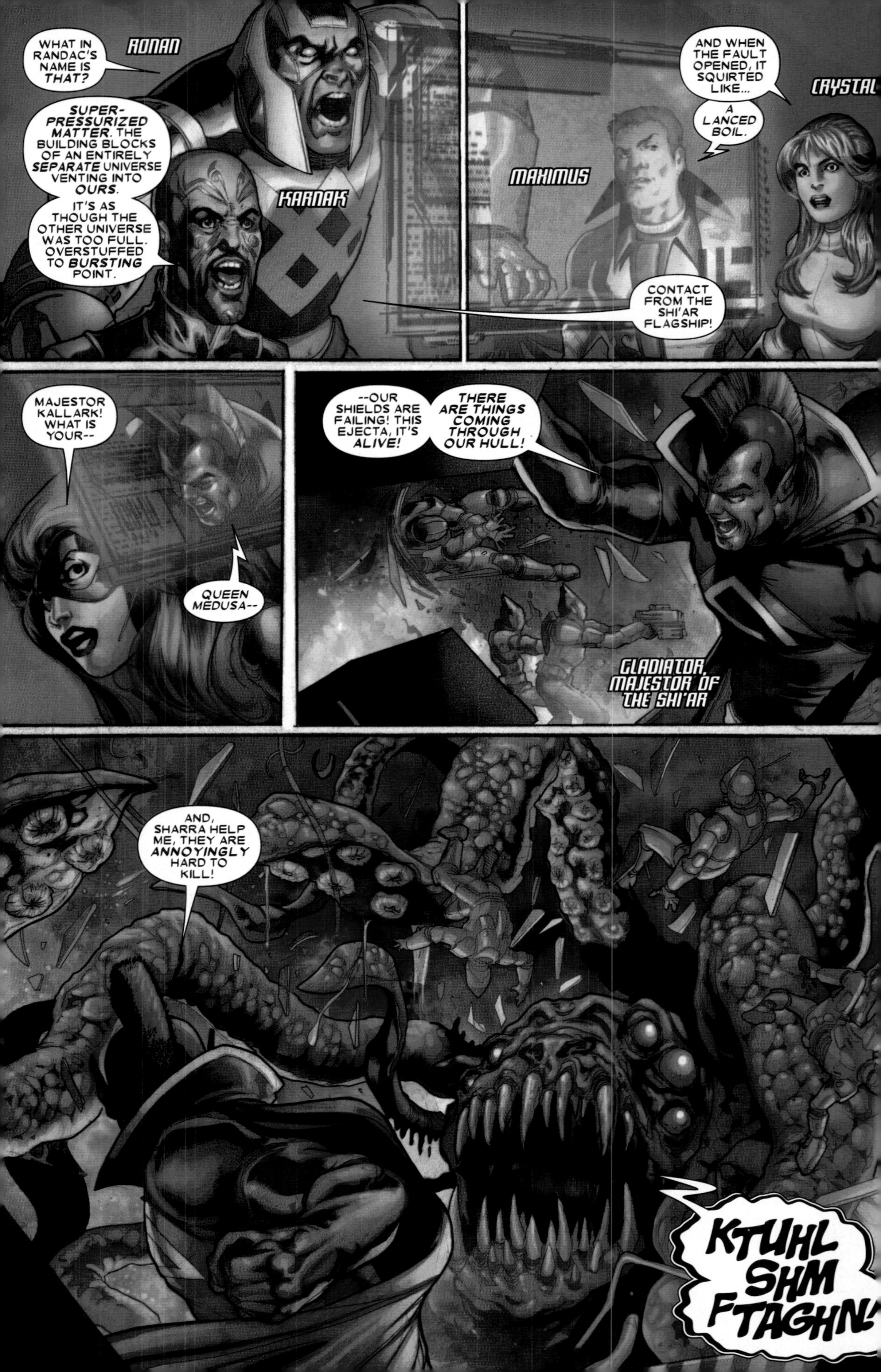
WHAT IN RANDAC'S NAME IS *THAT?*
RONAN
SUPER-PRESSURIZED MATTER. THE BUILDING BLOCKS OF AN ENTIRELY *SEPARATE* UNIVERSE VENTING INTO *OURS*.
IT'S AS THOUGH THE OTHER UNIVERSE WAS TOO FULL. OVERSTUFFED TO *BURSTING* POINT.
KARNAK
AND WHEN THE FAULT OPENED, IT SQUIRTED LIKE...
CRYSTAL
A LANCED BOIL.
MAXIMUS
CONTACT FROM THE SHI'AR FLAGSHIP!
MAJESTOR KALLARK! WHAT IS YOUR--
QUEEN MEDUSA--
--OUR SHIELDS ARE FAILING! THIS EJECTA, IT'S *ALIVE!*
THERE ARE THINGS COMING THROUGH OUR HULL!
GLADIATOR, MAJESTOR OF THE SHI'AR
AND, SHARRA HELP ME, THEY ARE *ANNOYINGLY* HARD TO KILL!
KTUHL SHM FTAGHN!

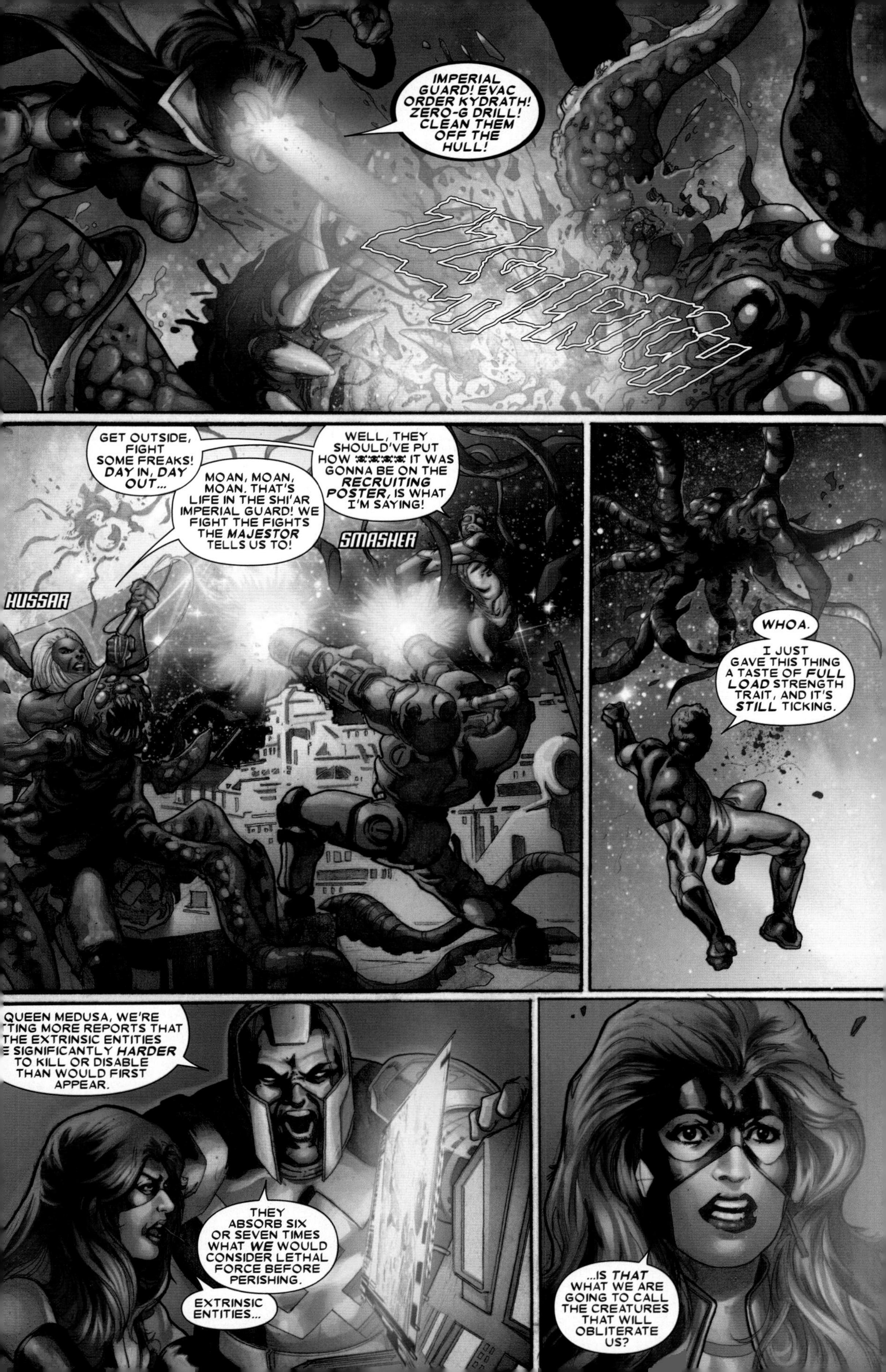
IMPERIAL GUARD! EVAC ORDER KYDRATH! ZERO-G DRILL! CLEAN THEM OFF THE HULL!
GET OUTSIDE, FIGHT SOME FREAKS! DAY IN, DAY OUT...
MOAN, MOAN, MOAN. THAT'S LIFE IN THE SHI'AR IMPERIAL GUARD! WE FIGHT THE FIGHTS THE MAJESTOR TELLS US TO!
WELL, THEY SHOULD'VE PUT HOW ✱✱✱ IT WAS GONNA BE ON THE RECRUITING POSTER, IS WHAT I'M SAYING!
SMASHER
HUSSAR
WHOA.
I JUST GAVE THIS THING A TASTE OF FULL LOAD STRENGTH TRAIT, AND IT'S STILL TICKING.
QUEEN MEDUSA, WE'RE TTING MORE REPORTS THAT THE EXTRINSIC ENTITIES E SIGNIFICANTLY HARDER TO KILL OR DISABLE THAN WOULD FIRST APPEAR.
THEY ABSORB SIX OR SEVEN TIMES WHAT WE WOULD CONSIDER LETHAL FORCE BEFORE PERISHING.
EXTRINSIC ENTITIES...
...IS THAT WHAT WE ARE GOING TO CALL THE CREATURES THAT WILL OBLITERATE US?

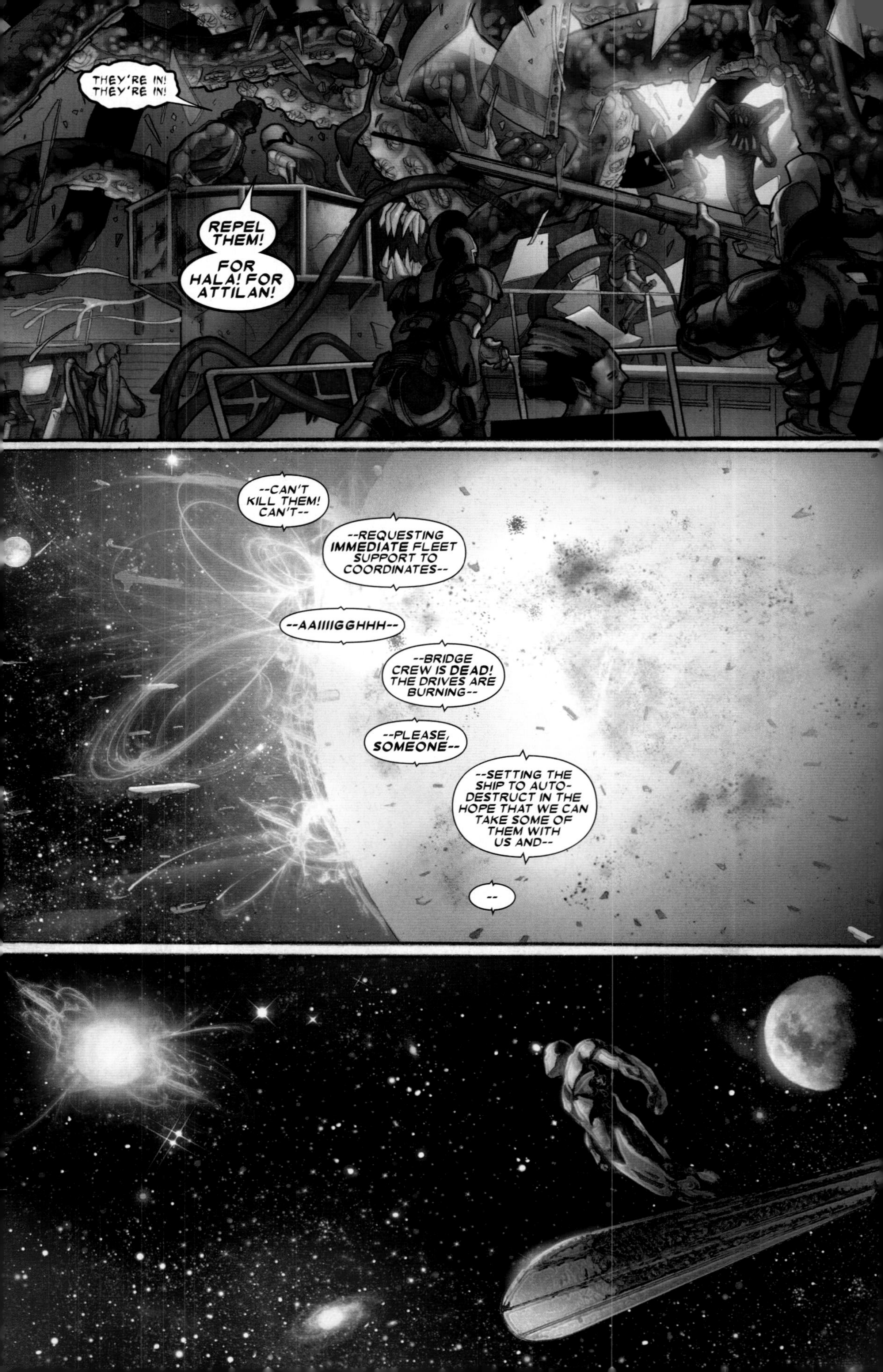
THEY'RE IN! THEY'RE IN!
REPEL THEM!
FOR HALA! FOR ATTILAN!
--CAN'T KILL THEM! CAN'T--
--REQUESTING IMMEDIATE FLEET SUPPORT TO COORDINATES--
--AAIIIIGGHHH--
--BRIDGE CREW IS DEAD! THE DRIVES ARE BURNING--
--PLEASE, SOMEONE--
--SETTING THE SHIP TO AUTO-DESTRUCT IN THE HOPE THAT WE CAN TAKE SOME OF THEM WITH US AND--
--

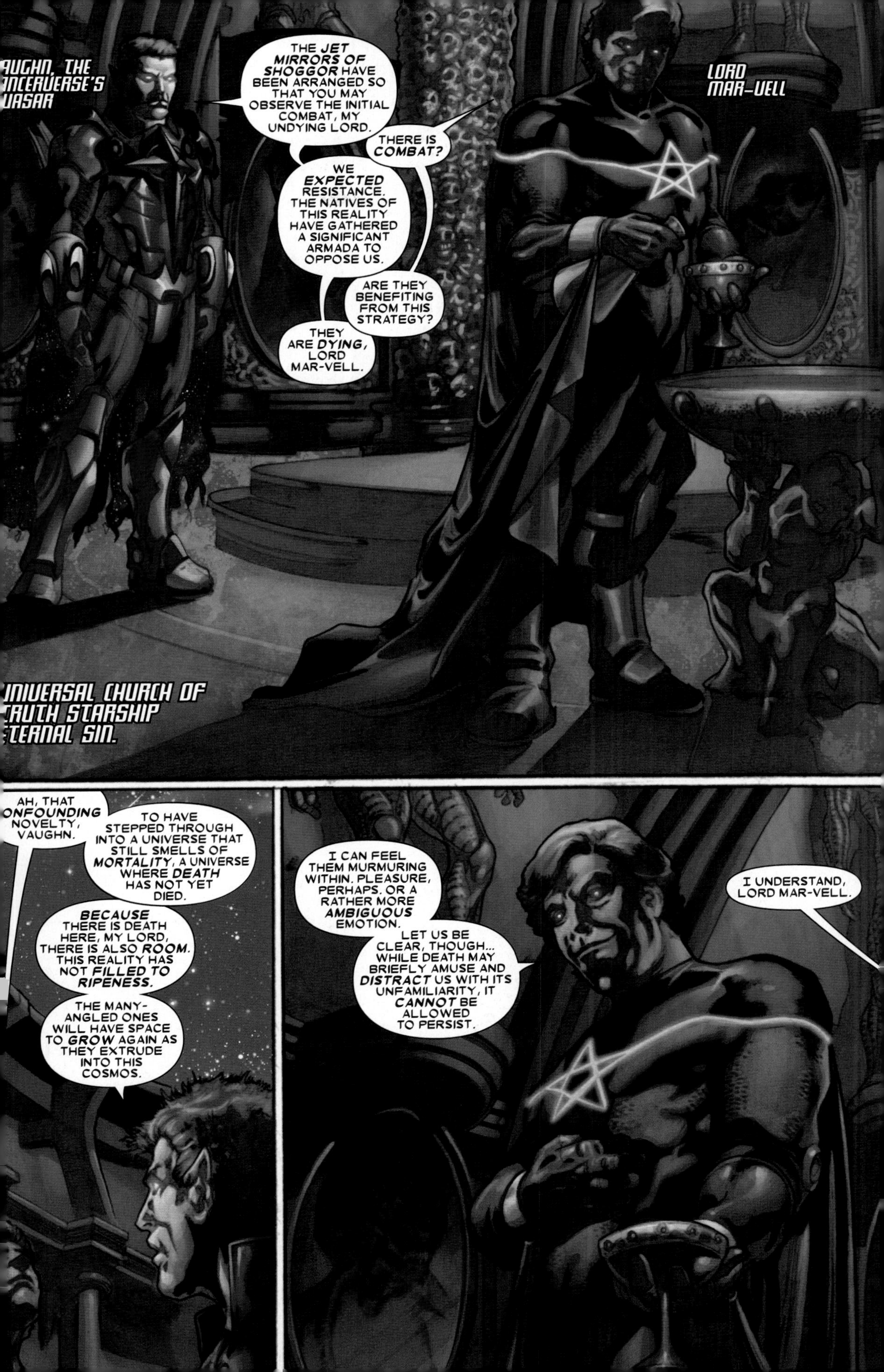

AUGHN, THE
NCERVERSE'S
UASAR
THE JET MIRRORS OF SHOGGOR HAVE BEEN ARRANGED SO THAT YOU MAY OBSERVE THE INITIAL COMBAT, MY UNDYING LORD.
LORD MAR-VELL
THERE IS COMBAT?
WE EXPECTED RESISTANCE. THE NATIVES OF THIS REALITY HAVE GATHERED A SIGNIFICANT ARMADA TO OPPOSE US.
ARE THEY BENEFITING FROM THIS STRATEGY?
THEY ARE DYING, LORD MAR-VELL.
NIVERSAL CHURCH OF
RUTH STARSHIP
TERNAL SIN.
AH, THAT ONFOUNDING NOVELTY, VAUGHN.
TO HAVE STEPPED THROUGH INTO A UNIVERSE THAT STILL SMELLS OF MORTALITY, A UNIVERSE WHERE DEATH HAS NOT YET DIED.
BECAUSE THERE IS DEATH HERE, MY LORD, THERE IS ALSO ROOM. THIS REALITY HAS NOT FILLED TO RIPENESS.
THE MANY-ANGLED ONES WILL HAVE SPACE TO GROW AGAIN AS THEY EXTRUDE INTO THIS COSMOS.
I CAN FEEL THEM MURMURING WITHIN. PLEASURE, PERHAPS. OR A RATHER MORE AMBIGUOUS EMOTION.
LET US BE CLEAR, THOUGH... WHILE DEATH MAY BRIEFLY AMUSE AND DISTRACT US WITH ITS UNFAMILIARITY, IT CANNOT BE ALLOWED TO PERSIST.
I UNDERSTAND, LORD MAR-VELL.

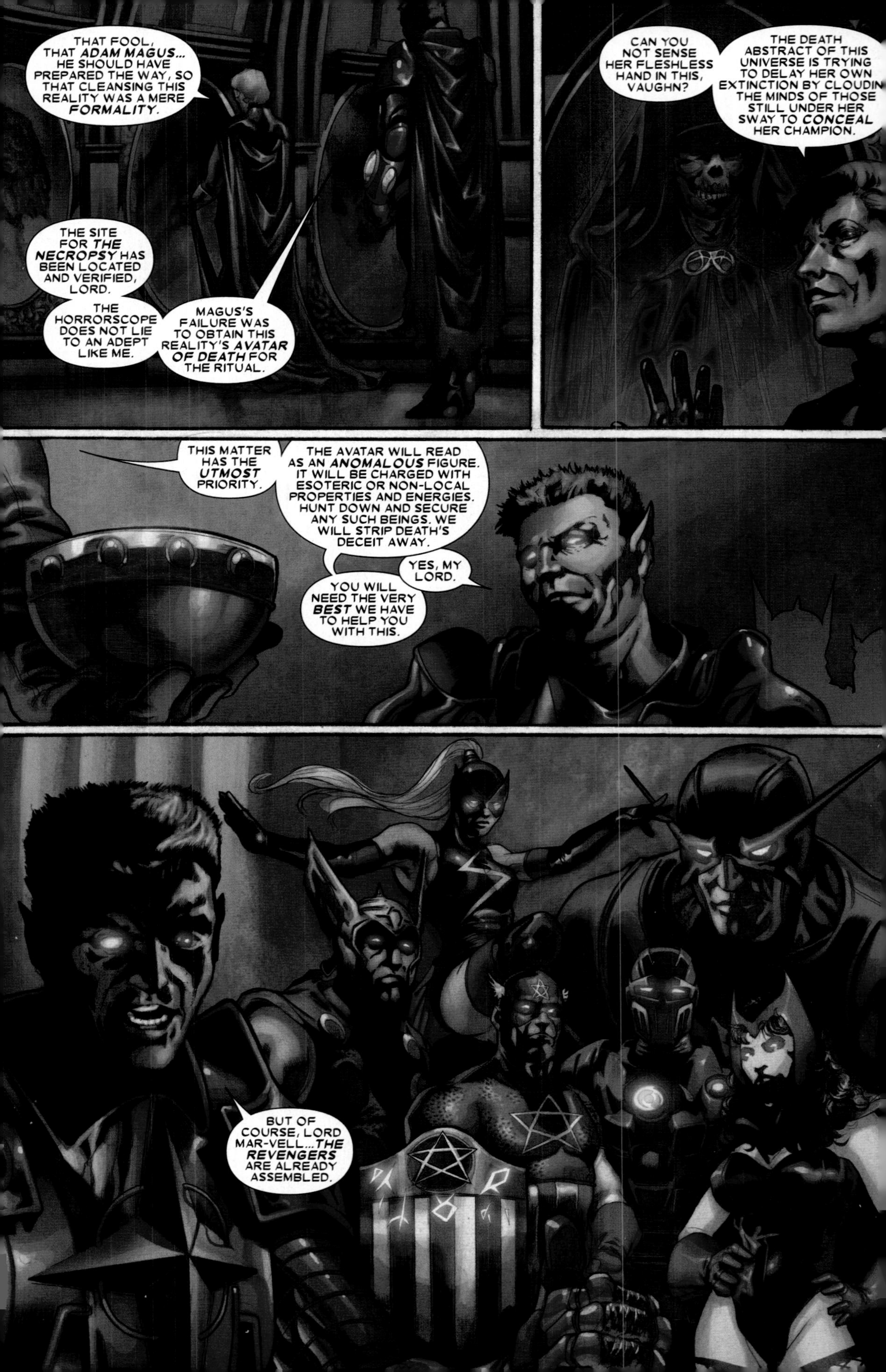
THAT FOOL, THAT ADAM MAGUS... HE SHOULD HAVE PREPARED THE WAY, SO THAT CLEANSING THIS REALITY WAS A MERE FORMALITY.
THE SITE FOR THE NECROPSY HAS BEEN LOCATED AND VERIFIED, LORD.
THE HORRORSCOPE DOES NOT LIE TO AN ADEPT LIKE ME.
MAGUS'S FAILURE WAS TO OBTAIN THIS REALITY'S AVATAR OF DEATH FOR THE RITUAL.
CAN YOU NOT SENSE HER FLESHLESS HAND IN THIS, VAUGHN?
THE DEATH ABSTRACT OF THIS UNIVERSE IS TRYING TO DELAY HER OWN EXTINCTION BY CLOUDIN THE MINDS OF THOSE STILL UNDER HER SWAY TO CONCEAL HER CHAMPION.
THIS MATTER HAS THE UTMOST PRIORITY.
THE AVATAR WILL READ AS AN ANOMALOUS FIGURE. IT WILL BE CHARGED WITH ESOTERIC OR NON-LOCAL PROPERTIES AND ENERGIES. HUNT DOWN AND SECURE ANY SUCH BEINGS. WE WILL STRIP DEATH'S DECEIT AWAY.
YES, MY LORD.
YOU WILL NEED THE VERY BEST WE HAVE TO HELP YOU WITH THIS.
BUT OF COURSE, LORD MAR-VELL...THE REVENGERS ARE ALREADY ASSEMBLED.

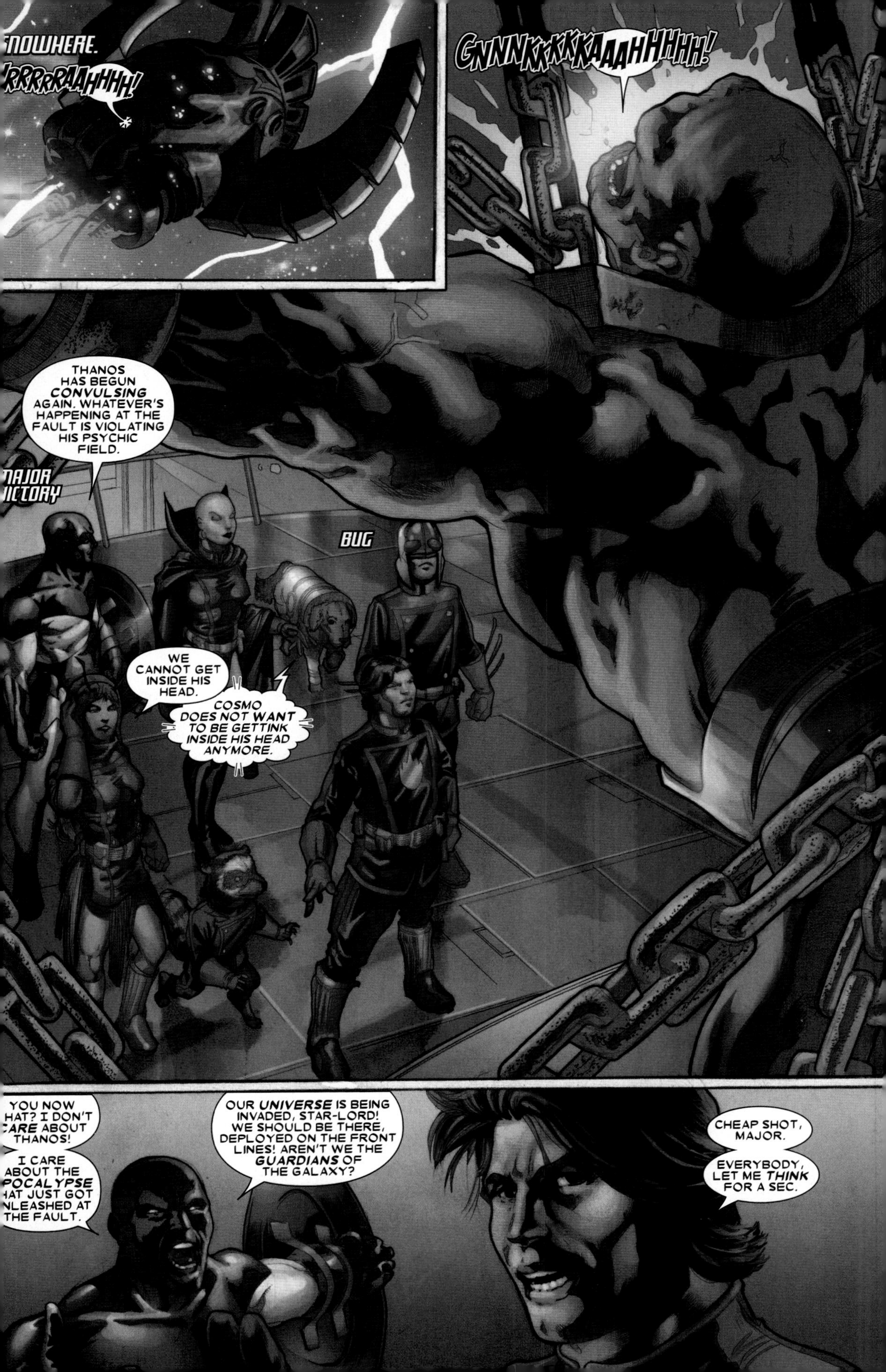

NOWHERE.
RRRRRAAHHHH!
GNNNKKKKKAAAHHHHH!
THANOS HAS BEGUN CONVULSING AGAIN. WHATEVER'S HAPPENING AT THE FAULT IS VIOLATING HIS PSYCHIC FIELD.
MAJOR VICTORY
BUG
WE CANNOT GET INSIDE HIS HEAD.
COSMO DOES NOT WANT TO BE GETTINK INSIDE HIS HEAD ANYMORE.
YOU NOW HAT? I DON'T CARE ABOUT THANOS!
I CARE ABOUT THE POCALYPSE HAT JUST GOT NLEASHED AT THE FAULT.
OUR UNIVERSE IS BEING INVADED, STAR-LORD! WE SHOULD BE THERE, DEPLOYED ON THE FRONT LINES! AREN'T WE THE GUARDIANS OF THE GALAXY?
CHEAP SHOT, MAJOR.
EVERYBODY, LET ME THINK FOR A SEC.

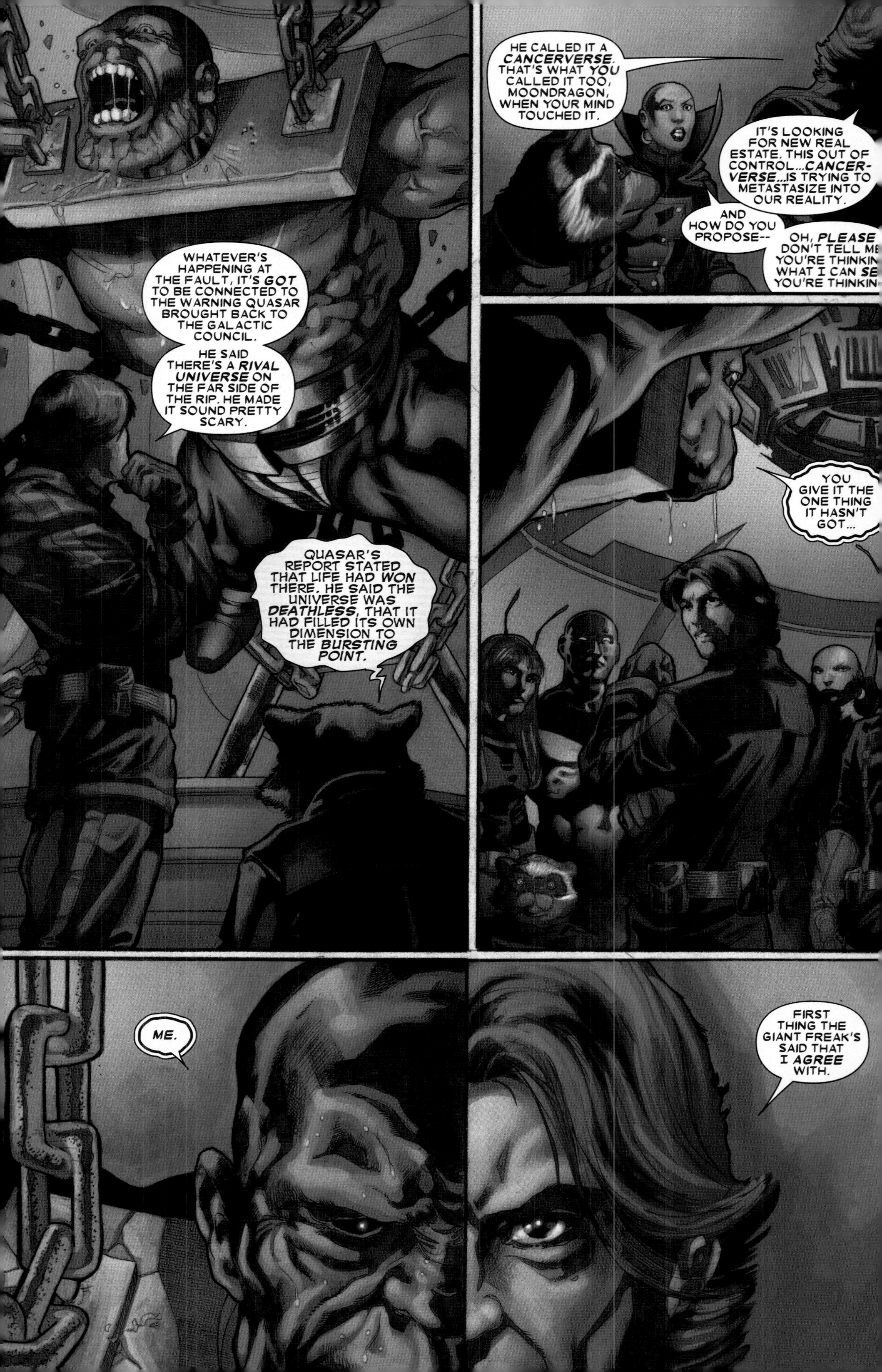

WHATEVER'S HAPPENING AT THE FAULT, IT'S *GOT* TO BE CONNECTED TO THE WARNING QUASAR BROUGHT BACK TO THE GALACTIC COUNCIL.
HE SAID THERE'S A *RIVAL UNIVERSE* ON THE FAR SIDE OF THE RIP. HE MADE IT SOUND PRETTY SCARY.
QUASAR'S REPORT STATED THAT LIFE HAD *WON* THERE. HE SAID THE UNIVERSE WAS *DEATHLESS*, THAT IT HAD FILLED ITS OWN DIMENSION TO THE *BURSTING POINT.*
HE CALLED IT A *CANCERVERSE*. THAT'S WHAT *YOU* CALLED IT TOO, MOONDRAGON, WHEN YOUR MIND TOUCHED IT.
IT'S LOOKING FOR NEW REAL ESTATE. THIS OUT OF CONTROL...*CANCER-VERSE*...IS TRYING TO METASTASIZE INTO OUR REALITY.
AND HOW DO YOU PROPOSE--
OH, *PLEASE* DON'T TELL ME YOU'RE THINKING WHAT I CAN *SEE* YOU'RE THINKING.
YOU GIVE IT THE ONE THING IT HASN'T GOT...
ME.
FIRST THING THE GIANT FREAK'S SAID THAT I *AGREE* WITH.

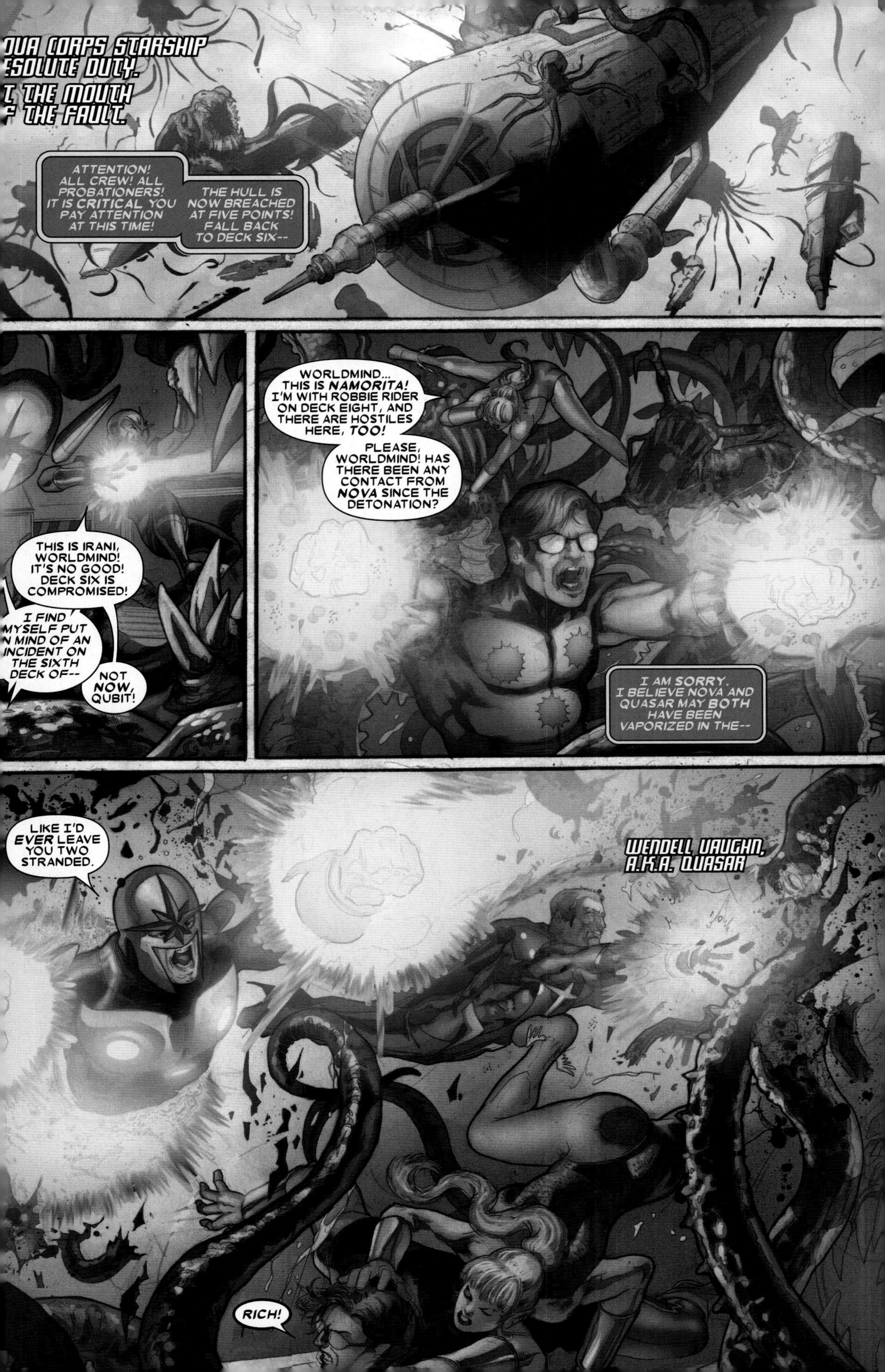

OVA CORPS STARSHIP
ESOLUTE DUTY.
T THE MOUTH
F THE FAULT.
ATTENTION! ALL CREW! ALL PROBATIONERS! IT IS CRITICAL YOU PAY ATTENTION AT THIS TIME!
THE HULL IS NOW BREACHED AT FIVE POINTS! FALL BACK TO DECK SIX--
THIS IS IRANI, WORLDMIND! IT'S NO GOOD! DECK SIX IS COMPROMISED!
I FIND MYSELF PUT N MIND OF AN INCIDENT ON THE SIXTH DECK OF--
NOT NOW, QUBIT!
WORLDMIND... THIS IS NAMORITA! I'M WITH ROBBIE RIDER ON DECK EIGHT, AND THERE ARE HOSTILES HERE, TOO!
PLEASE, WORLDMIND! HAS THERE BEEN ANY CONTACT FROM NOVA SINCE THE DETONATION?
I AM SORRY. I BELIEVE NOVA AND QUASAR MAY BOTH HAVE BEEN VAPORIZED IN THE--
LIKE I'D EVER LEAVE YOU TWO STRANDED.
WENDELL VAUGHN, A.K.A. QUASAR
RICH!

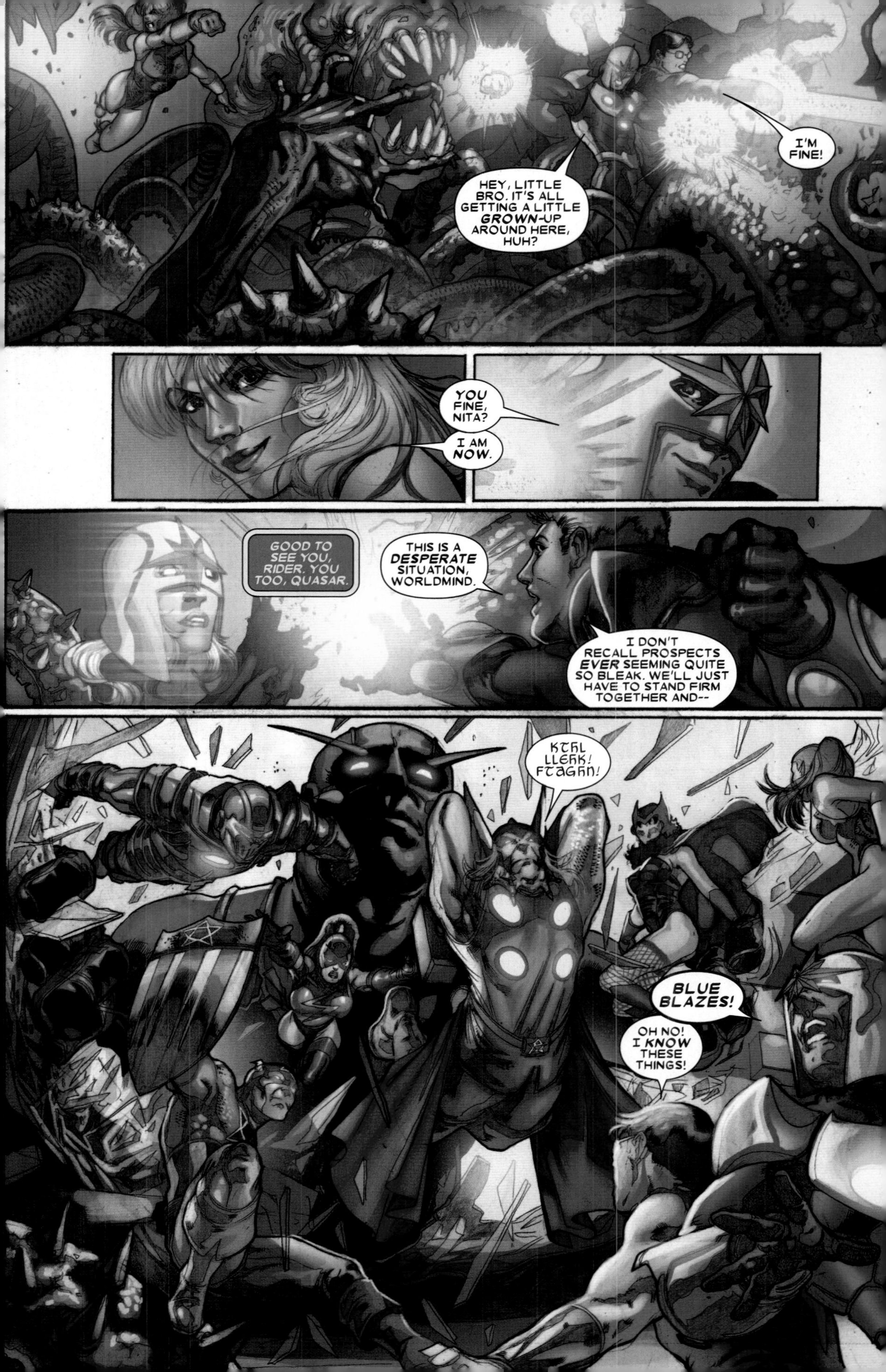
HEY, LITTLE BRO. IT'S ALL GETTING A LITTLE GROWN-UP AROUND HERE, HUH?
I'M FINE!
YOU FINE, NITA?
I AM NOW.
GOOD TO SEE YOU, RIDER. YOU TOO, QUASAR.
THIS IS A DESPERATE SITUATION, WORLDMIND.
I DON'T RECALL PROSPECTS EVER SEEMING QUITE SO BLEAK. WE'LL JUST HAVE TO STAND FIRM TOGETHER AND--
KTHL LLEHK! FTAGHN!
BLUE BLAZES!
OH NO! I KNOW THESE THINGS!

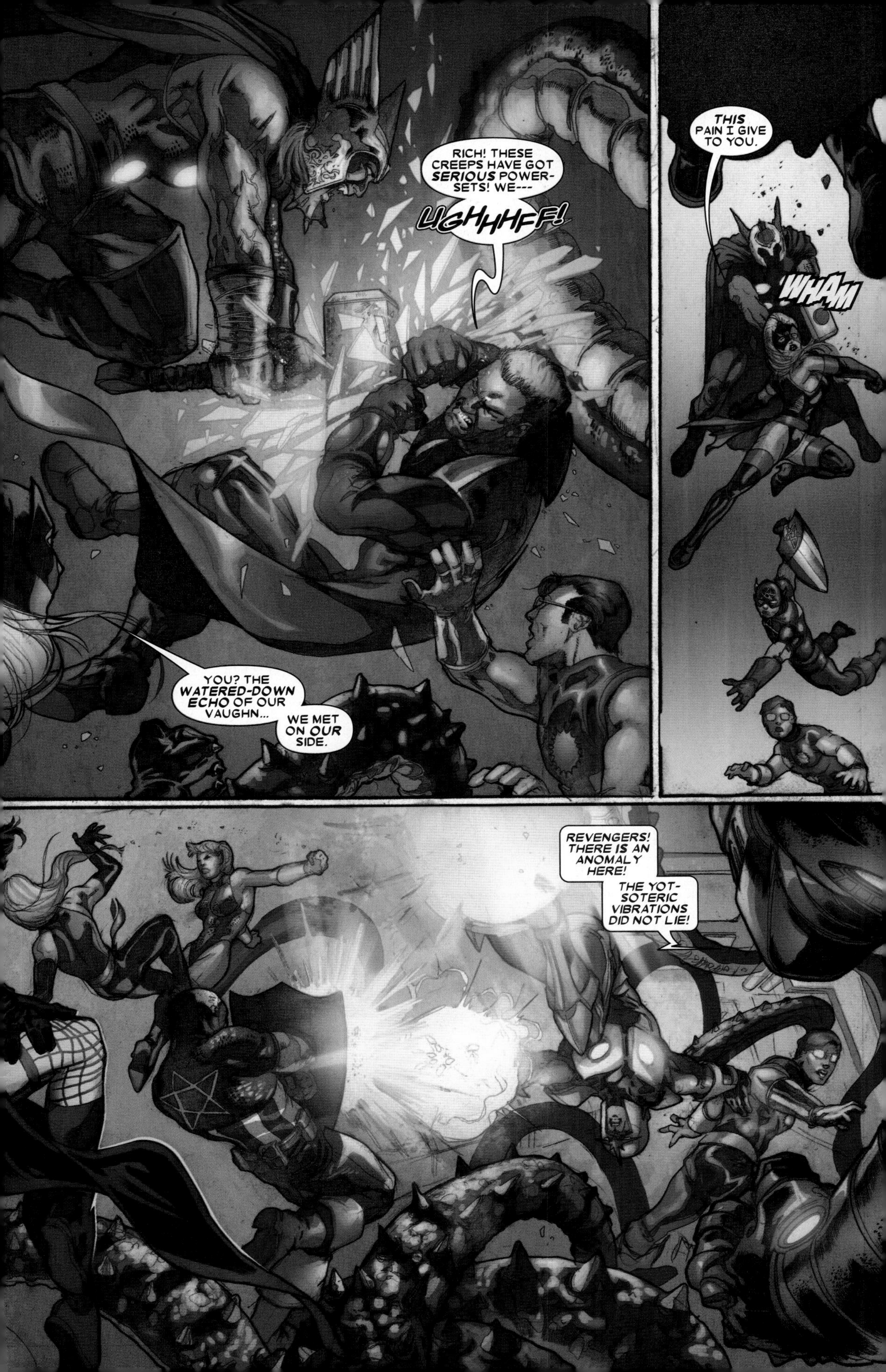
RICH! THESE CREEPS HAVE GOT SERIOUS POWER-SETS! WE---
UGHHHFF!
YOU? THE WATERED-DOWN ECHO OF OUR VAUGHN...
WE MET ON OUR SIDE.
THIS PAIN I GIVE TO YOU.
WHAM
REVENGERS! THERE IS AN ANOMALY HERE!
THE YOT-SOTERIC VIBRATIONS DID NOT LIE!

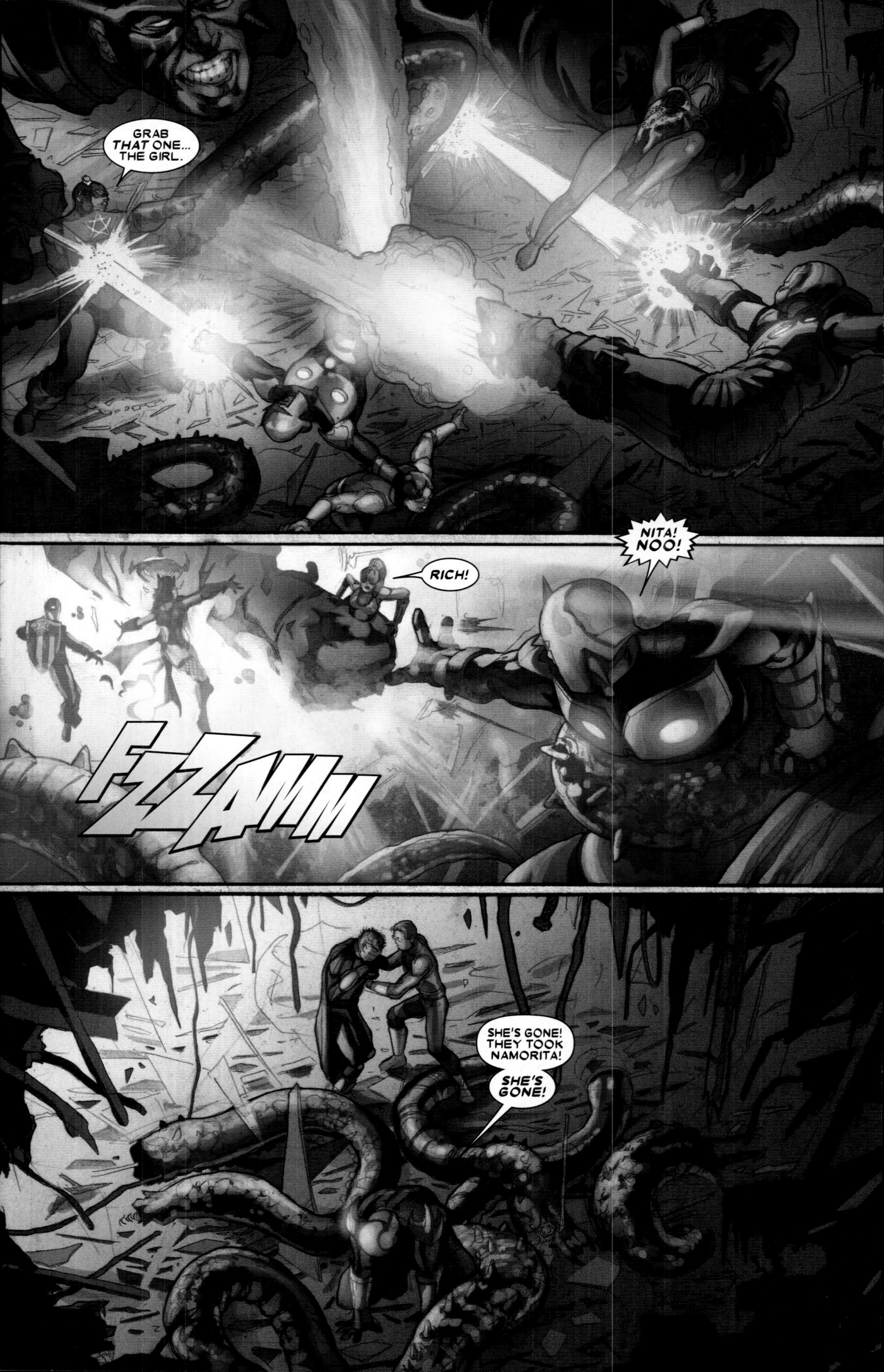
GRAB THAT ONE... THE GIRL.
NITA! NOO!
RICH!
FZZAMM
SHE'S GONE! THEY TOOK NAMORITA!
SHE'S GONE!

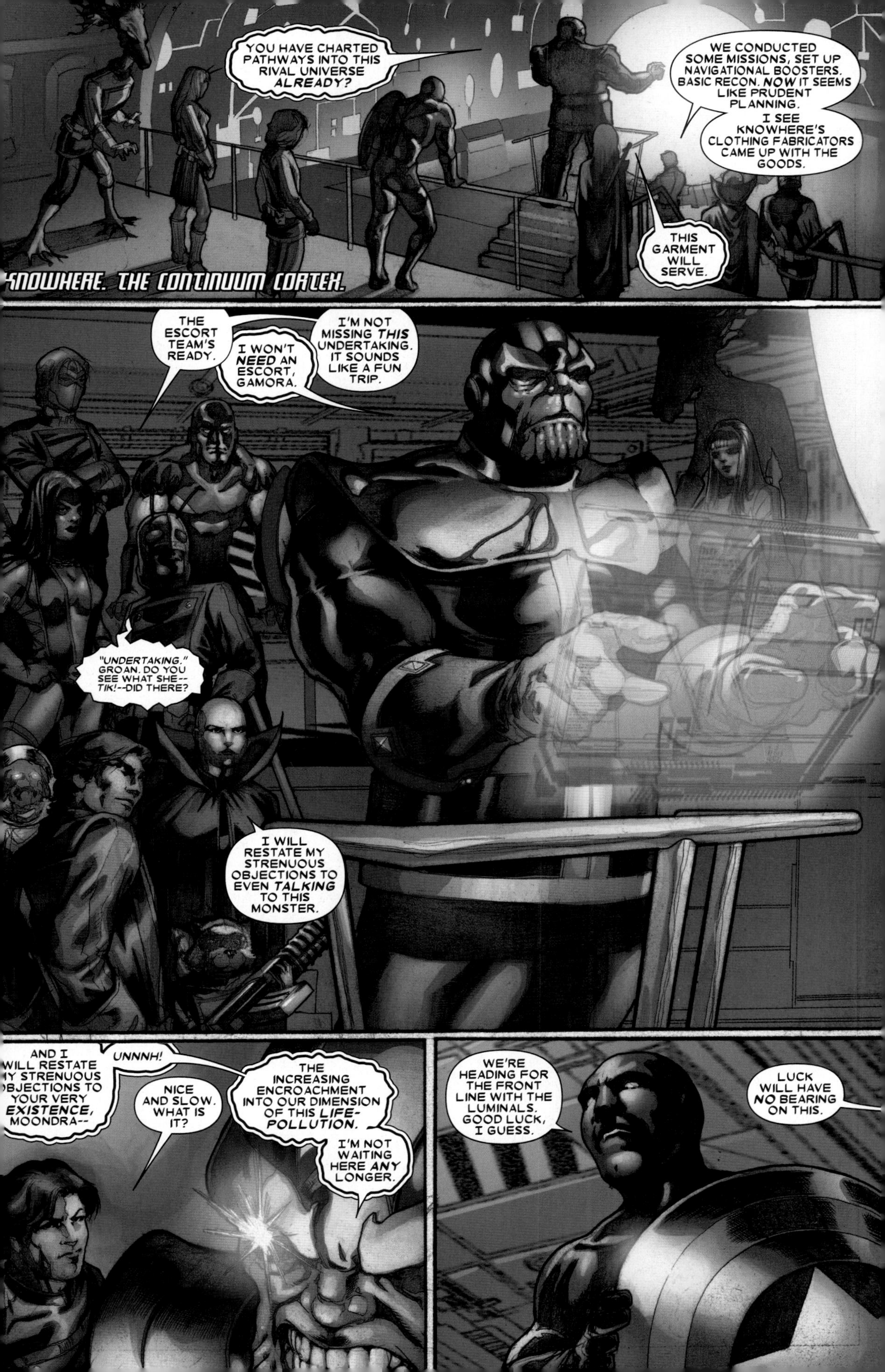
YOU HAVE CHARTED PATHWAYS INTO THIS RIVAL UNIVERSE ALREADY?
WE CONDUCTED SOME MISSIONS, SET UP NAVIGATIONAL BOOSTERS. BASIC RECON. NOW IT SEEMS LIKE PRUDENT PLANNING.
I SEE KNOWHERE'S CLOTHING FABRICATORS CAME UP WITH THE GOODS.
THIS GARMENT WILL SERVE.
KNOWHERE. THE CONTINUUM CORTEX.
THE ESCORT TEAM'S READY.
I WON'T NEED AN ESCORT, GAMORA.
I'M NOT MISSING THIS UNDERTAKING. IT SOUNDS LIKE A FUN TRIP.
"UNDERTAKING." GROAN. DO YOU SEE WHAT SHE--TIK!--DID THERE?
I WILL RESTATE MY STRENUOUS OBJECTIONS TO EVEN TALKING TO THIS MONSTER.
AND I WILL RESTATE MY STRENUOUS OBJECTIONS TO YOUR VERY EXISTENCE, MOONDRA--
UNNNH!
NICE AND SLOW. WHAT IS IT?
THE INCREASING ENCROACHMENT INTO OUR DIMENSION OF THIS LIFE-POLLUTION.
I'M NOT WAITING HERE ANY LONGER.
WE'RE HEADING FOR THE FRONT LINE WITH THE LUMINALS. GOOD LUCK, I GUESS.
LUCK WILL HAVE NO BEARING ON THIS.

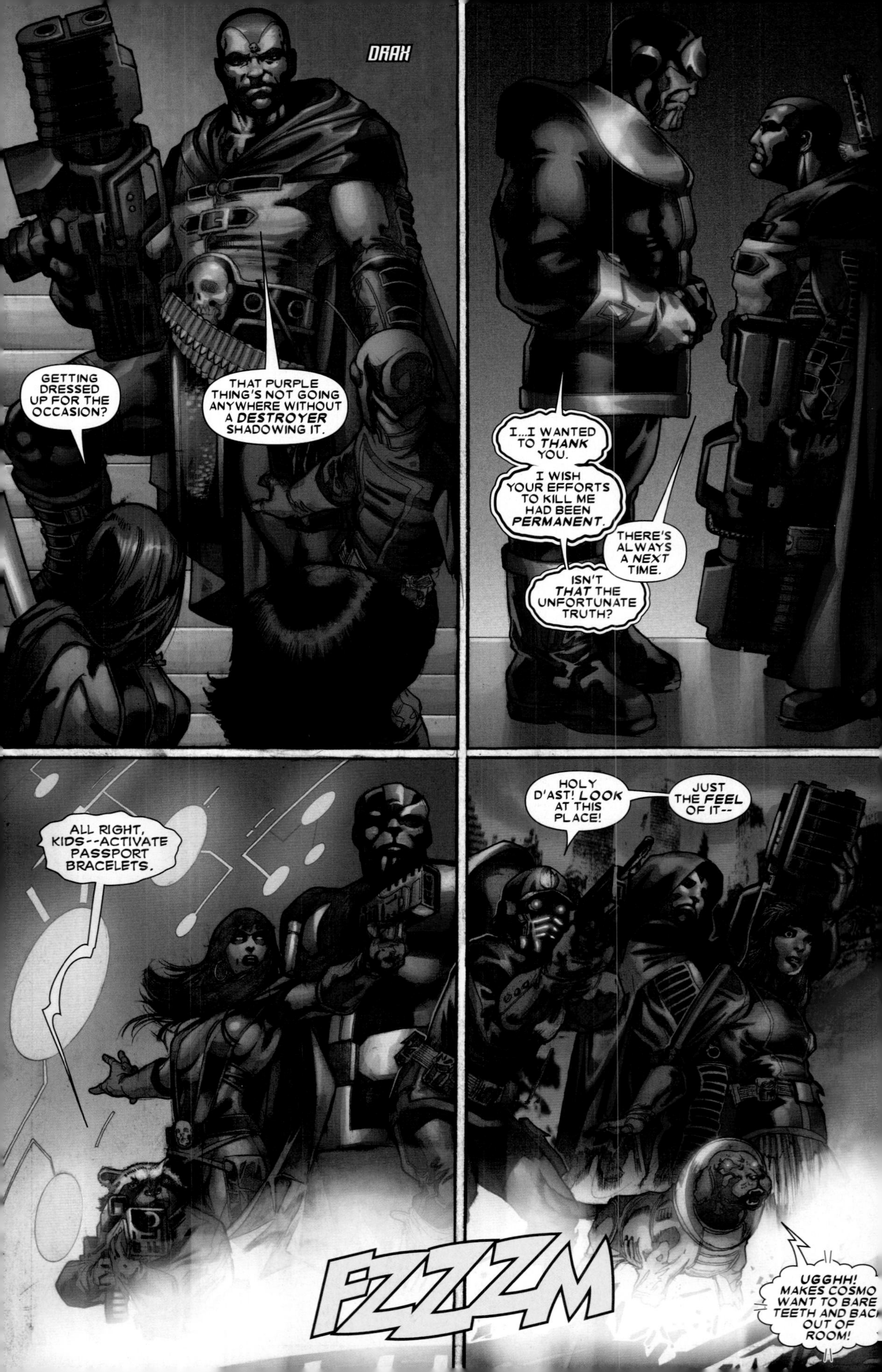
DRAX
GETTING DRESSED UP FOR THE OCCASION?
THAT PURPLE THING'S NOT GOING ANYWHERE WITHOUT A DESTROYER SHADOWING IT.
I...I WANTED TO THANK YOU.
I WISH YOUR EFFORTS TO KILL ME HAD BEEN PERMANENT.
THERE'S ALWAYS A NEXT TIME.
ISN'T THAT THE UNFORTUNATE TRUTH?
ALL RIGHT, KIDS--ACTIVATE PASSPORT BRACELETS.
HOLY D'AST! LOOK AT THIS PLACE!
JUST THE FEEL OF IT--
FZZZM
UGGHH! MAKES COSMO WANT TO BARE TEETH AND BAC OUT OF ROOM!

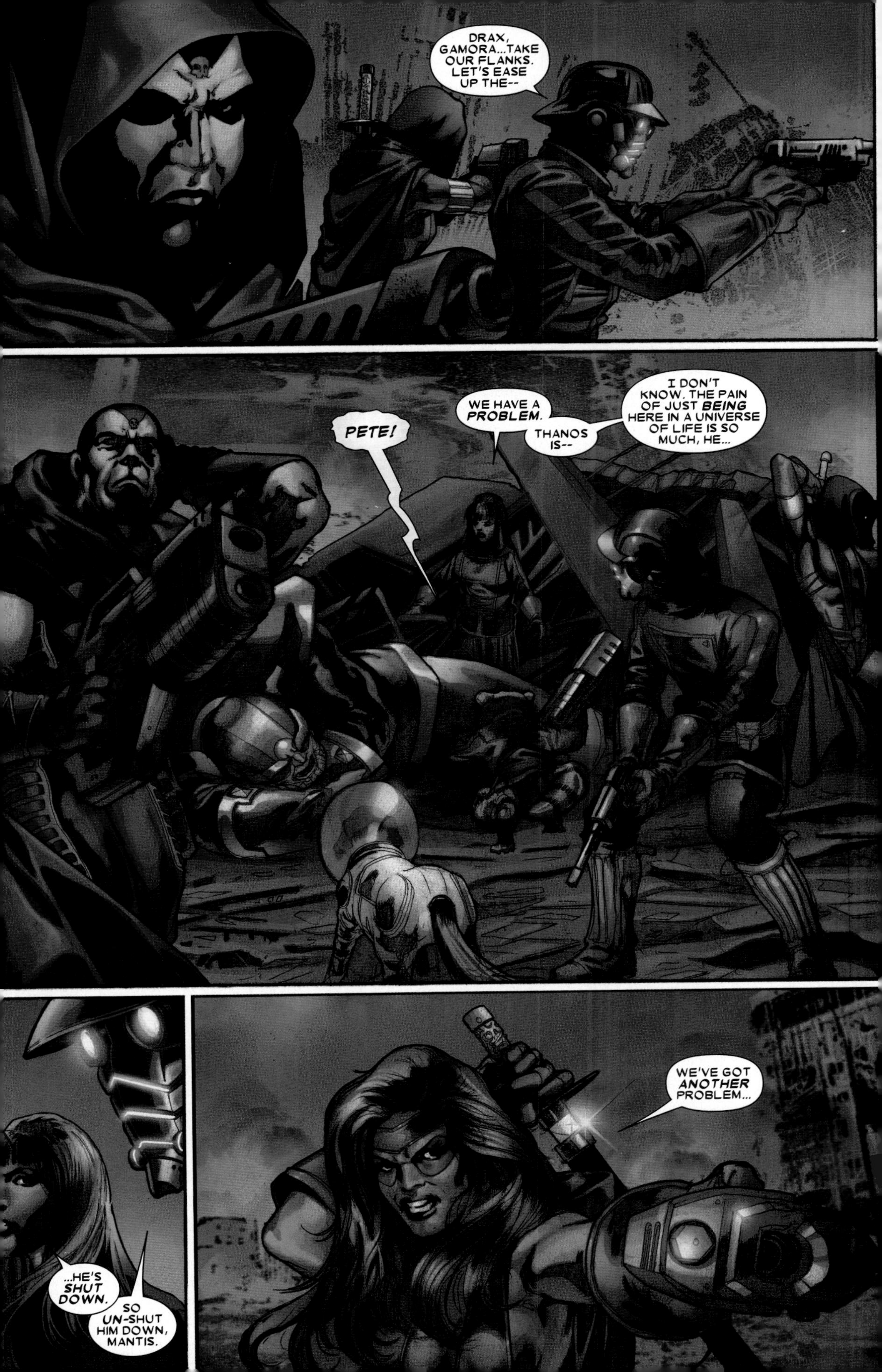
DRAX, GAMORA...TAKE OUR FLANKS. LET'S EASE UP THE--
PETE!
WE HAVE A *PROBLEM*.
THANOS IS--
I DON'T KNOW. THE PAIN OF JUST *BEING* HERE IN A UNIVERSE OF LIFE IS SO MUCH, HE...
...HE'S *SHUT DOWN*.
SO *UN*-SHUT HIM DOWN, MANTIS.
WE'VE GOT *ANOTHER* PROBLEM...

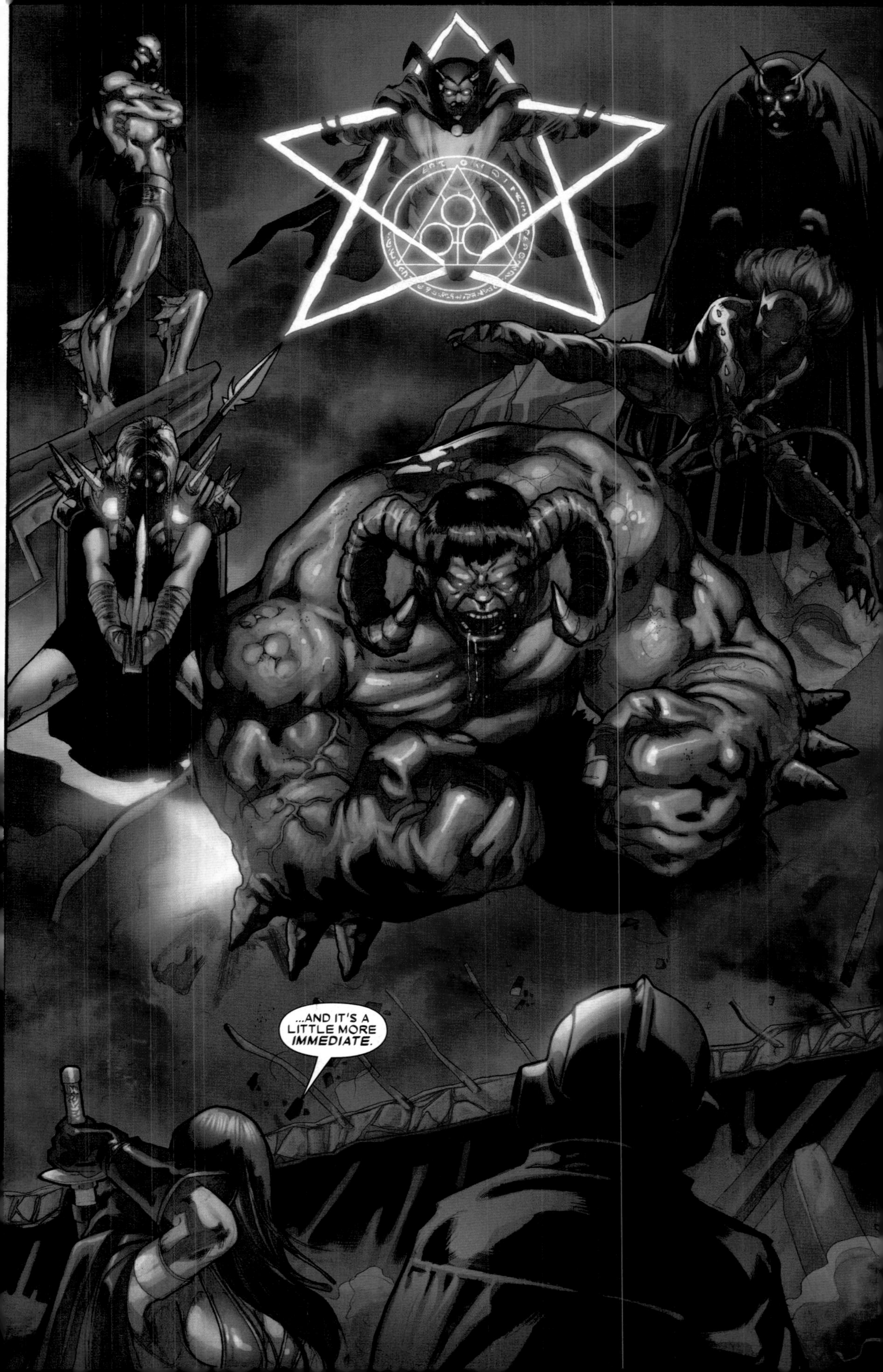
...AND IT'S A LITTLE MORE IMMEDIATE.

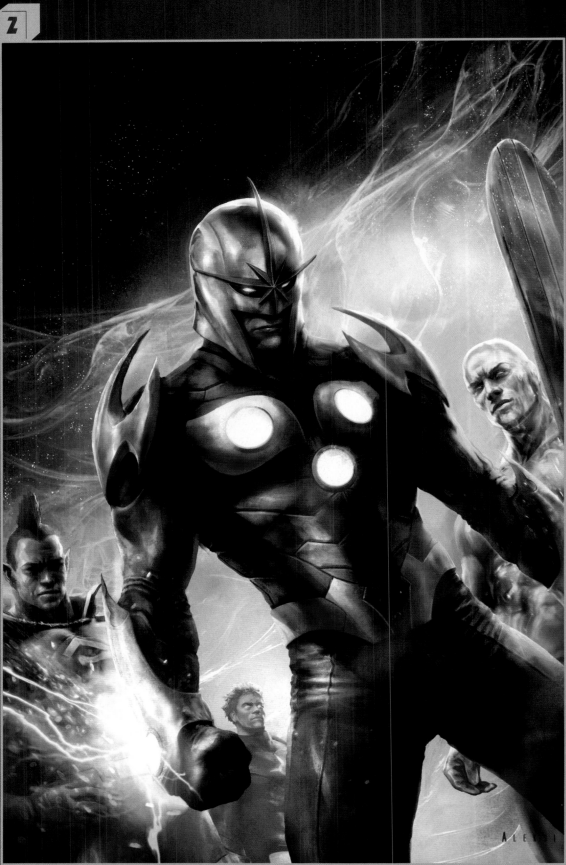

ATTENTION-- HOSTILE, EIGHT METERS! TARGETING!

ATTENTION--TWO HOSTILES, FIVE AND SEVEN METERS! TARGETING!

ATTENTION-- HOSTILE CLOSING FROM BEHIND!

NOVA! ARE YOU PAYING ATTENTION?!

ON IT, WORLDMIND! PULSE-FIRE, LEFT HAND, FULL GRAVIMETRIC!

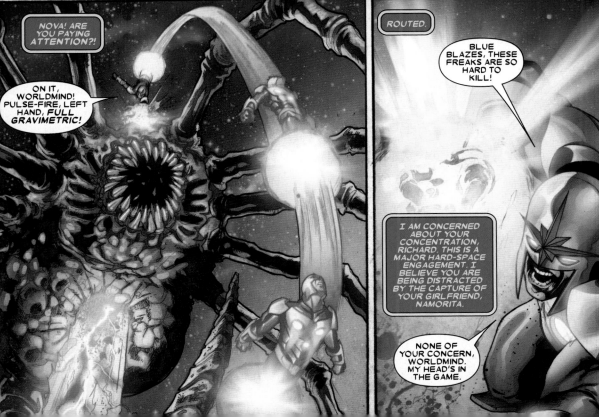

ROUTED.

BLUE BLAZES, THESE FREAKS ARE SO HARD TO KILL!

I AM CONCERNED ABOUT YOUR CONCENTRATION, RICHARD. THIS IS A MAJOR HARD-SPACE ENGAGEMENT. I BELIEVE YOU ARE BEING DISTRACTED BY THE CAPTURE OF YOUR GIRLFRIEND, NAMORITA.

NONE OF YOUR CONCERN, WORLDMIND. MY HEAD'S IN THE GAME.

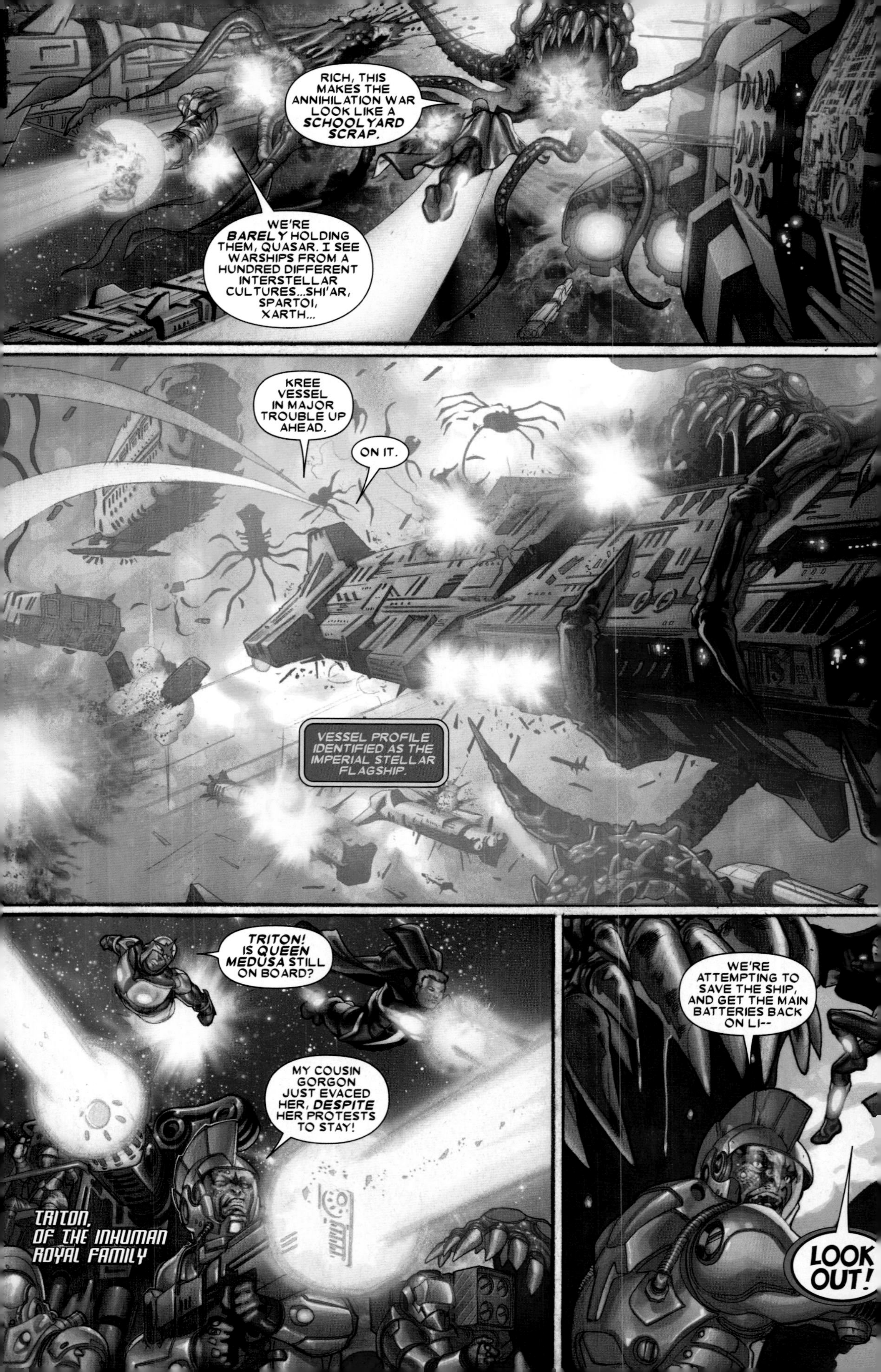
RICH, THIS MAKES THE ANNIHILATION WAR LOOK LIKE A SCHOOLYARD SCRAP.
WE'RE BARELY HOLDING THEM, QUASAR. I SEE WARSHIPS FROM A HUNDRED DIFFERENT INTERSTELLAR CULTURES...SHI'AR, SPARTOI, XARTH...
KREE VESSEL IN MAJOR TROUBLE UP AHEAD.
ON IT.
VESSEL PROFILE IDENTIFIED AS THE IMPERIAL STELLAR FLAGSHIP.
TRITON! IS QUEEN MEDUSA STILL ON BOARD?
MY COUSIN GORGON JUST EVACED HER, DESPITE HER PROTESTS TO STAY!
TRITON, OF THE INHUMAN ROYAL FAMILY
WE'RE ATTEMPTING TO SAVE THE SHIP, AND GET THE MAIN BATTERIES BACK ON LI--
LOOK OUT!

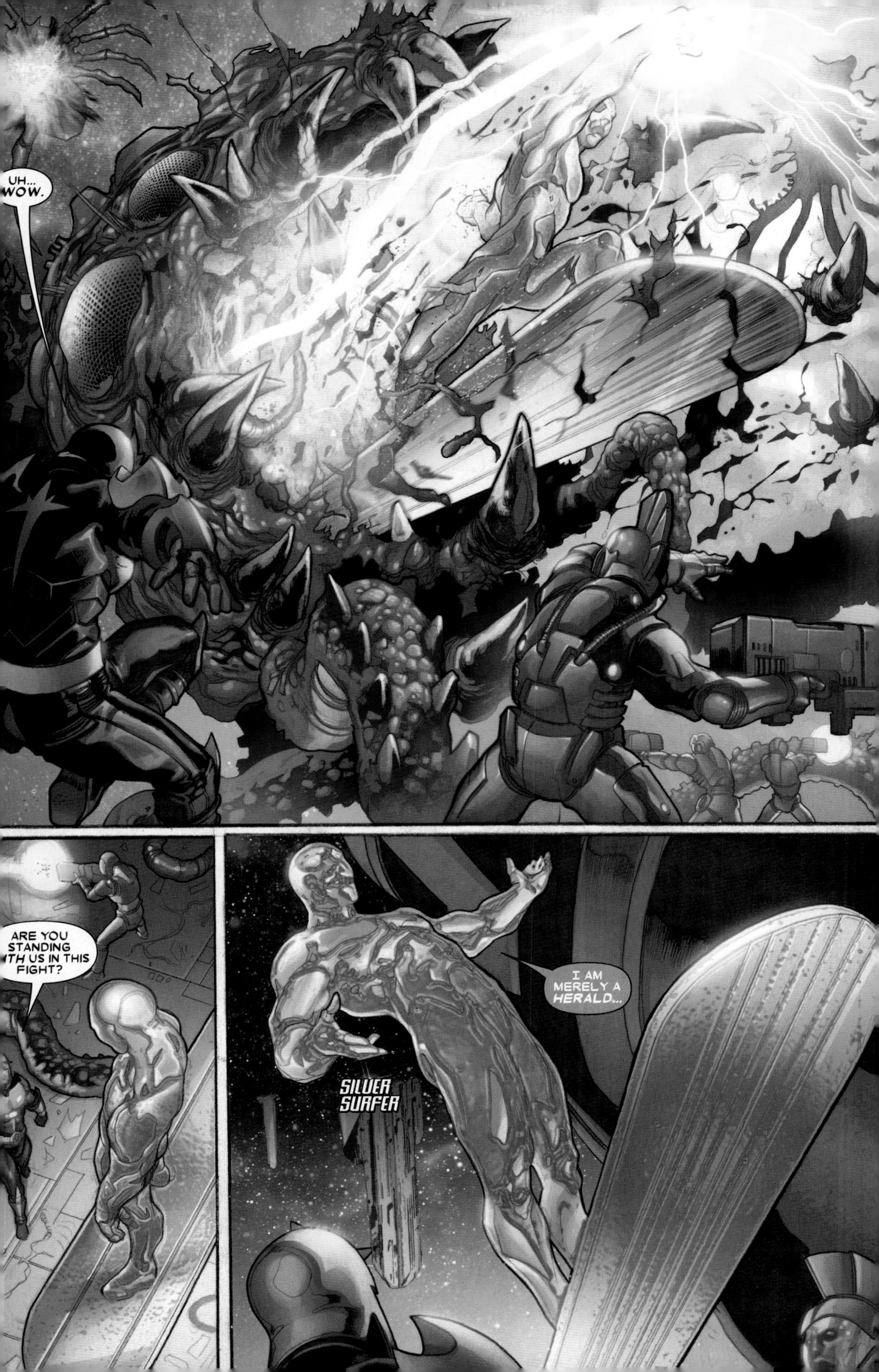
UH... WOW.
ARE YOU STANDING ITH US IN THIS FIGHT?
I AM MERELY A *HERALD*...
SILVER SURFER

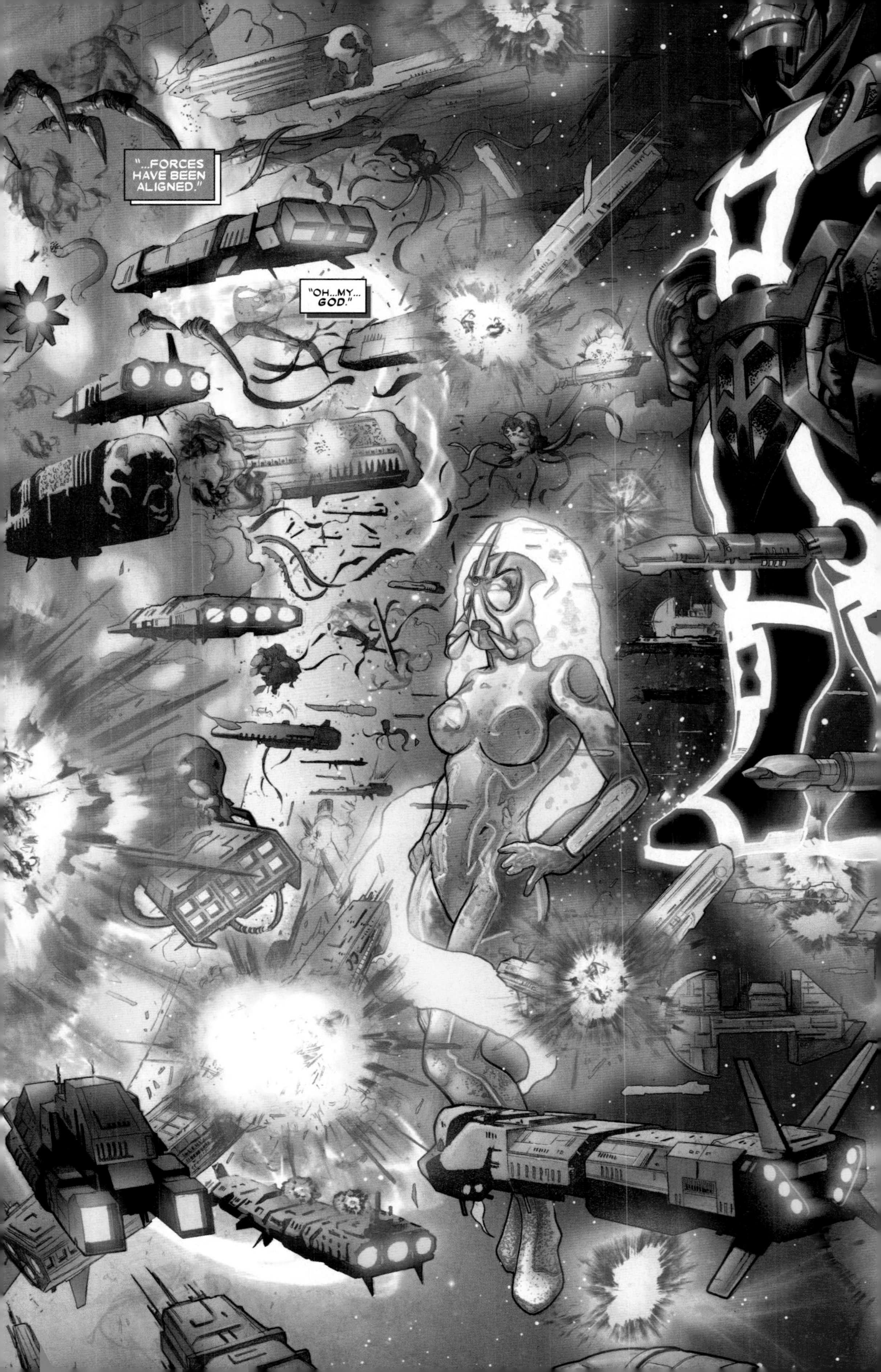
"...FORCES HAVE BEEN ALIGNED."
"OH...MY... GOD."

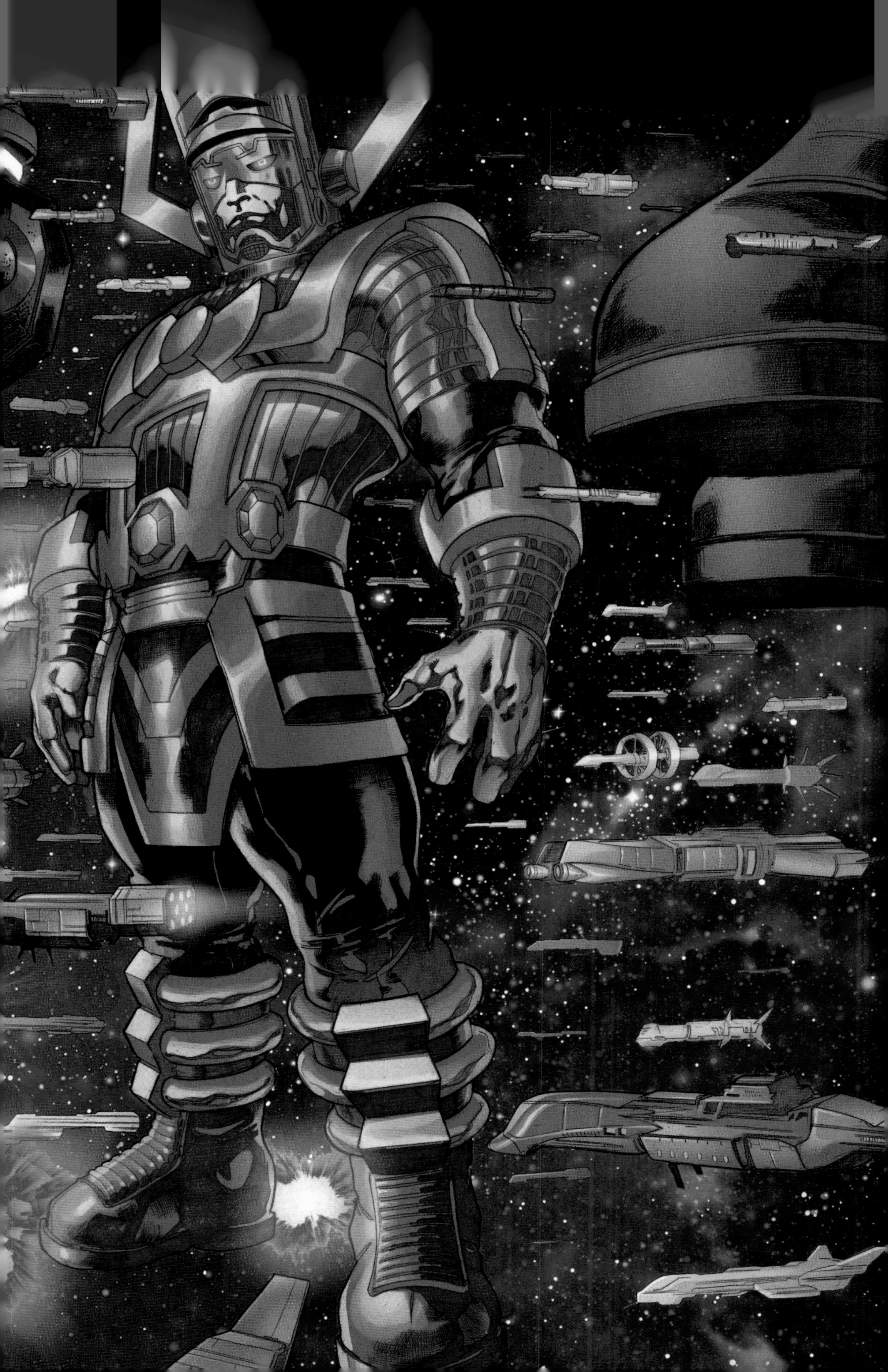

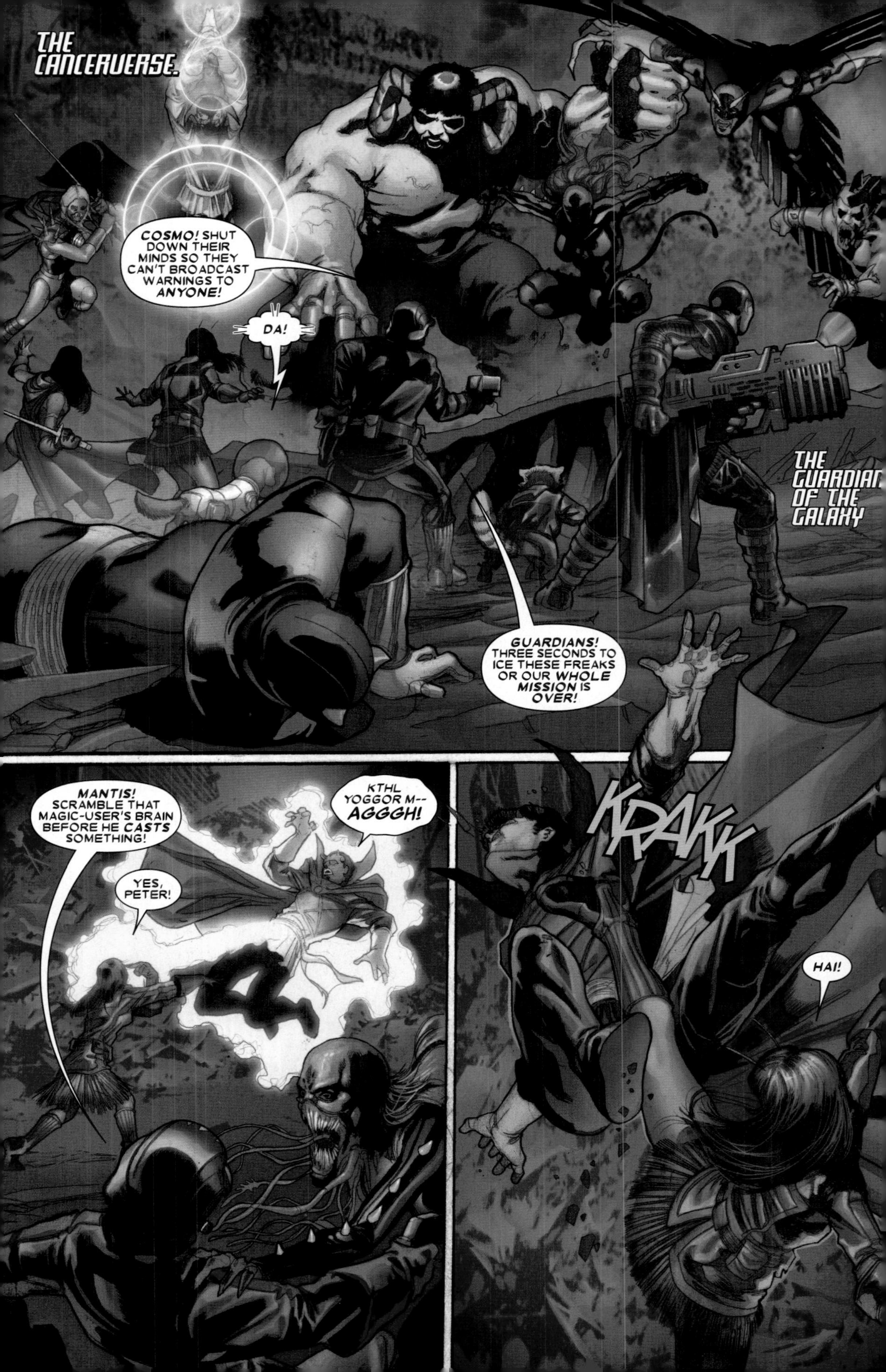
THE CANCERVERSE.
COSMO! SHUT DOWN THEIR MINDS SO THEY CAN'T BROADCAST WARNINGS TO ANYONE!
DA!
THE GUARDIANS OF THE GALAXY
GUARDIANS! THREE SECONDS TO ICE THESE FREAKS OR OUR WHOLE MISSION IS OVER!
MANTIS! SCRAMBLE THAT MAGIC-USER'S BRAIN BEFORE HE CASTS SOMETHING!
KTHL YOGGOR M-- AGGGH!
YES, PETER!
KRAKK
HAI!

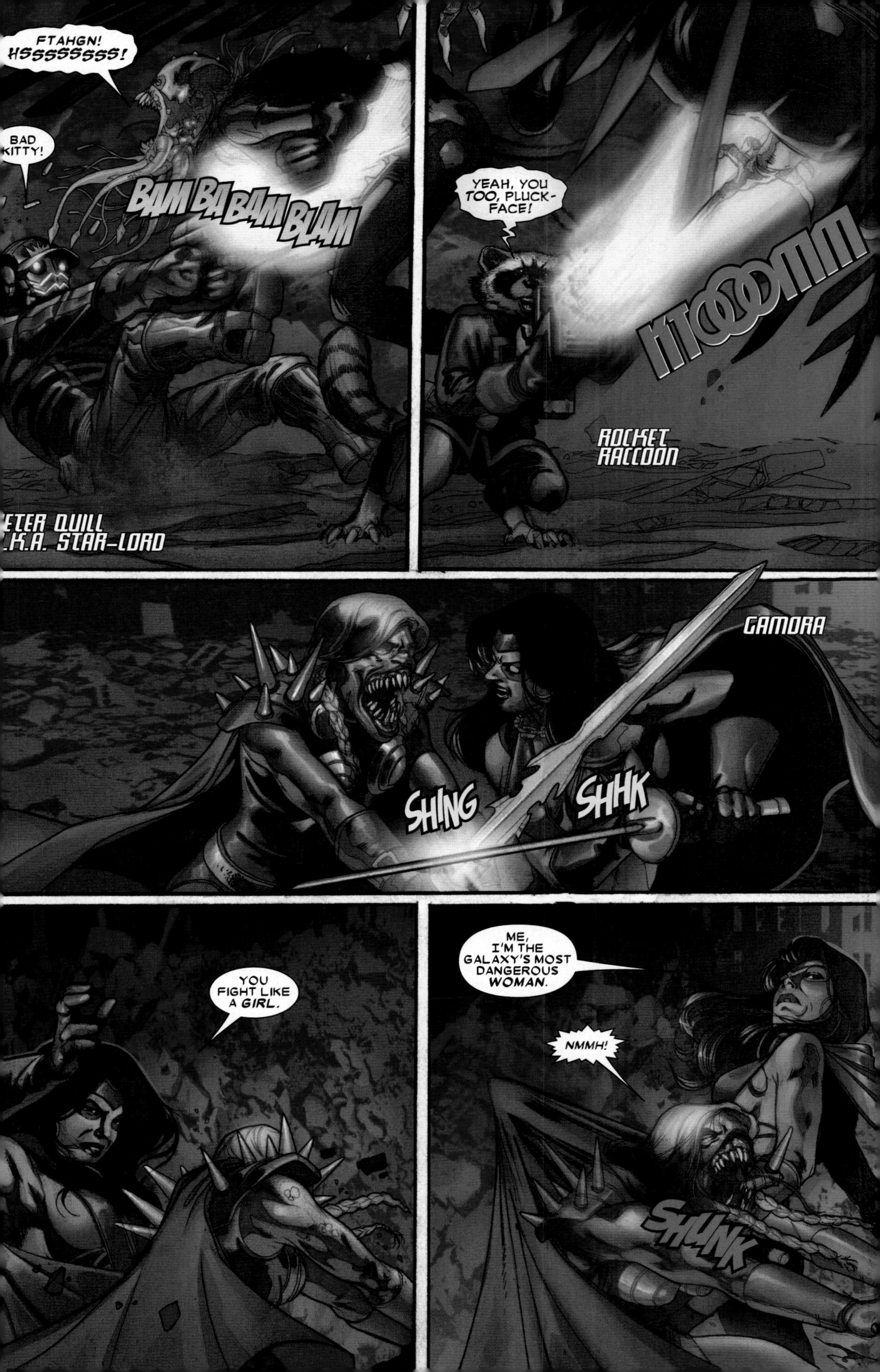
FTAHGN! HSSSSSSSS!
BAD KITTY!
BAM BA BAM BLAM
ETER QUILL
.K.A. STAR-LORD
YEAH, YOU TOO, PLUCK-FACE!
KTOOOMM
ROCKET RACCOON
GAMORA
SHING
SHHK
YOU FIGHT LIKE A GIRL.
ME, I'M THE GALAXY'S MOST DANGEROUS WOMAN.
NMMH!
SHUNK

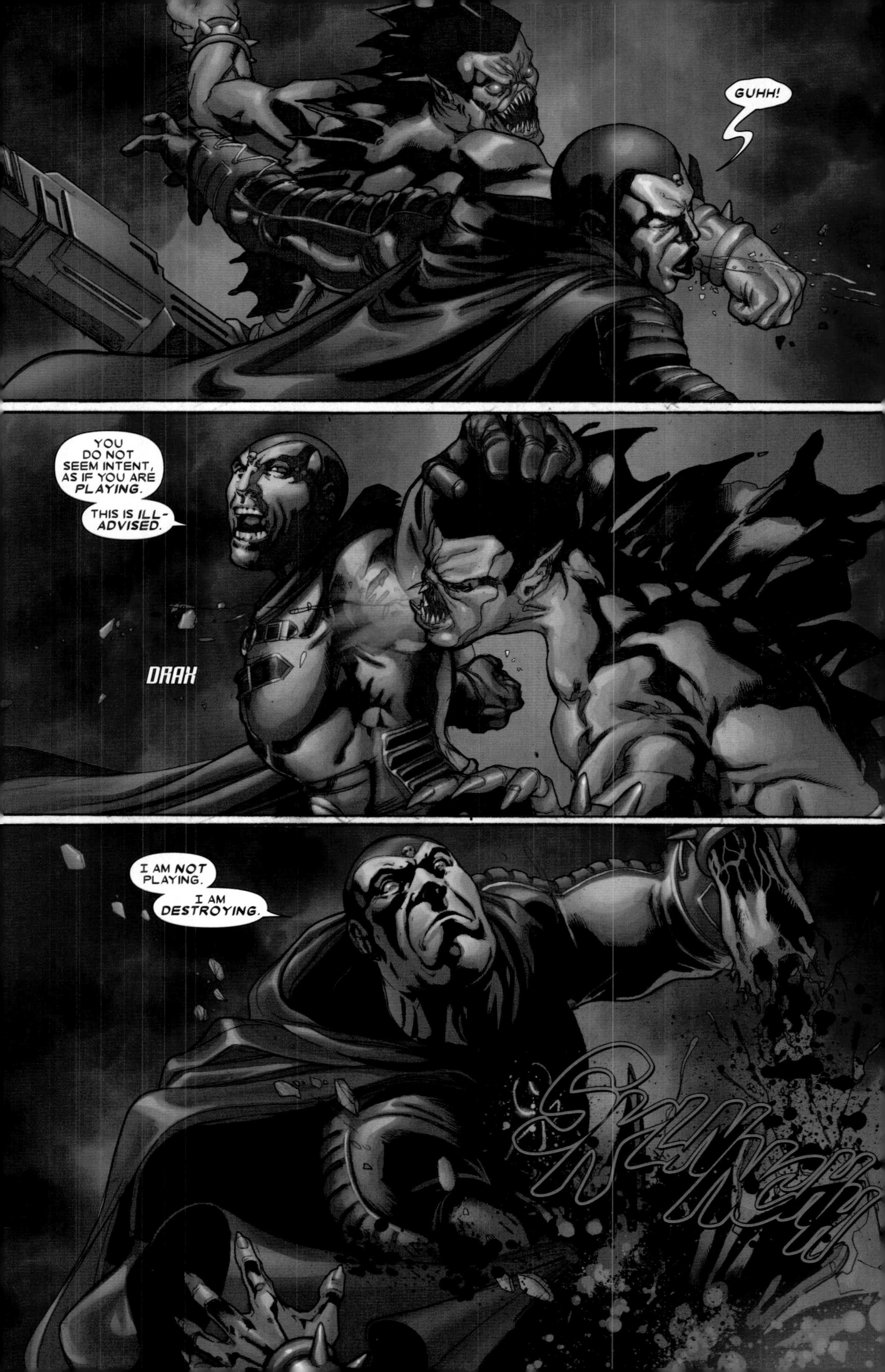
GUHH!
YOU DO NOT SEEM INTENT, AS IF YOU ARE PLAYING.
THIS IS ILL-ADVISED.
DRAX
I AM NOT PLAYING.
I AM DESTROYING.

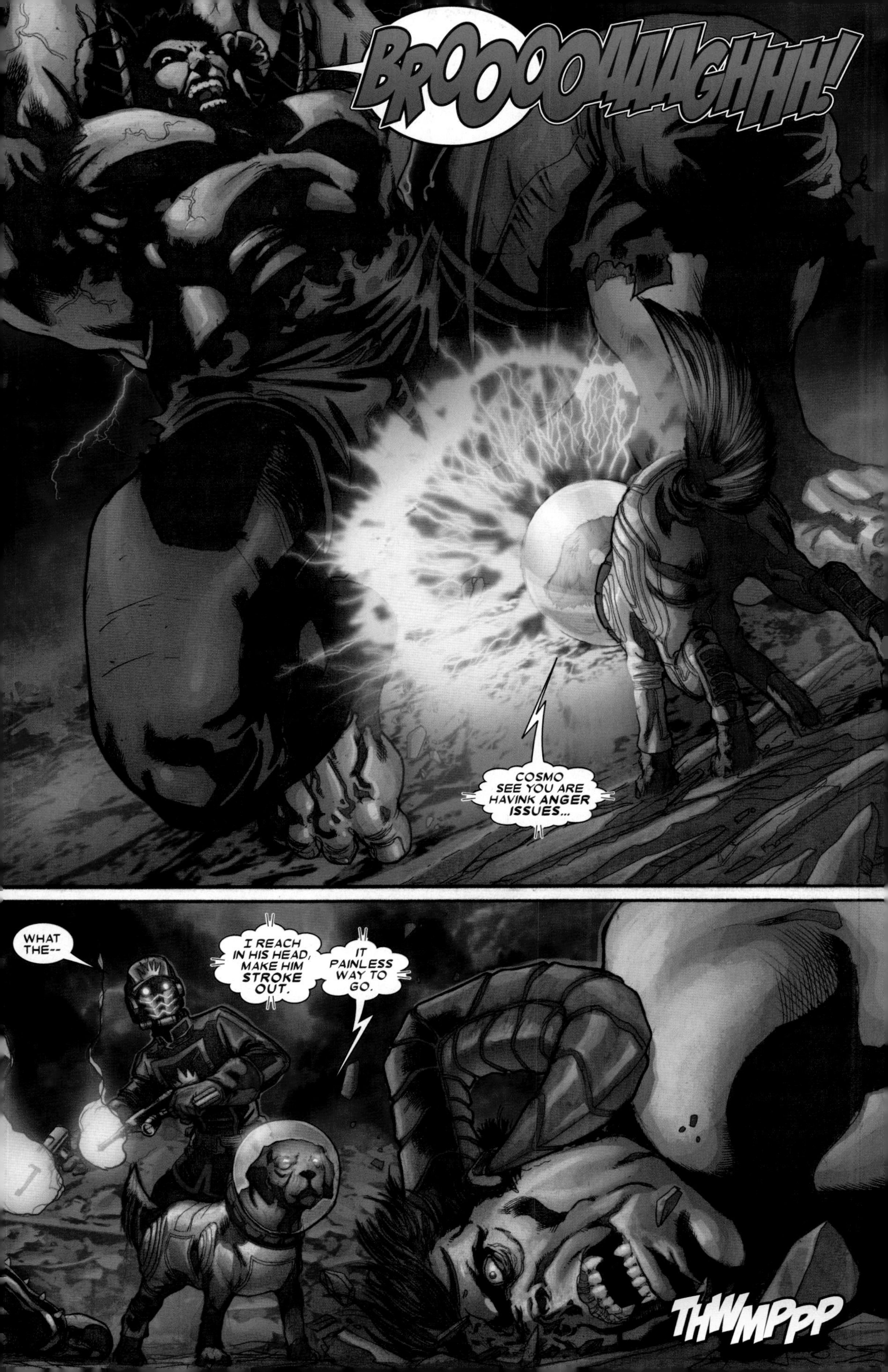
BROOOOOAAAGHHH!
COSMO SEE YOU ARE HAVINK ANGER ISSUES...
WHAT THE--
I REACH IN HIS HEAD, MAKE HIM STROKE OUT.
IT PAINLESS WAY TO GO.
THWMPPP

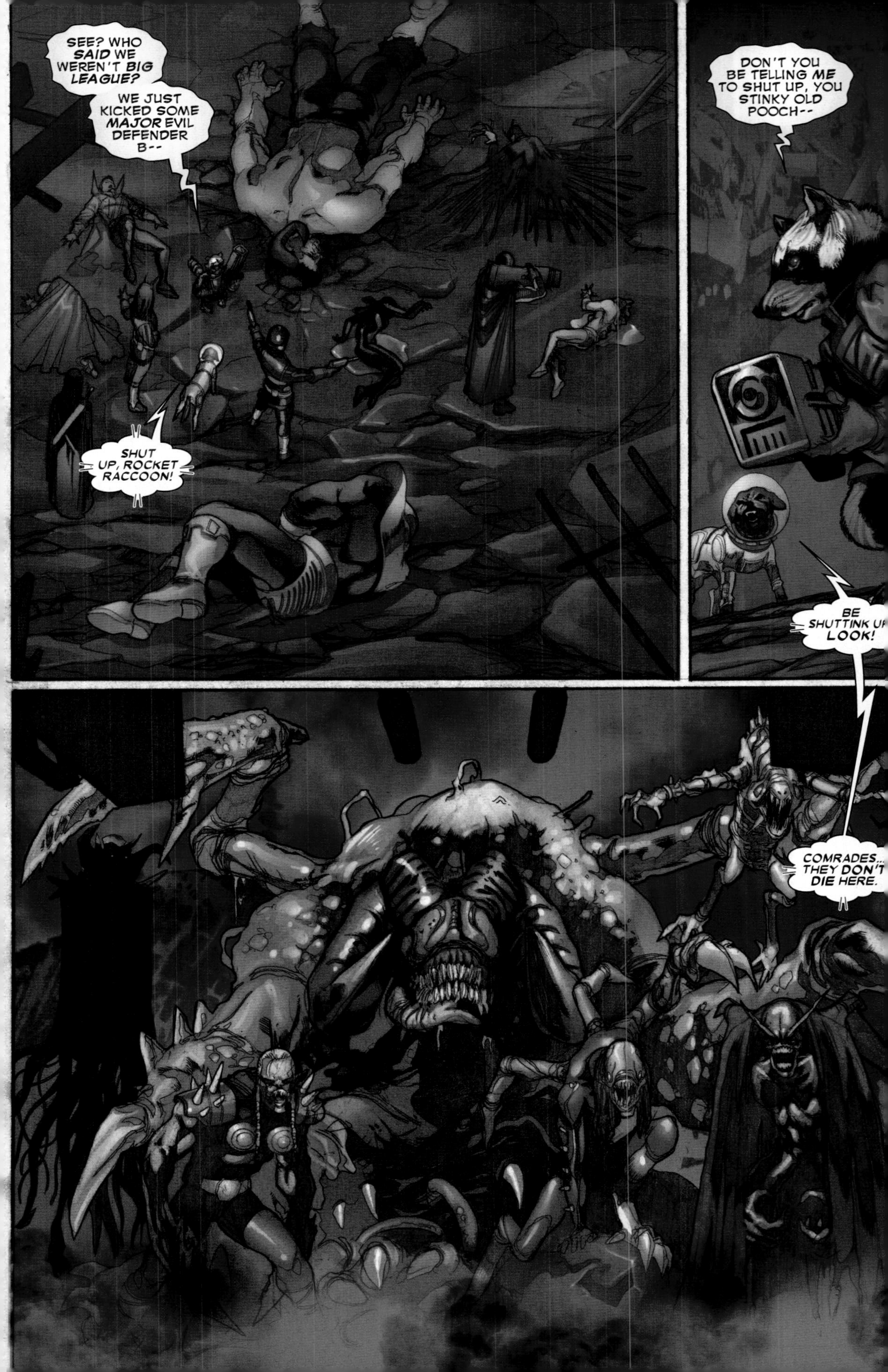
SEE? WHO SAID WE WEREN'T BIG LEAGUE?
WE JUST KICKED SOME MAJOR EVIL DEFENDER B--
SHUT UP, ROCKET RACCOON!
DON'T YOU BE TELLING ME TO SHUT UP, YOU STINKY OLD POOCH--
BE SHUTTINK UP! LOOK!
COMRADES... THEY DON'T DIE HERE.

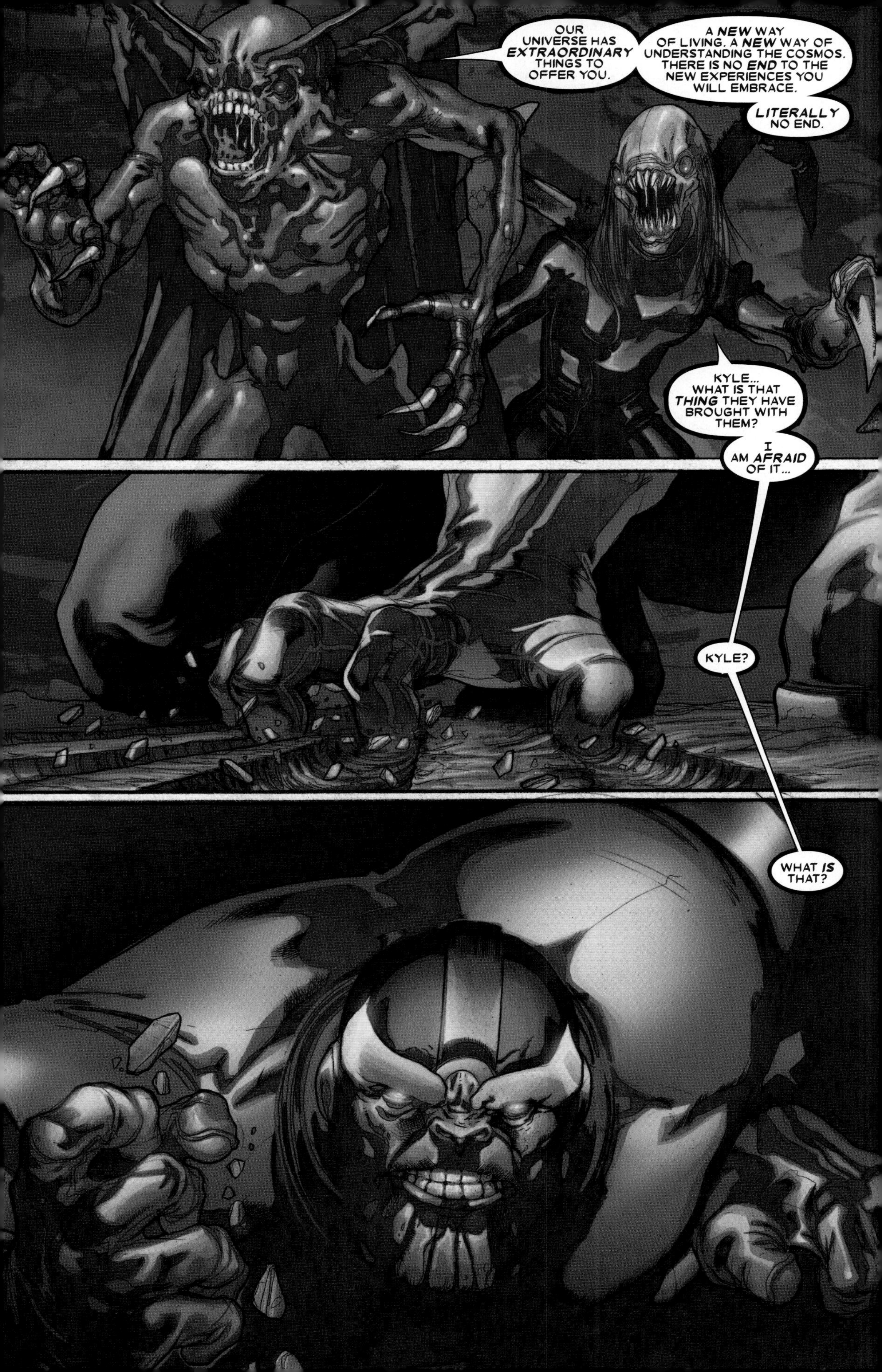
OUR UNIVERSE HAS EXTRAORDINARY THINGS TO OFFER YOU.
A NEW WAY OF LIVING. A NEW WAY OF UNDERSTANDING THE COSMOS. THERE IS NO END TO THE NEW EXPERIENCES YOU WILL EMBRACE.
LITERALLY NO END.
KYLE... WHAT IS THAT THING THEY HAVE BROUGHT WITH THEM?
I AM AFRAID OF IT...
KYLE?
WHAT IS THAT?

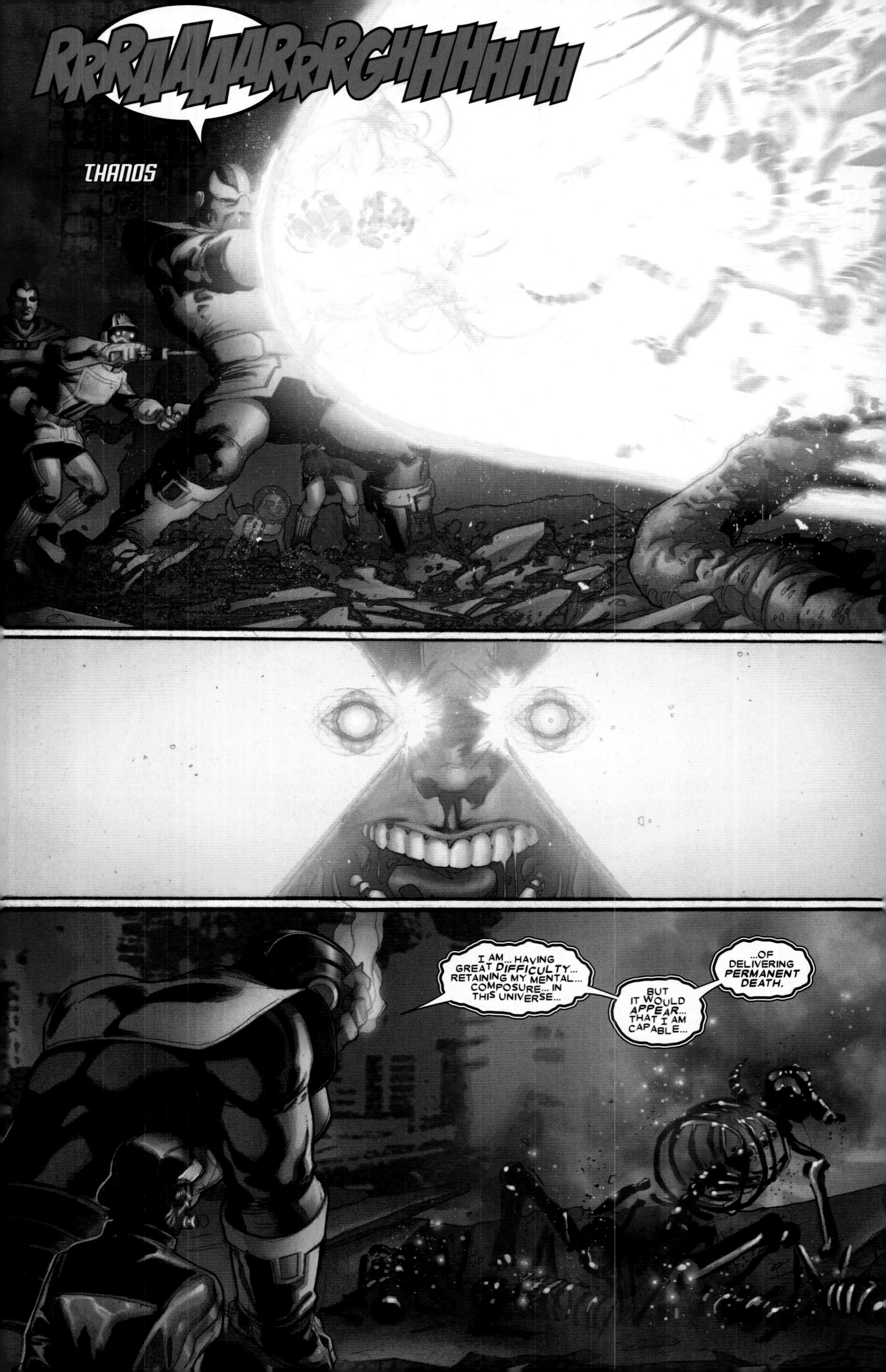
RRRAAAARRRGHHHHHH
THANOS
I AM... HAVING GREAT DIFFICULTY... RETAINING MY MENTAL... COMPOSURE... IN THIS UNIVERSE...
BUT IT WOULD APPEAR... THAT I AM CAPABLE...
...OF DELIVERING PERMANENT DEATH.

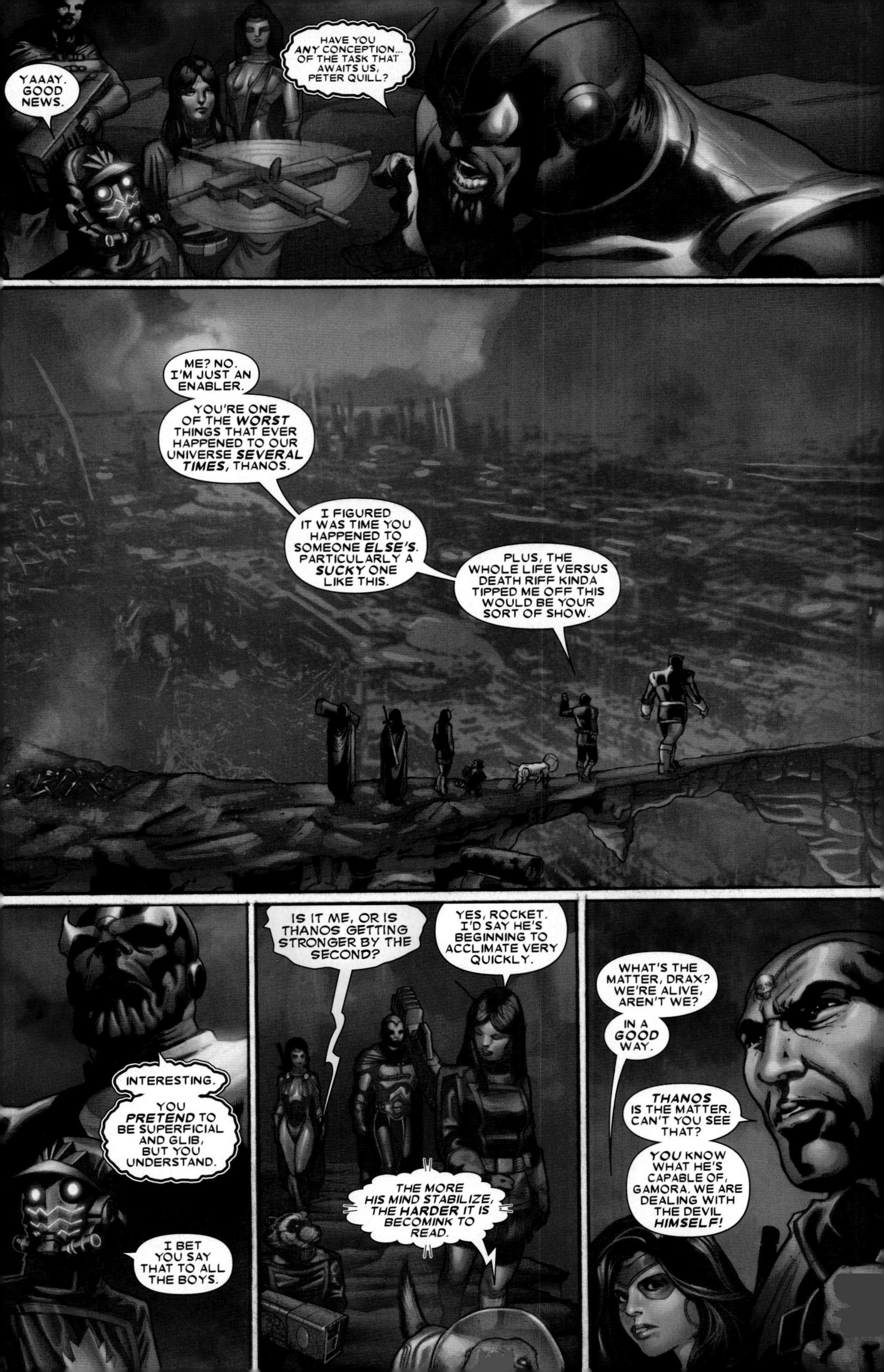
YAAAY. GOOD NEWS.
HAVE YOU ANY CONCEPTION... OF THE TASK THAT AWAITS US, PETER QUILL?
ME? NO. I'M JUST AN ENABLER.
YOU'RE ONE OF THE WORST THINGS THAT EVER HAPPENED TO OUR UNIVERSE SEVERAL TIMES, THANOS.
I FIGURED IT WAS TIME YOU HAPPENED TO SOMEONE ELSE'S. PARTICULARLY A SUCKY ONE LIKE THIS.
PLUS, THE WHOLE LIFE VERSUS DEATH RIFF KINDA TIPPED ME OFF THIS WOULD BE YOUR SORT OF SHOW.
INTERESTING.
YOU PRETEND TO BE SUPERFICIAL AND GLIB, BUT YOU UNDERSTAND.
I BET YOU SAY THAT TO ALL THE BOYS.
IS IT ME, OR IS THANOS GETTING STRONGER BY THE SECOND?
YES, ROCKET. I'D SAY HE'S BEGINNING TO ACCLIMATE VERY QUICKLY.
THE MORE HIS MIND STABILIZE, THE HARDER IT IS BECOMINK TO READ.
WHAT'S THE MATTER, DRAX? WE'RE ALIVE, AREN'T WE?
IN A GOOD WAY.
THANOS IS THE MATTER. CAN'T YOU SEE THAT?
YOU KNOW WHAT HE'S CAPABLE OF, GAMORA. WE ARE DEALING WITH THE DEVIL HIMSELF!

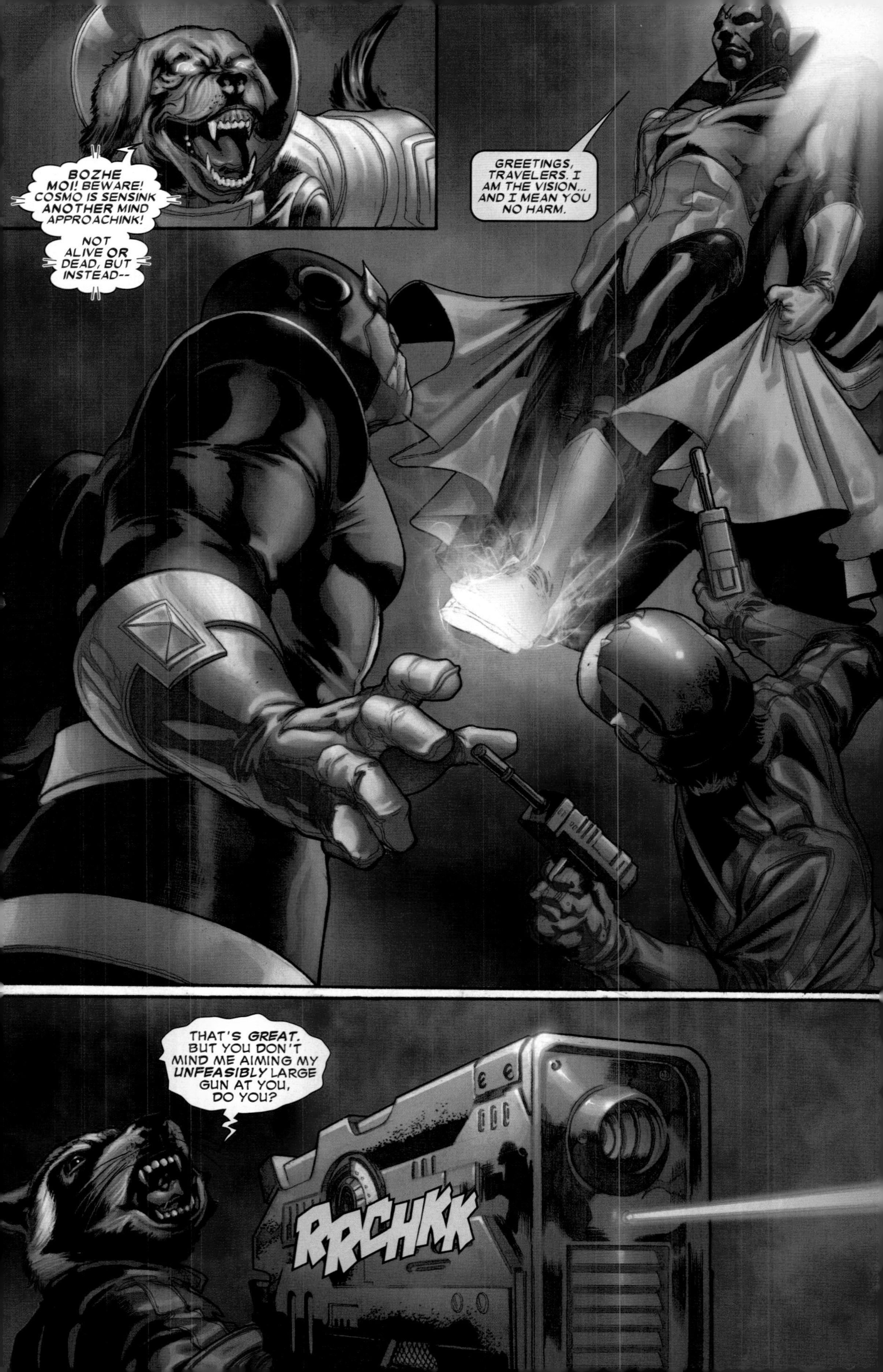
BOZHE MOI! BEWARE! COSMO IS SENSINK ANOTHER MIND APPROACHINK!
NOT ALIVE OR DEAD, BUT INSTEAD--
GREETINGS, TRAVELERS. I AM THE VISION... AND I MEAN YOU NO HARM.
THAT'S GREAT. BUT YOU DON'T MIND ME AIMING MY UNFEASIBLY LARGE GUN AT YOU, DO YOU?
RRCHKK

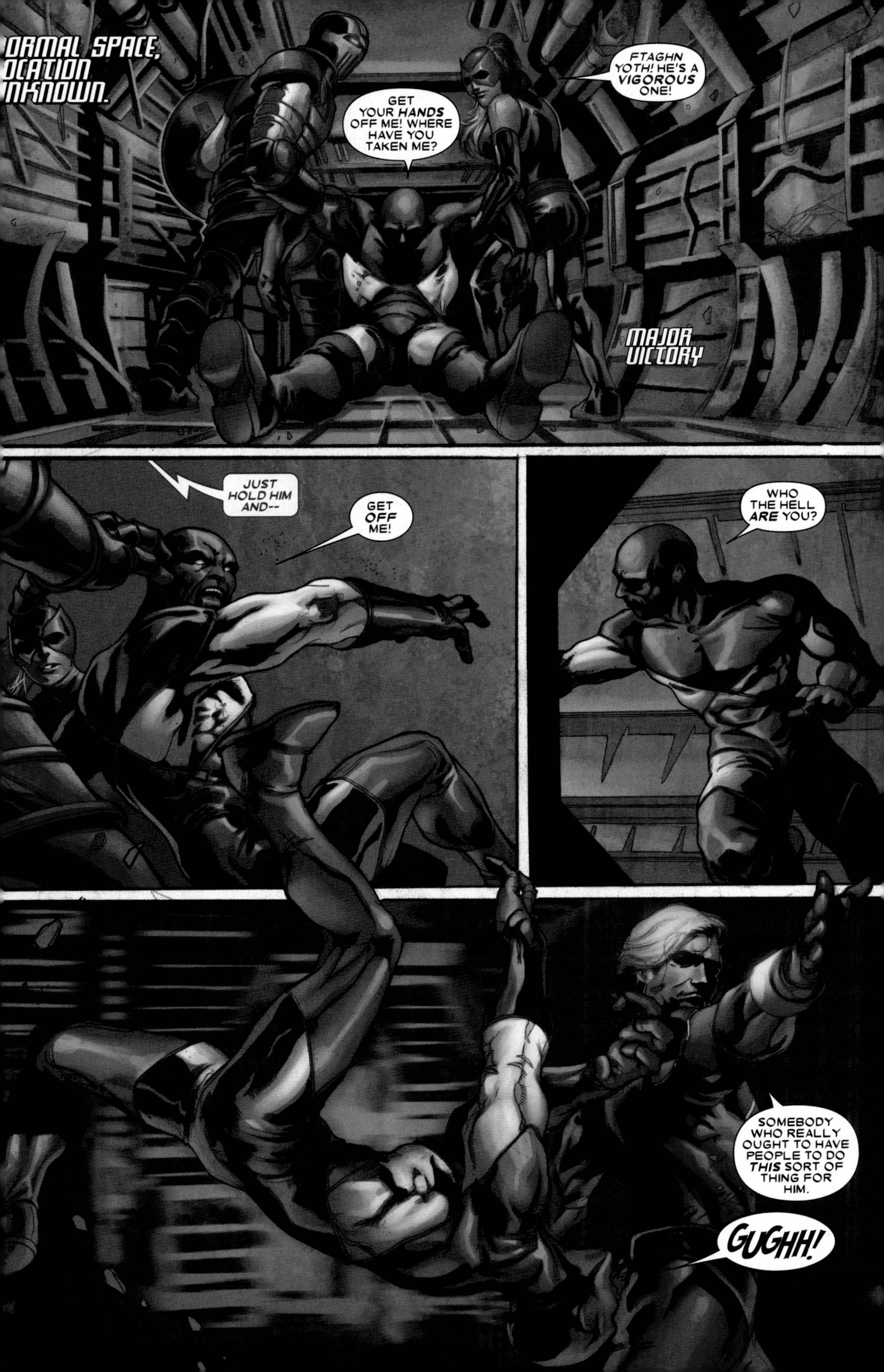

ORMAL SPACE, OCATION NKNOWN.
GET YOUR HANDS OFF ME! WHERE HAVE YOU TAKEN ME?
FTAGHN YOTH! HE'S A VIGOROUS ONE!
MAJOR VICTORY
JUST HOLD HIM AND--
GET OFF ME!
WHO THE HELL ARE YOU?
SOMEBODY WHO REALLY OUGHT TO HAVE PEOPLE TO DO THIS SORT OF THING FOR HIM.
GUGHH!

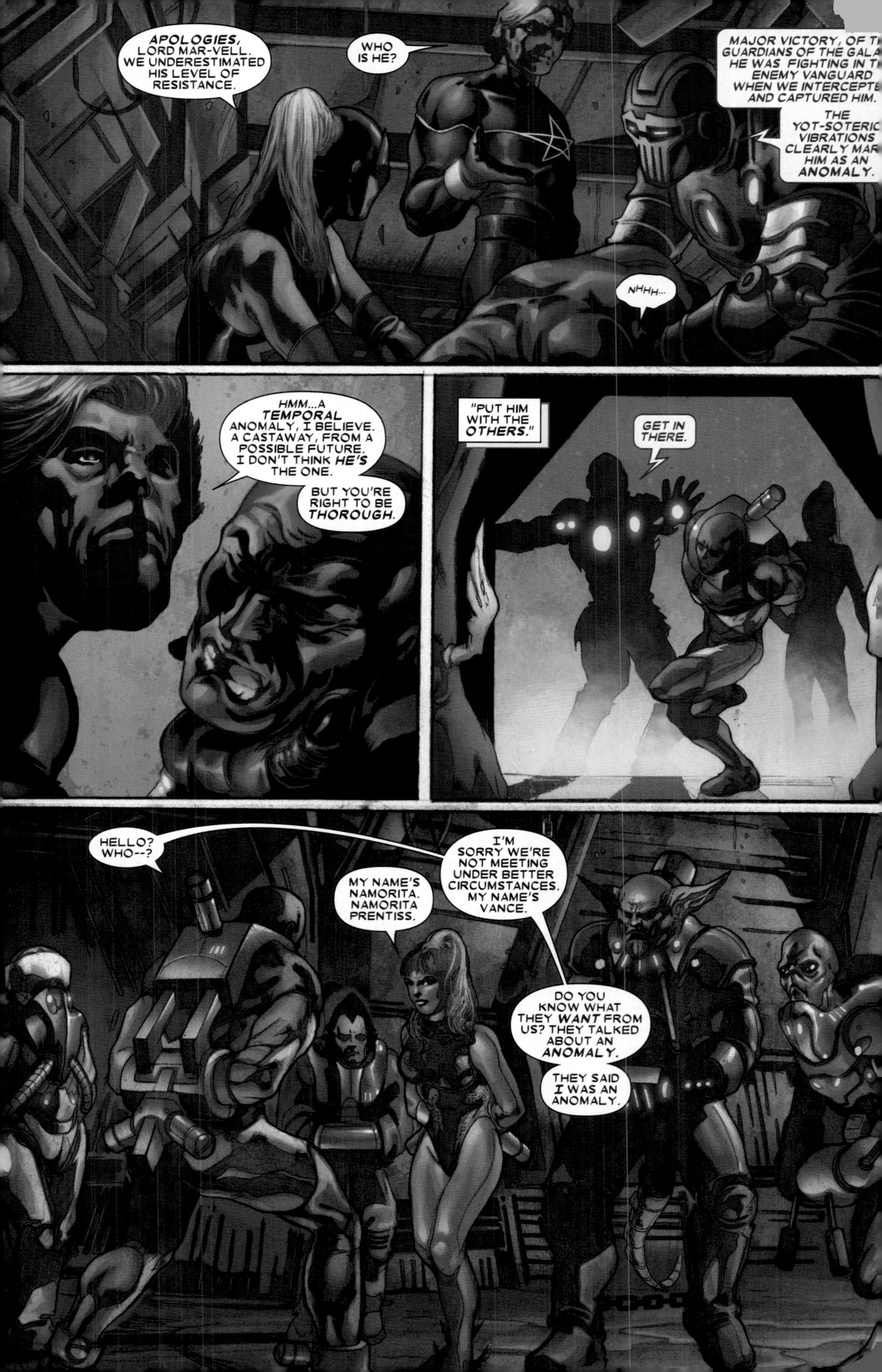
APOLOGIES, LORD MAR-VELL. WE UNDERESTIMATED HIS LEVEL OF RESISTANCE.
WHO IS HE?
MAJOR VICTORY, OF THE GUARDIANS OF THE GALA... HE WAS FIGHTING IN T... ENEMY VANGUARD WHEN WE INTERCEPTE... AND CAPTURED HIM.
THE YOT-SOTERIC VIBRATIONS CLEARLY MAR... HIM AS AN ANOMALY.
NHHH...
HMM...A TEMPORAL ANOMALY, I BELIEVE. A CASTAWAY, FROM A POSSIBLE FUTURE. I DON'T THINK HE'S THE ONE.
BUT YOU'RE RIGHT TO BE THOROUGH.
"PUT HIM WITH THE OTHERS."
GET IN THERE.
HELLO? WHO--?
I'M SORRY WE'RE NOT MEETING UNDER BETTER CIRCUMSTANCES. MY NAME'S VANCE.
MY NAME'S NAMORITA. NAMORITA PRENTISS.
DO YOU KNOW WHAT THEY WANT FROM US? THEY TALKED ABOUT AN ANOMALY.
THEY SAID I WAS AN ANOMALY.

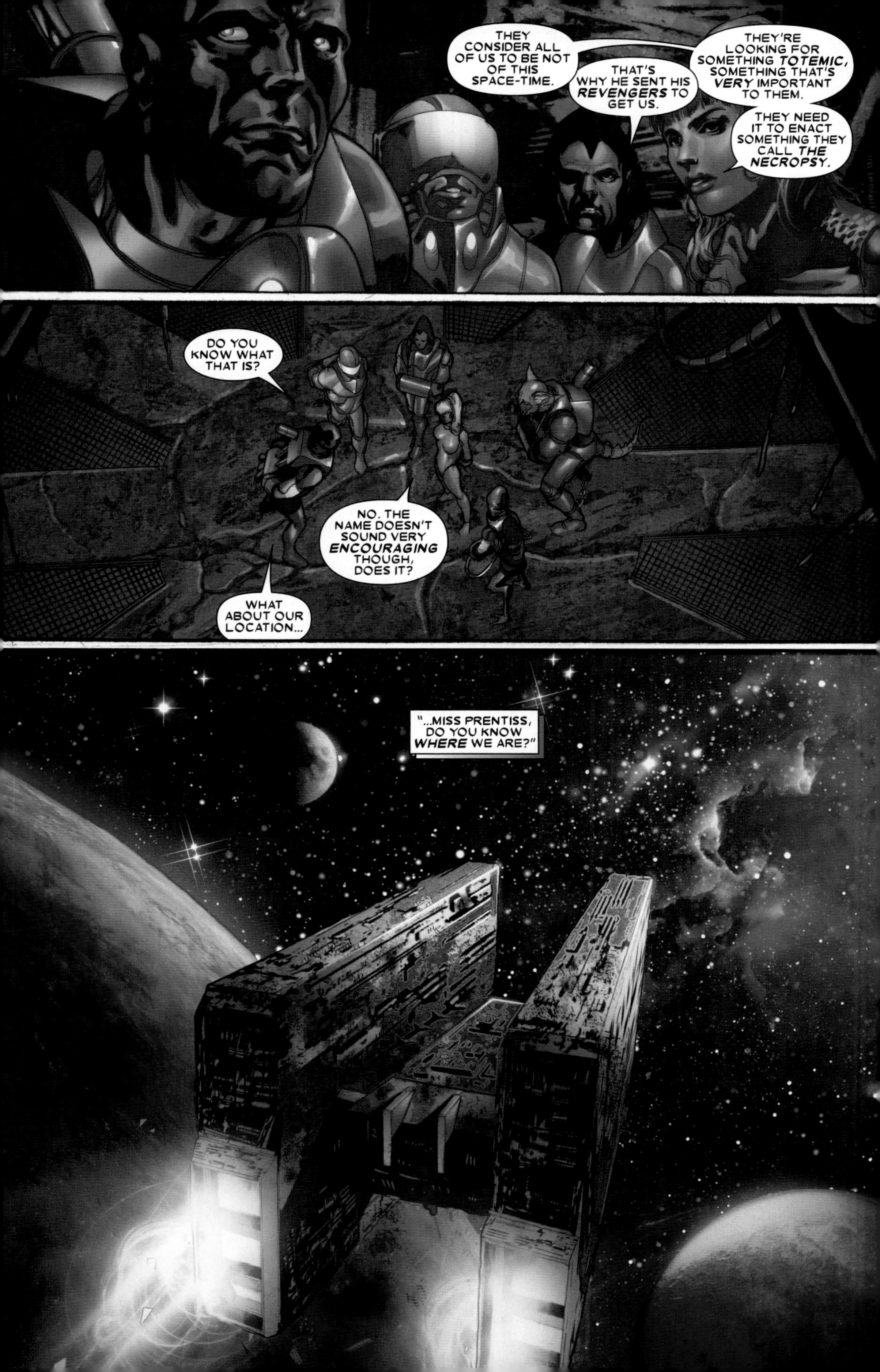
THEY CONSIDER ALL OF US TO BE NOT OF THIS SPACE-TIME.
THAT'S WHY HE SENT HIS *REVENGERS* TO GET US.
THEY'RE LOOKING FOR SOMETHING *TOTEMIC,* SOMETHING THAT'S *VERY* IMPORTANT TO THEM.
THEY NEED IT TO ENACT SOMETHING THEY CALL *THE NECROPSY.*
DO YOU KNOW WHAT THAT *IS*?
NO. THE NAME DOESN'T SOUND VERY *ENCOURAGING* THOUGH, DOES IT?
WHAT ABOUT OUR LOCATION...
"...MISS PRENTISS, DO YOU KNOW *WHERE* WE ARE?"

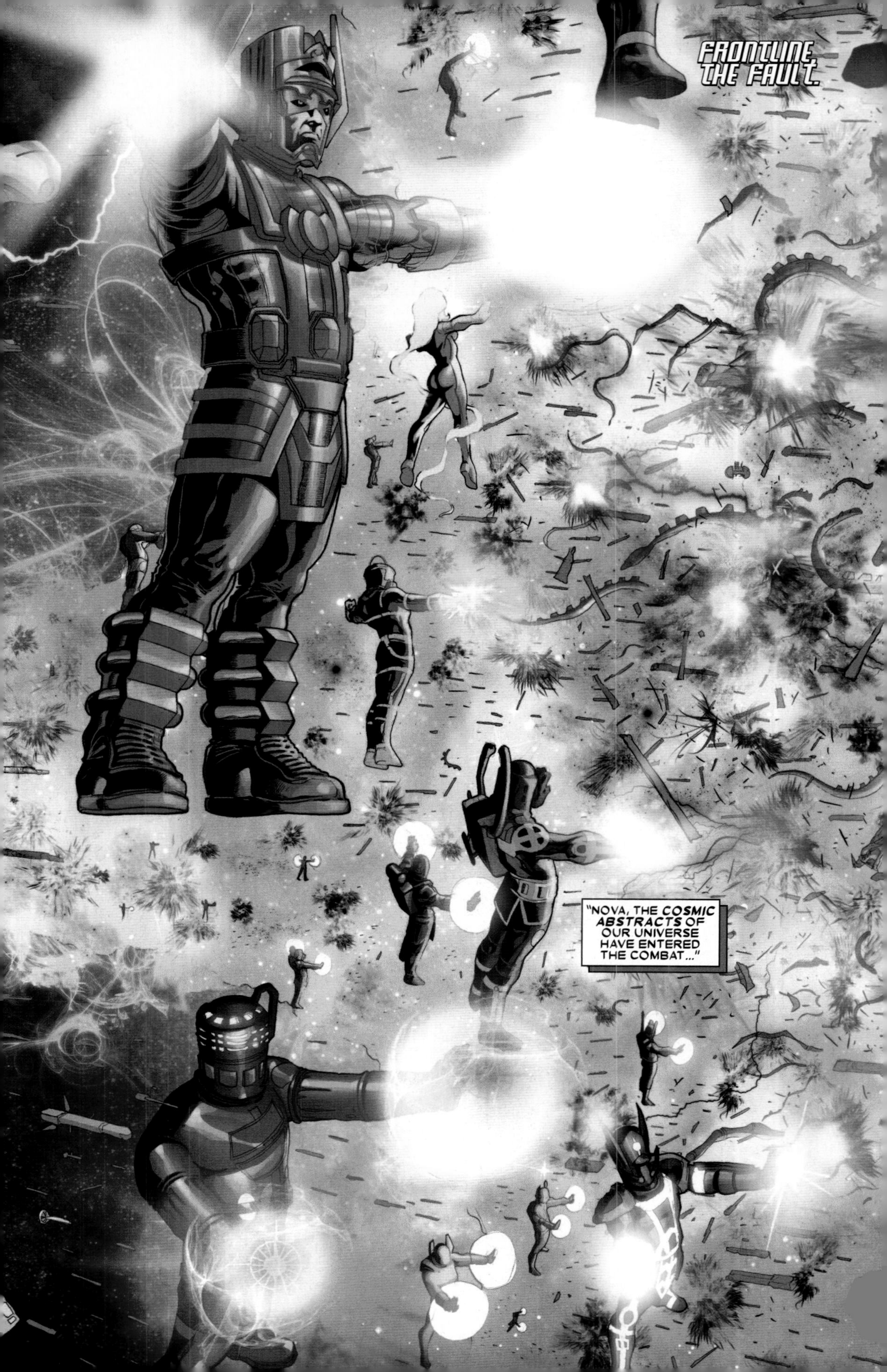
FRONTLINE THE FAULT.
"NOVA, THE COSMIC ABSTRACTS OF OUR UNIVERSE HAVE ENTERED THE COMBAT..."

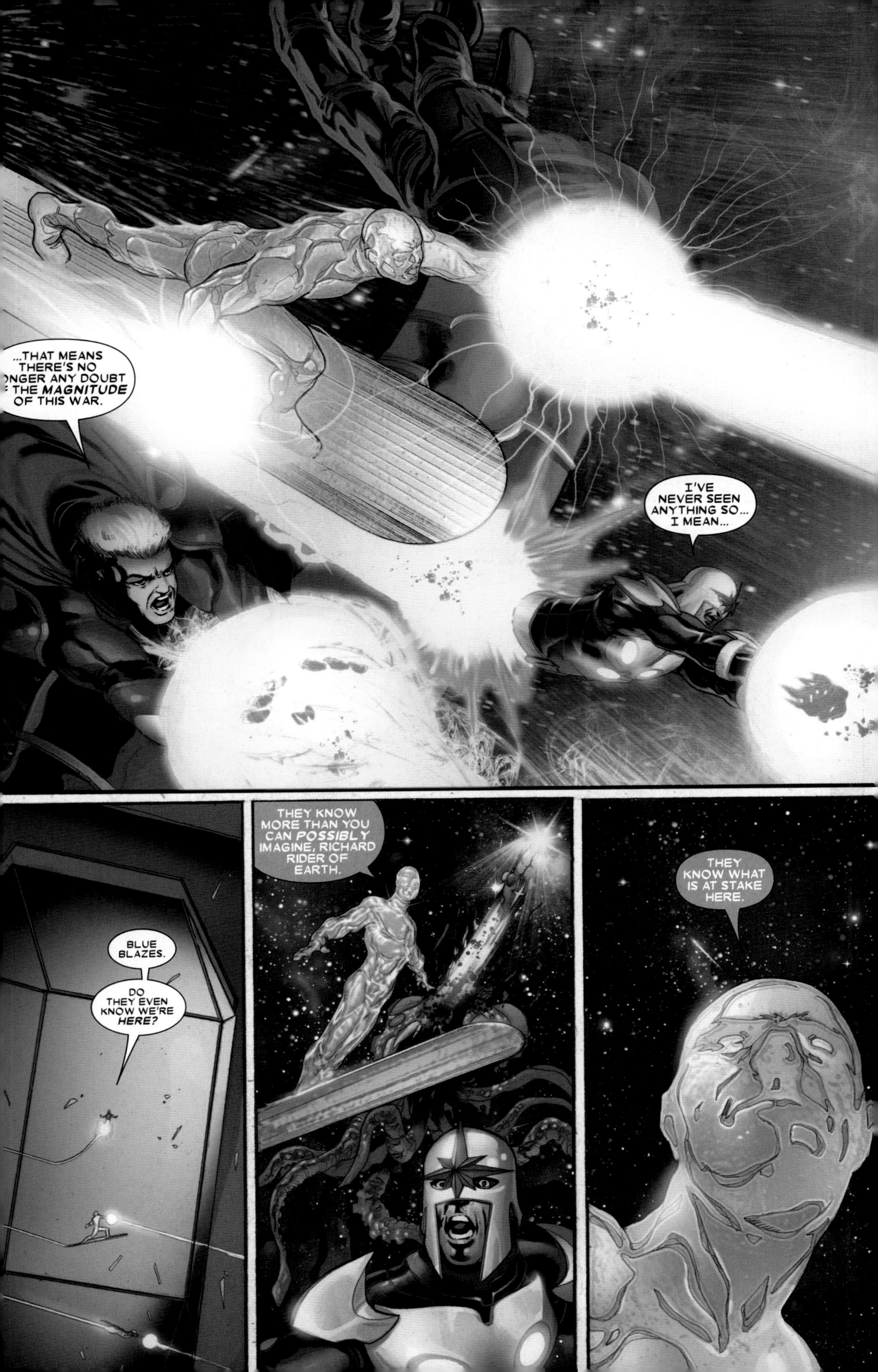
...THAT MEANS THERE'S NO LONGER ANY DOUBT OF THE MAGNITUDE OF THIS WAR.
I'VE NEVER SEEN ANYTHING SO... I MEAN...
BLUE BLAZES.
DO THEY EVEN KNOW WE'RE HERE?
THEY KNOW MORE THAN YOU CAN POSSIBLY IMAGINE, RICHARD RIDER OF EARTH.
THEY KNOW WHAT IS AT STAKE HERE.

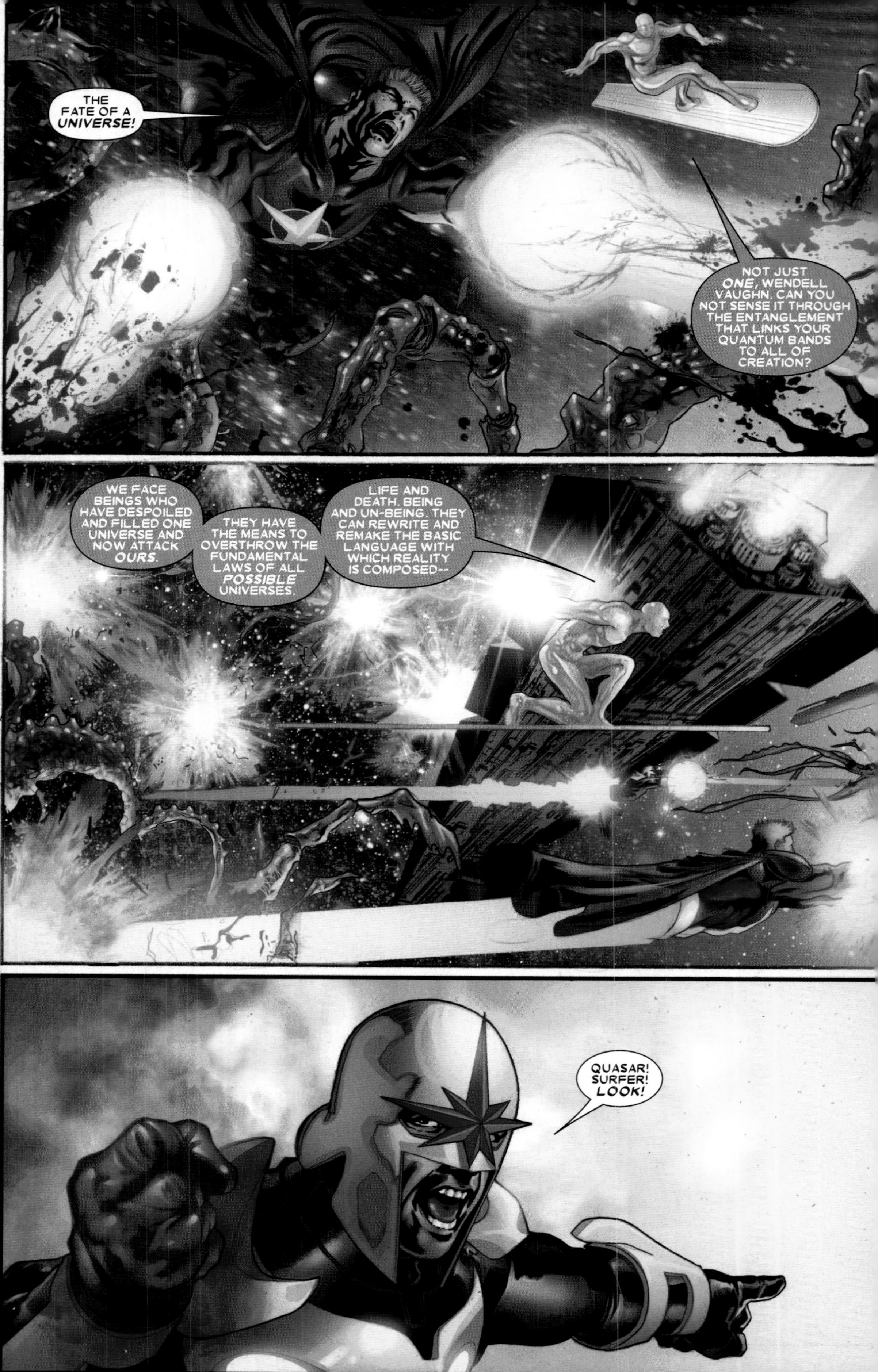
THE FATE OF A UNIVERSE!
NOT JUST ONE, WENDELL VAUGHN. CAN YOU NOT SENSE IT THROUGH THE ENTANGLEMENT THAT LINKS YOUR QUANTUM BANDS TO ALL OF CREATION?
WE FACE BEINGS WHO HAVE DESPOILED AND FILLED ONE UNIVERSE AND NOW ATTACK OURS.
THEY HAVE THE MEANS TO OVERTHROW THE FUNDAMENTAL LAWS OF ALL POSSIBLE UNIVERSES.
LIFE AND DEATH. BEING AND UN-BEING. THEY CAN REWRITE AND REMAKE THE BASIC LANGUAGE WITH WHICH REALITY IS COMPOSED--
QUASAR! SURFER! LOOK!

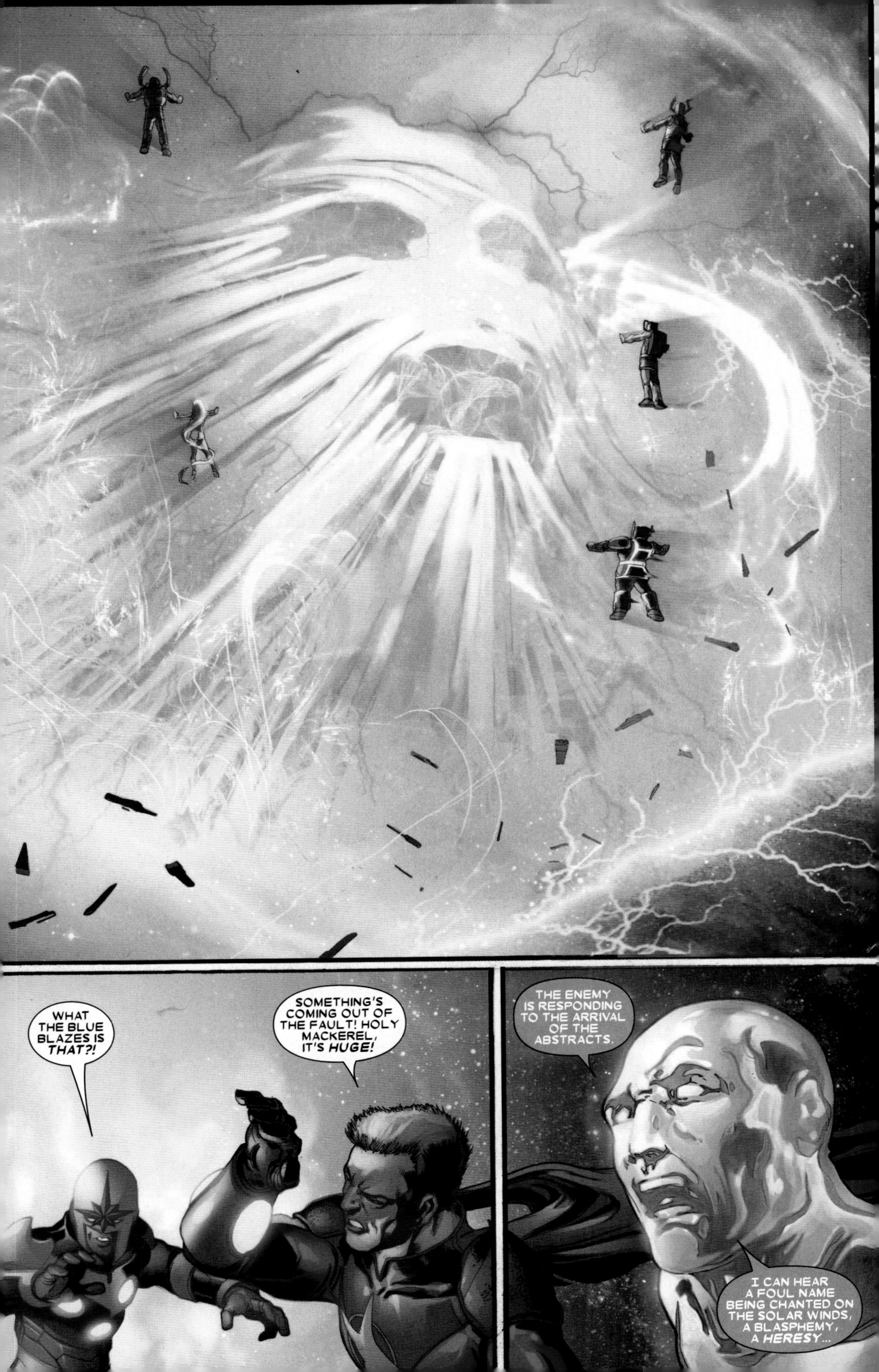
WHAT THE BLUE BLAZES IS THAT?!
SOMETHING'S COMING OUT OF THE FAULT! HOLY MACKEREL, IT'S HUGE!
THE ENEMY IS RESPONDING TO THE ARRIVAL OF THE ABSTRACTS.
I CAN HEAR A FOUL NAME BEING CHANTED ON THE SOLAR WINDS, A BLASPHEMY, A HERESY...

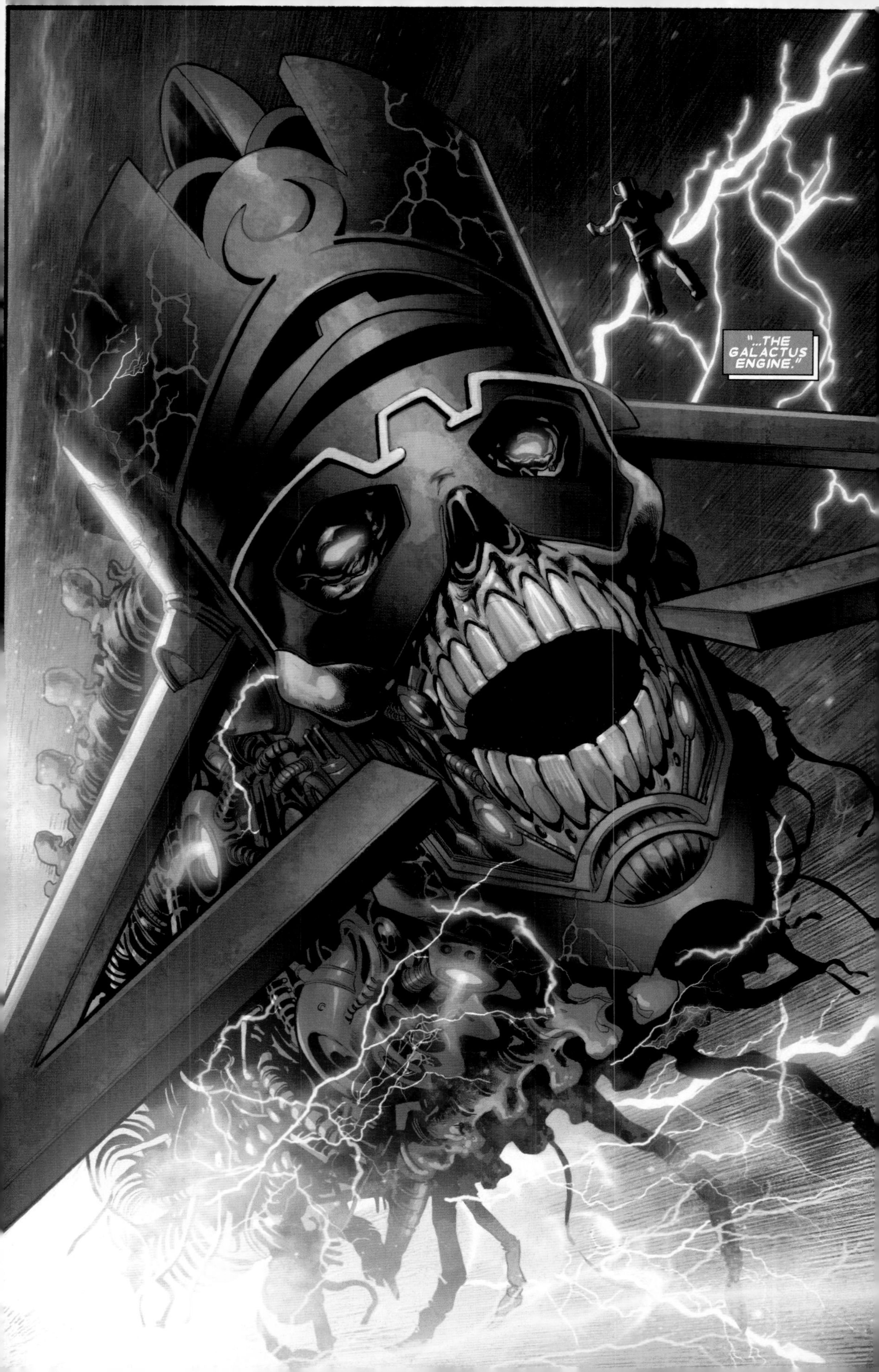
"...THE GALACTUS ENGINE."

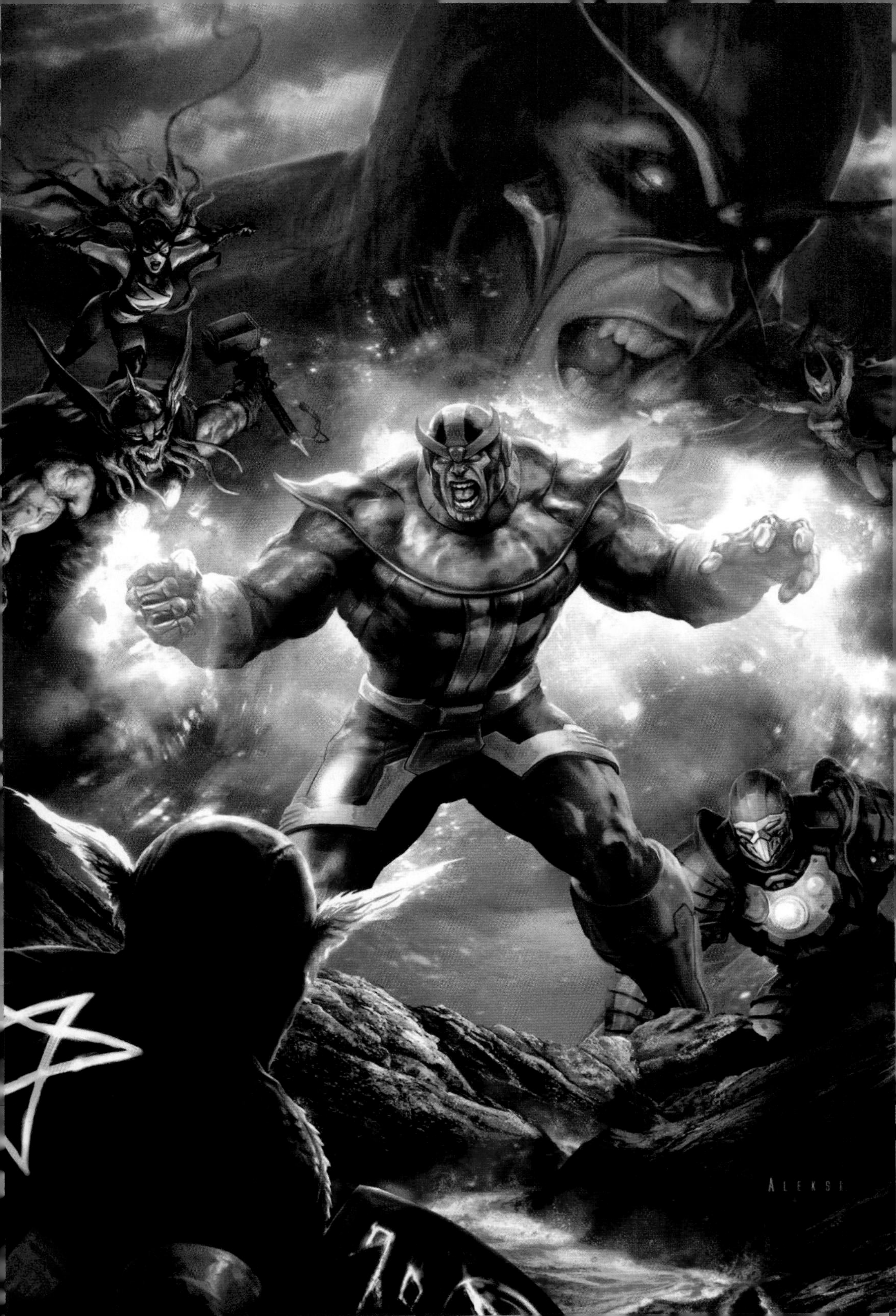
ALEKSI

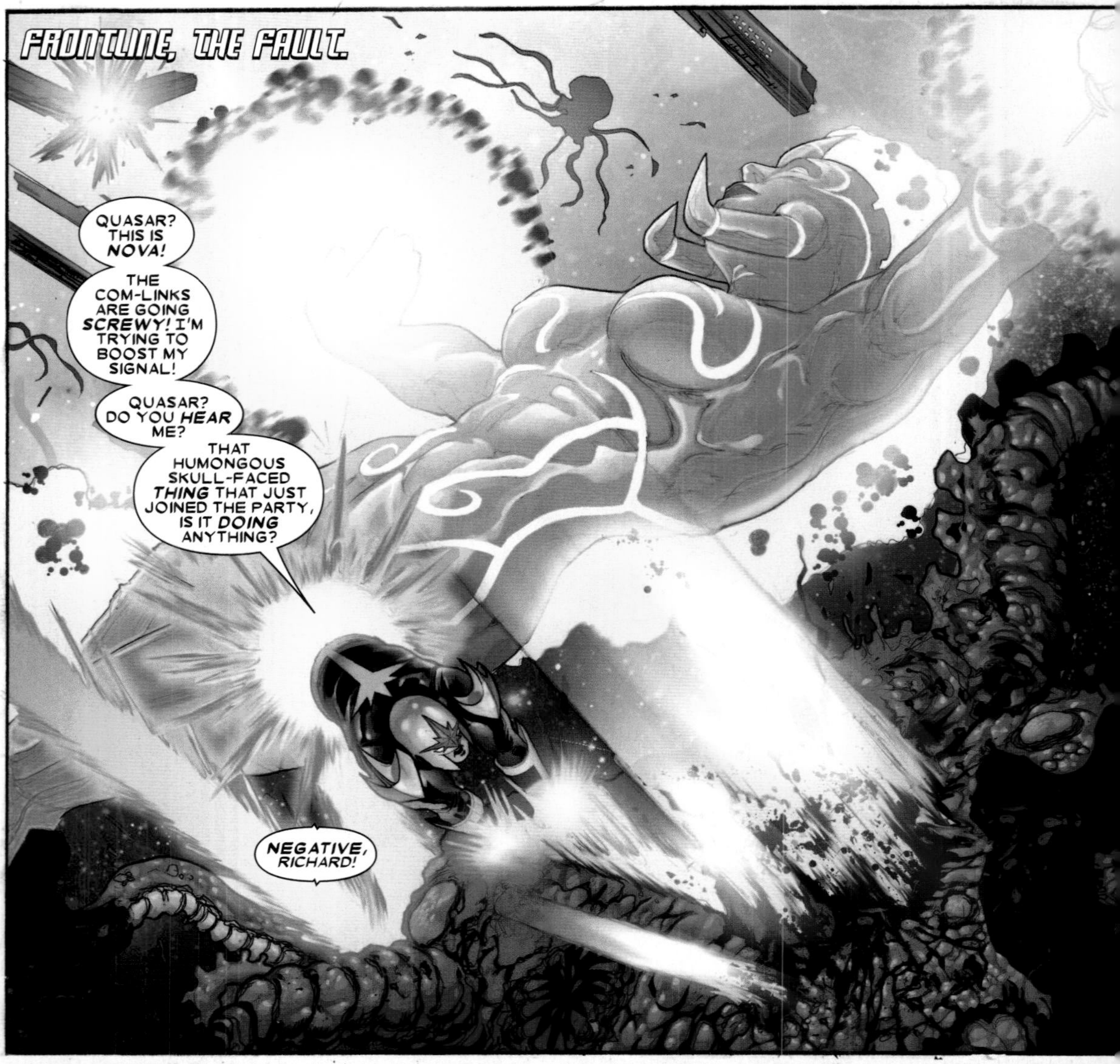
FRONTLINE, THE FAULT.
QUASAR? THIS IS NOVA!
THE COM-LINKS ARE GOING SCREWY! I'M TRYING TO BOOST MY SIGNAL!
QUASAR? DO YOU HEAR ME?
THAT HUMONGOUS SKULL-FACED THING THAT JUST JOINED THE PARTY, IS IT DOING ANYTHING?
NEGATIVE, RICHARD!

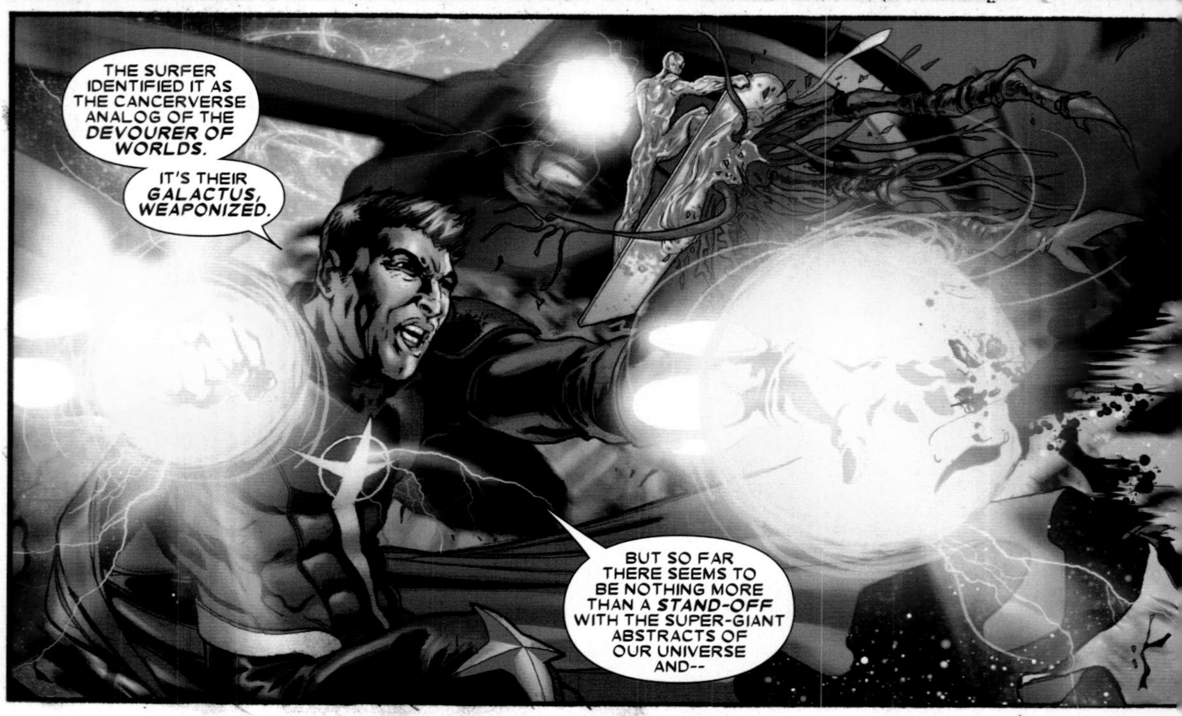
THE SURFER IDENTIFIED IT AS THE CANCERVERSE ANALOG OF THE DEVOURER OF WORLDS.
IT'S THEIR GALACTUS, WEAPONIZED.
BUT SO FAR THERE SEEMS TO BE NOTHING MORE THAN A STAND-OFF WITH THE SUPER-GIANT ABSTRACTS OF OUR UNIVERSE AND--

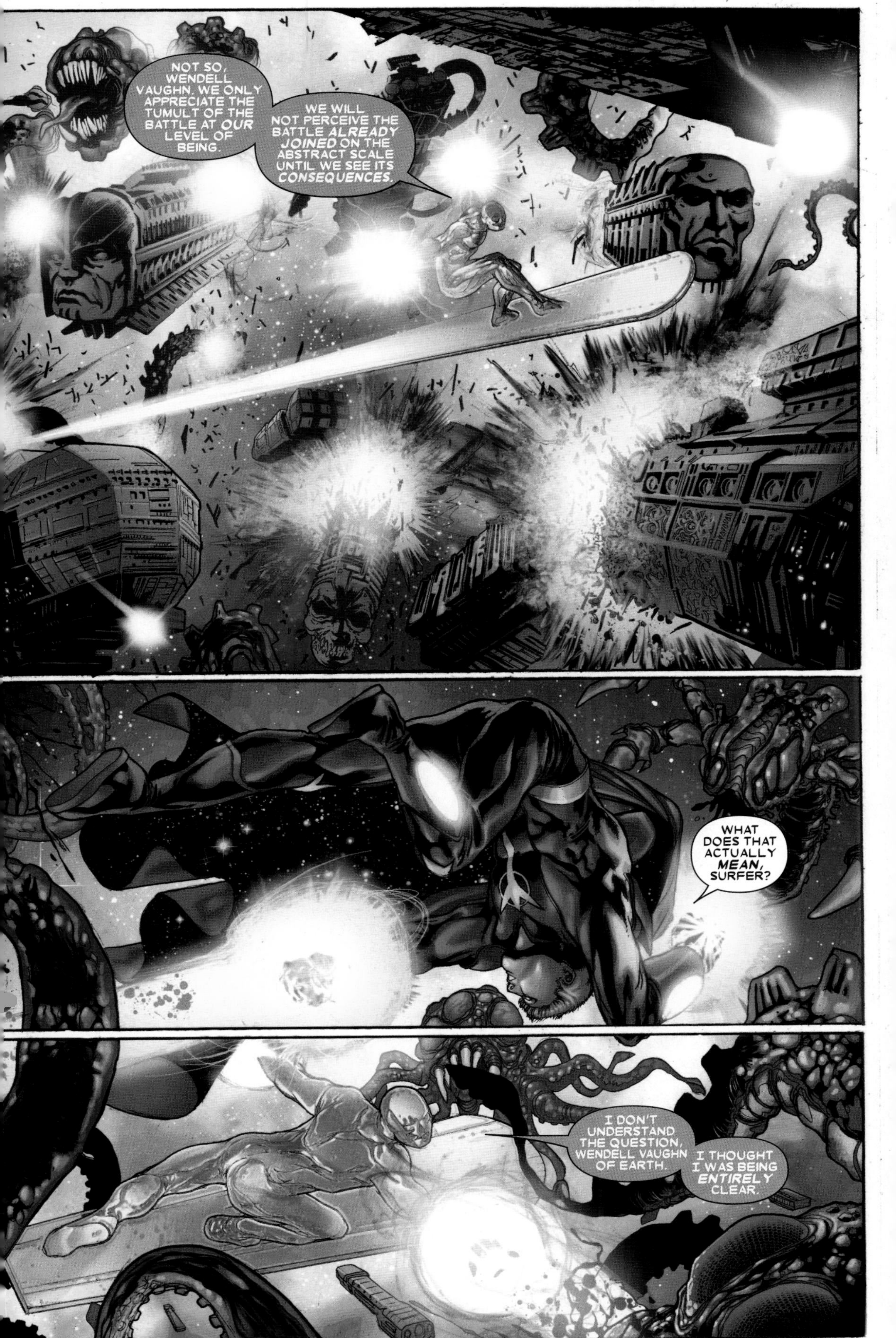
NOT SO, WENDELL VAUGHN. WE ONLY APPRECIATE THE TUMULT OF THE BATTLE AT OUR LEVEL OF BEING.
WE WILL NOT PERCEIVE THE BATTLE ALREADY JOINED ON THE ABSTRACT SCALE UNTIL WE SEE ITS CONSEQUENCES.
WHAT DOES THAT ACTUALLY MEAN, SURFER?
I DON'T UNDERSTAND THE QUESTION, WENDELL VAUGHN OF EARTH.
I THOUGHT I WAS BEING ENTIRELY CLEAR.

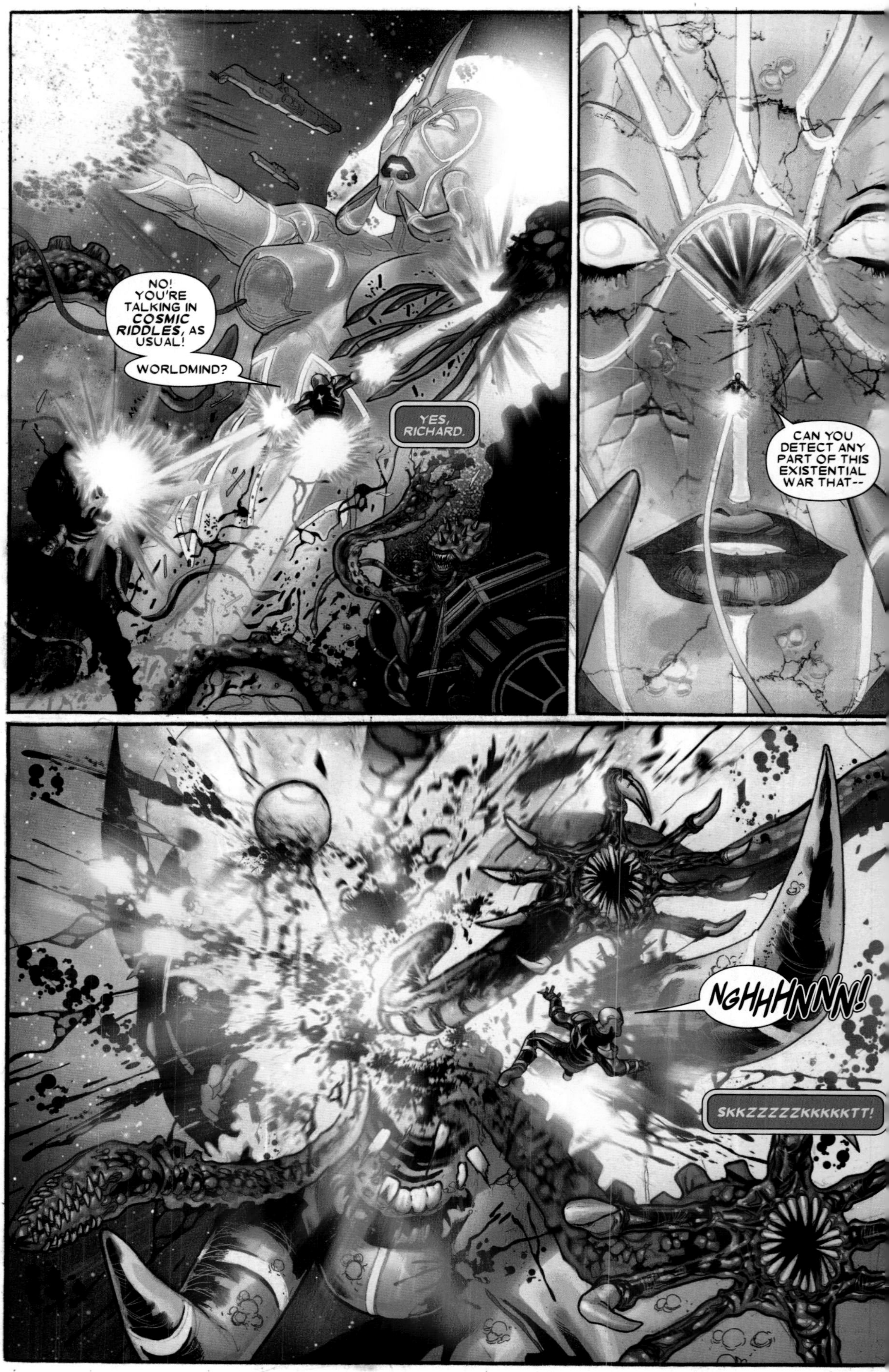
NO! YOU'RE TALKING IN COSMIC RIDDLES, AS USUAL!
WORLDMIND?
YES, RICHARD.
CAN YOU DETECT ANY PART OF THIS EXISTENTIAL WAR THAT--
NGHHHNNN!
SKKZZZZZKKKKKTT!

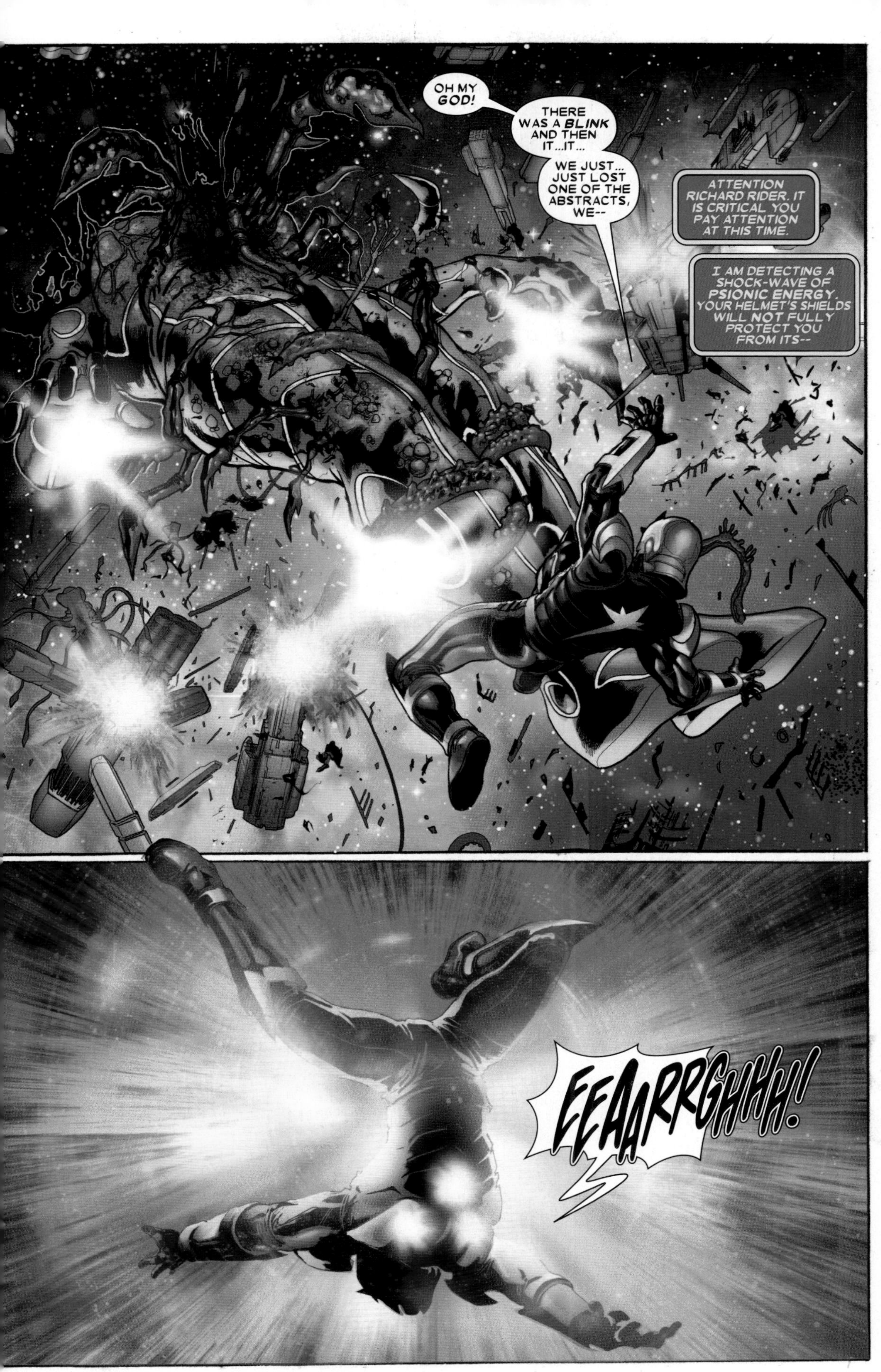

OH MY GOD!
THERE WAS A BLINK AND THEN IT...IT...
WE JUST... JUST LOST ONE OF THE ABSTRACTS, WE--
ATTENTION RICHARD RIDER. IT IS CRITICAL YOU PAY ATTENTION AT THIS TIME.
I AM DETECTING A SHOCK-WAVE OF PSIONIC ENERGY. YOUR HELMET'S SHIELDS WILL NOT FULLY PROTECT YOU FROM ITS--
EEAARRGHHH!

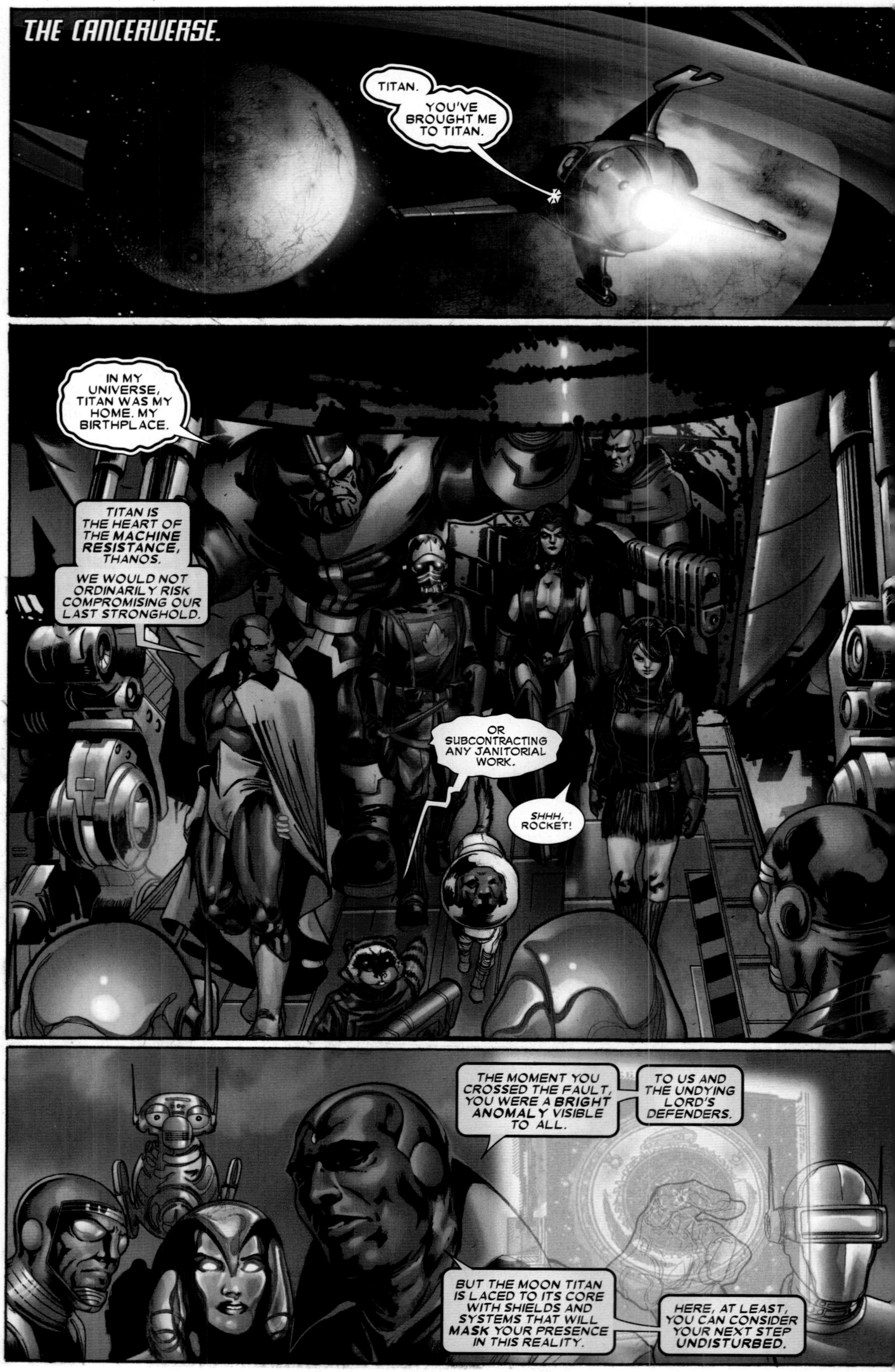
THE CANCERVERSE.
TITAN.
YOU'VE BROUGHT ME TO TITAN.
IN MY UNIVERSE, TITAN WAS MY HOME. MY BIRTHPLACE.
TITAN IS THE HEART OF THE MACHINE RESISTANCE, THANOS.
WE WOULD NOT ORDINARILY RISK COMPROMISING OUR LAST STRONGHOLD.
OR SUBCONTRACTING ANY JANITORIAL WORK.
SHHH, ROCKET!
THE MOMENT YOU CROSSED THE FAULT, YOU WERE A BRIGHT ANOMALY VISIBLE TO ALL.
TO US AND THE UNDYING LORD'S DEFENDERS.
BUT THE MOON TITAN IS LACED TO ITS CORE WITH SHIELDS AND SYSTEMS THAT WILL MASK YOUR PRESENCE IN THIS REALITY.
HERE, AT LEAST, YOU CAN CONSIDER YOUR NEXT STEP UNDISTURBED.

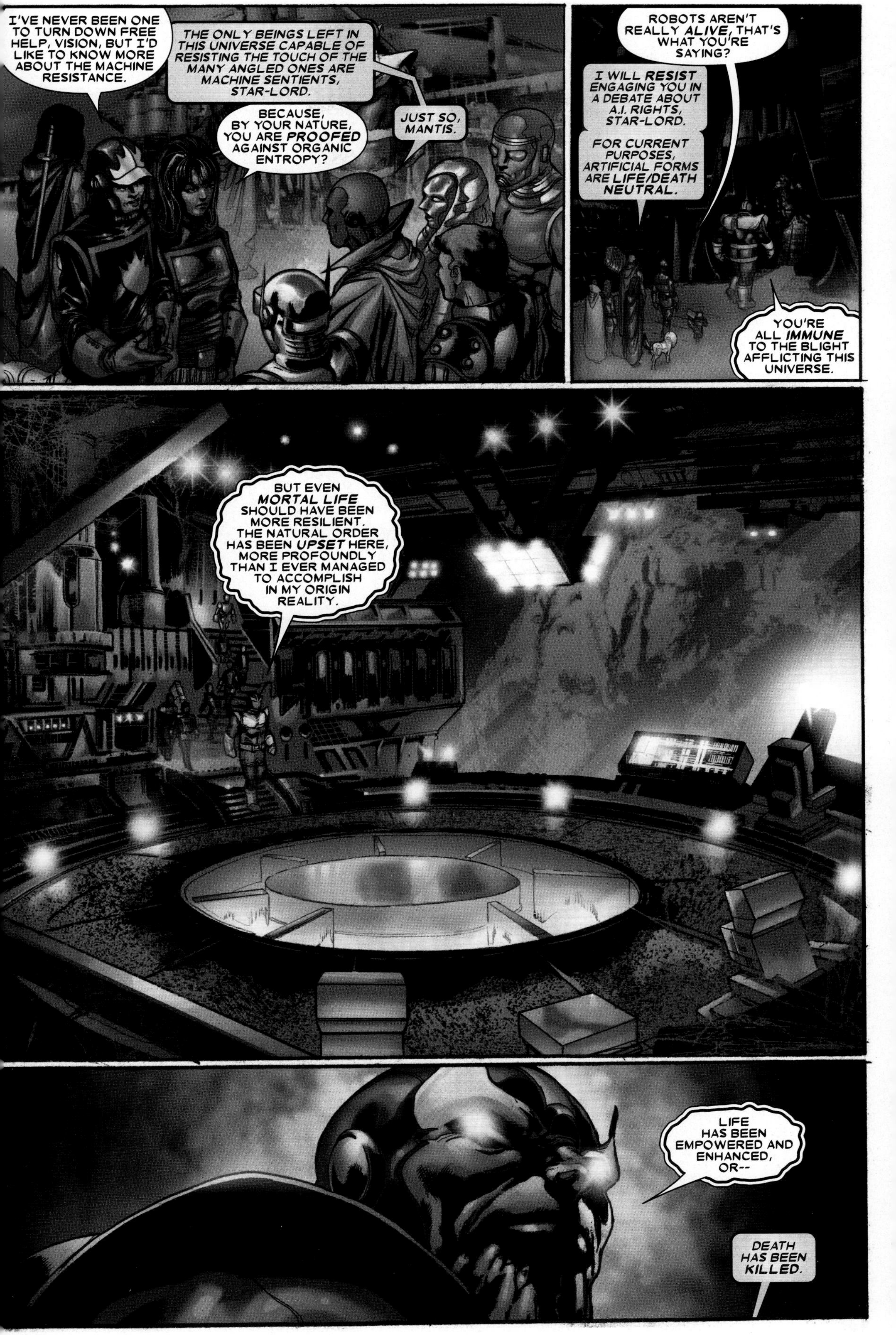

I'VE NEVER BEEN ONE TO TURN DOWN FREE HELP, VISION, BUT I'D LIKE TO KNOW MORE ABOUT THE MACHINE RESISTANCE.
THE ONLY BEINGS LEFT IN THIS UNIVERSE CAPABLE OF RESISTING THE TOUCH OF THE MANY ANGLED ONES ARE MACHINE SENTIENTS, STAR-LORD.
BECAUSE, BY YOUR NATURE, YOU ARE PROOFED AGAINST ORGANIC ENTROPY?
JUST SO, MANTIS.
ROBOTS AREN'T REALLY ALIVE, THAT'S WHAT YOU'RE SAYING?
I WILL RESIST ENGAGING YOU IN A DEBATE ABOUT A.I. RIGHTS, STAR-LORD.
FOR CURRENT PURPOSES, ARTIFICIAL FORMS ARE LIFE/DEATH NEUTRAL.
YOU'RE ALL IMMUNE TO THE BLIGHT AFFLICTING THIS UNIVERSE.
BUT EVEN MORTAL LIFE SHOULD HAVE BEEN MORE RESILIENT. THE NATURAL ORDER HAS BEEN UPSET HERE, MORE PROFOUNDLY THAN I EVER MANAGED TO ACCOMPLISH IN MY ORIGIN REALITY.
LIFE HAS BEEN EMPOWERED AND ENHANCED, OR--
DEATH HAS BEEN KILLED.

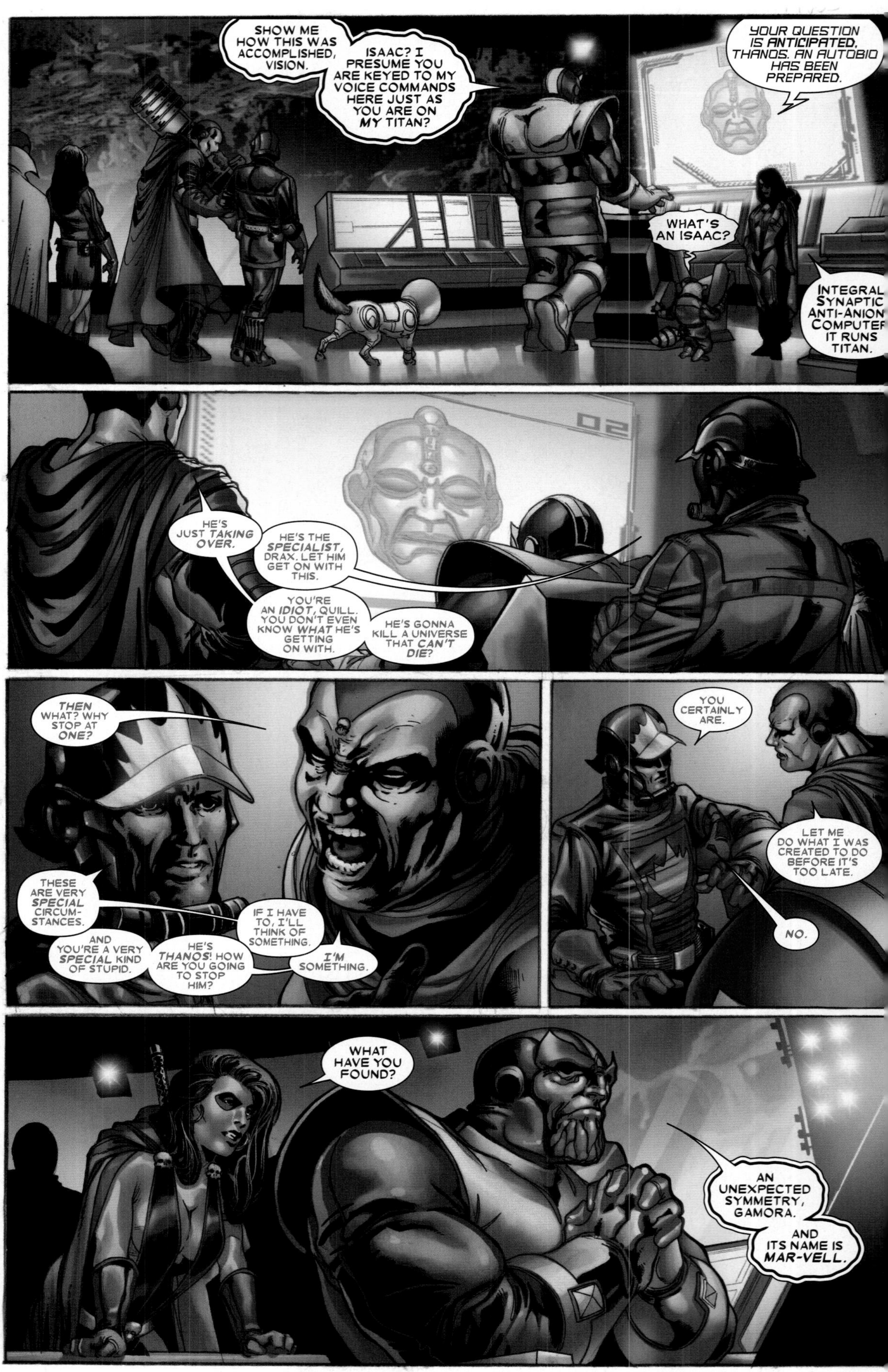
SHOW ME HOW THIS WAS ACCOMPLISHED, VISION.
ISAAC? I PRESUME YOU ARE KEYED TO MY VOICE COMMANDS HERE JUST AS YOU ARE ON MY TITAN?
YOUR QUESTION IS ANTICIPATED, THANOS. AN AUTOBIO HAS BEEN PREPARED.
WHAT'S AN ISAAC?
INTEGRAL SYNAPTIC ANTI-ANION COMPUTER IT RUNS TITAN.
HE'S JUST TAKING OVER.
HE'S THE SPECIALIST, DRAX. LET HIM GET ON WITH THIS.
YOU'RE AN IDIOT, QUILL. YOU DON'T EVEN KNOW WHAT HE'S GETTING ON WITH.
HE'S GONNA KILL A UNIVERSE THAT CAN'T DIE?
THEN WHAT? WHY STOP AT ONE?
THESE ARE VERY SPECIAL CIRCUM-STANCES.
AND YOU'RE A VERY SPECIAL KIND OF STUPID.
HE'S THANOS! HOW ARE YOU GOING TO STOP HIM?
IF I HAVE TO, I'LL THINK OF SOMETHING.
I'M SOMETHING.
YOU CERTAINLY ARE.
LET ME DO WHAT I WAS CREATED TO DO BEFORE IT'S TOO LATE.
NO.
WHAT HAVE YOU FOUND?
AN UNEXPECTED SYMMETRY, GAMORA.
AND ITS NAME IS MAR-VELL.

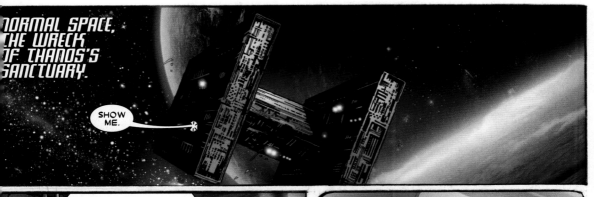

NORMAL SPACE, THE WRECK OF THANOS'S SANCTUARY.
SHOW ME.
LORD MAR-VELL, THE RESEARCH I CONDUCTED IN PREPARATION FOR YOUR ARRIVAL HERE REVEALED A SIMPLE DISCONTINUITY.
HE DIED, DIDN'T HE, VAUGHN? THE MAR-VELL IN THIS UNIVERSE ALLOWED HIMSELF TO DIE.
HIS ACCEPTANCE OF DEATH WAS SEEN AS SELFLESS AND COURAGEOUS, LORD.
HE DIED AS HE LIVED, AS ONE OF THEIR MOST CELEBRATED HEROES.
WAS IT CANCER, OR ARE OUR HISTORIES MORE PARALLEL?
IT WAS CANCER, LORD.
HE WAS BELOVED, LIKE YOU. ADMIRED EVEN BY HIS ENEMIES, LIKE YOU.
WHEN THE SHOCKING DIAGNOSIS WAS MADE, EVERY EFFORT WAS EXPENDED TO CHANGE THE PROGNOSIS. THE HIGHEST SCIENCE, EVEN SORCERY, WAS EMPLOYED.
AS IN YOUR CASE, THE KREE-FORGED NEGA-BANDS, THE SOURCE OF YOUR POWER, WERE THE STUMBLING BLOCK.
AND AT THAT POINT, THE GREAT AND THE GOOD OF THIS INSIPID UNIVERSE SIMPLY GAVE UP ON HIM, AND ALLOWED HIM TO PASS OUT OF LIFE'S REALM AS THOUGH IT WAS SOMETHING NOBLE AND VALUABLE.
THEY WERE TOO BUSY WORRYING ABOUT HOW SAD THEY WERE SUPPOSED TO LOOK TO EVEN BEGIN TO EXPLORE OTHER OPTIONS.

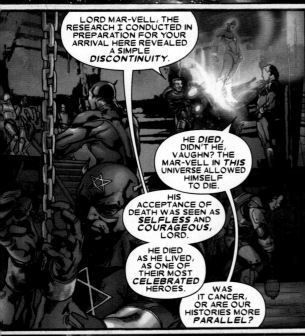

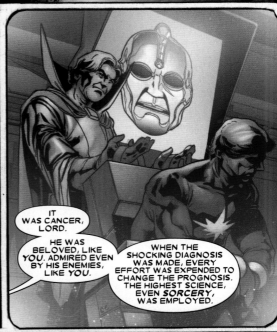

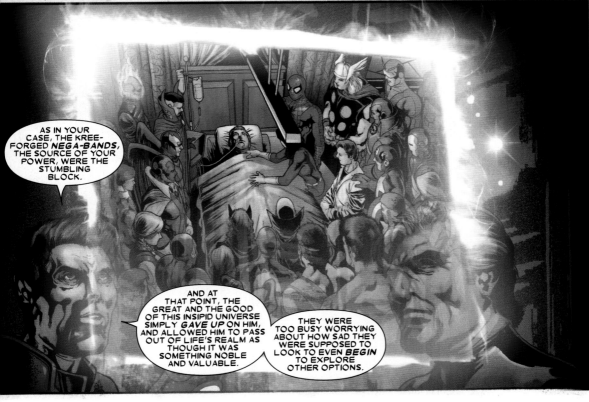

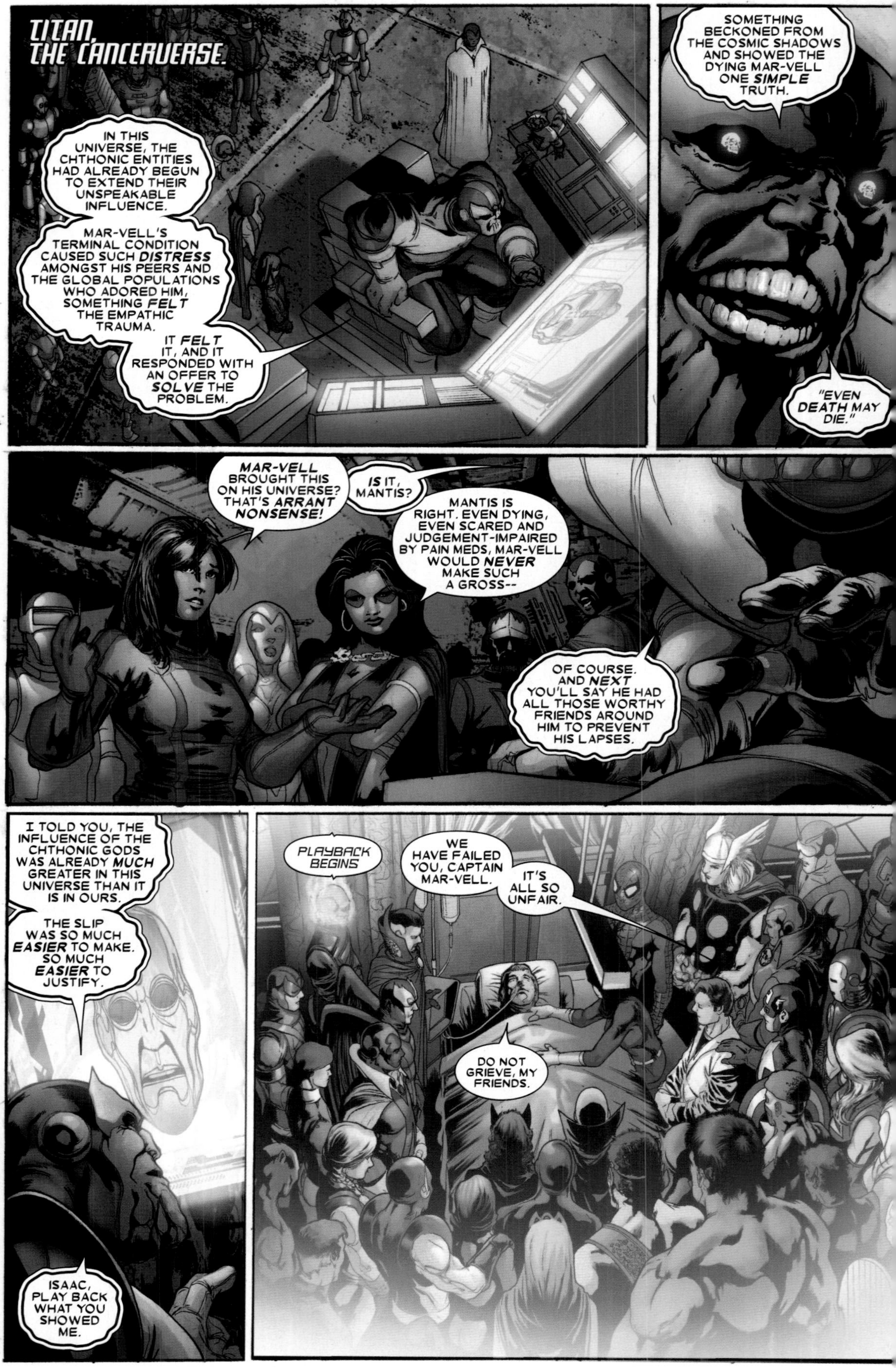
TITAN, THE CANCERVERSE.
IN THIS UNIVERSE, THE CHTHONIC ENTITIES HAD ALREADY BEGUN TO EXTEND THEIR UNSPEAKABLE INFLUENCE.
MAR-VELL'S TERMINAL CONDITION CAUSED SUCH DISTRESS AMONGST HIS PEERS AND THE GLOBAL POPULATIONS WHO ADORED HIM, SOMETHING FELT THE EMPATHIC TRAUMA.
IT FELT IT, AND IT RESPONDED WITH AN OFFER TO SOLVE THE PROBLEM.
SOMETHING BECKONED FROM THE COSMIC SHADOWS AND SHOWED THE DYING MAR-VELL ONE SIMPLE TRUTH.
"EVEN DEATH MAY DIE."
MAR-VELL BROUGHT THIS ON HIS UNIVERSE? THAT'S ARRANT NONSENSE!
IS IT, MANTIS?
MANTIS IS RIGHT. EVEN DYING, EVEN SCARED AND JUDGEMENT-IMPAIRED BY PAIN MEDS, MAR-VELL WOULD NEVER MAKE SUCH A GROSS--
OF COURSE. AND NEXT YOU'LL SAY HE HAD ALL THOSE WORTHY FRIENDS AROUND HIM TO PREVENT HIS LAPSES.
I TOLD YOU, THE INFLUENCE OF THE CHTHONIC GODS WAS ALREADY MUCH GREATER IN THIS UNIVERSE THAN IT IS IN OURS.
THE SLIP WAS SO MUCH EASIER TO MAKE. SO MUCH EASIER TO JUSTIFY.
ISAAC, PLAY BACK WHAT YOU SHOWED ME.
PLAYBACK BEGINS
WE HAVE FAILED YOU, CAPTAIN MAR-VELL.
IT'S ALL SO UNFAIR.
DO NOT GRIEVE, MY FRIENDS.

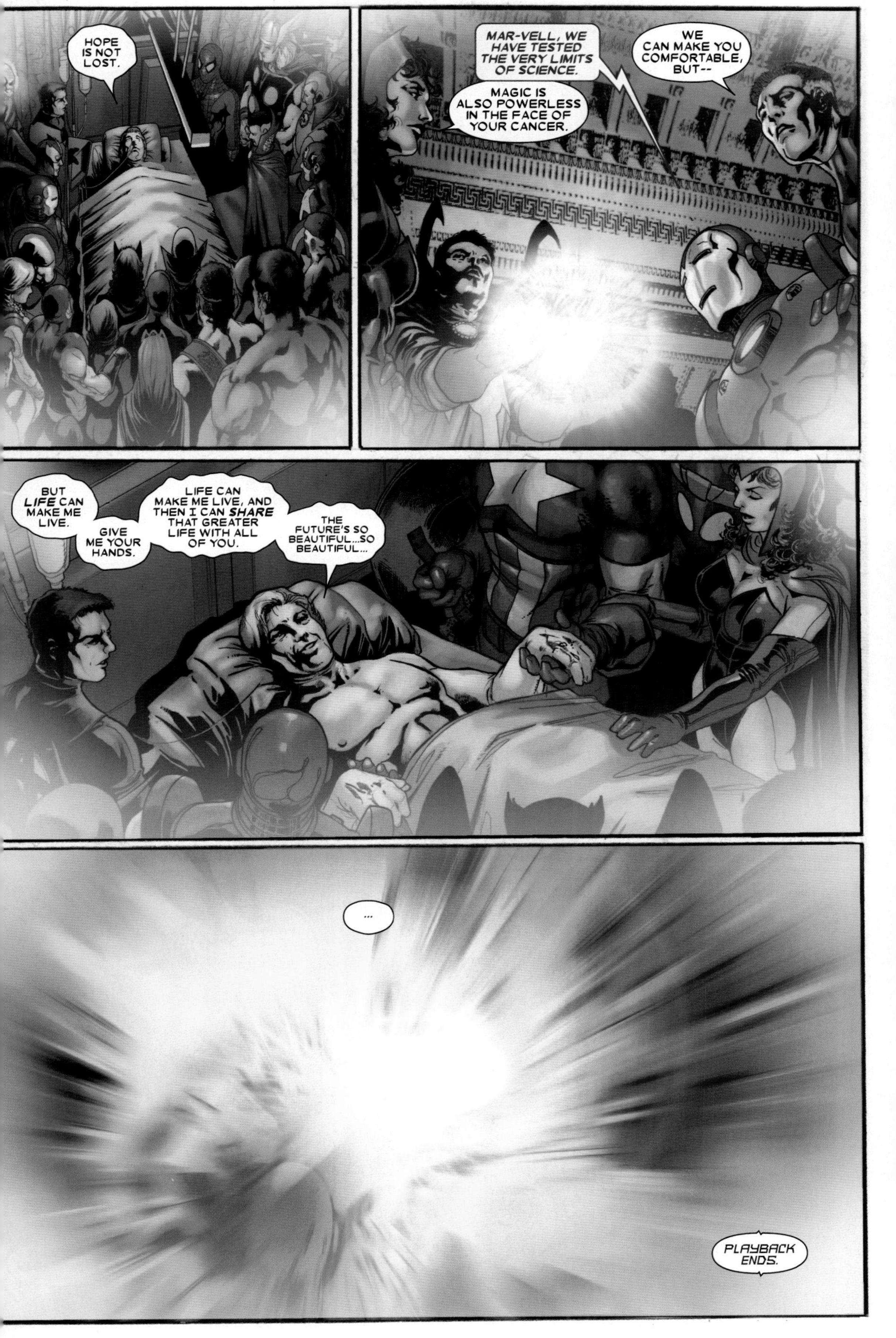
HOPE IS NOT LOST.
MAR-VELL, WE HAVE TESTED THE VERY LIMITS OF SCIENCE.
WE CAN MAKE YOU COMFORTABLE, BUT--
MAGIC IS ALSO POWERLESS IN THE FACE OF YOUR CANCER.
BUT LIFE CAN MAKE ME LIVE.
GIVE ME YOUR HANDS.
LIFE CAN MAKE ME LIVE, AND THEN I CAN SHARE THAT GREATER LIFE WITH ALL OF YOU.
THE FUTURE'S SO BEAUTIFUL...SO BEAUTIFUL...
...
PLAYBACK ENDS.

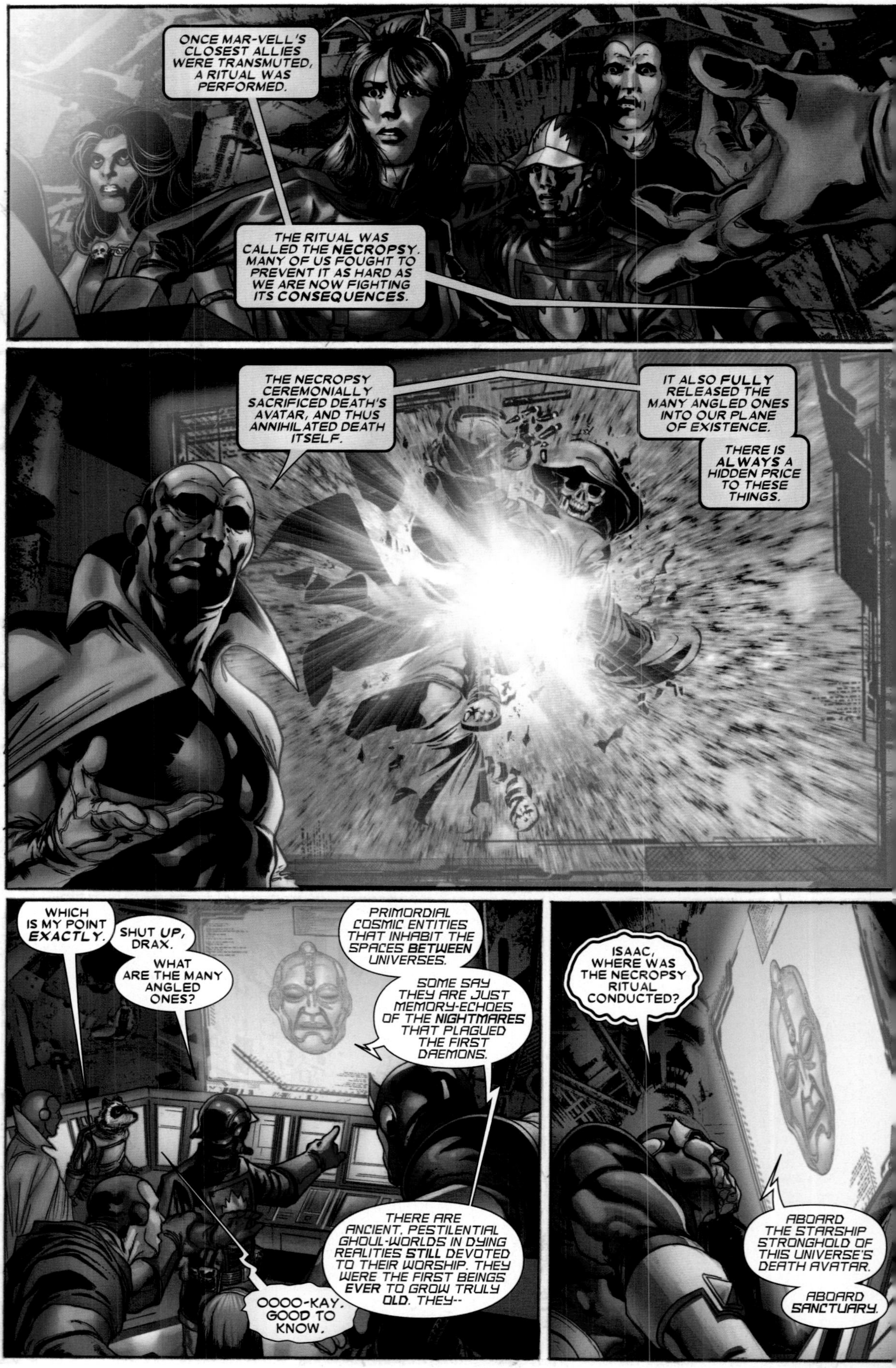
ONCE MAR-VELL'S CLOSEST ALLIES WERE TRANSMUTED, A RITUAL WAS PERFORMED.
THE RITUAL WAS CALLED THE NECROPSY. MANY OF US FOUGHT TO PREVENT IT AS HARD AS WE ARE NOW FIGHTING ITS CONSEQUENCES.
THE NECROPSY CEREMONIALLY SACRIFICED DEATH'S AVATAR, AND THUS ANNIHILATED DEATH ITSELF.
IT ALSO FULLY RELEASED THE MANY ANGLED ONES INTO OUR PLANE OF EXISTENCE.
THERE IS ALWAYS A HIDDEN PRICE TO THESE THINGS.
WHICH IS MY POINT EXACTLY.
SHUT UP, DRAX.
WHAT ARE THE MANY ANGLED ONES?
PRIMORDIAL COSMIC ENTITIES THAT INHABIT THE SPACES BETWEEN UNIVERSES.
SOME SAY THEY ARE JUST MEMORY-ECHOES OF THE NIGHTMARES THAT PLAGUED THE FIRST DAEMONS.
THERE ARE ANCIENT, PESTILENTIAL GHOUL-WORLDS IN DYING REALITIES STILL DEVOTED TO THEIR WORSHIP. THEY WERE THE FIRST BEINGS EVER TO GROW TRULY OLD. THEY--
OOOO-KAY. GOOD TO KNOW.
ISAAC, WHERE WAS THE NECROPSY RITUAL CONDUCTED?
ABOARD THE STARSHIP STRONGHOLD OF THIS UNIVERSE'S DEATH AVATAR.
ABOARD SANCTUARY.

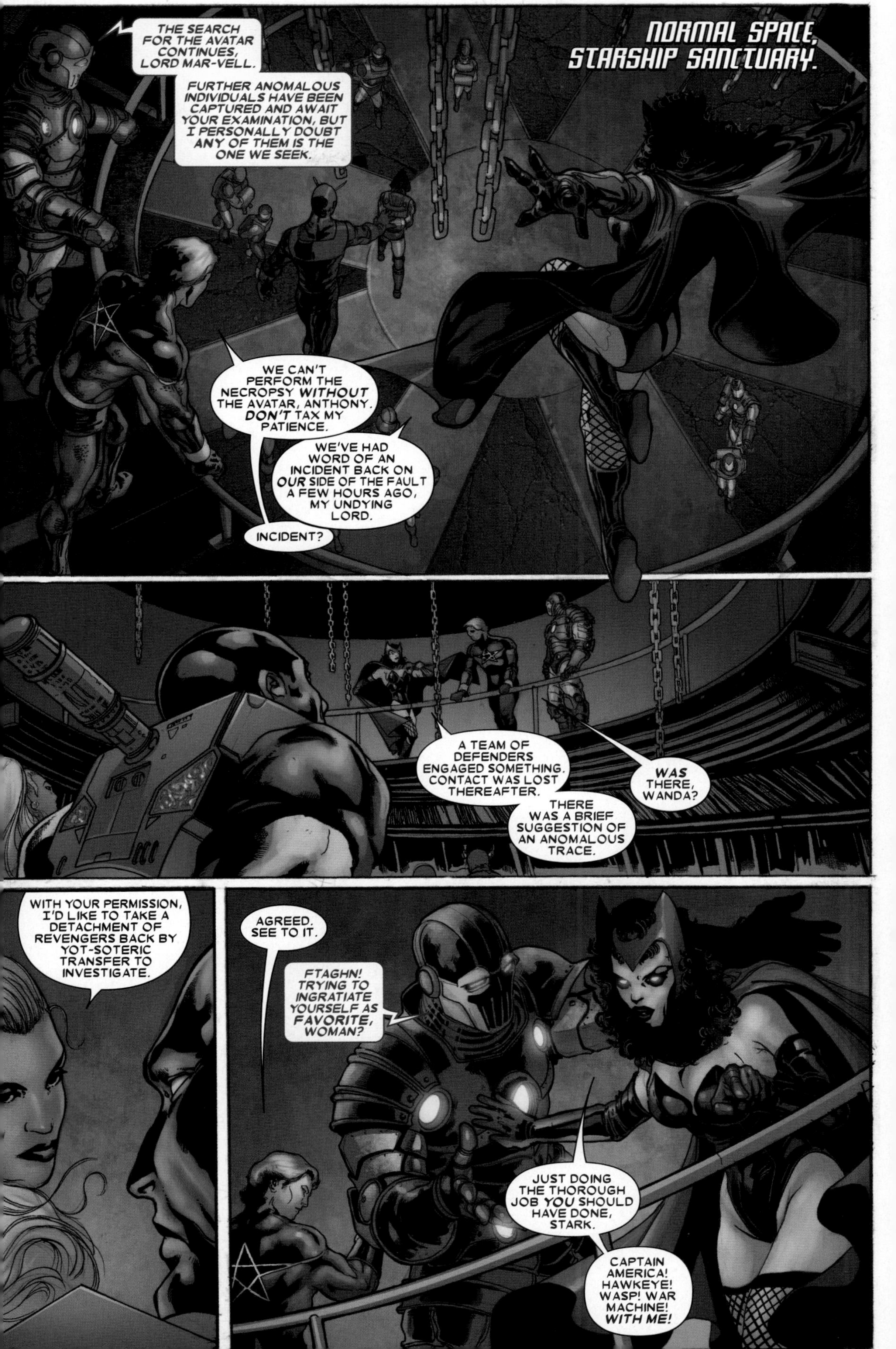
NORMAL SPACE, STARSHIP SANCTUARY.
THE SEARCH FOR THE AVATAR CONTINUES, LORD MAR-VELL.
FURTHER ANOMALOUS INDIVIDUALS HAVE BEEN CAPTURED AND AWAIT YOUR EXAMINATION, BUT I PERSONALLY DOUBT ANY OF THEM IS THE ONE WE SEEK.
WE CAN'T PERFORM THE NECROPSY WITHOUT THE AVATAR, ANTHONY. DON'T TAX MY PATIENCE.
WE'VE HAD WORD OF AN INCIDENT BACK ON OUR SIDE OF THE FAULT A FEW HOURS AGO, MY UNDYING LORD.
INCIDENT?
A TEAM OF DEFENDERS ENGAGED SOMETHING. CONTACT WAS LOST THEREAFTER.
WAS THERE, WANDA?
THERE WAS A BRIEF SUGGESTION OF AN ANOMALOUS TRACE.
WITH YOUR PERMISSION, I'D LIKE TO TAKE A DETACHMENT OF REVENGERS BACK BY YOT-SOTERIC TRANSFER TO INVESTIGATE.
AGREED. SEE TO IT.
FTAGHN! TRYING TO INGRATIATE YOURSELF AS FAVORITE, WOMAN?
JUST DOING THE THOROUGH JOB YOU SHOULD HAVE DONE, STARK.
CAPTAIN AMERICA! HAWKEYE! WASP! WAR MACHINE! WITH ME!

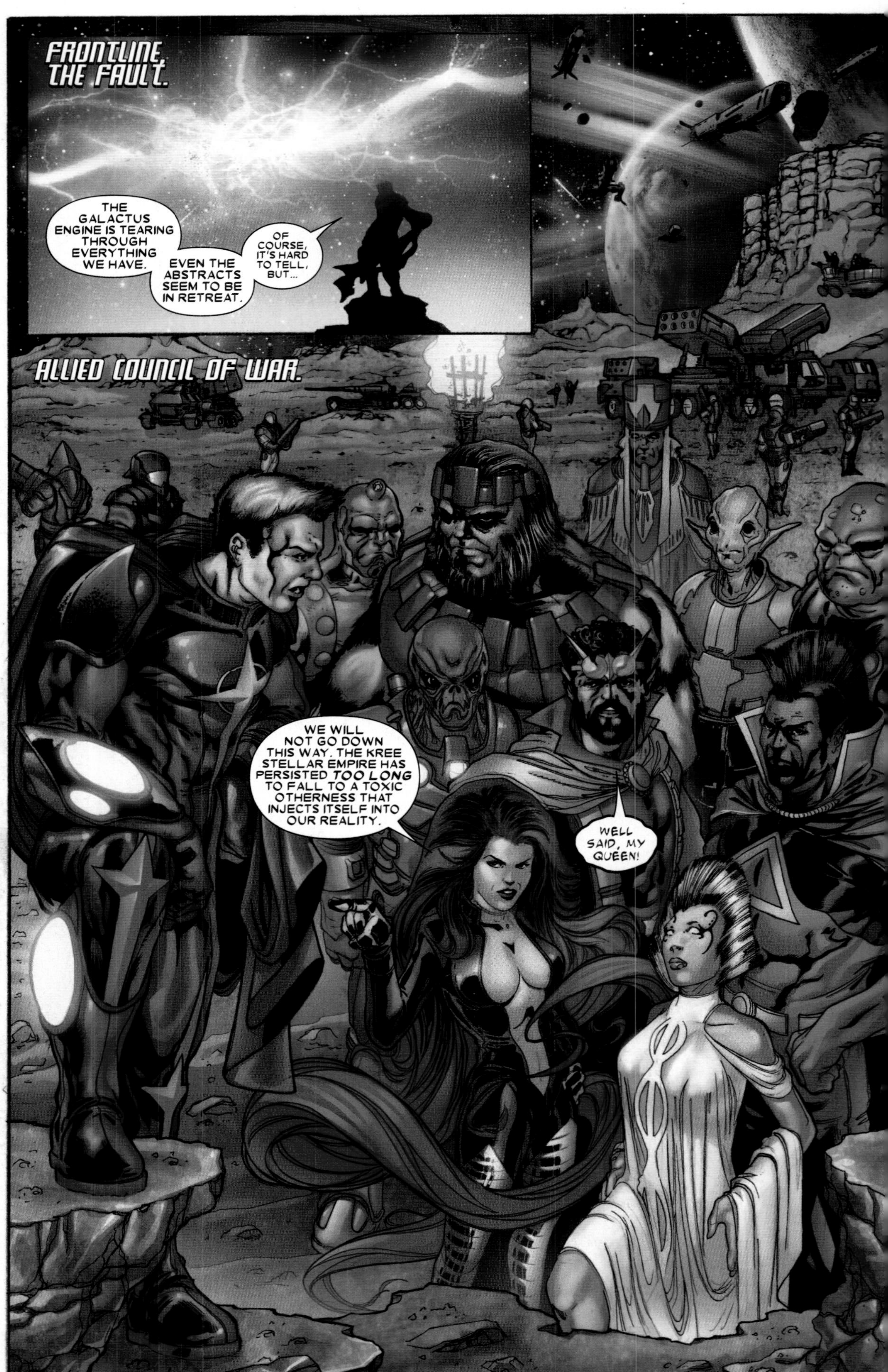

FRONTLINE, THE FAULT.
THE GALACTUS ENGINE IS TEARING THROUGH EVERYTHING WE HAVE.
EVEN THE ABSTRACTS SEEM TO BE IN RETREAT.
OF COURSE, IT'S HARD TO TELL, BUT...
ALLIED COUNCIL OF WAR.
WE WILL NOT GO DOWN THIS WAY. THE KREE STELLAR EMPIRE HAS PERSISTED TOO LONG TO FALL TO A TOXIC OTHERNESS THAT INJECTS ITSELF INTO OUR REALITY.
WELL SAID, MY QUEEN!

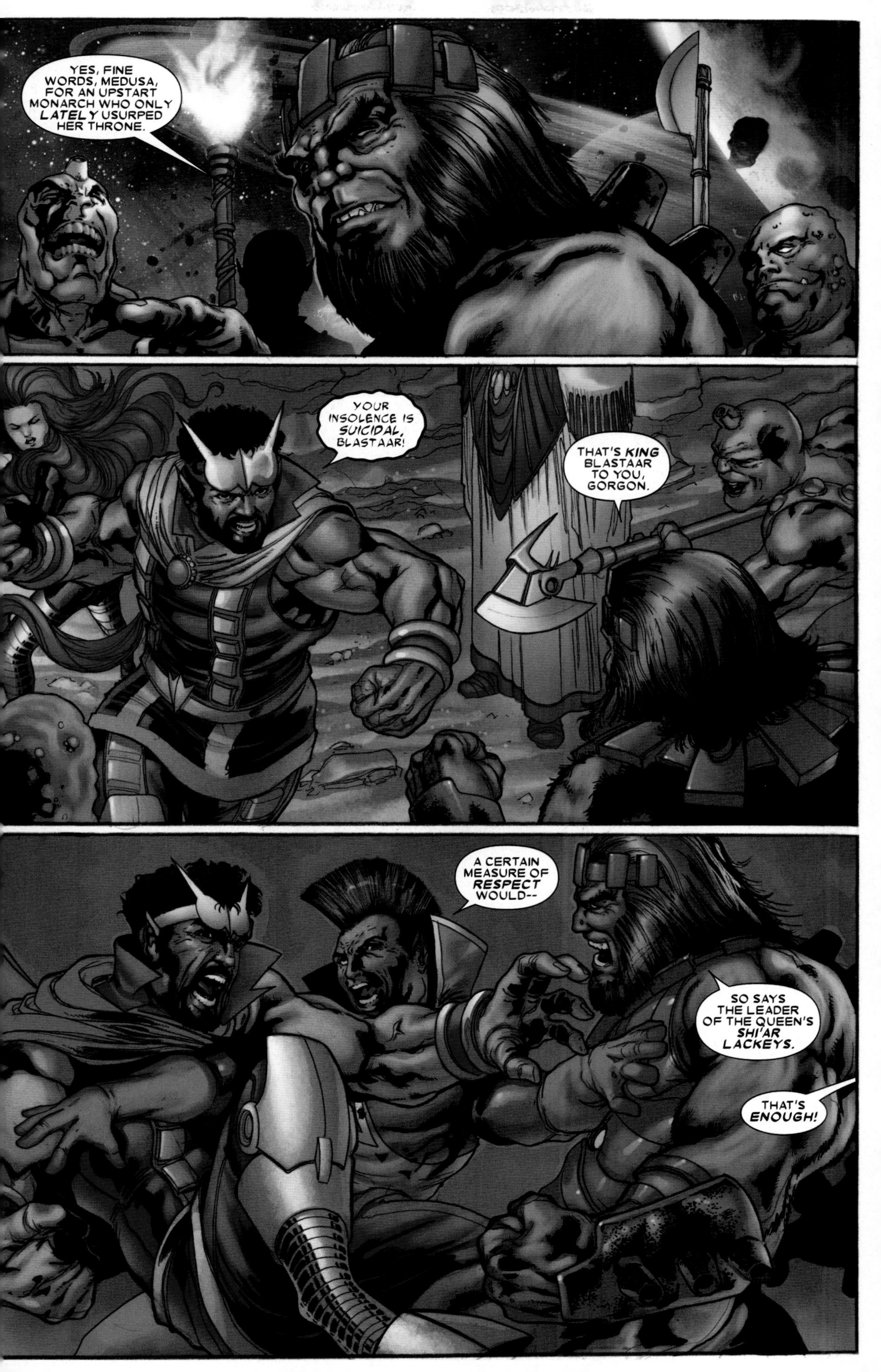

YES, FINE WORDS, MEDUSA, FOR AN UPSTART MONARCH WHO ONLY LATELY USURPED HER THRONE.
YOUR INSOLENCE IS SUICIDAL, BLASTAAR!
THAT'S KING BLASTAAR TO YOU, GORGON.
A CERTAIN MEASURE OF RESPECT WOULD--
SO SAYS THE LEADER OF THE QUEEN'S SHI'AR LACKEYS.
THAT'S ENOUGH!

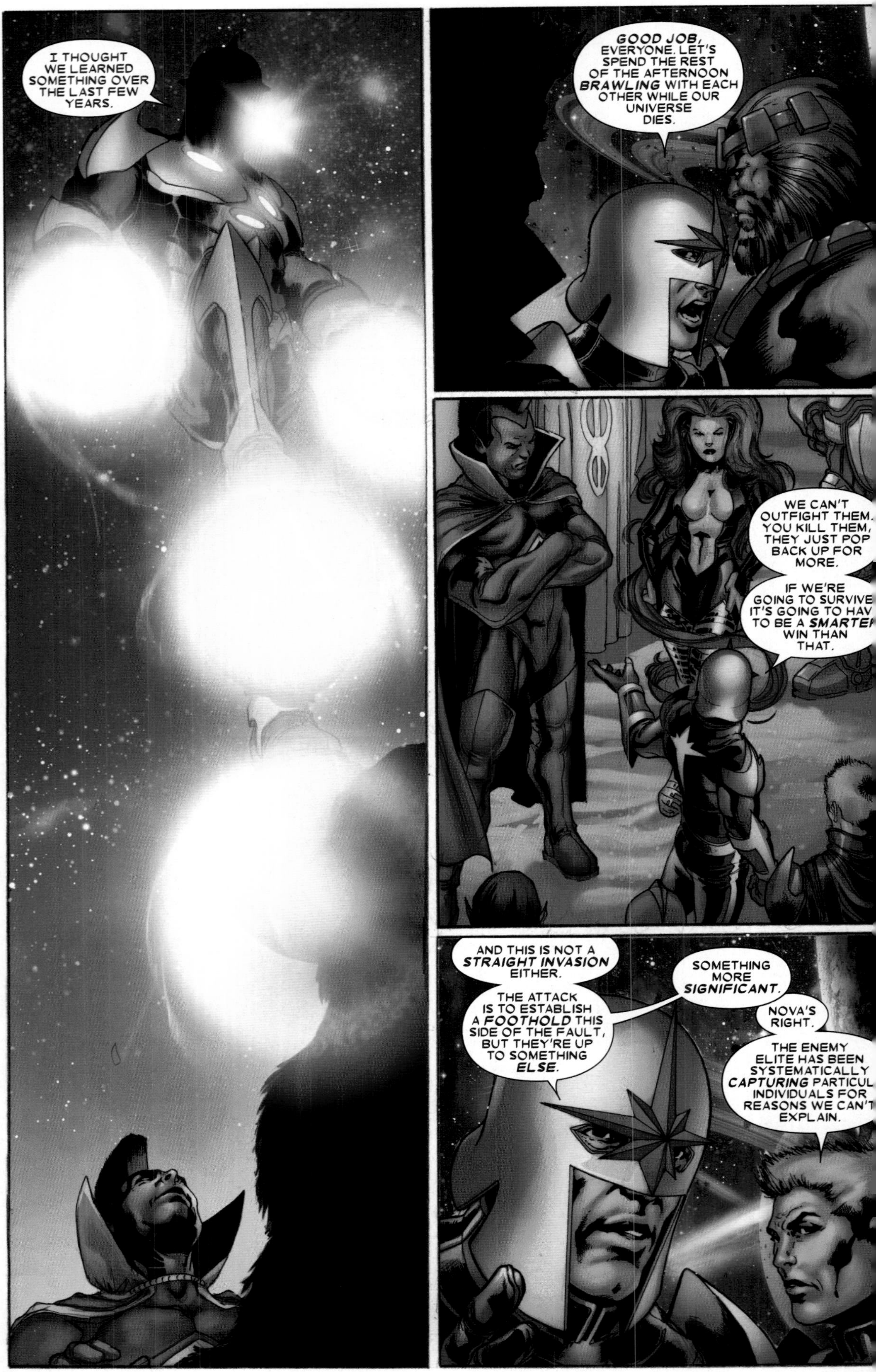
I THOUGHT WE LEARNED SOMETHING OVER THE LAST FEW YEARS.
GOOD JOB, EVERYONE. LET'S SPEND THE REST OF THE AFTERNOON BRAWLING WITH EACH OTHER WHILE OUR UNIVERSE DIES.
WE CAN'T OUTFIGHT THEM. YOU KILL THEM, THEY JUST POP BACK UP FOR MORE.
IF WE'RE GOING TO SURVIVE IT'S GOING TO HAV TO BE A SMARTE WIN THAN THAT.
AND THIS IS NOT A STRAIGHT INVASION EITHER.
THE ATTACK IS TO ESTABLISH A FOOTHOLD THIS SIDE OF THE FAULT, BUT THEY'RE UP TO SOMETHING ELSE.
SOMETHING MORE SIGNIFICANT.
NOVA'S RIGHT.
THE ENEMY ELITE HAS BEEN SYSTEMATICALLY CAPTURING PARTICUL INDIVIDUALS FOR REASONS WE CAN'T EXPLAIN.

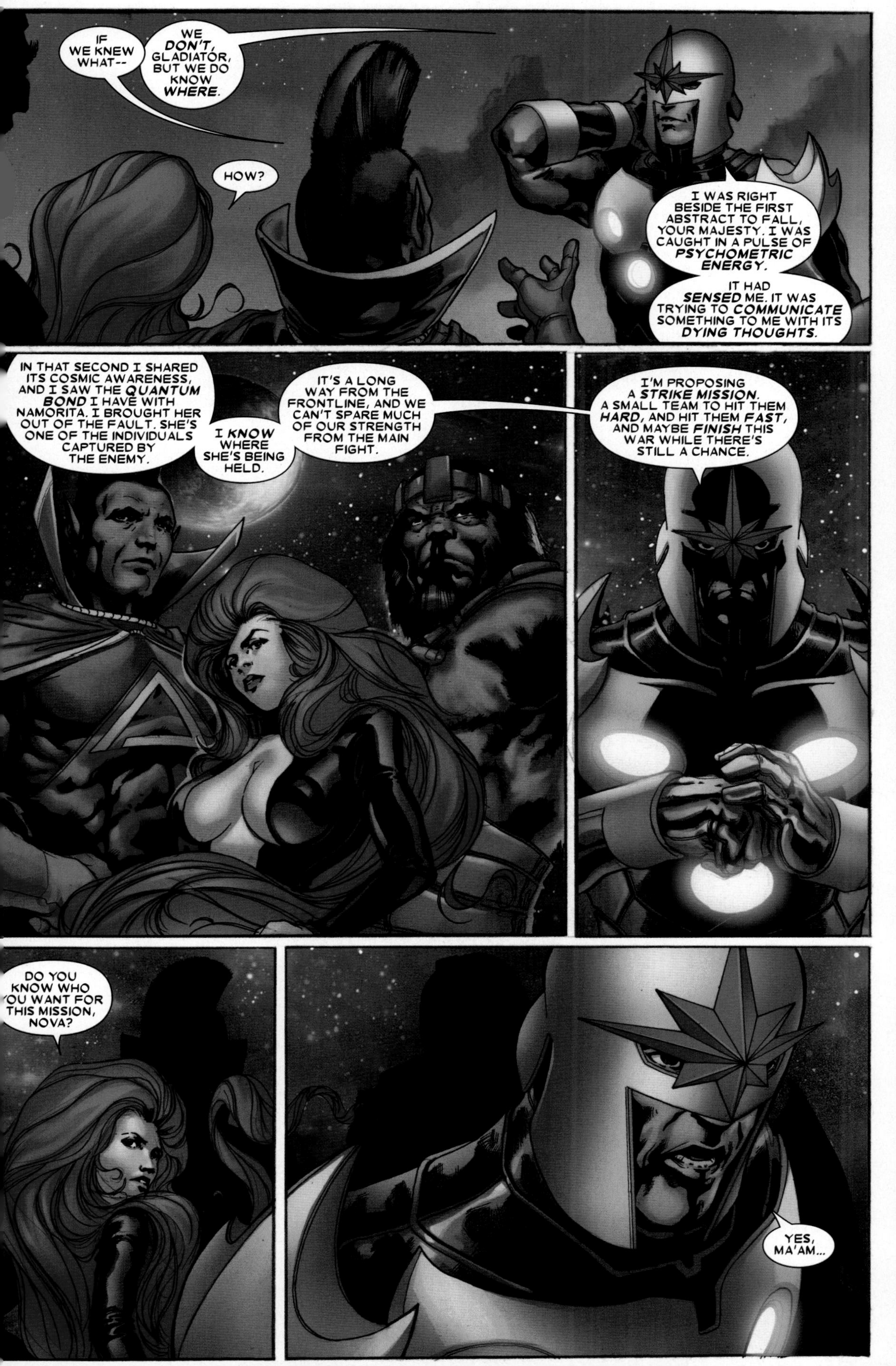
IF WE KNEW WHAT--
WE DON'T, GLADIATOR, BUT WE DO KNOW WHERE.
HOW?
I WAS RIGHT BESIDE THE FIRST ABSTRACT TO FALL, YOUR MAJESTY. I WAS CAUGHT IN A PULSE OF PSYCHOMETRIC ENERGY.
IT HAD SENSED ME. IT WAS TRYING TO COMMUNICATE SOMETHING TO ME WITH ITS DYING THOUGHTS.
IN THAT SECOND I SHARED ITS COSMIC AWARENESS, AND I SAW THE QUANTUM BOND I HAVE WITH NAMORITA. I BROUGHT HER OUT OF THE FAULT. SHE'S ONE OF THE INDIVIDUALS CAPTURED BY THE ENEMY.
I KNOW WHERE SHE'S BEING HELD.
IT'S A LONG WAY FROM THE FRONTLINE, AND WE CAN'T SPARE MUCH OF OUR STRENGTH FROM THE MAIN FIGHT.
I'M PROPOSING A STRIKE MISSION. A SMALL TEAM TO HIT THEM HARD, AND HIT THEM FAST, AND MAYBE FINISH THIS WAR WHILE THERE'S STILL A CHANCE.
DO YOU KNOW WHO YOU WANT FOR THIS MISSION, NOVA?
YES, MA'AM...

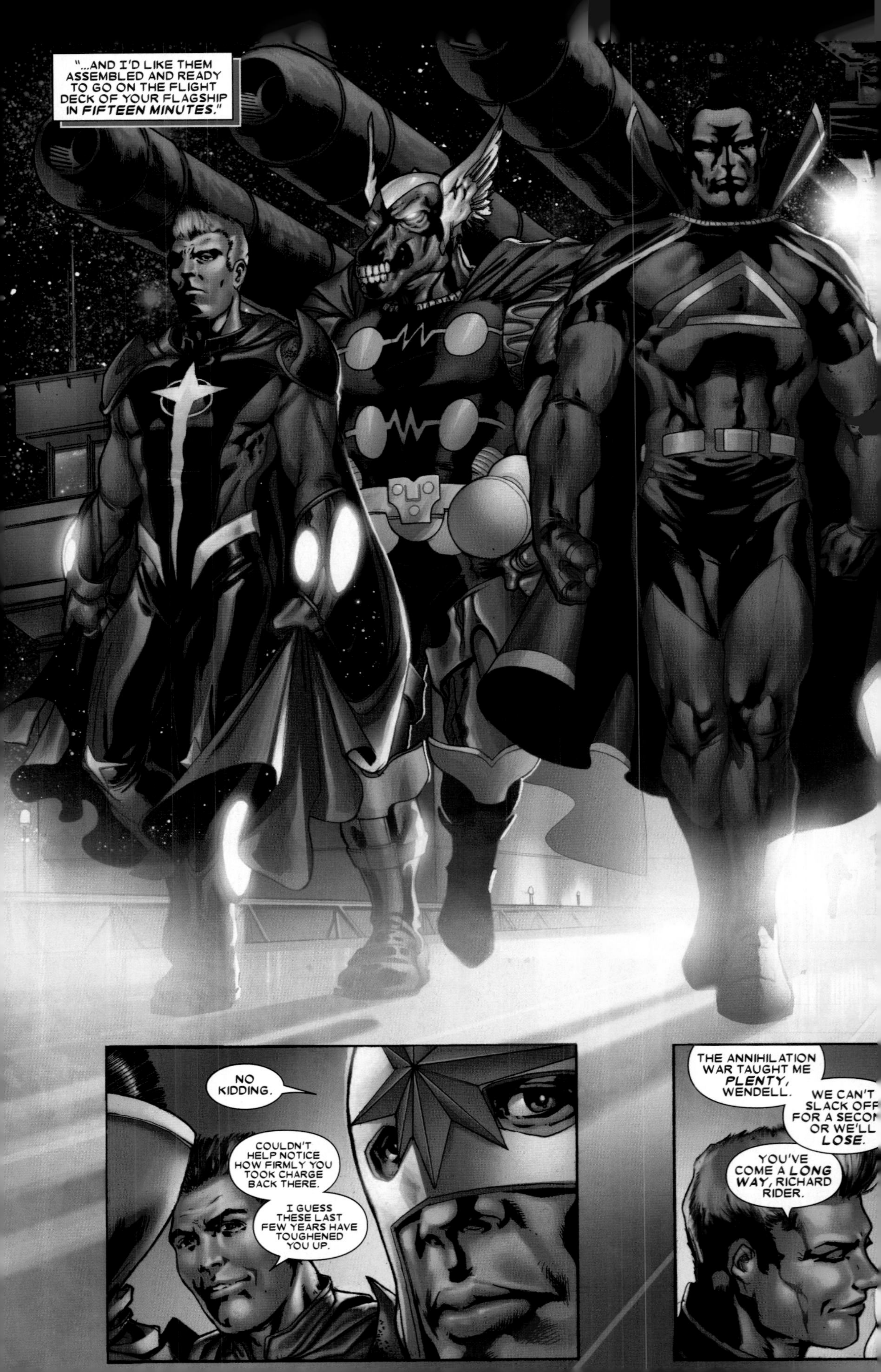
"...AND I'D LIKE THEM ASSEMBLED AND READY TO GO ON THE FLIGHT DECK OF YOUR FLAGSHIP IN *FIFTEEN MINUTES*."
NO KIDDING.
COULDN'T HELP NOTICE HOW FIRMLY YOU TOOK CHARGE BACK THERE.
I GUESS THESE LAST FEW YEARS HAVE TOUGHENED YOU UP.
THE ANNIHILATION WAR TAUGHT ME *PLENTY*, WENDELL.
WE CAN'T SLACK OFF FOR A SECON OR WE'LL *LOSE*.
YOU'VE COME A *LONG WAY*, RICHARD RIDER.

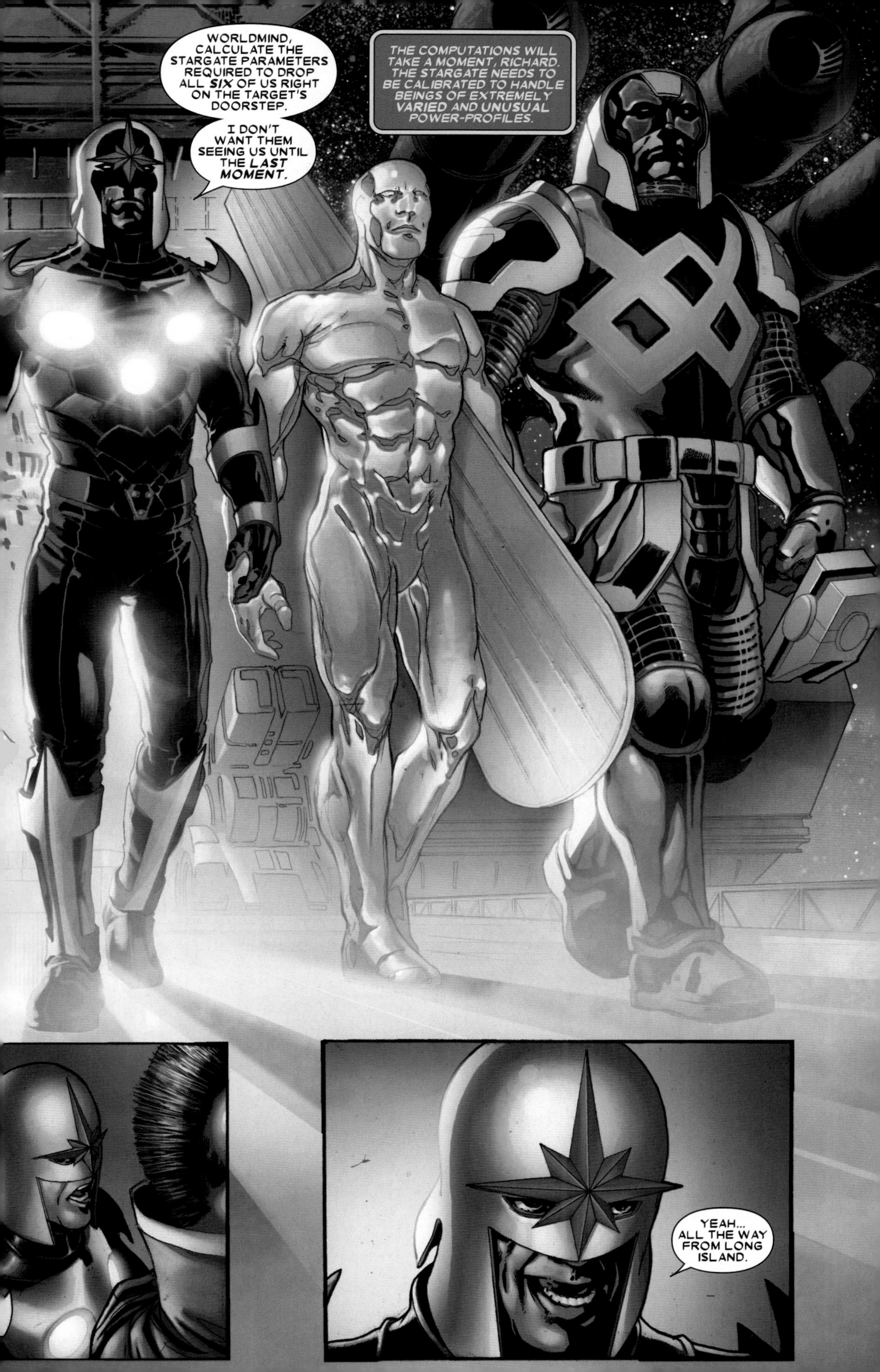
WORLDMIND, CALCULATE THE STARGATE PARAMETERS REQUIRED TO DROP ALL SIX OF US RIGHT ON THE TARGET'S DOORSTEP.
I DON'T WANT THEM SEEING US UNTIL THE LAST MOMENT.
THE COMPUTATIONS WILL TAKE A MOMENT, RICHARD. THE STARGATE NEEDS TO BE CALIBRATED TO HANDLE BEINGS OF EXTREMELY VARIED AND UNUSUAL POWER-PROFILES.
YEAH... ALL THE WAY FROM LONG ISLAND.

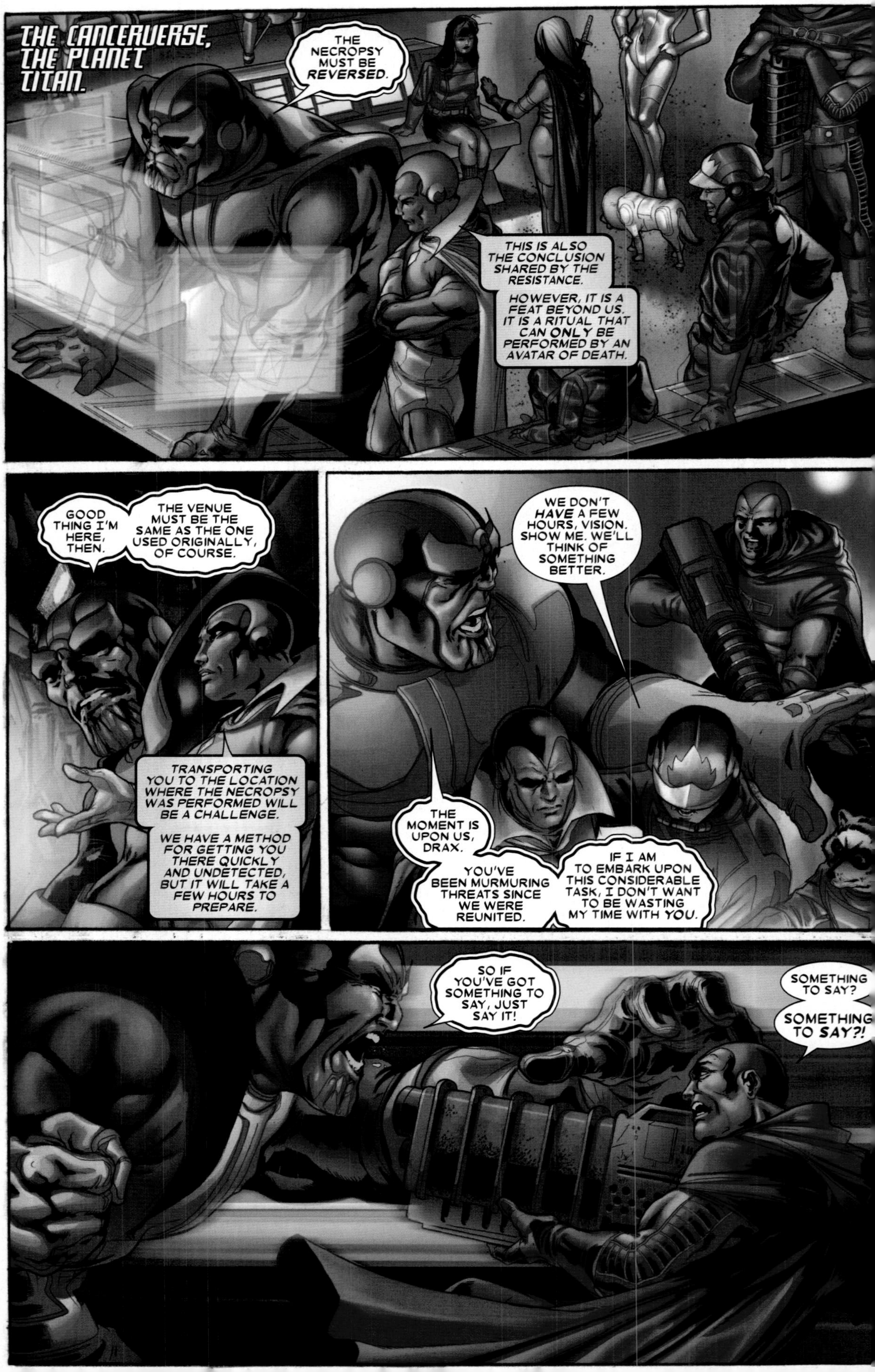
THE CANCERVERSE, THE PLANET TITAN.
THE NECROPSY MUST BE REVERSED.
THIS IS ALSO THE CONCLUSION SHARED BY THE RESISTANCE.
HOWEVER, IT IS A FEAT BEYOND US. IT IS A RITUAL THAT CAN ONLY BE PERFORMED BY AN AVATAR OF DEATH.
GOOD THING I'M HERE, THEN.
THE VENUE MUST BE THE SAME AS THE ONE USED ORIGINALLY, OF COURSE.
TRANSPORTING YOU TO THE LOCATION WHERE THE NECROPSY WAS PERFORMED WILL BE A CHALLENGE.
WE HAVE A METHOD FOR GETTING YOU THERE QUICKLY AND UNDETECTED, BUT IT WILL TAKE A FEW HOURS TO PREPARE.
WE DON'T HAVE A FEW HOURS, VISION. SHOW ME. WE'LL THINK OF SOMETHING BETTER.
THE MOMENT IS UPON US, DRAX.
YOU'VE BEEN MURMURING THREATS SINCE WE WERE REUNITED.
IF I AM TO EMBARK UPON THIS CONSIDERABLE TASK, I DON'T WANT TO BE WASTING MY TIME WITH YOU.
SO IF YOU'VE GOT SOMETHING TO SAY, JUST SAY IT!
SOMETHING TO SAY?
SOMETHING TO SAY?!

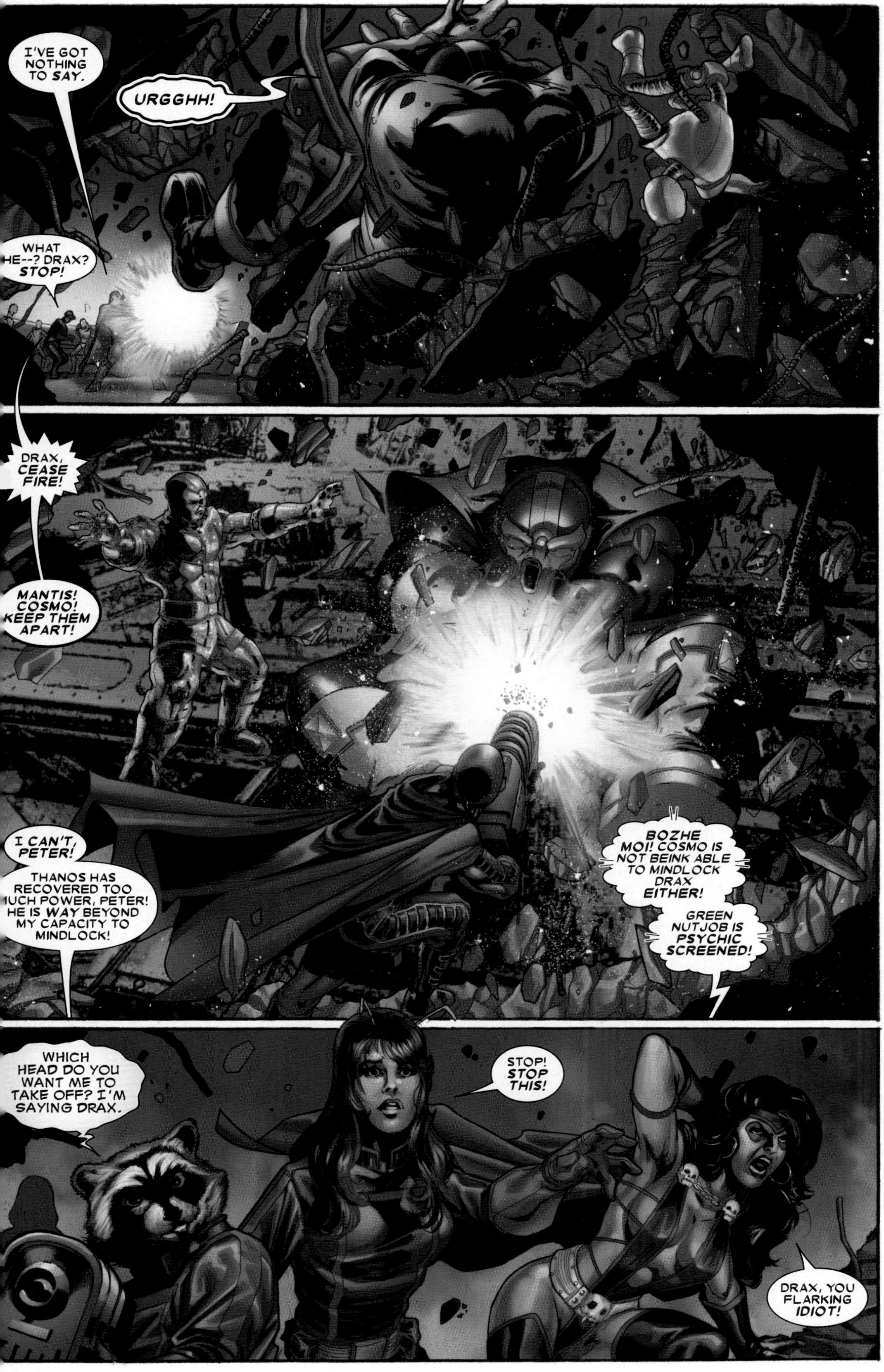I'VE GOT NOTHING TO SAY.
URGGHH!
WHAT HE--? DRAX? STOP!
DRAX, CEASE FIRE!
MANTIS! COSMO! KEEP THEM APART!
I CAN'T, PETER!
THANOS HAS RECOVERED TOO MUCH POWER, PETER! HE IS WAY BEYOND MY CAPACITY TO MINDLOCK!
BOZHE MOI! COSMO IS NOT BEINK ABLE TO MINDLOCK DRAX EITHER!
GREEN NUTJOB IS PSYCHIC SCREENED!
WHICH HEAD DO YOU WANT ME TO TAKE OFF? I'M SAYING DRAX.
STOP! STOP THIS!
DRAX, YOU FLARKING IDIOT!

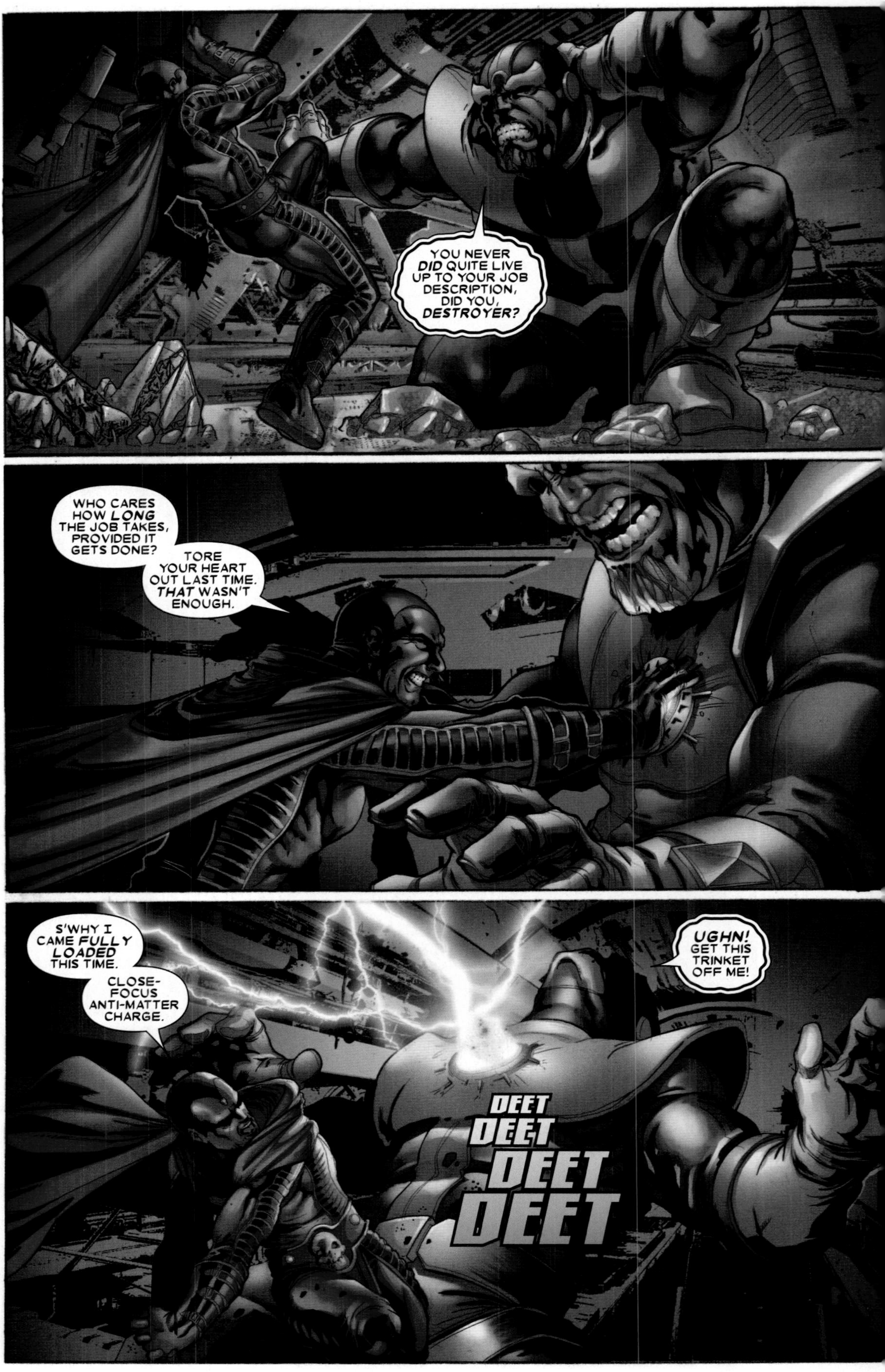
YOU NEVER DID QUITE LIVE UP TO YOUR JOB DESCRIPTION, DID YOU, DESTROYER?
WHO CARES HOW LONG THE JOB TAKES, PROVIDED IT GETS DONE?
TORE YOUR HEART OUT LAST TIME. THAT WASN'T ENOUGH.
S'WHY I CAME FULLY LOADED THIS TIME.
CLOSE-FOCUS ANTI-MATTER CHARGE.
UGHN! GET THIS TRINKET OFF ME!
DEET DEET DEET DEET

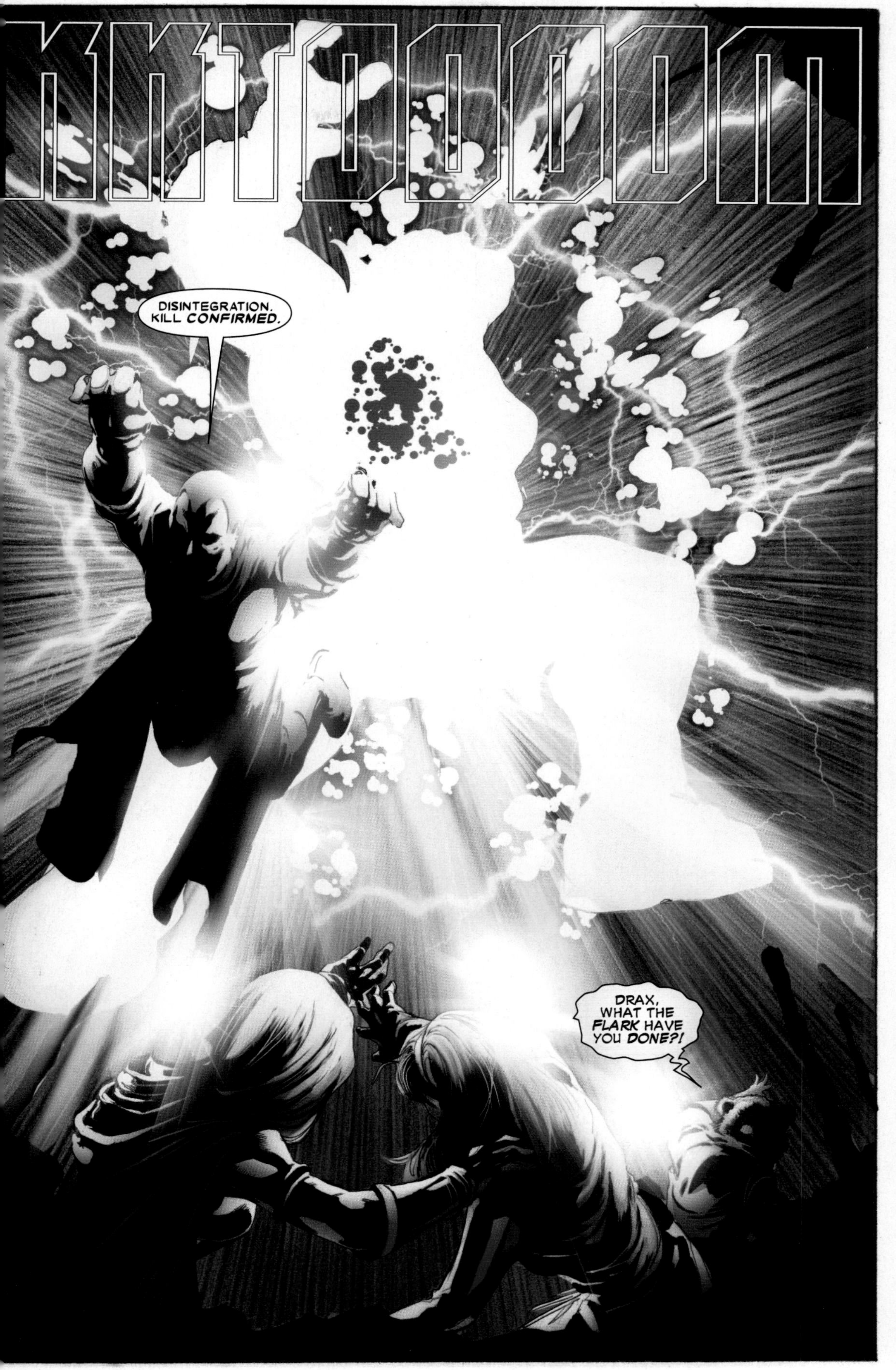
KKTOOOOM
DISINTEGRATION. KILL CONFIRMED.
DRAX, WHAT THE FLARK HAVE YOU DONE?!

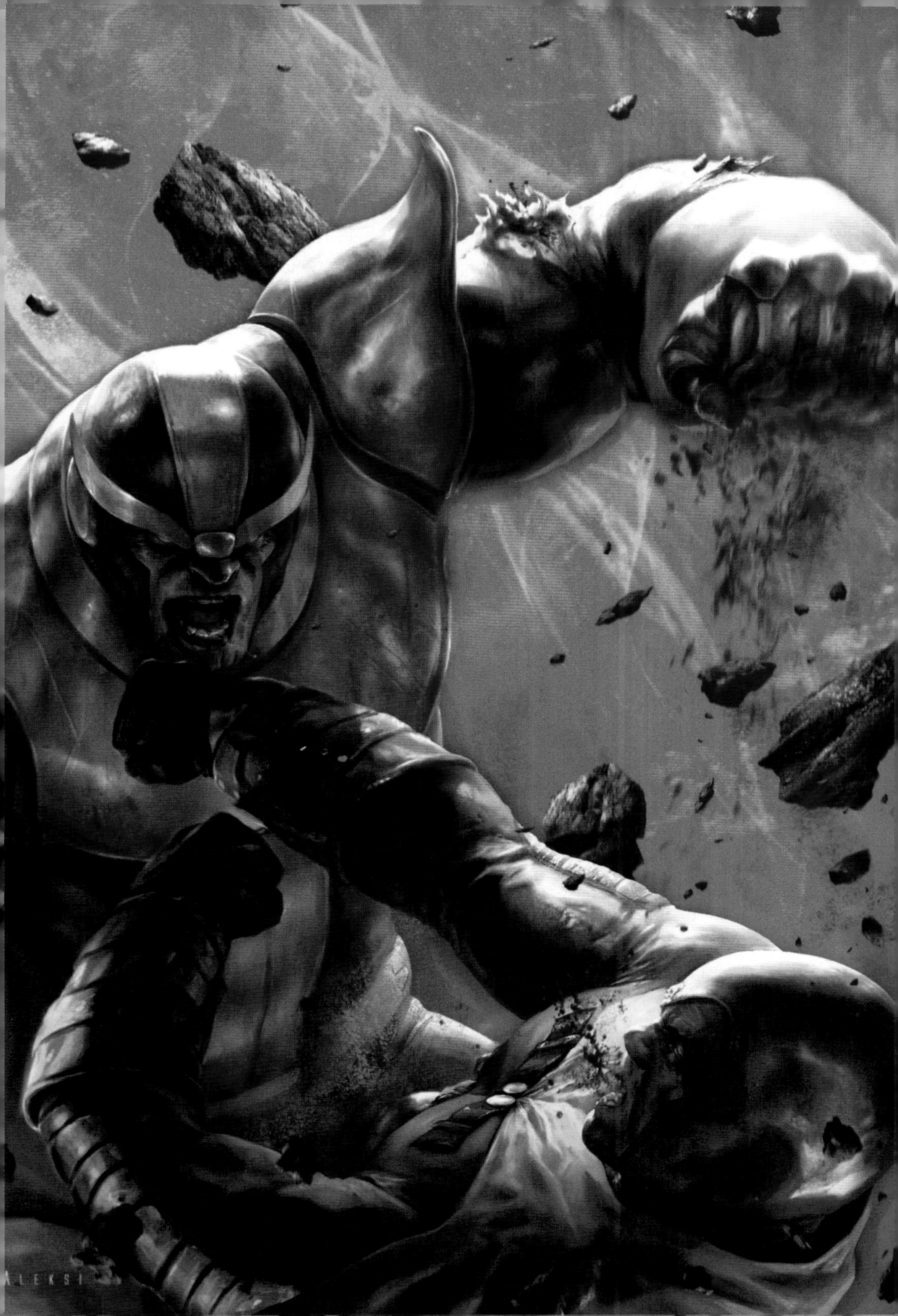
ALEKSI

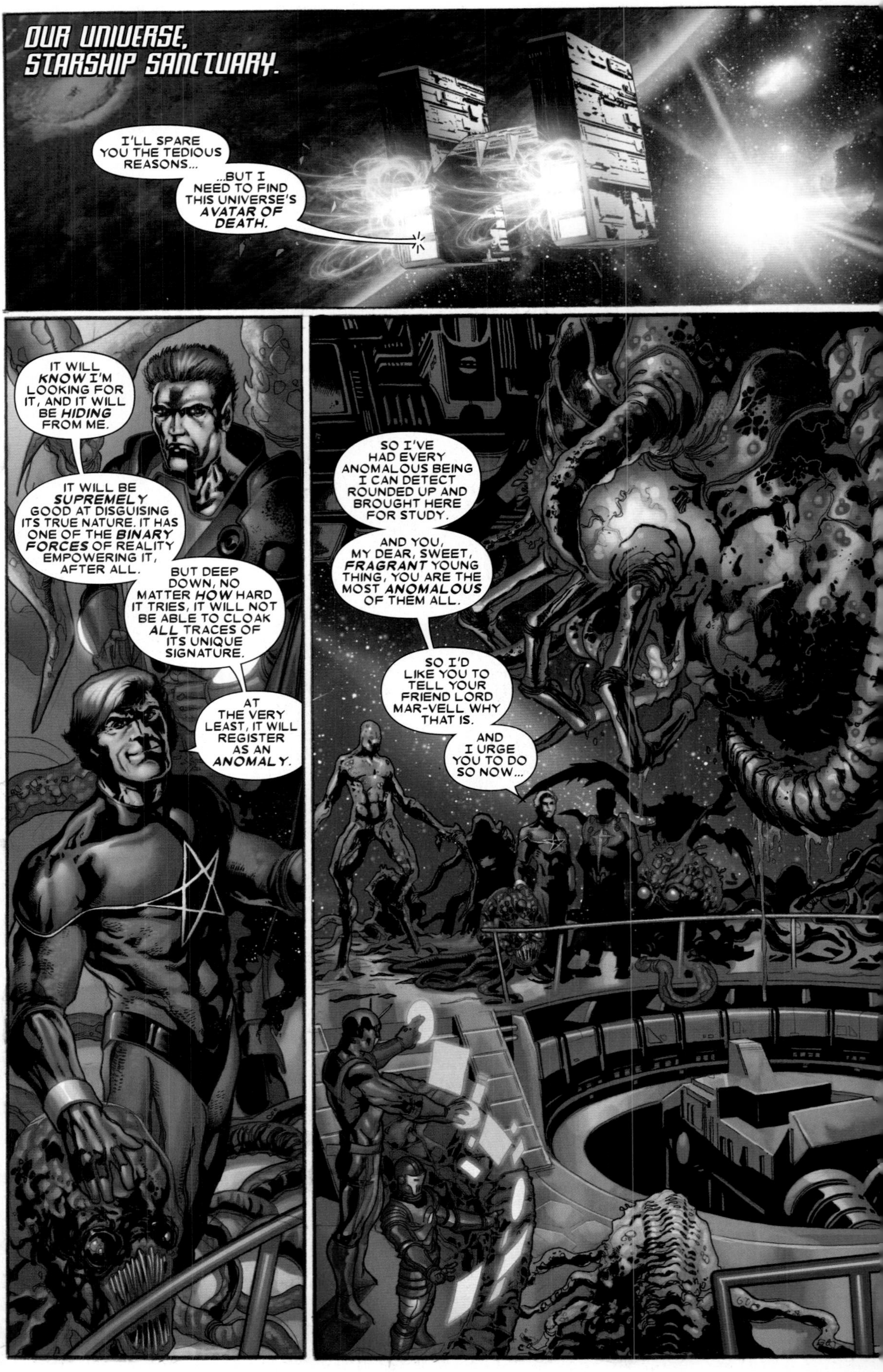
OUR UNIVERSE, STARSHIP SANCTUARY.
I'LL SPARE YOU THE TEDIOUS REASONS...
...BUT I NEED TO FIND THIS UNIVERSE'S AVATAR OF DEATH.
IT WILL KNOW I'M LOOKING FOR IT, AND IT WILL BE HIDING FROM ME.
IT WILL BE SUPREMELY GOOD AT DISGUISING ITS TRUE NATURE. IT HAS ONE OF THE BINARY FORCES OF REALITY EMPOWERING IT, AFTER ALL.
BUT DEEP DOWN, NO MATTER HOW HARD IT TRIES, IT WILL NOT BE ABLE TO CLOAK ALL TRACES OF ITS UNIQUE SIGNATURE.
AT THE VERY LEAST, IT WILL REGISTER AS AN ANOMALY.
SO I'VE HAD EVERY ANOMALOUS BEING I CAN DETECT ROUNDED UP AND BROUGHT HERE FOR STUDY.
AND YOU, MY DEAR, SWEET, FRAGRANT YOUNG THING, YOU ARE THE MOST ANOMALOUS OF THEM ALL.
SO I'D LIKE YOU TO TELL YOUR FRIEND LORD MAR-VELL WHY THAT IS.
AND I URGE YOU TO DO SO NOW...

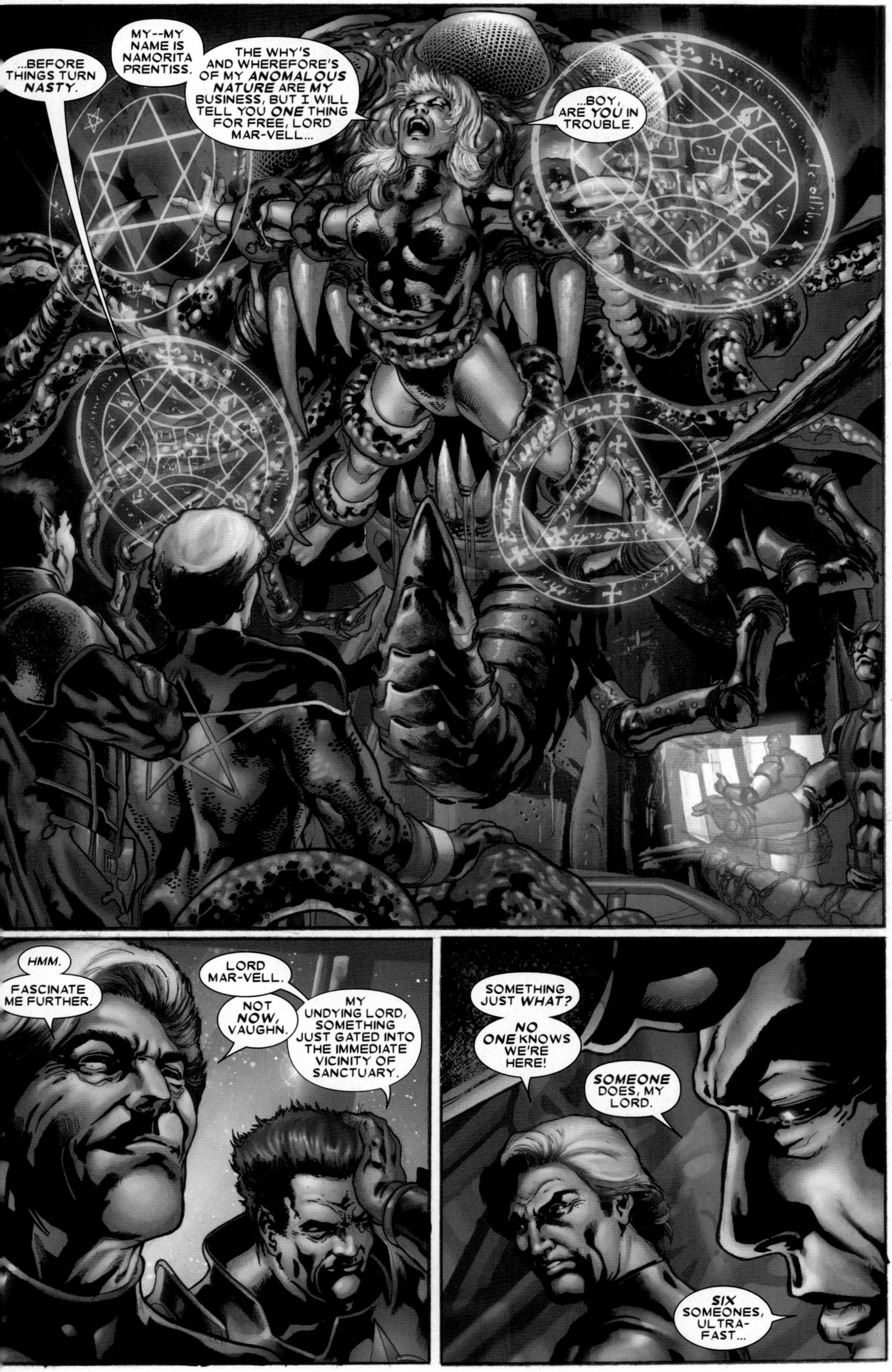
...BEFORE THINGS TURN NASTY.
MY--MY NAME IS NAMORITA PRENTISS.
THE WHY'S AND WHEREFORE'S OF MY ANOMALOUS NATURE ARE MY BUSINESS, BUT I WILL TELL YOU ONE THING FOR FREE, LORD MAR-VELL...
...BOY, ARE YOU IN TROUBLE.
HMM.
FASCINATE ME FURTHER.
LORD MAR-VELL.
NOT NOW, VAUGHN.
MY UNDYING LORD, SOMETHING JUST GATED INTO THE IMMEDIATE VICINITY OF SANCTUARY.
SOMETHING JUST WHAT?
NO ONE KNOWS WE'RE HERE!
SOMEONE DOES, MY LORD.
SIX SOMEONES, ULTRA-FAST...

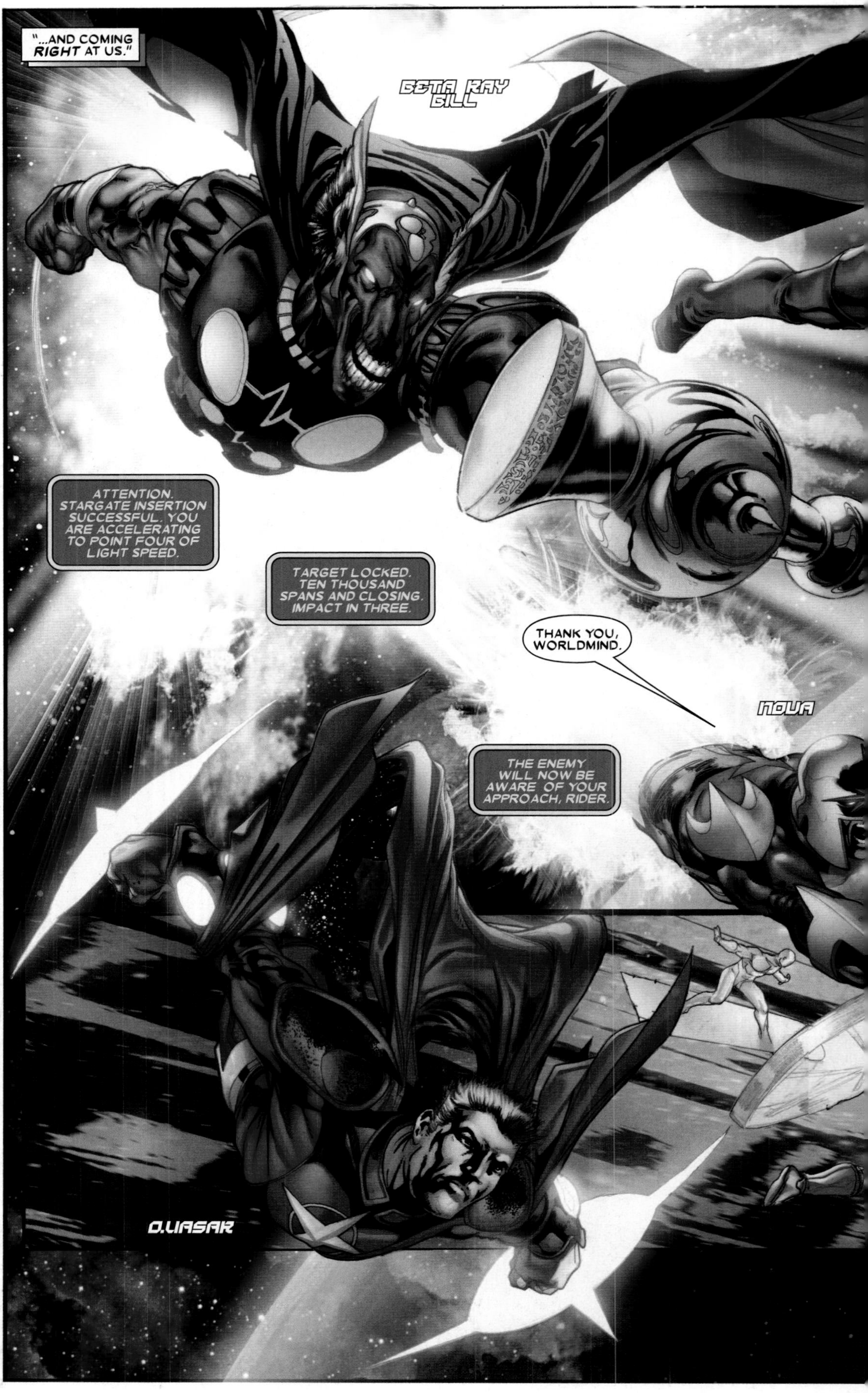
"...AND COMING RIGHT AT US."
BETA RAY BILL
ATTENTION. STARGATE INSERTION SUCCESSFUL. YOU ARE ACCELERATING TO POINT FOUR OF LIGHT SPEED.
TARGET LOCKED. TEN THOUSAND SPANS AND CLOSING. IMPACT IN THREE.
THANK YOU, WORLDMIND.
NOVA
THE ENEMY WILL NOW BE AWARE OF YOUR APPROACH, RIDER.
QUASAR

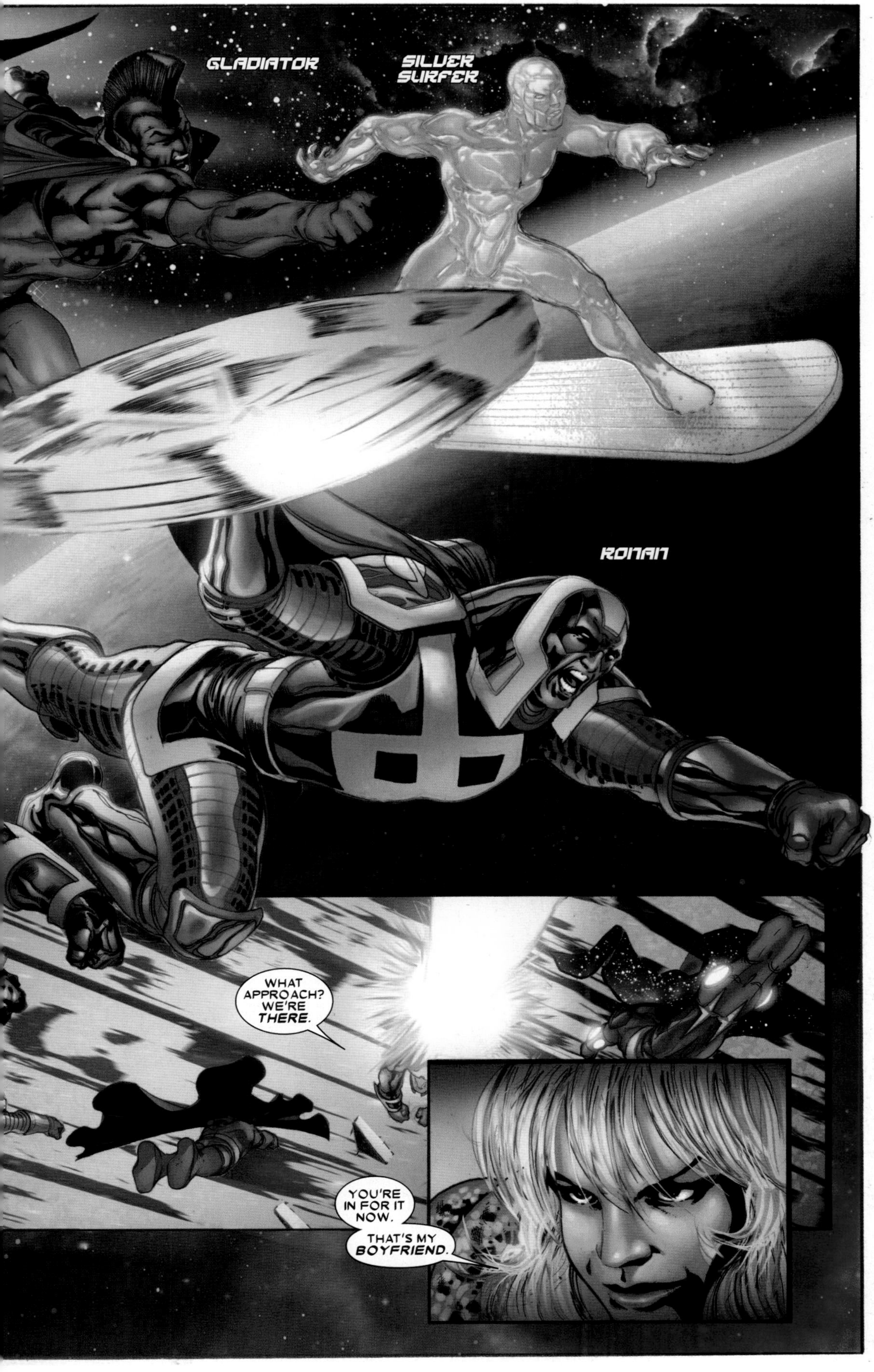
GLADIATOR
SILVER SURFER
RONAN
WHAT APPROACH? WE'RE *THERE*.
YOU'RE IN FOR IT NOW.
THAT'S MY *BOYFRIEND*.

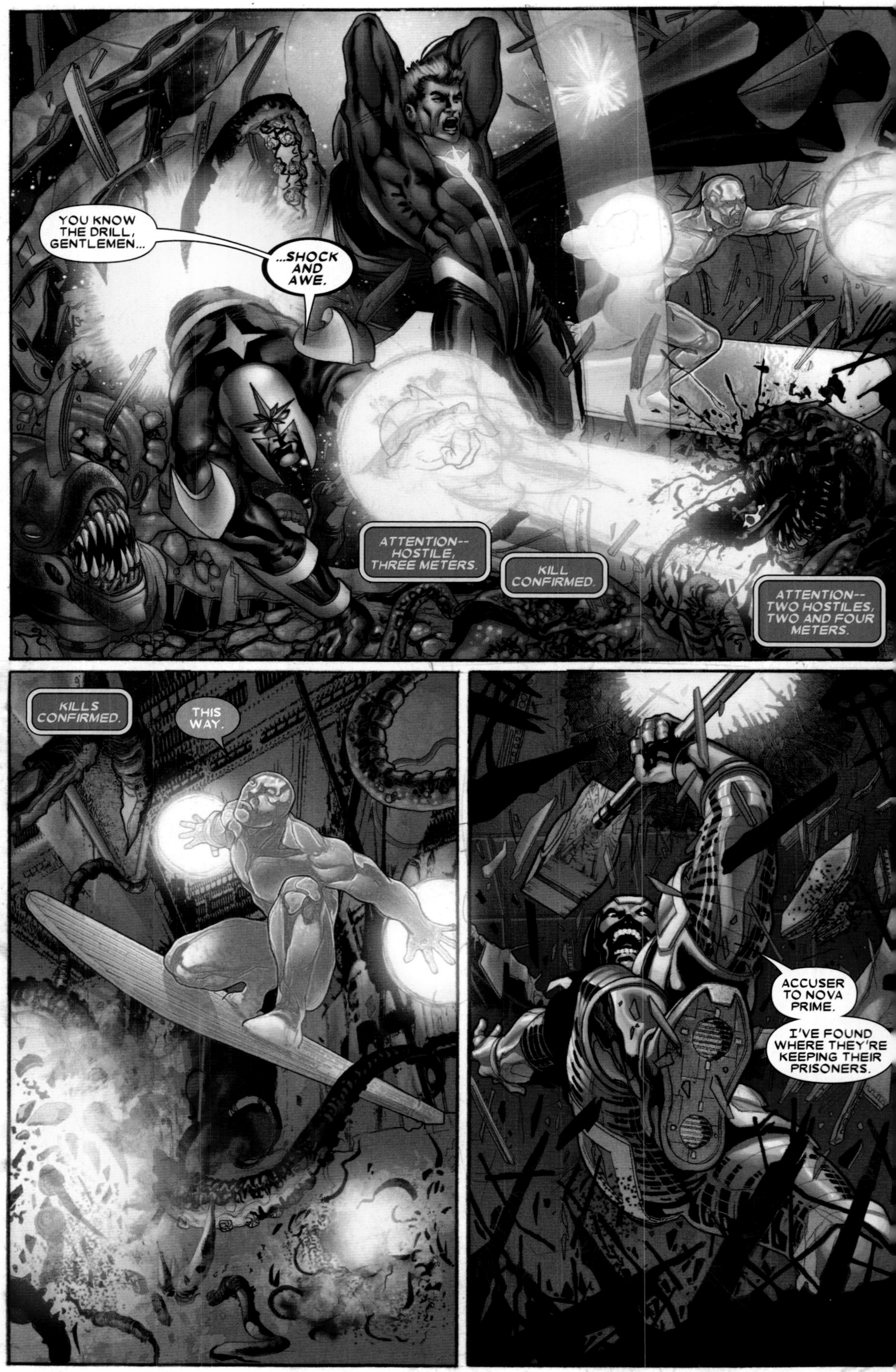
YOU KNOW THE DRILL, GENTLEMEN...
...SHOCK AND AWE.
ATTENTION-- HOSTILE, THREE METERS.
KILL CONFIRMED.
ATTENTION-- TWO HOSTILES, TWO AND FOUR METERS.
KILLS CONFIRMED.
THIS WAY.
ACCUSER TO NOVA PRIME.
I'VE FOUND WHERE THEY'RE KEEPING THEIR PRISONERS.

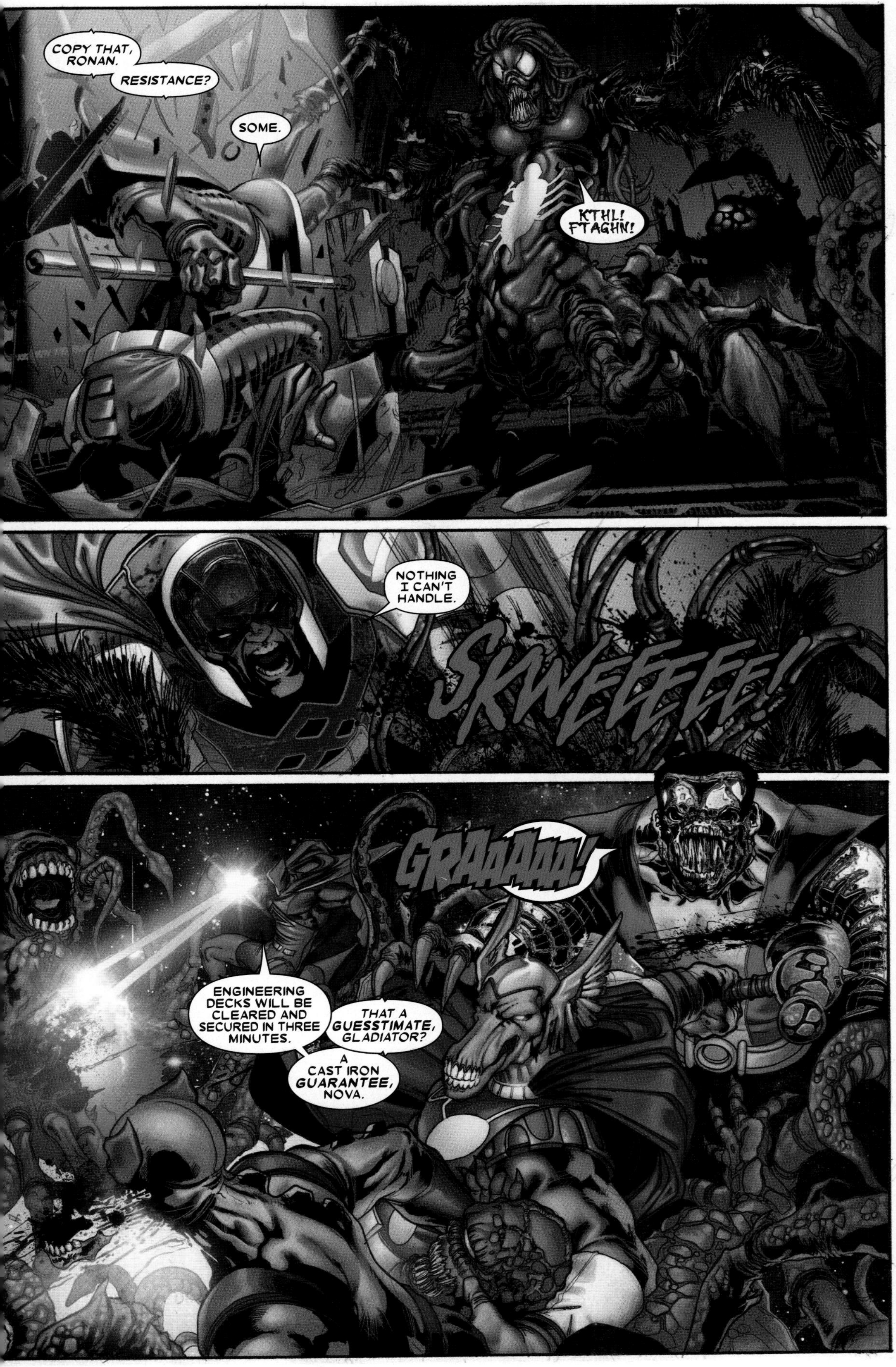
COPY THAT, RONAN.
RESISTANCE?
SOME.
KTHL! FTAGHN!
NOTHING I CAN'T HANDLE.
SKWEEEEE!
GRAAAAA!
ENGINEERING DECKS WILL BE CLEARED AND SECURED IN THREE MINUTES.
THAT A GUESSTIMATE, GLADIATOR?
A CAST IRON GUARANTEE, NOVA.

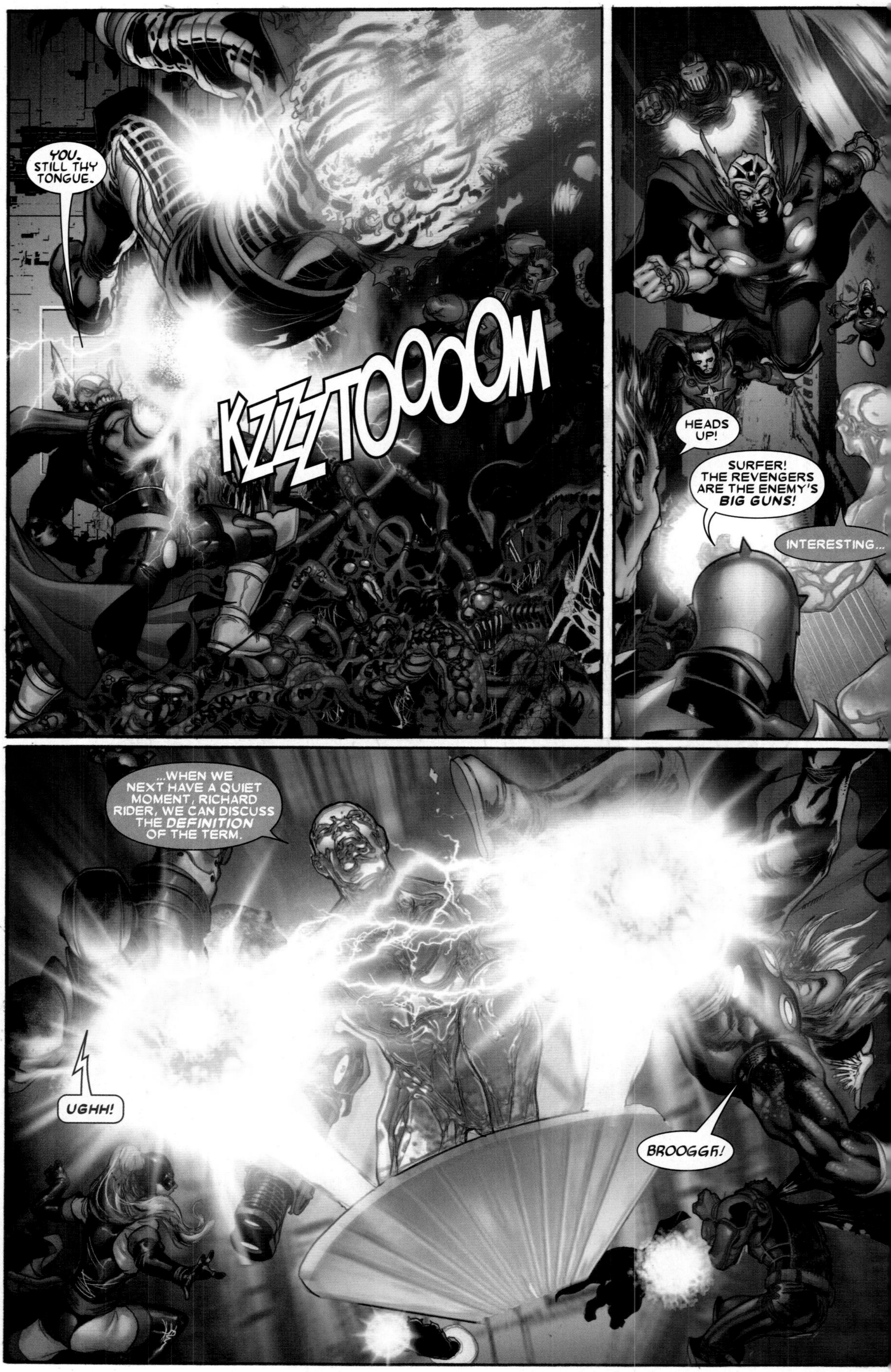
YOU. STILL THY TONGUE.
KZZZTOOOOM
HEADS UP!
SURFER! THE REVENGERS ARE THE ENEMY'S BIG GUNS!
INTERESTING...
...WHEN WE NEXT HAVE A QUIET MOMENT, RICHARD RIDER, WE CAN DISCUSS THE DEFINITION OF THE TERM.
UGHH!
BROOGGH!

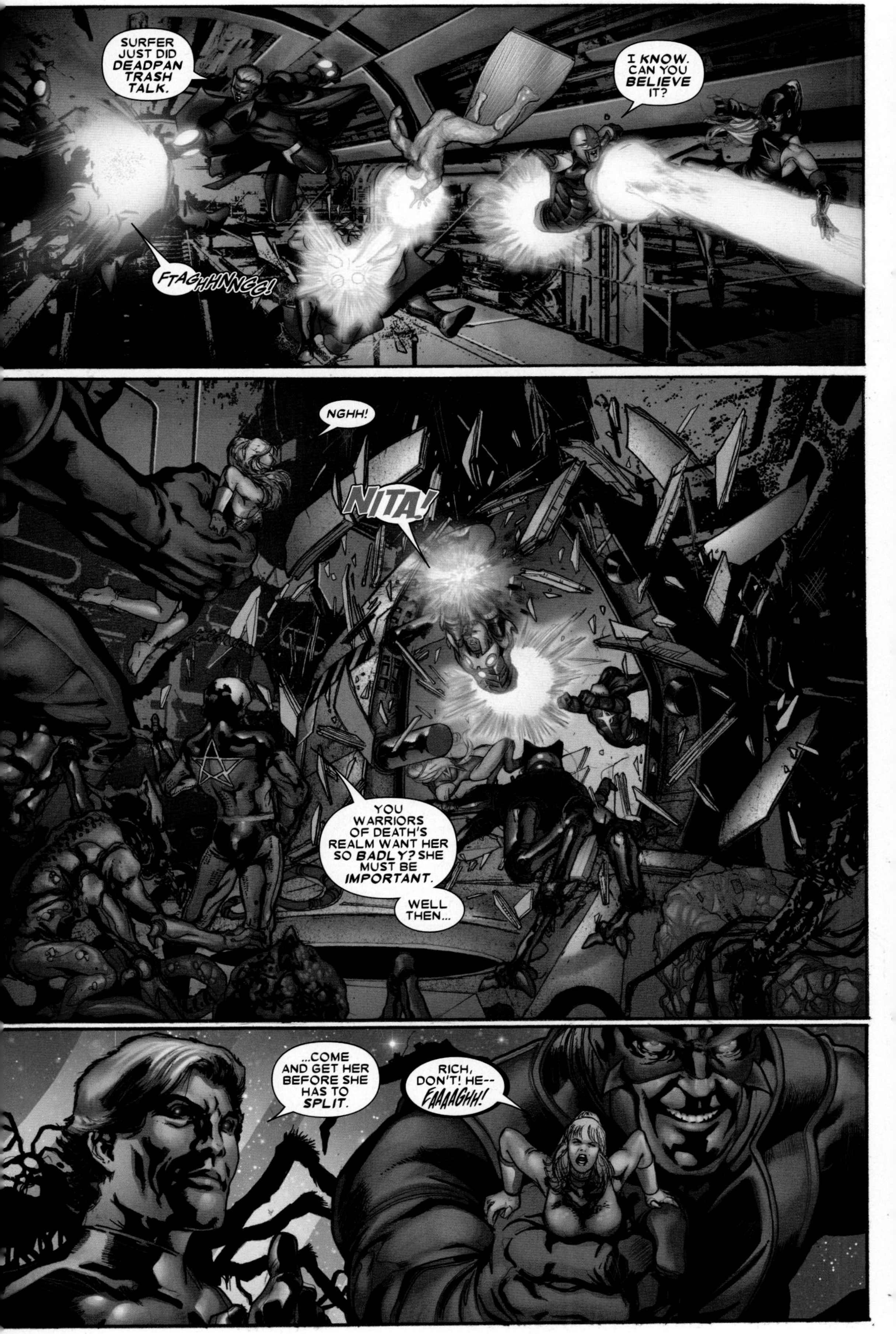
SURFER JUST DID DEADPAN TRASH TALK.
I KNOW. CAN YOU BELIEVE IT?
FTAGHHNNGG!
NGHH!
NITA!
YOU WARRIORS OF DEATH'S REALM WANT HER SO BADLY? SHE MUST BE IMPORTANT.
WELL THEN...
...COME AND GET HER BEFORE SHE HAS TO SPLIT.
RICH, DON'T! HE-- EAAAAGHH!

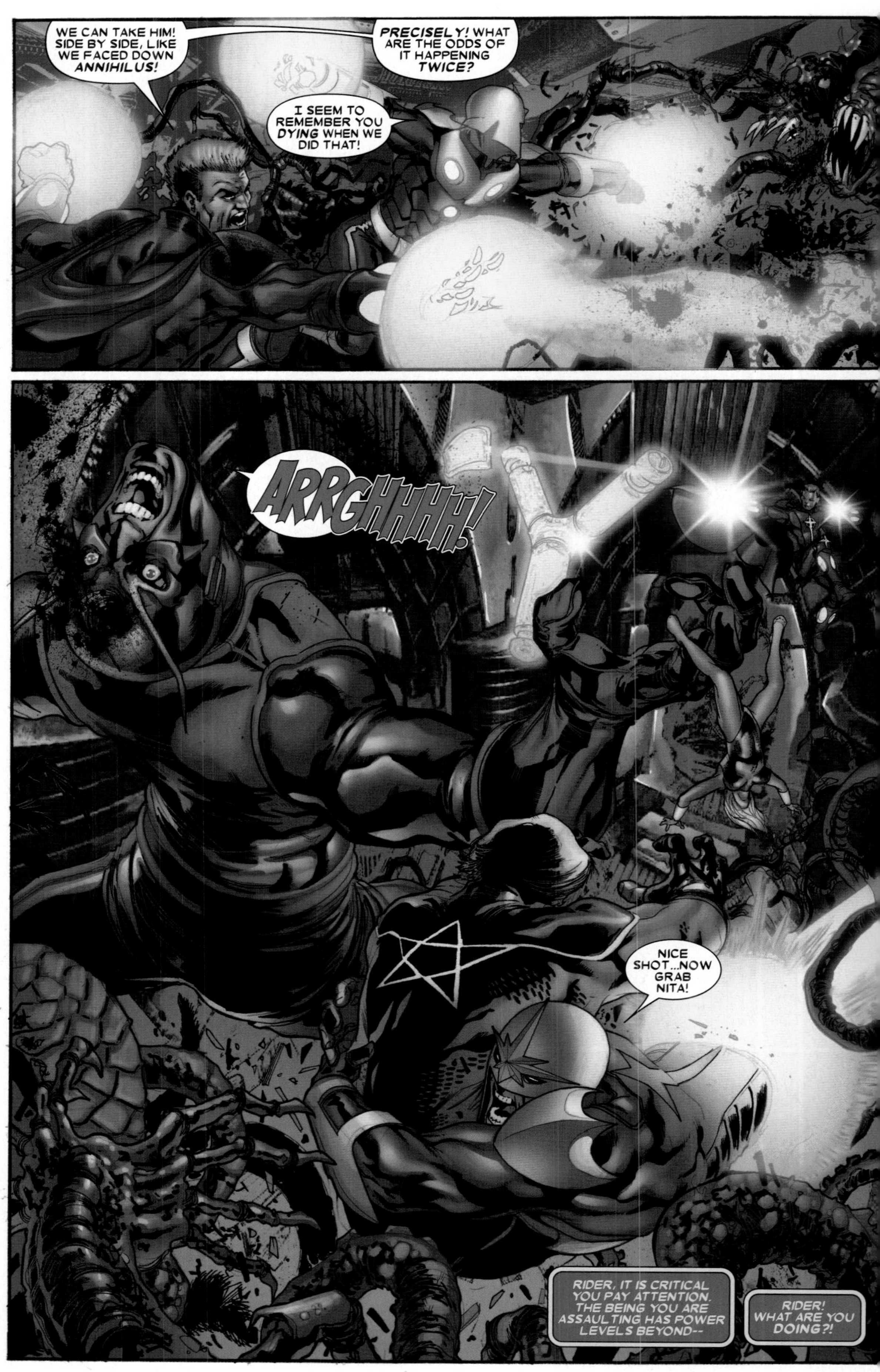
WE CAN TAKE HIM! SIDE BY SIDE, LIKE WE FACED DOWN ANNIHILUS!
PRECISELY! WHAT ARE THE ODDS OF IT HAPPENING TWICE?
I SEEM TO REMEMBER YOU DYING WHEN WE DID THAT!
ARRGHHHH!
NICE SHOT...NOW GRAB NITA!
RIDER, IT IS CRITICAL YOU PAY ATTENTION. THE BEING YOU ARE ASSAULTING HAS POWER LEVELS BEYOND--
RIDER! WHAT ARE YOU DOING?!

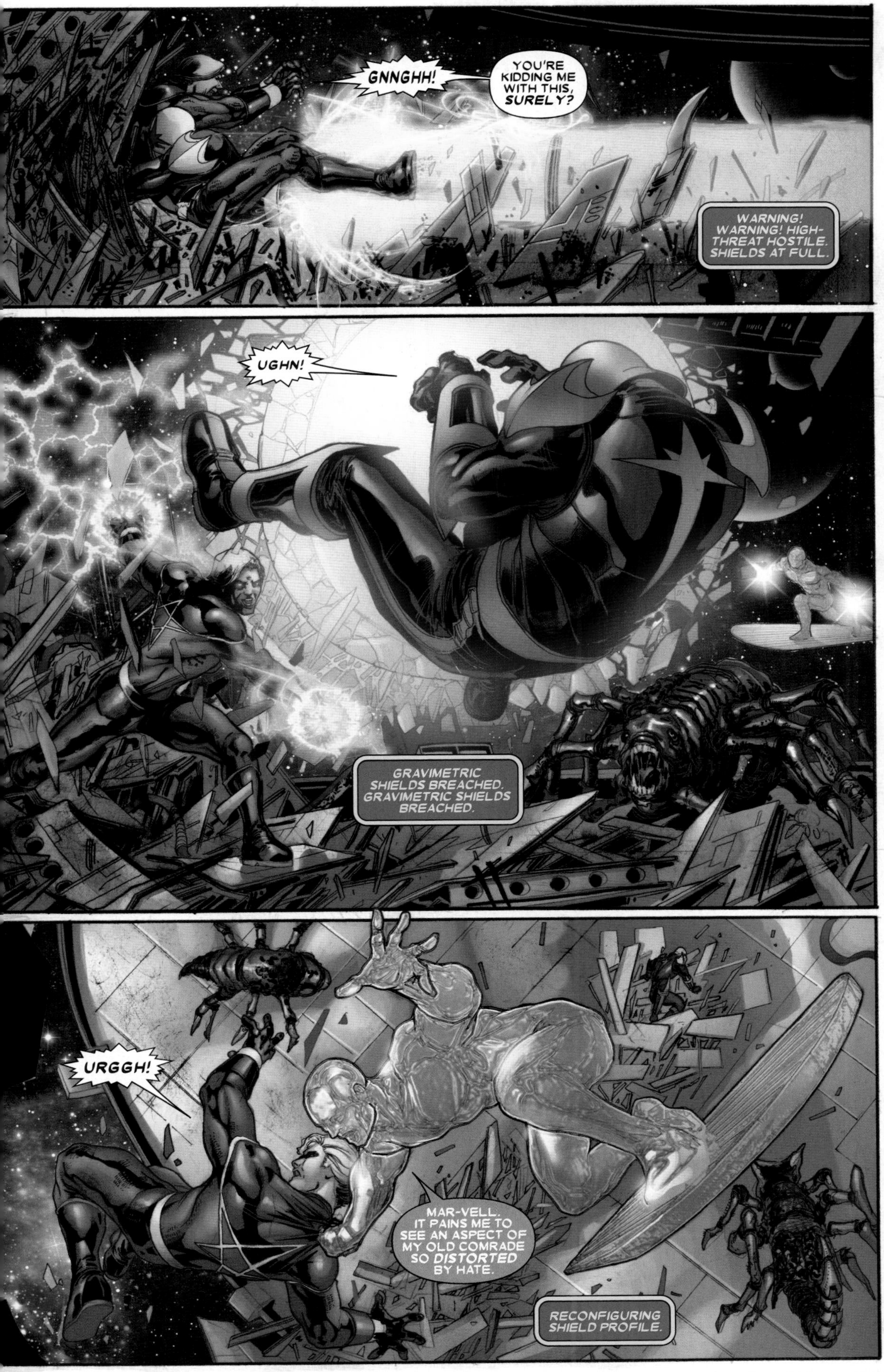
GNNGHH!
YOU'RE KIDDING ME WITH THIS, SURELY?
WARNING! WARNING! HIGH-THREAT HOSTILE. SHIELDS AT FULL.
UGHN!
GRAVIMETRIC SHIELDS BREACHED. GRAVIMETRIC SHIELDS BREACHED.
URGGH!
MAR-VELL. IT PAINS ME TO SEE AN ASPECT OF MY OLD COMRADE SO DISTORTED BY HATE.
RECONFIGURING SHIELD PROFILE.

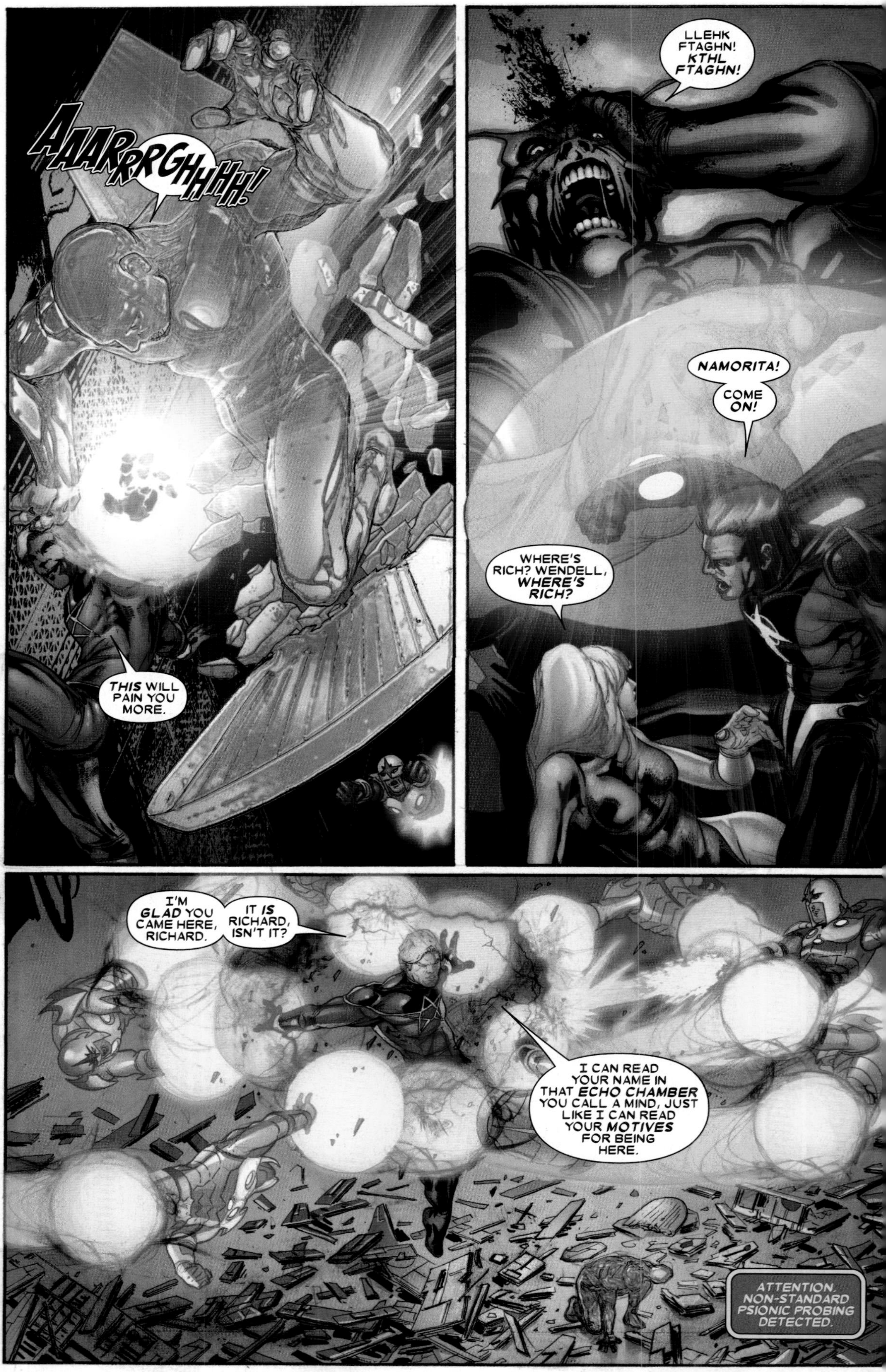
AAARRRGHHHH!
THIS WILL PAIN YOU MORE.
LLEHK FTAGHN! KTHL FTAGHN!
NAMORITA!
COME ON!
WHERE'S RICH? WENDELL, WHERE'S RICH?
I'M GLAD YOU CAME HERE, RICHARD.
IT IS RICHARD, ISN'T IT?
I CAN READ YOUR NAME IN THAT ECHO CHAMBER YOU CALL A MIND, JUST LIKE I CAN READ YOUR MOTIVES FOR BEING HERE.
ATTENTION. NON-STANDARD PSIONIC PROBING DETECTED.

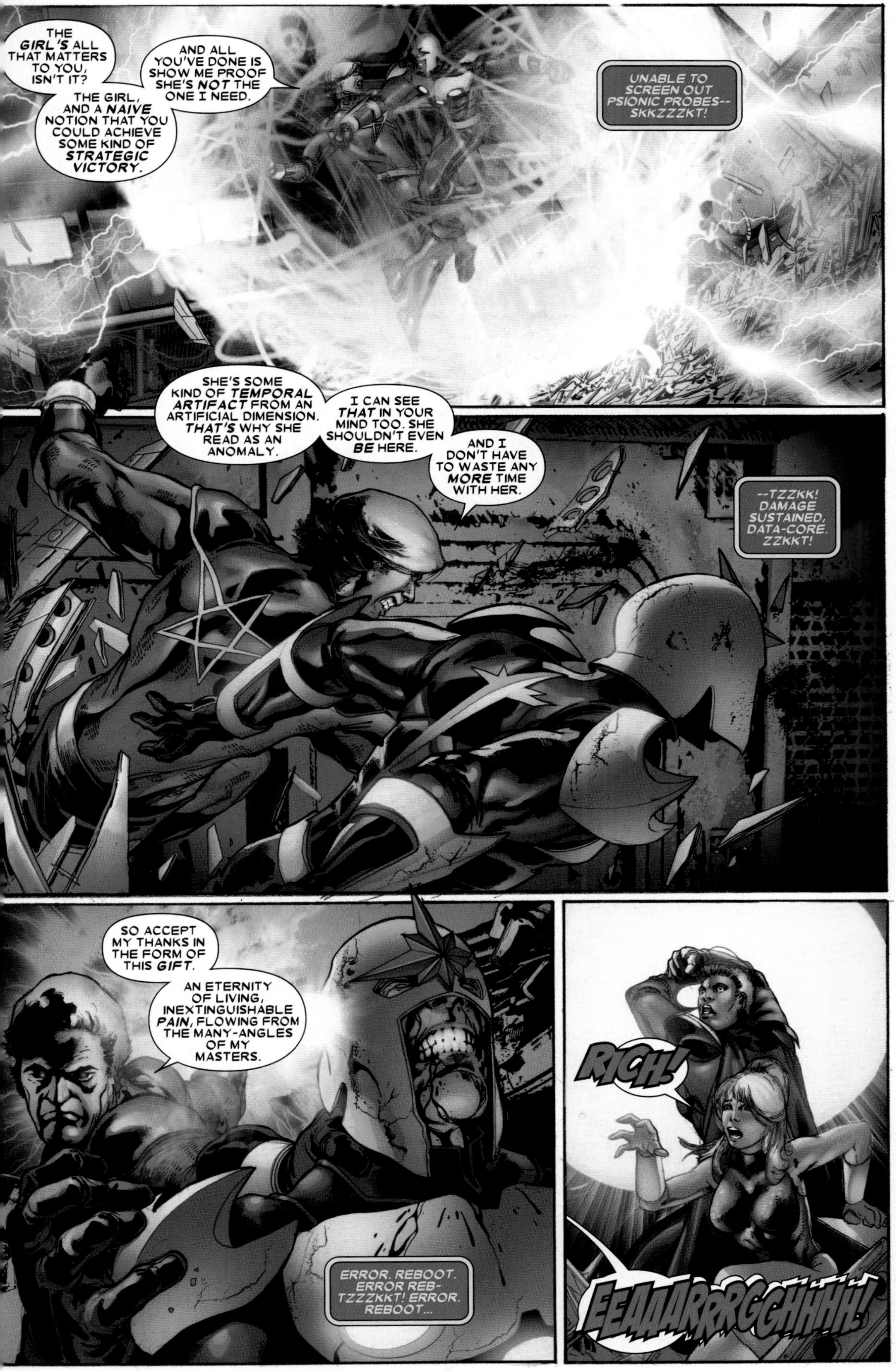
THE GIRL'S ALL THAT MATTERS TO YOU, ISN'T IT?
THE GIRL, AND A NAIVE NOTION THAT YOU COULD ACHIEVE SOME KIND OF STRATEGIC VICTORY.
AND ALL YOU'VE DONE IS SHOW ME PROOF SHE'S NOT THE ONE I NEED.
UNABLE TO SCREEN OUT PSIONIC PROBES-- SKKZZZKT!
SHE'S SOME KIND OF TEMPORAL ARTIFACT FROM AN ARTIFICIAL DIMENSION. THAT'S WHY SHE READ AS AN ANOMALY.
I CAN SEE THAT IN YOUR MIND TOO. SHE SHOULDN'T EVEN BE HERE.
AND I DON'T HAVE TO WASTE ANY MORE TIME WITH HER.
--TZZKK! DAMAGE SUSTAINED, DATA-CORE. ZZKKT!
SO ACCEPT MY THANKS IN THE FORM OF THIS GIFT.
AN ETERNITY OF LIVING, INEXTINGUISHABLE PAIN, FLOWING FROM THE MANY-ANGLES OF MY MASTERS.
ERROR. REBOOT. ERROR REB-TZZZKKT! ERROR. REBOOT...
RICH!
EEAAARRRGGHHHH!

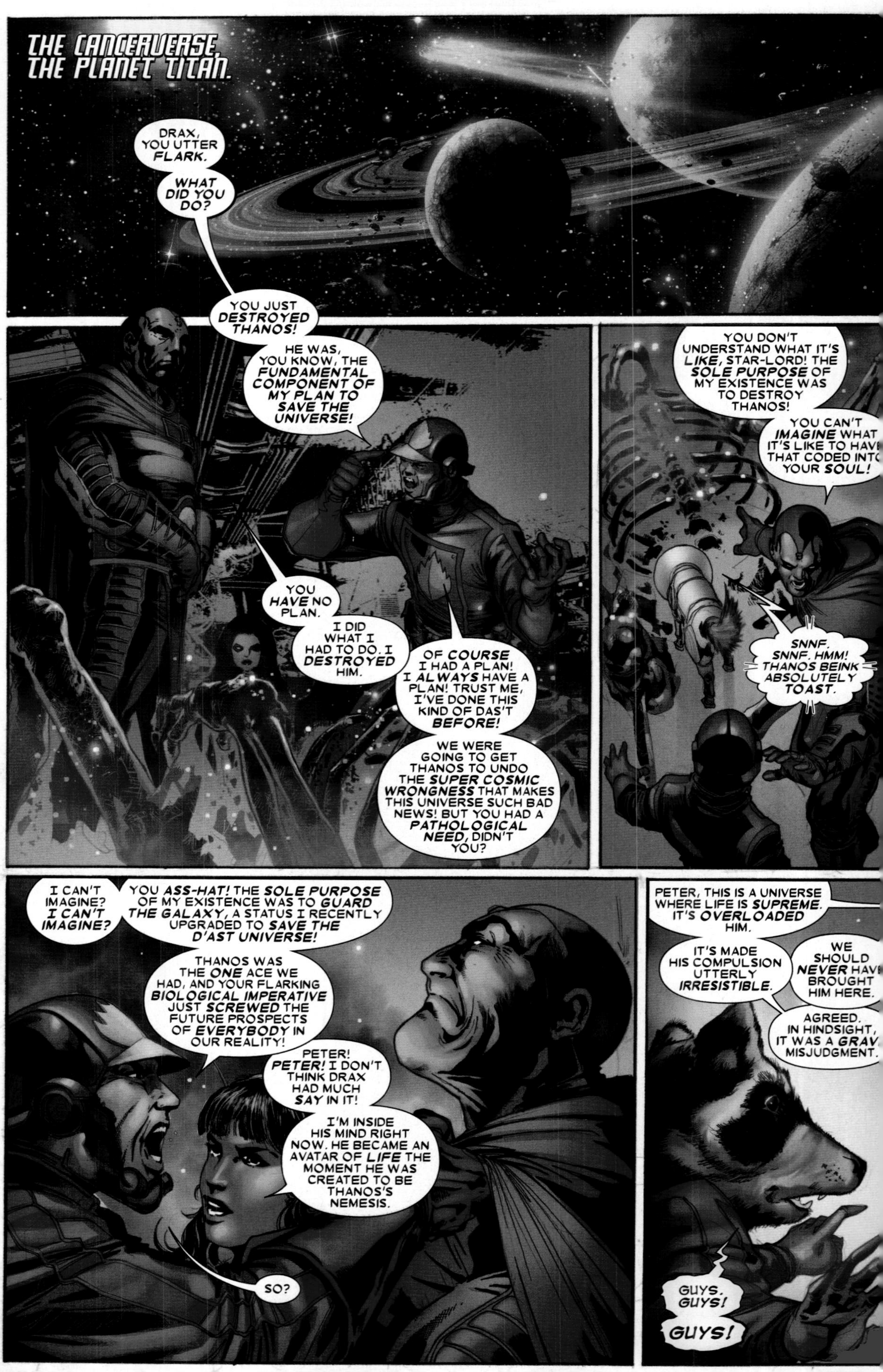
THE CANCERVERSE, THE PLANET TITAN.
DRAX, YOU UTTER FLARK.
WHAT DID YOU DO?
YOU JUST DESTROYED THANOS!
HE WAS, YOU KNOW, THE FUNDAMENTAL COMPONENT OF MY PLAN TO SAVE THE UNIVERSE!
YOU HAVE NO PLAN.
I DID WHAT I HAD TO DO. I DESTROYED HIM.
OF COURSE I HAD A PLAN! I ALWAYS HAVE A PLAN! TRUST ME, I'VE DONE THIS KIND OF DAS'T BEFORE!
WE WERE GOING TO GET THANOS TO UNDO THE SUPER COSMIC WRONGNESS THAT MAKES THIS UNIVERSE SUCH BAD NEWS! BUT YOU HAD A PATHOLOGICAL NEED, DIDN'T YOU?
YOU DON'T UNDERSTAND WHAT IT'S LIKE, STAR-LORD! THE SOLE PURPOSE OF MY EXISTENCE WAS TO DESTROY THANOS!
YOU CAN'T IMAGINE WHAT IT'S LIKE TO HAVE THAT CODED INTO YOUR SOUL!
SNNF. SNNF. HMM! THANOS BEINK ABSOLUTELY TOAST.
I CAN'T IMAGINE? I CAN'T IMAGINE?
YOU ASS-HAT! THE SOLE PURPOSE OF MY EXISTENCE WAS TO GUARD THE GALAXY, A STATUS I RECENTLY UPGRADED TO SAVE THE D'AST UNIVERSE!
THANOS WAS THE ONE ACE WE HAD, AND YOUR FLARKING BIOLOGICAL IMPERATIVE JUST SCREWED THE FUTURE PROSPECTS OF EVERYBODY IN OUR REALITY!
PETER! PETER! I DON'T THINK DRAX HAD MUCH SAY IN IT!
I'M INSIDE HIS MIND RIGHT NOW. HE BECAME AN AVATAR OF LIFE THE MOMENT HE WAS CREATED TO BE THANOS'S NEMESIS.
SO?
PETER, THIS IS A UNIVERSE WHERE LIFE IS SUPREME. IT'S OVERLOADED HIM.
IT'S MADE HIS COMPULSION UTTERLY IRRESISTIBLE.
WE SHOULD NEVER HAVE BROUGHT HIM HERE.
AGREED. IN HINDSIGHT, IT WAS A GRAVE MISJUDGMENT.
GUYS, GUYS!
GUYS!

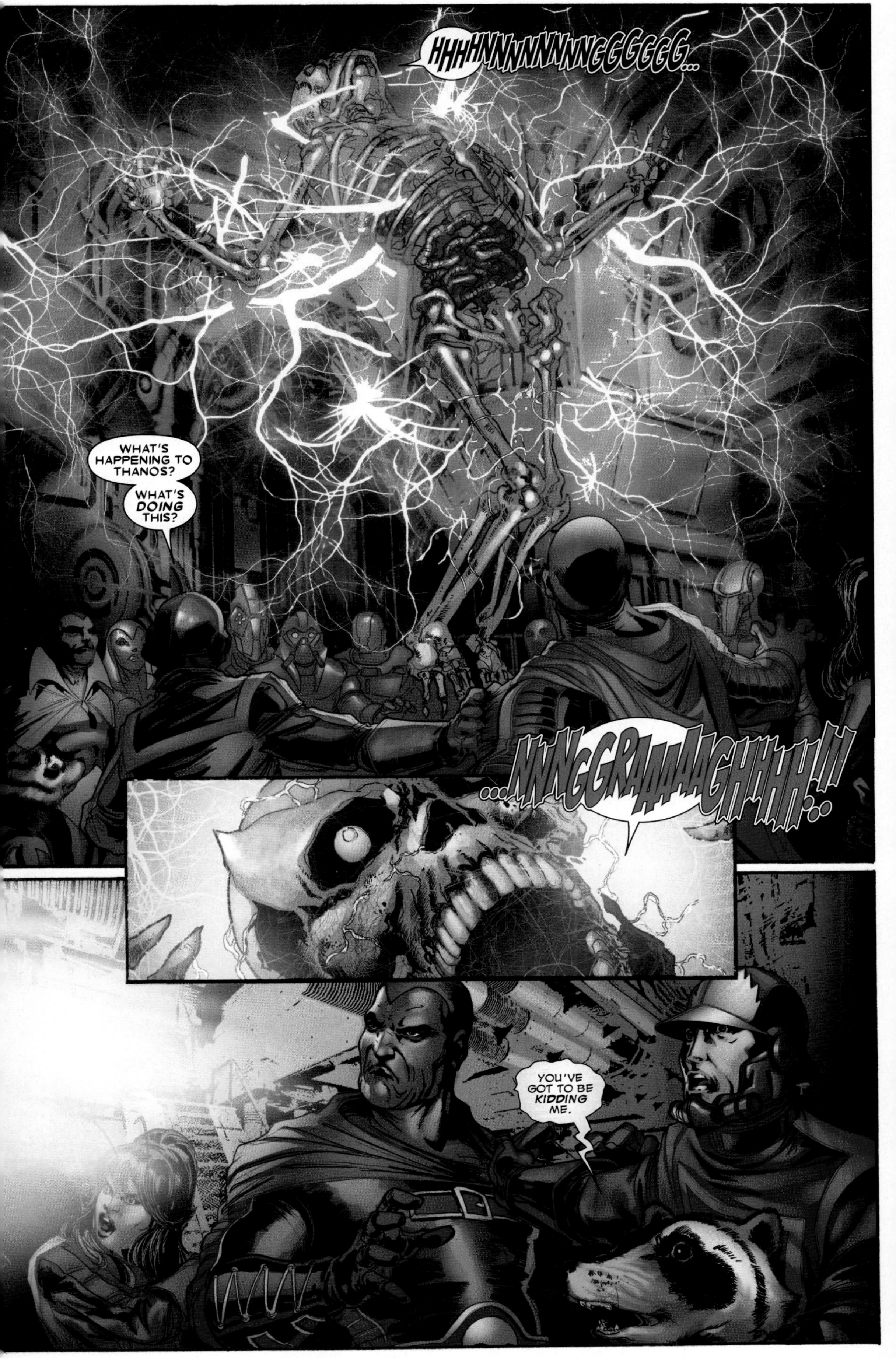
HHHHNNNNNNNNGGGGGG...
WHAT'S HAPPENING TO THANOS?
WHAT'S DOING THIS?
...NNNGGRAAAAAGHHHH!!!
YOU'VE GOT TO BE KIDDING ME.

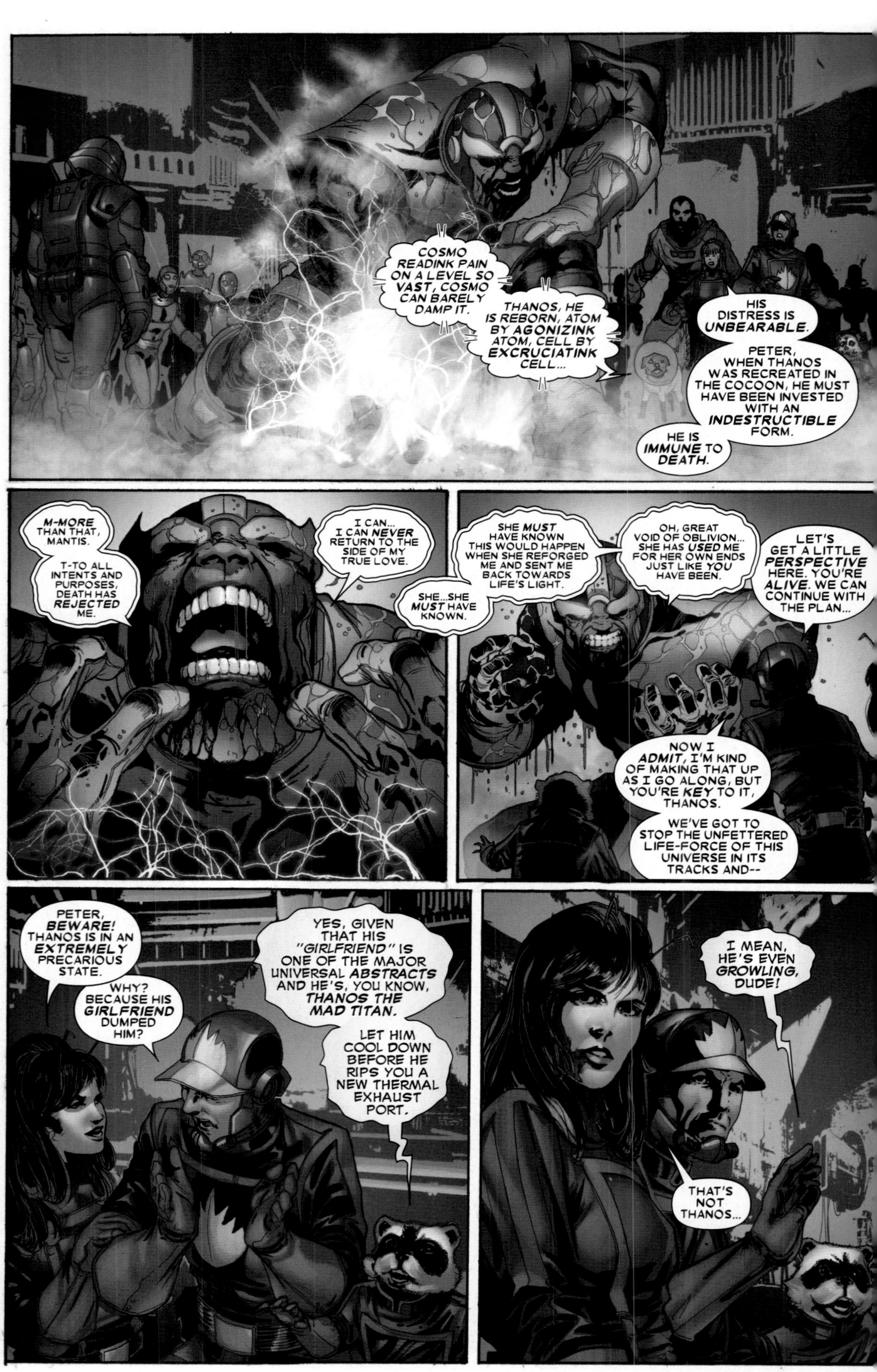
COSMO READINK PAIN ON A LEVEL SO VAST, COSMO CAN BARELY DAMP IT.
THANOS, HE IS REBORN, ATOM BY AGONIZINK ATOM, CELL BY EXCRUCIATINK CELL...
HIS DISTRESS IS UNBEARABLE.
PETER, WHEN THANOS WAS RECREATED IN THE COCOON, HE MUST HAVE BEEN INVESTED WITH AN INDESTRUCTIBLE FORM.
HE IS IMMUNE TO DEATH.
M-MORE THAN THAT, MANTIS.
T-TO ALL INTENTS AND PURPOSES, DEATH HAS REJECTED ME.
I CAN... I CAN NEVER RETURN TO THE SIDE OF MY TRUE LOVE.
SHE MUST HAVE KNOWN THIS WOULD HAPPEN WHEN SHE REFORGED ME AND SENT ME BACK TOWARDS LIFE'S LIGHT.
SHE...SHE MUST HAVE KNOWN.
OH, GREAT VOID OF OBLIVION... SHE HAS USED ME FOR HER OWN ENDS JUST LIKE YOU HAVE BEEN.
LET'S GET A LITTLE PERSPECTIVE HERE. YOU'RE ALIVE. WE CAN CONTINUE WITH THE PLAN...
NOW I ADMIT, I'M KIND OF MAKING THAT UP AS I GO ALONG, BUT YOU'RE KEY TO IT, THANOS.
WE'VE GOT TO STOP THE UNFETTERED LIFE-FORCE OF THIS UNIVERSE IN ITS TRACKS AND--
PETER, BEWARE! THANOS IS IN AN EXTREMELY PRECARIOUS STATE.
WHY? BECAUSE HIS GIRLFRIEND DUMPED HIM?
YES, GIVEN THAT HIS "GIRLFRIEND" IS ONE OF THE MAJOR UNIVERSAL ABSTRACTS AND HE'S, YOU KNOW, THANOS THE MAD TITAN.
LET HIM COOL DOWN BEFORE HE RIPS YOU A NEW THERMAL EXHAUST PORT.
I MEAN, HE'S EVEN GROWLING, DUDE!
THAT'S NOT THANOS...

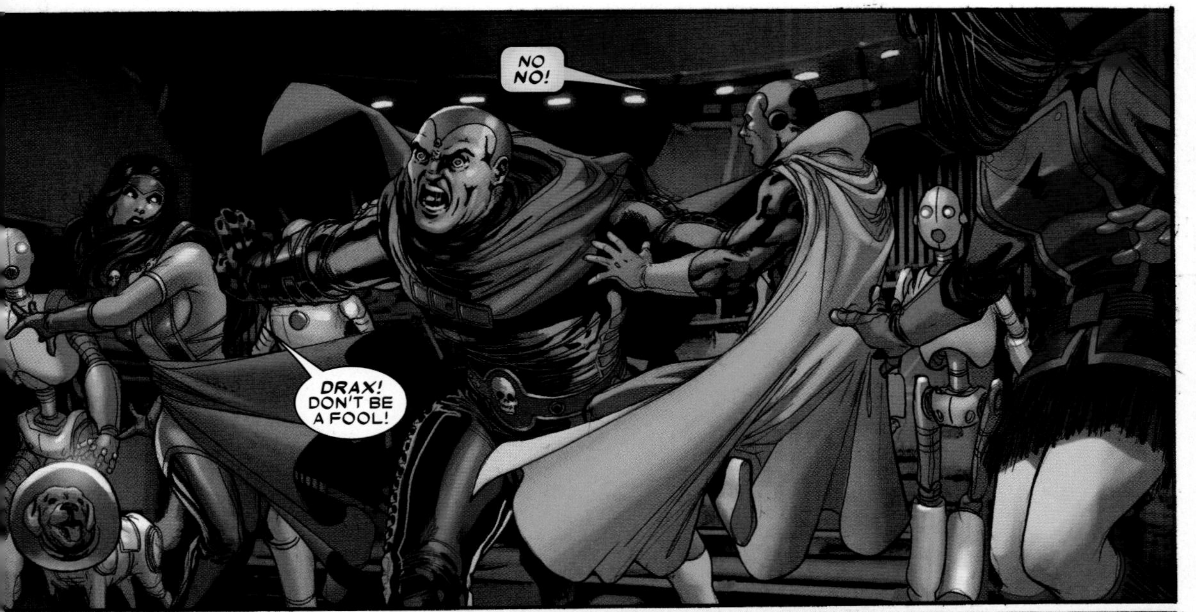
NO NO!
DRAX! DON'T BE A FOOL!
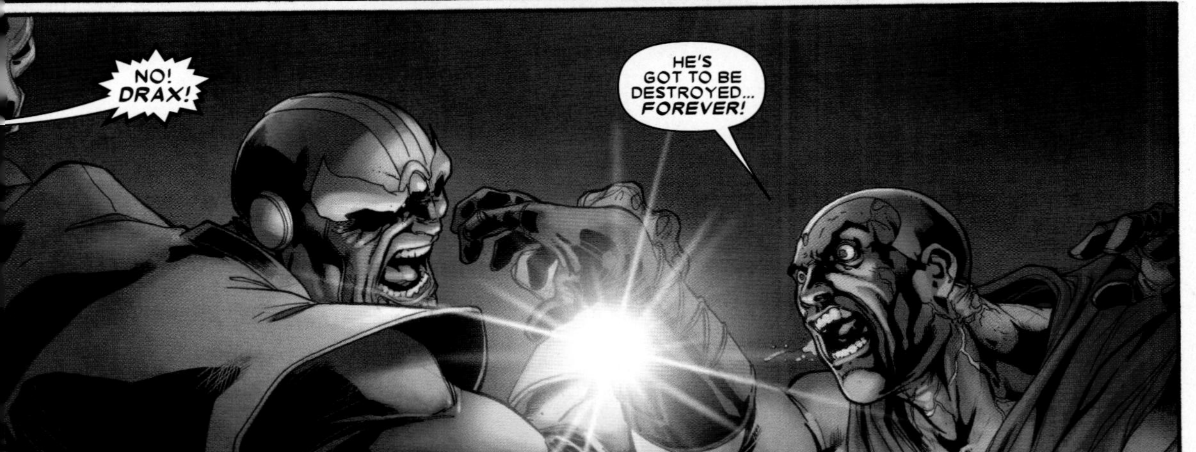
NO! DRAX!
HE'S GOT TO BE DESTROYED... FOREVER!
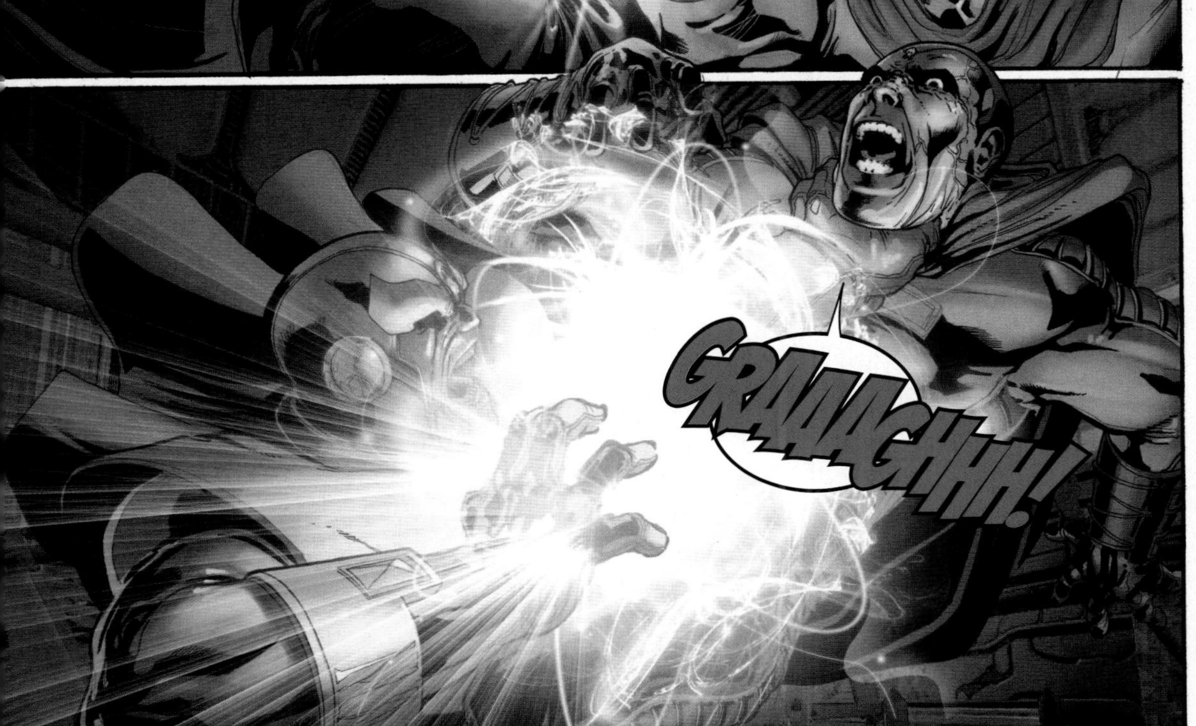
GRAAAAGHHH!

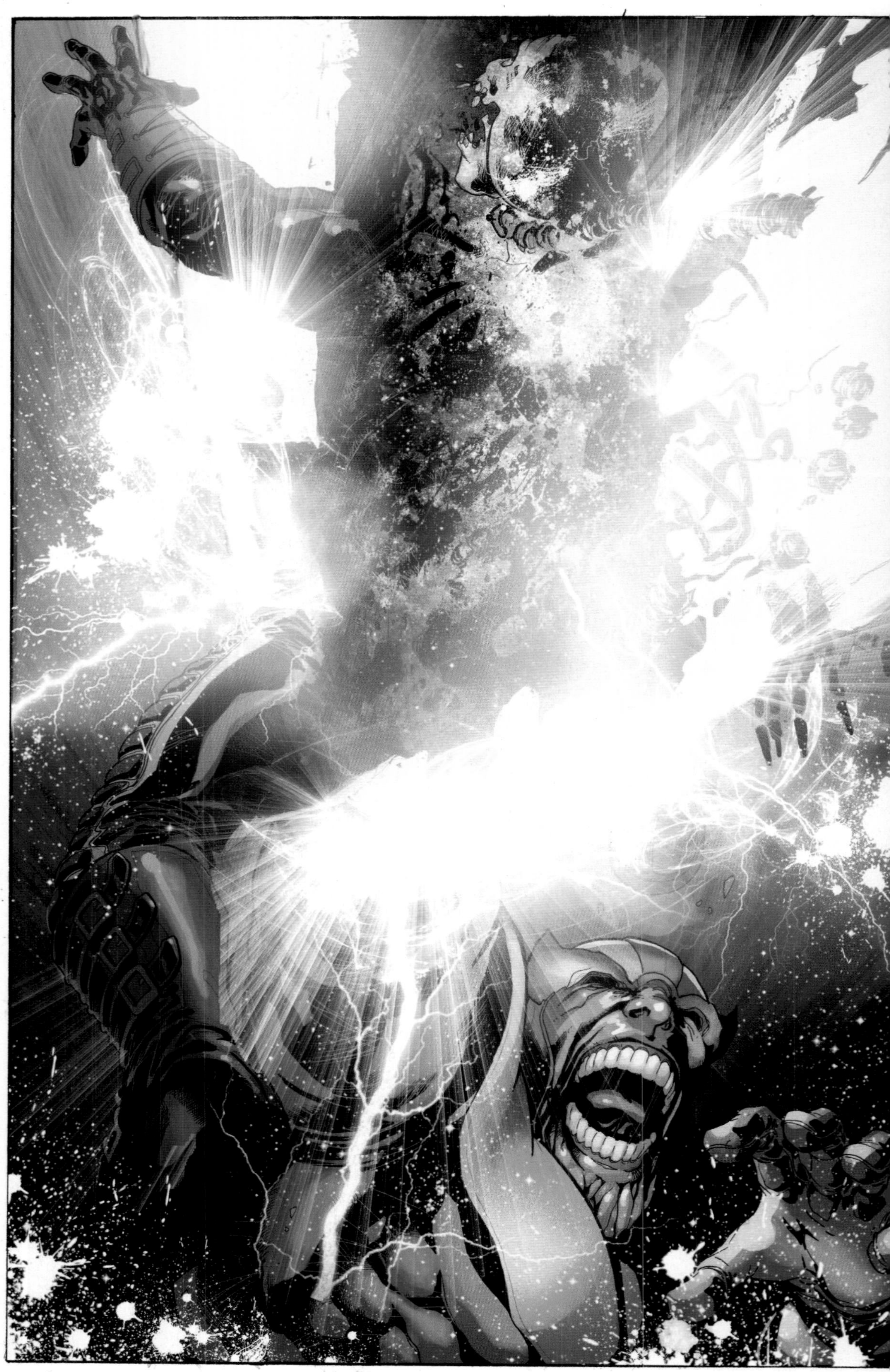

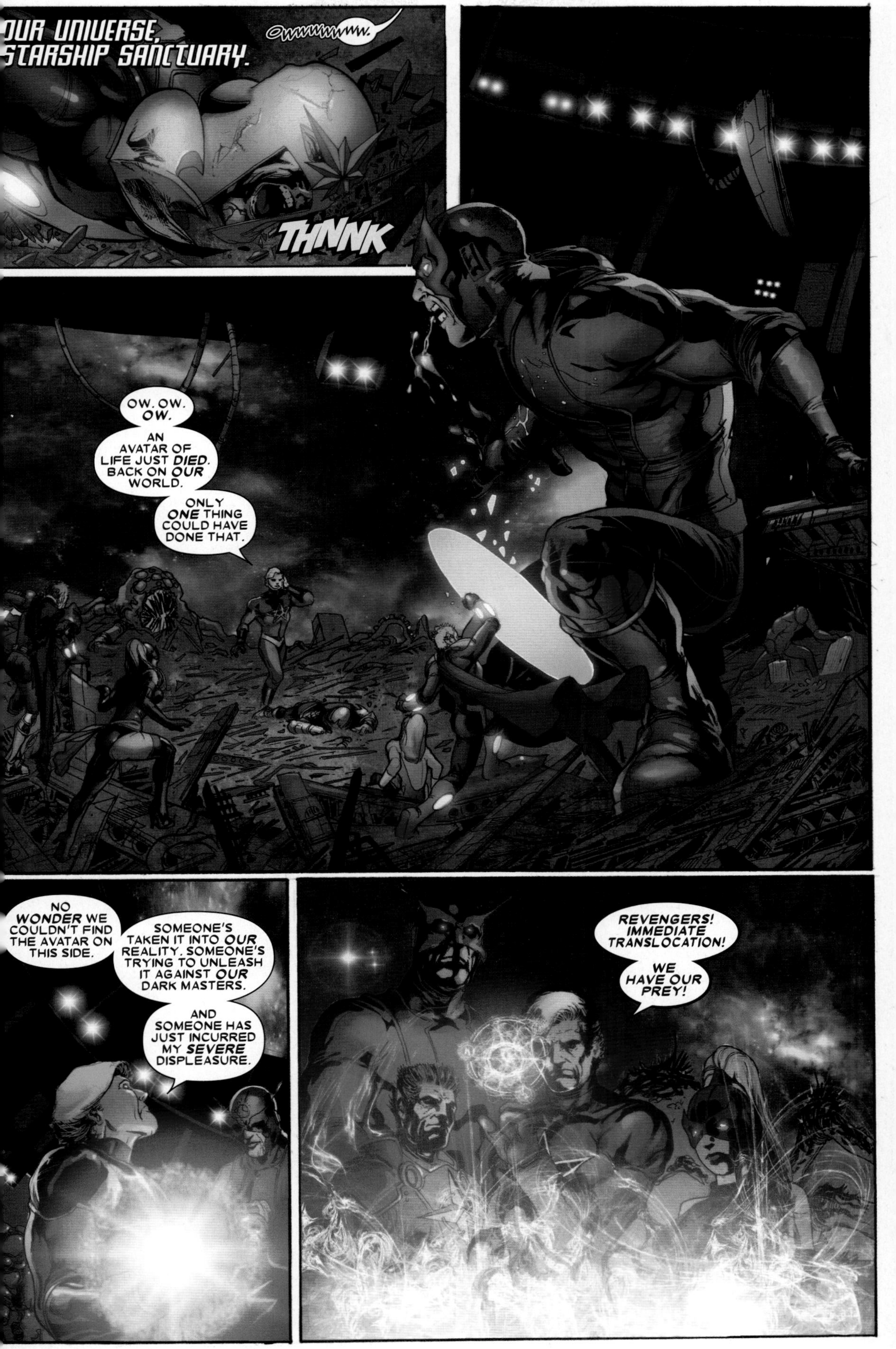
OUR UNIVERSE, STARSHIP SANCTUARY.
OWWWWWWW.
THNNK
OW. OW. OW.
AN AVATAR OF LIFE JUST DIED. BACK ON OUR WORLD.
ONLY ONE THING COULD HAVE DONE THAT.
NO WONDER WE COULDN'T FIND THE AVATAR ON THIS SIDE.
SOMEONE'S TAKEN IT INTO OUR REALITY. SOMEONE'S TRYING TO UNLEASH IT AGAINST OUR DARK MASTERS.
AND SOMEONE HAS JUST INCURRED MY SEVERE DISPLEASURE.
REVENGERS! IMMEDIATE TRANSLOCATION!
WE HAVE OUR PREY!

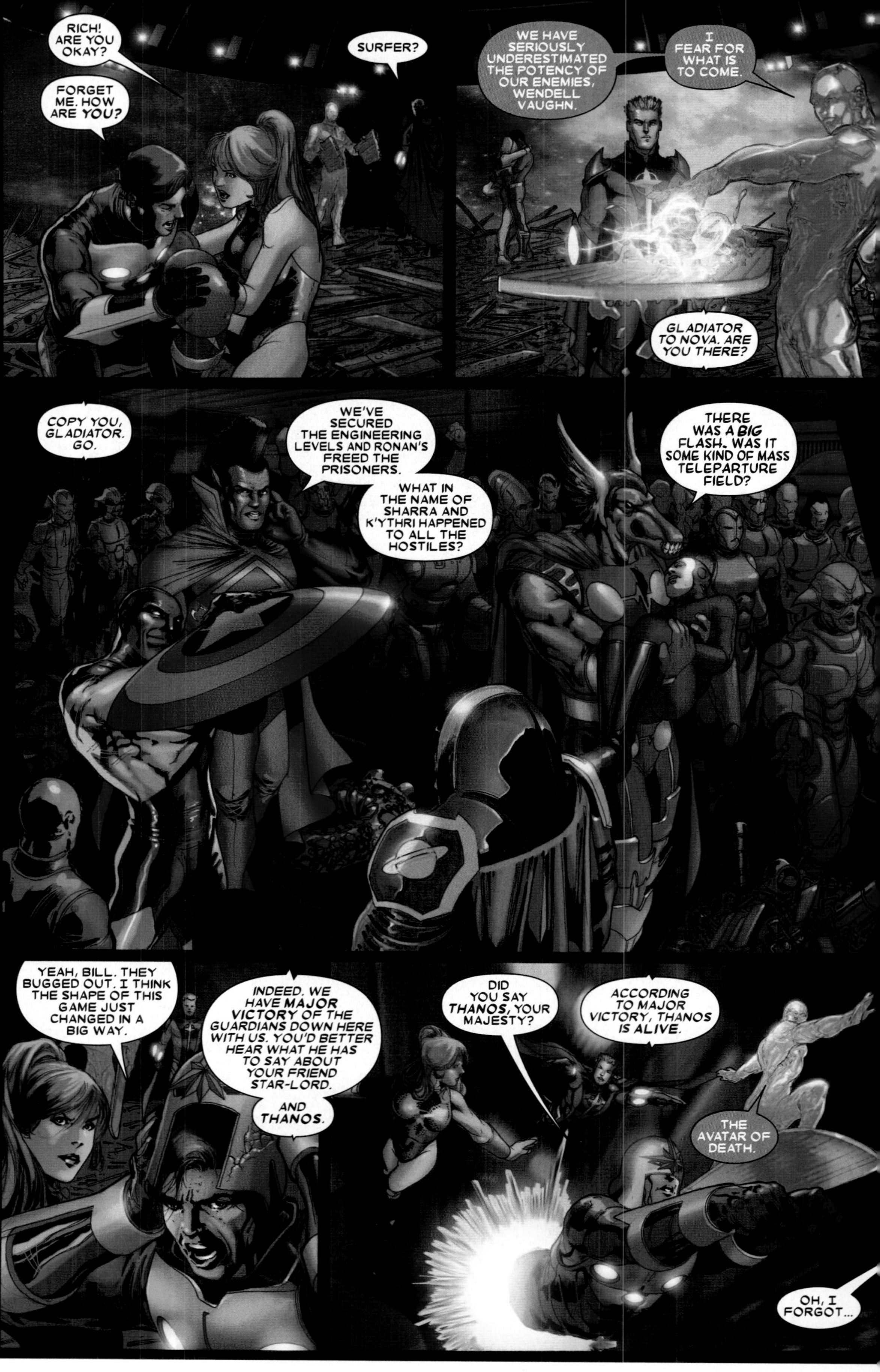
RICH! ARE YOU OKAY?
FORGET ME. HOW ARE YOU?
SURFER?
WE HAVE SERIOUSLY UNDERESTIMATED THE POTENCY OF OUR ENEMIES, WENDELL VAUGHN.
I FEAR FOR WHAT IS TO COME.
GLADIATOR TO NOVA. ARE YOU THERE?
COPY YOU, GLADIATOR. GO.
WE'VE SECURED THE ENGINEERING LEVELS AND RONAN'S FREED THE PRISONERS.
WHAT IN THE NAME OF SHARRA AND K'YTHRI HAPPENED TO ALL THE HOSTILES?
THERE WAS A BIG FLASH. WAS IT SOME KIND OF MASS TELEPARTURE FIELD?
YEAH, BILL. THEY BUGGED OUT. I THINK THE SHAPE OF THIS GAME JUST CHANGED IN A BIG WAY.
INDEED. WE HAVE MAJOR VICTORY OF THE GUARDIANS DOWN HERE WITH US. YOU'D BETTER HEAR WHAT HE HAS TO SAY ABOUT YOUR FRIEND STAR-LORD.
AND THANOS.
DID YOU SAY THANOS, YOUR MAJESTY?
ACCORDING TO MAJOR VICTORY, THANOS IS ALIVE.
THE AVATAR OF DEATH.
OH, I FORGOT...

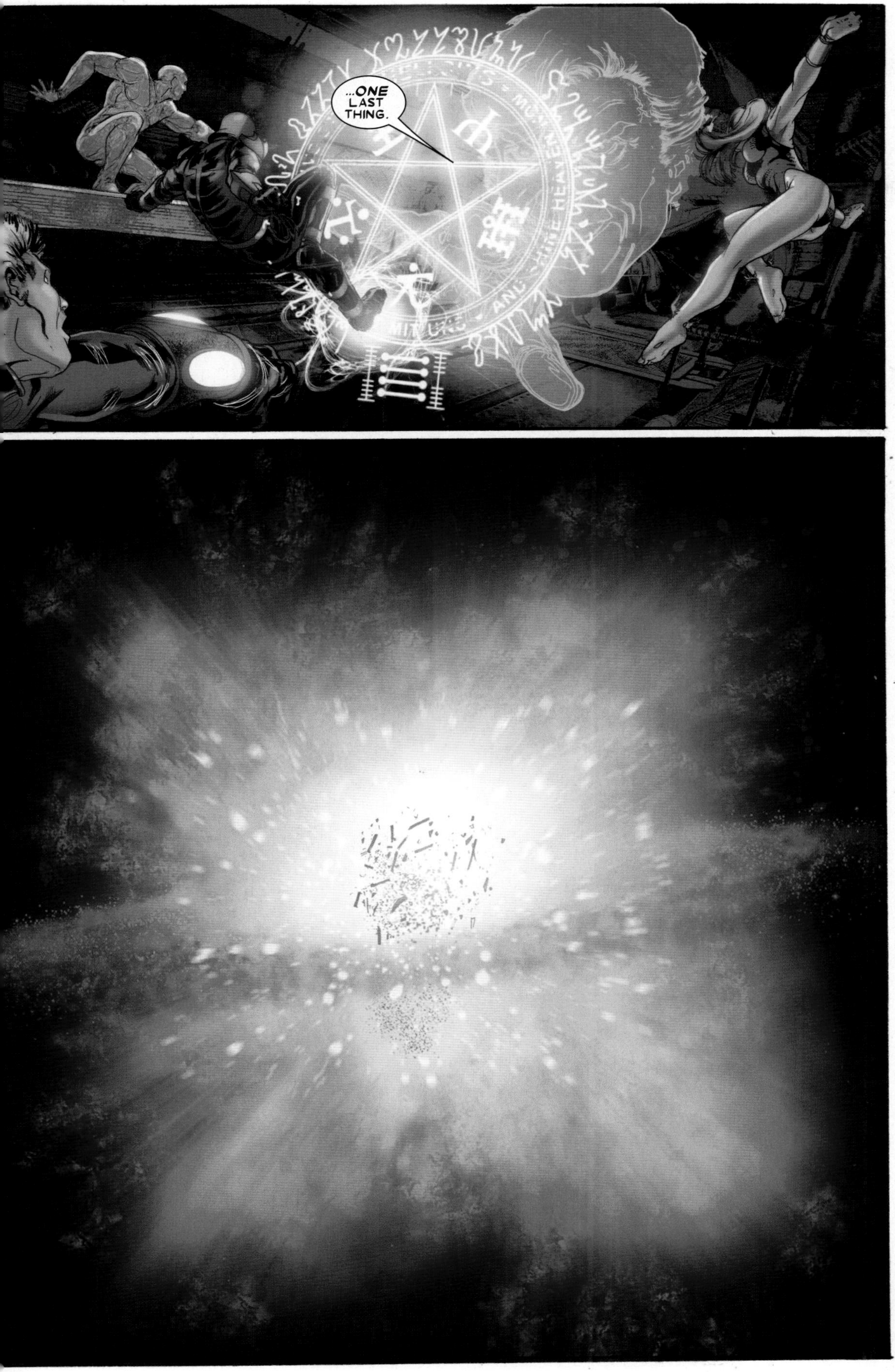
...ONE LAST THING.

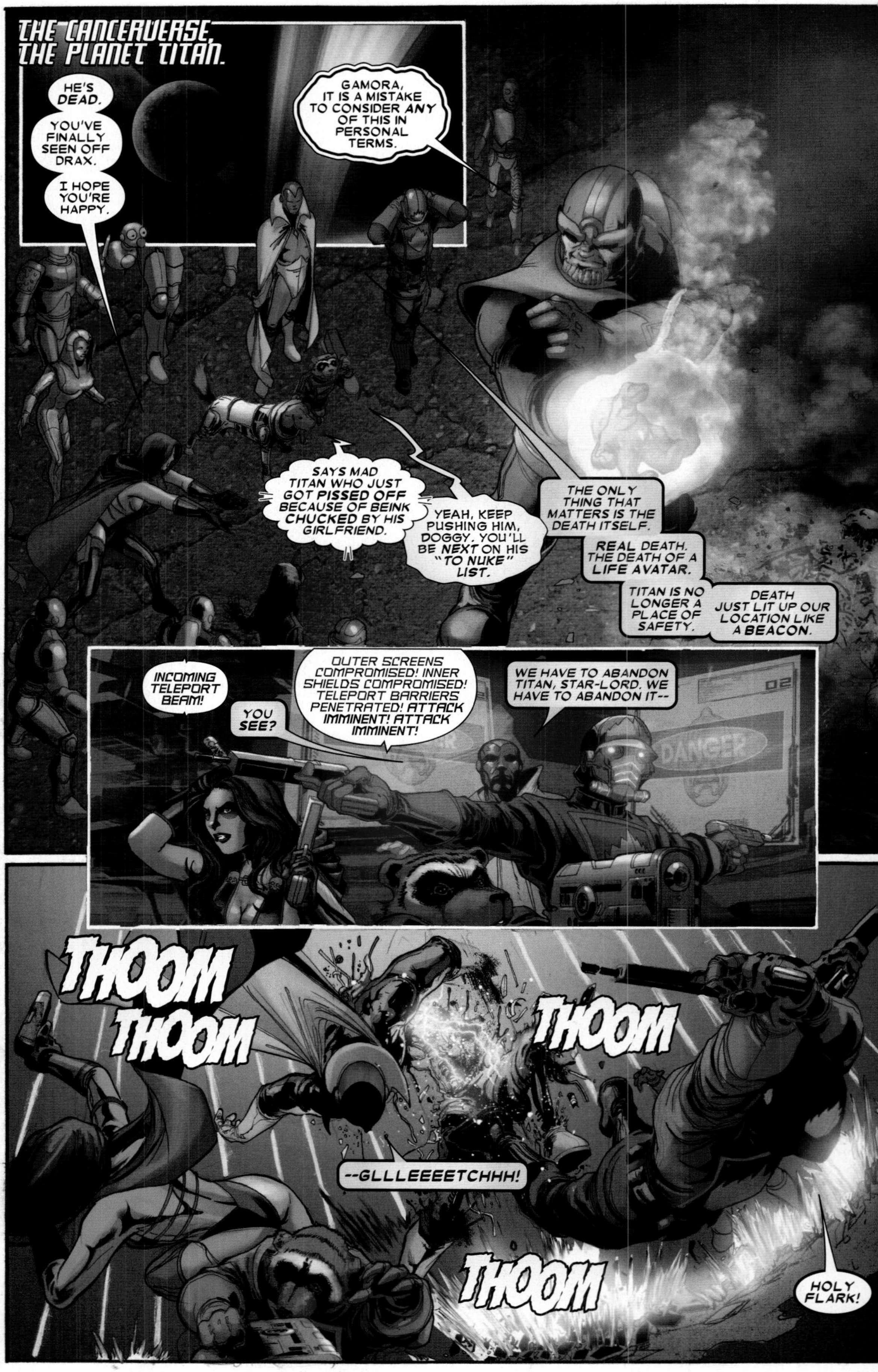
THE CANCERVERSE, THE PLANET TITAN.
HE'S DEAD.
YOU'VE FINALLY SEEN OFF DRAX.
I HOPE YOU'RE HAPPY.
GAMORA, IT IS A MISTAKE TO CONSIDER ANY OF THIS IN PERSONAL TERMS.
SAYS MAD TITAN WHO JUST GOT PISSED OFF BECAUSE OF BEINK CHUCKED BY HIS GIRLFRIEND.
YEAH, KEEP PUSHING HIM, DOGGY. YOU'LL BE NEXT ON HIS "TO NUKE" LIST.
THE ONLY THING THAT MATTERS IS THE DEATH ITSELF.
REAL DEATH. THE DEATH OF A LIFE AVATAR.
TITAN IS NO LONGER A PLACE OF SAFETY.
DEATH JUST LIT UP OUR LOCATION LIKE A BEACON.
INCOMING TELEPORT BEAM!
OUTER SCREENS COMPROMISED! INNER SHIELDS COMPROMISED! TELEPORT BARRIERS PENETRATED! ATTACK IMMINENT! ATTACK IMMINENT!
YOU SEE?
WE HAVE TO ABANDON TITAN, STAR-LORD. WE HAVE TO ABANDON IT--
DANGER
THOOM
THOOM
THOOM
--GLLLEEEETCHHH!
THOOM
HOLY FLARK!

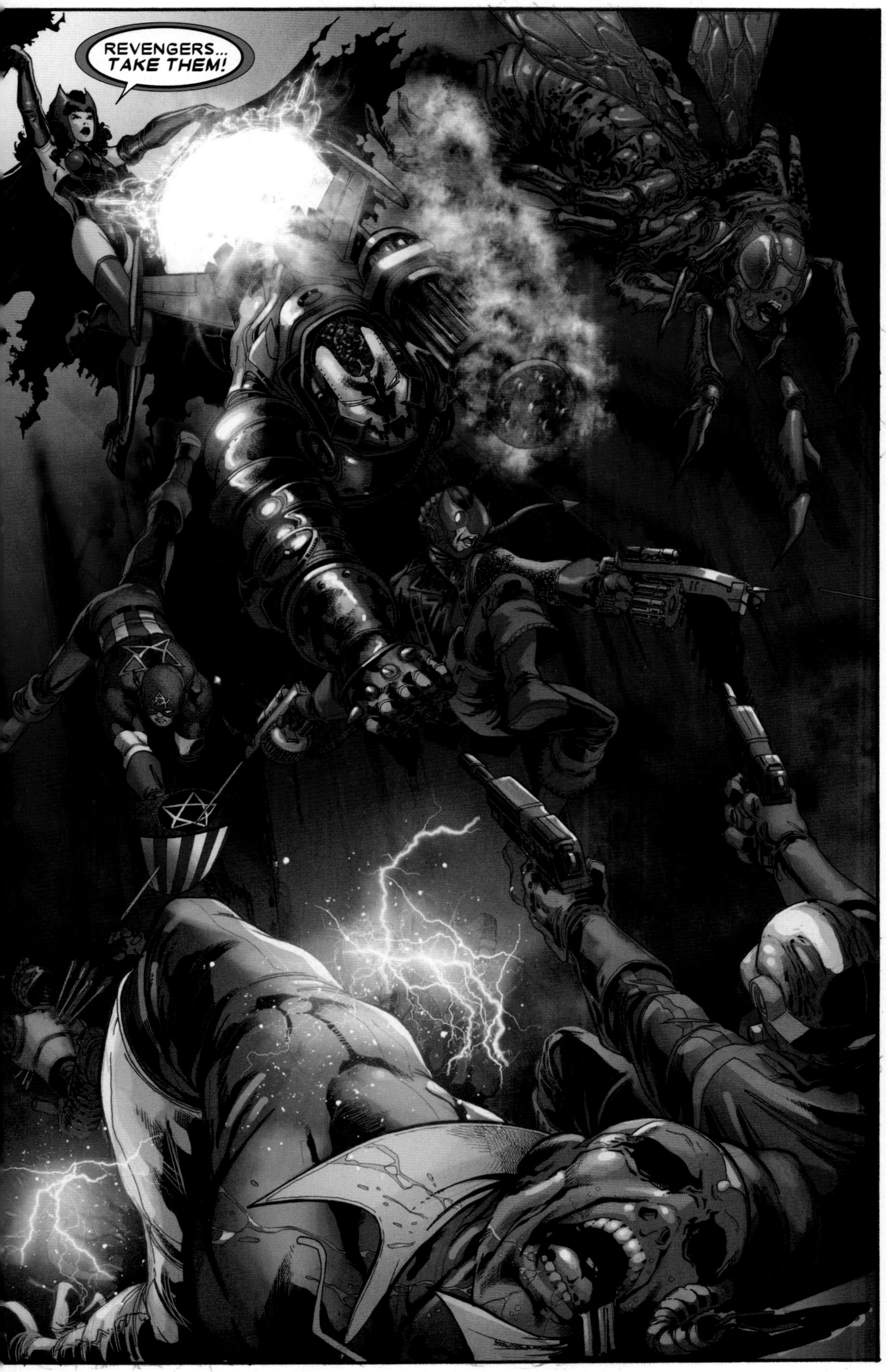
REVENGERS... TAKE THEM!

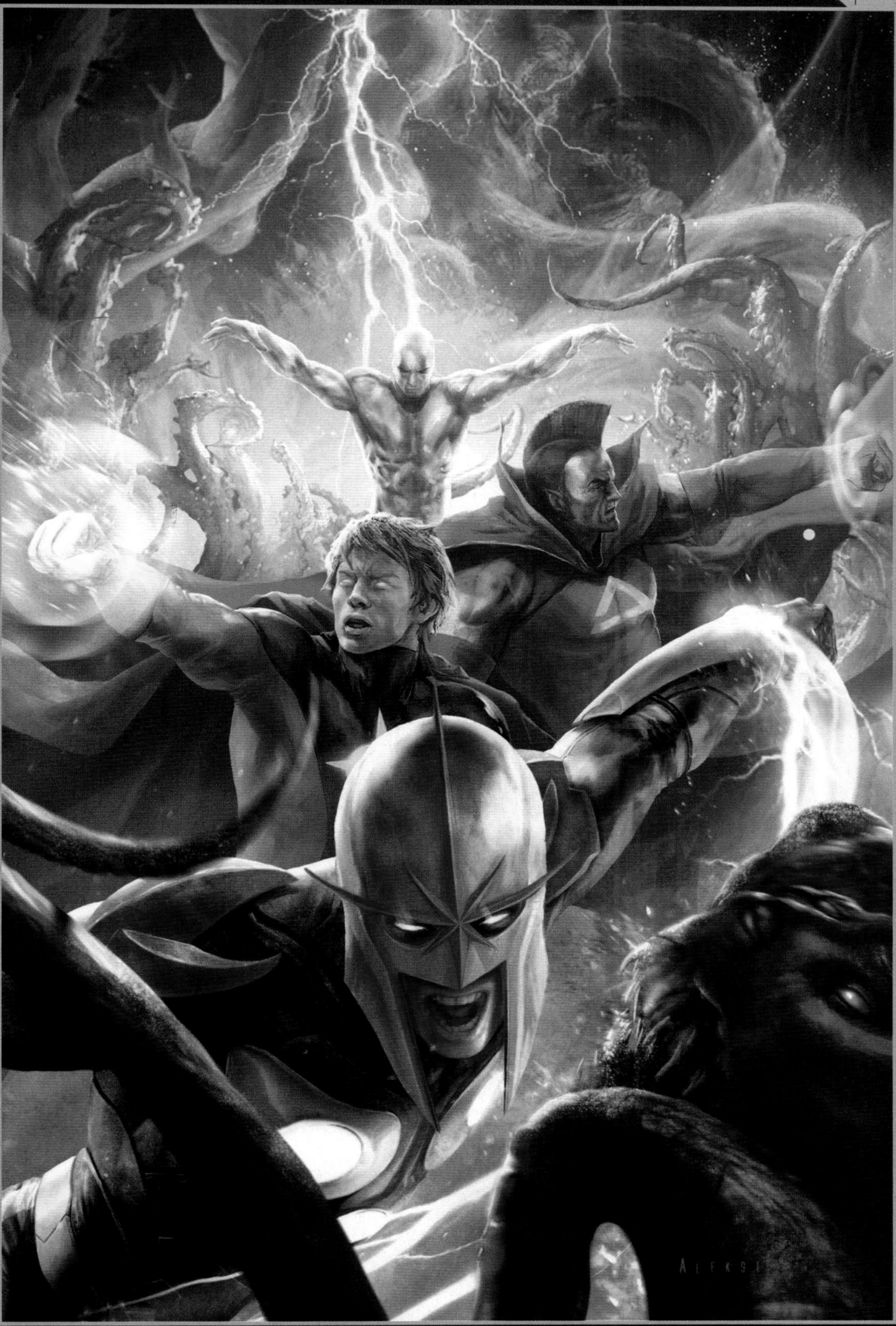
ALEKSI

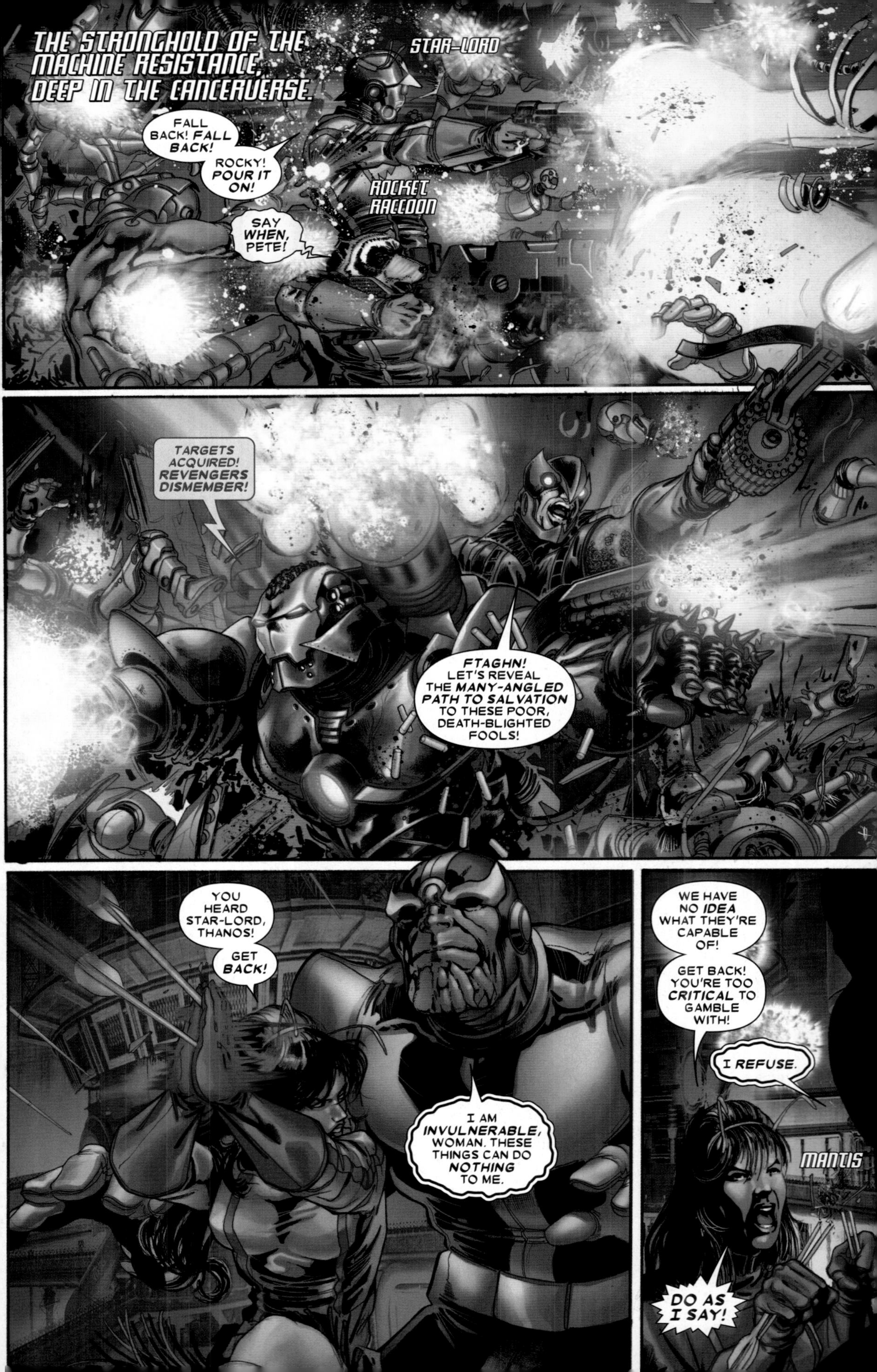
THE STRONGHOLD OF THE MACHINE RESISTANCE, DEEP IN THE CANCERVERSE.
STAR-LORD
FALL BACK! FALL BACK!
ROCKY! POUR IT ON!
ROCKET RACCOON
SAY WHEN, PETE!
TARGETS ACQUIRED! REVENGERS DISMEMBER!
FTAGHN! LET'S REVEAL THE MANY-ANGLED PATH TO SALVATION TO THESE POOR, DEATH-BLIGHTED FOOLS!
YOU HEARD STAR-LORD, THANOS!
GET BACK!
I AM INVULNERABLE, WOMAN. THESE THINGS CAN DO NOTHING TO ME.
WE HAVE NO IDEA WHAT THEY'RE CAPABLE OF!
GET BACK! YOU'RE TOO CRITICAL TO GAMBLE WITH!
I REFUSE.
MANTIS
DO AS I SAY!

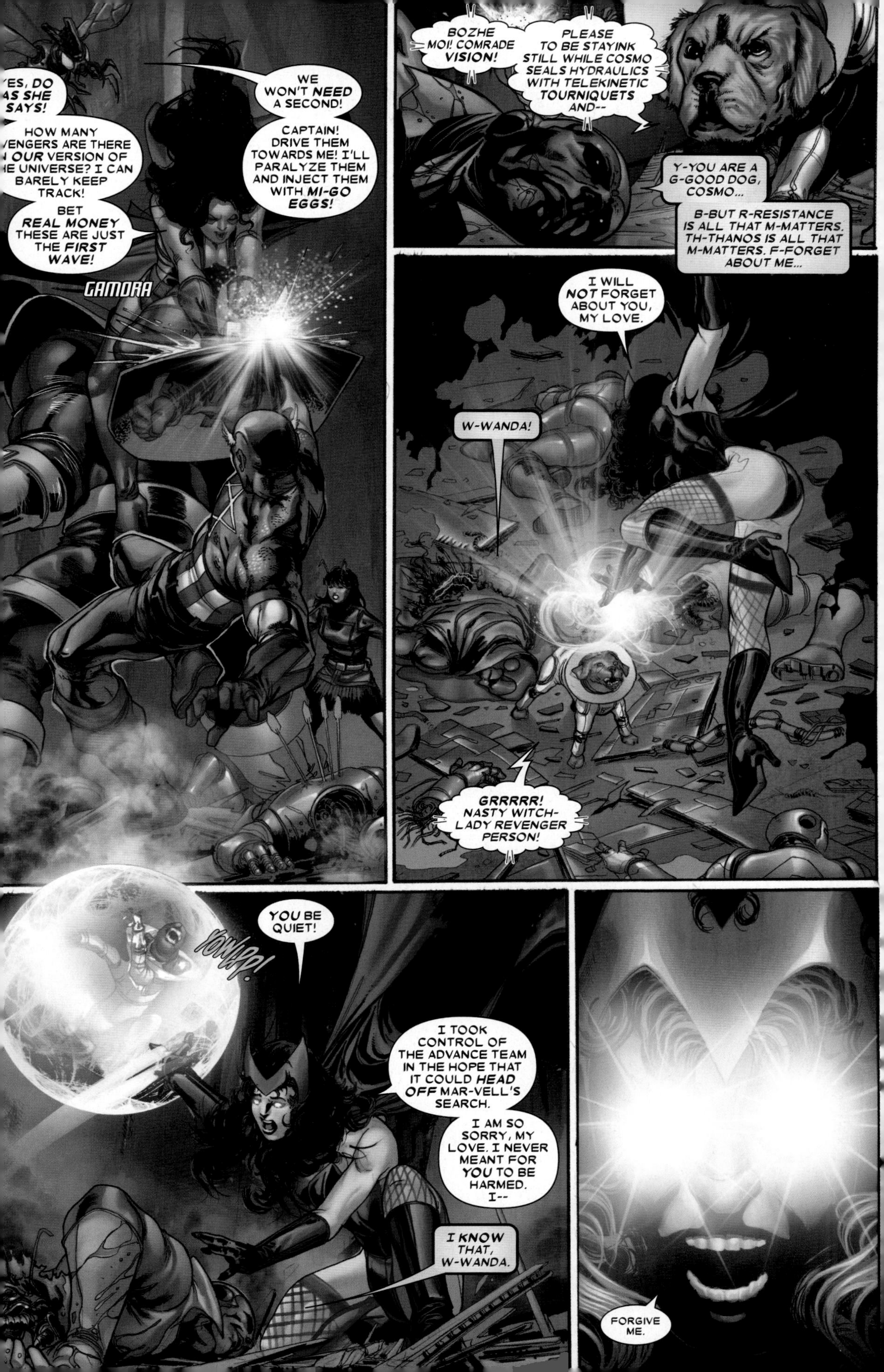

YES, DO AS SHE SAYS!
HOW MANY AVENGERS ARE THERE IN OUR VERSION OF THE UNIVERSE? I CAN BARELY KEEP TRACK!
BET REAL MONEY THESE ARE JUST THE FIRST WAVE!
WE WON'T NEED A SECOND!
CAPTAIN! DRIVE THEM TOWARDS ME! I'LL PARALYZE THEM AND INJECT THEM WITH MI-GO EGGS!
GAMORA
BOZHE MOI! COMRADE VISION!
PLEASE TO BE STAYINK STILL WHILE COSMO SEALS HYDRAULICS WITH TELEKINETIC TOURNIQUETS AND--
Y-YOU ARE A G-GOOD DOG, COSMO...
B-BUT R-RESISTANCE IS ALL THAT M-MATTERS. TH-THANOS IS ALL THAT M-MATTERS. F-FORGET ABOUT ME...
I WILL NOT FORGET ABOUT YOU, MY LOVE.
W-WANDA!
GRRRRR! NASTY WITCH-LADY REVENGER PERSON!
YOU BE QUIET!
YOWLP!
I TOOK CONTROL OF THE ADVANCE TEAM IN THE HOPE THAT IT COULD HEAD OFF MAR-VELL'S SEARCH.
I AM SO SORRY, MY LOVE. I NEVER MEANT FOR YOU TO BE HARMED. I--
I KNOW THAT, W-WANDA.
FORGIVE ME.

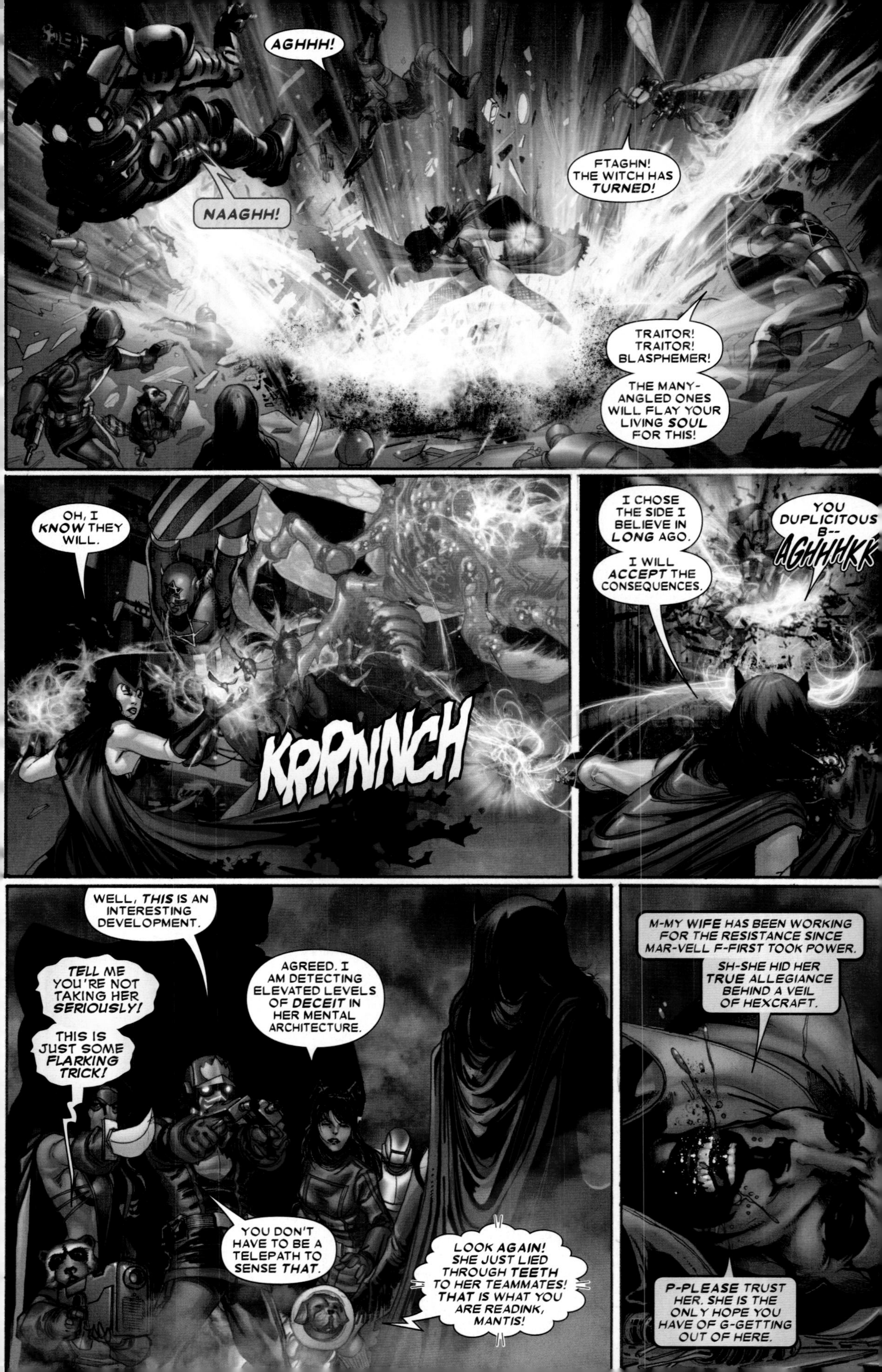
AGHHH!
NAAGHH!
FTAGHN! THE WITCH HAS TURNED!
TRAITOR! TRAITOR! BLASPHEMER!
THE MANY-ANGLED ONES WILL FLAY YOUR LIVING SOUL FOR THIS!
OH, I KNOW THEY WILL.
KRRNNCH
I CHOSE THE SIDE I BELIEVE IN LONG AGO.
I WILL ACCEPT THE CONSEQUENCES.
YOU DUPLICITOUS B--
AGHHHKK
WELL, THIS IS AN INTERESTING DEVELOPMENT.
TELL ME YOU'RE NOT TAKING HER SERIOUSLY!
THIS IS JUST SOME FLARKING TRICK!
AGREED. I AM DETECTING ELEVATED LEVELS OF DECEIT IN HER MENTAL ARCHITECTURE.
YOU DON'T HAVE TO BE A TELEPATH TO SENSE THAT.
LOOK AGAIN! SHE JUST LIED THROUGH TEETH TO HER TEAMMATES! THAT IS WHAT YOU ARE READINK, MANTIS!
M-MY WIFE HAS BEEN WORKING FOR THE RESISTANCE SINCE MAR-VELL F-FIRST TOOK POWER.
SH-SHE HID HER TRUE ALLEGIANCE BEHIND A VEIL OF HEXCRAFT.
P-PLEASE TRUST HER. SHE IS THE ONLY HOPE YOU HAVE OF G-GETTING OUT OF HERE.

WE HAVE WAITED A *LONG* TIME FOR A CHANCE LIKE THIS. YOU GUARDIANS HAVE BROUGHT US AN OPPORTUNITY WE CANNOT *AFFORD* TO MISS.

THIS IS WHY WE HAVE SHOWN OUR HAND TODAY. YOU ARE THE *AVATAR OF DEATH* LORD MAR-VELL SEEKS.

I NEED TO REACH THE SITE WHERE THE *NECROPSY RITUAL* WAS PERFORMED.

CAN YOU TRANSPORT ME THERE?

YES, IF I EXHAUST MY POWERS.

THESE REVENGERS WILL RECOVER WITHIN MINUTES, AND MORE ARE ON THEIR WAY.

I THOUGHT YOU WERE *RESIGNED* TO THE CONSEQUENCES?

F COURSE. WAS JUST A TEMENT OF CT, NOT A MPLAINT.

I WILL UFFER AT MY SBAND'S SIDE, NSUMED BY THE INITE HORROR F THE ELDER GODS.

IF I AM SUCCESSFUL, THAT SUFFERING WILL BE *FINITE.*

HEY! *HELLO?* PERSON IN *ACTUAL CHARGE* HERE? I CALL THE SHOTS!

YOU HAVEN'T BEEN IN CHARGE OF ANYTHING SINCE WE *STARTED* DOWN THIS ROAD, QUILL.

YOU ARE OF *NO CONSEQUENCE.* NONE OF YOU ARE.

SHEESH! STOP IT WITH THE *COMPLIMENTS!* YOU'LL SWELL MY HEAD!

SEND US TO THE SITE OF THE NECROPSY, LIKE HE SAID.

I'M REALLY SORRY THAT THE BAD GUYS ARE GOING TO FLARK YOU UP, BUT THERE'S *TOO MUCH* AT STAKE.

LORD MAR-VELL IS MOMENTS AWAY FROM ARRIVING. I CAN SMELL HIS STINK ON THE COSMIC WINDS.

GOOD LUCK. DO *NOT* WASTE THIS FINAL CHANCE.

NOW HOLD ON...

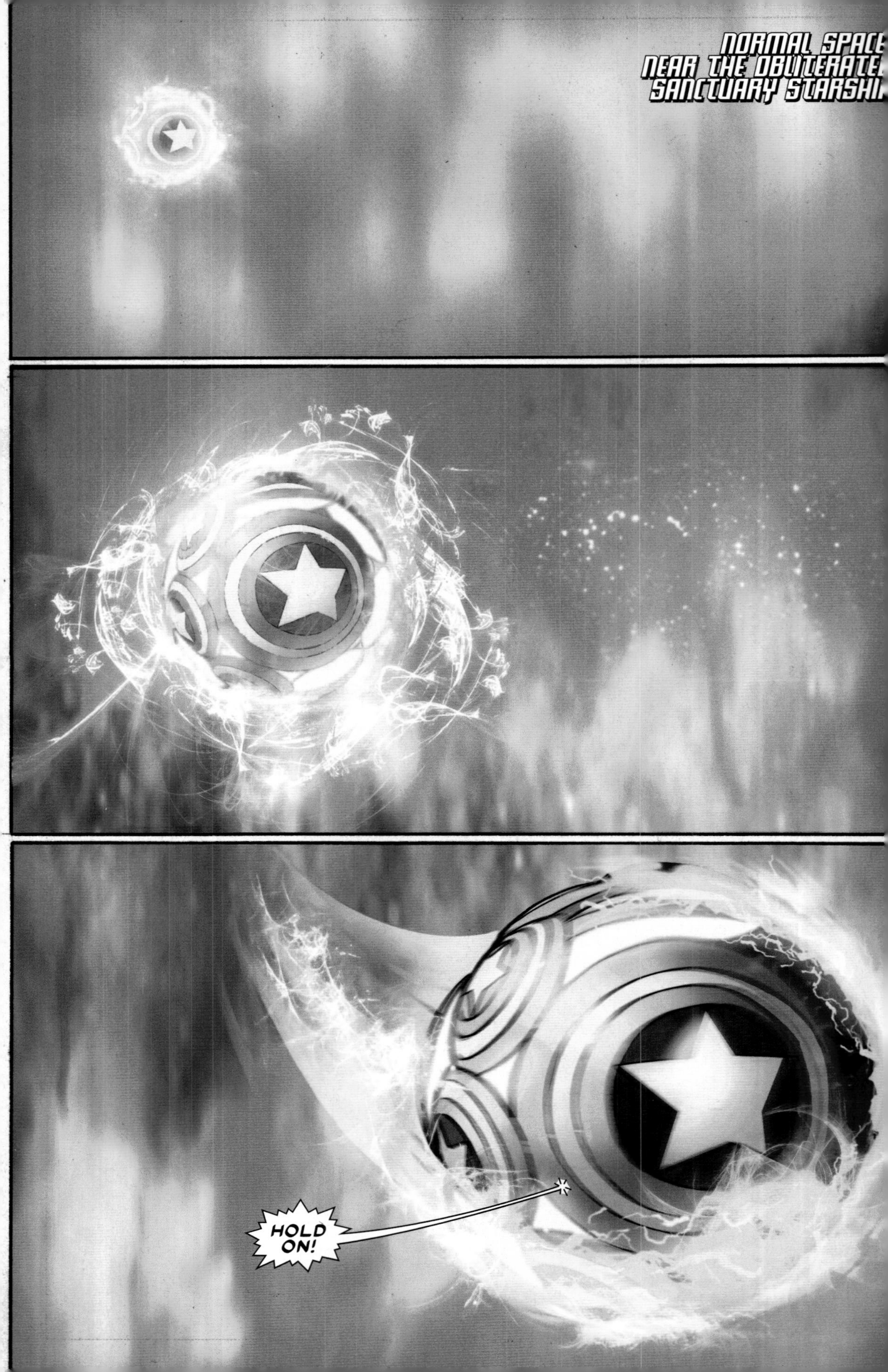
NORMAL SPACE
NEAR THE OBLITERATED
SANCTUARY STARSHIP
HOLD ON!

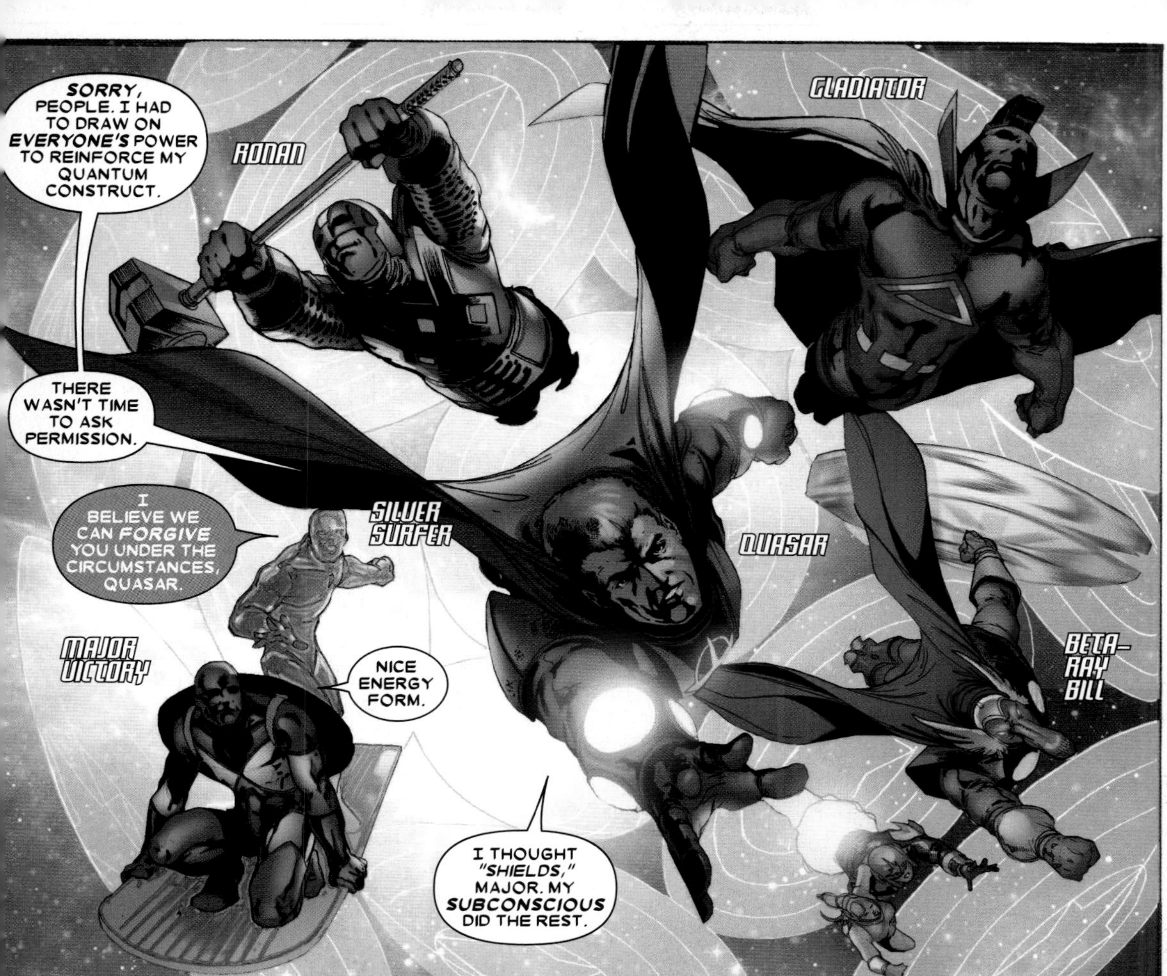
SORRY, PEOPLE. I HAD TO DRAW ON EVERYONE'S POWER TO REINFORCE MY QUANTUM CONSTRUCT.
RONAN
GLADIATOR
THERE WASN'T TIME TO ASK PERMISSION.
I BELIEVE WE CAN FORGIVE YOU UNDER THE CIRCUMSTANCES, QUASAR.
SILVER SURFER
QUASAR
MAJOR VICTORY
NICE ENERGY FORM.
BETA-RAY BILL
I THOUGHT "SHIELDS," MAJOR. MY SUBCONSCIOUS DID THE REST.

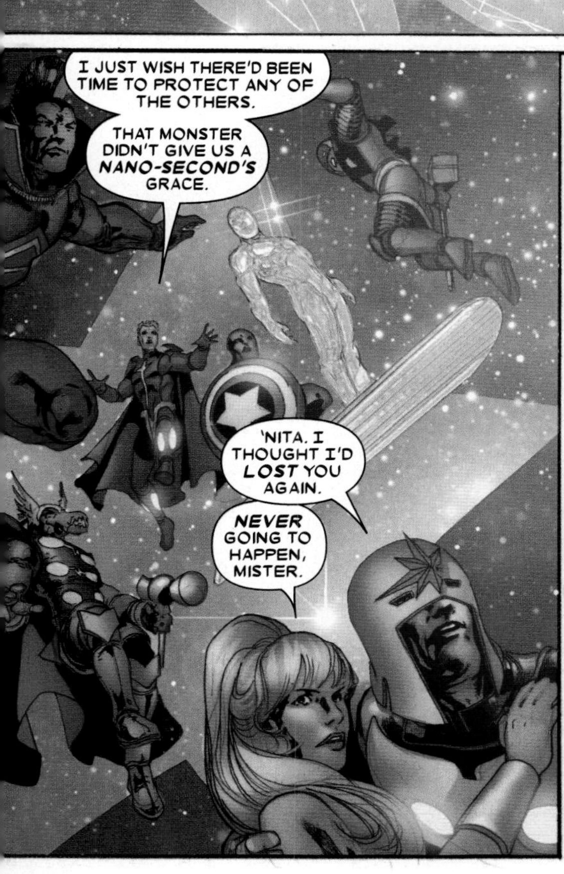
I JUST WISH THERE'D BEEN TIME TO PROTECT ANY OF THE OTHERS.
THAT MONSTER DIDN'T GIVE US A NANO-SECOND'S GRACE.
'NITA. I THOUGHT I'D LOST YOU AGAIN.
NEVER GOING TO HAPPEN, MISTER.

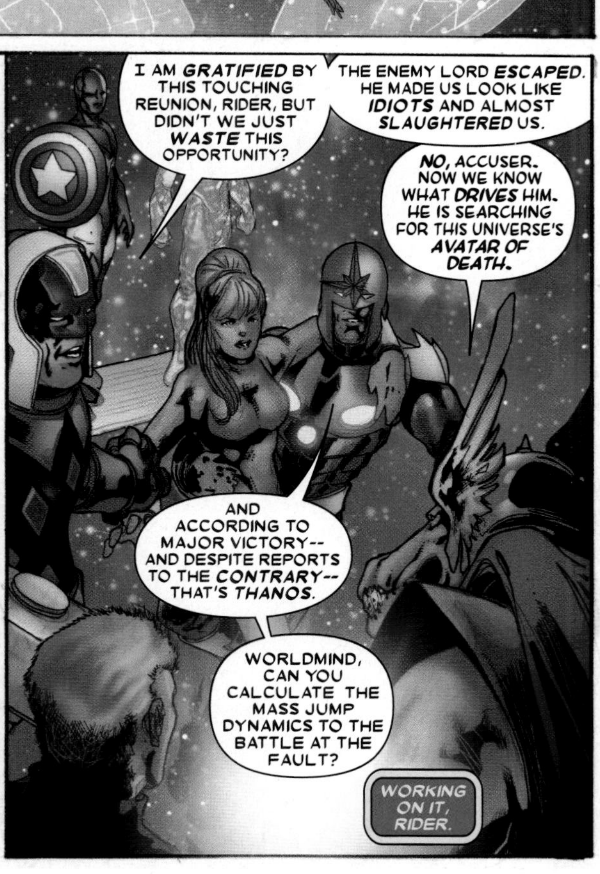
I AM GRATIFIED BY THIS TOUCHING REUNION, RIDER, BUT DIDN'T WE JUST WASTE THIS OPPORTUNITY?
THE ENEMY LORD ESCAPED. HE MADE US LOOK LIKE IDIOTS AND ALMOST SLAUGHTERED US.
NO, ACCUSER. NOW WE KNOW WHAT DRIVES HIM. HE IS SEARCHING FOR THIS UNIVERSE'S AVATAR OF DEATH.
AND ACCORDING TO MAJOR VICTORY-- AND DESPITE REPORTS TO THE CONTRARY-- THAT'S THANOS.
WORLDMIND, CAN YOU CALCULATE THE MASS JUMP DYNAMICS TO THE BATTLE AT THE FAULT?
WORKING ON IT, RIDER.

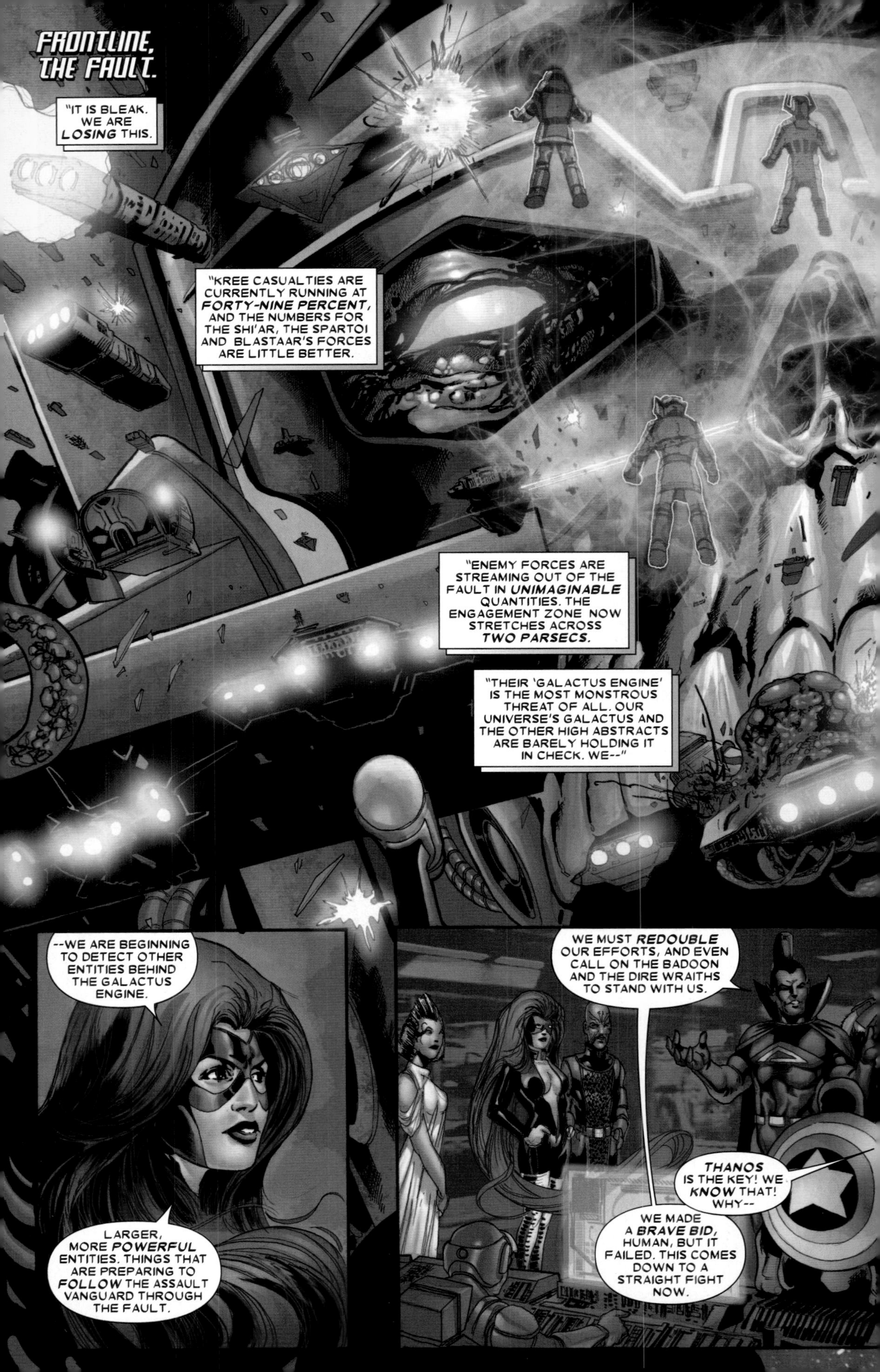
FRONTLINE, THE FAULT.
"IT IS BLEAK. WE ARE LOSING THIS.
"KREE CASUALTIES ARE CURRENTLY RUNNING AT FORTY-NINE PERCENT, AND THE NUMBERS FOR THE SHI'AR, THE SPARTOI AND BLASTAAR'S FORCES ARE LITTLE BETTER.
"ENEMY FORCES ARE STREAMING OUT OF THE FAULT IN UNIMAGINABLE QUANTITIES. THE ENGAGEMENT ZONE NOW STRETCHES ACROSS TWO PARSECS.
"THEIR 'GALACTUS ENGINE' IS THE MOST MONSTROUS THREAT OF ALL. OUR UNIVERSE'S GALACTUS AND THE OTHER HIGH ABSTRACTS ARE BARELY HOLDING IT IN CHECK. WE--"
--WE ARE BEGINNING TO DETECT OTHER ENTITIES BEHIND THE GALACTUS ENGINE.
LARGER, MORE POWERFUL ENTITIES. THINGS THAT ARE PREPARING TO FOLLOW THE ASSAULT VANGUARD THROUGH THE FAULT.
WE MUST REDOUBLE OUR EFFORTS, AND EVEN CALL ON THE BADOON AND THE DIRE WRAITHS TO STAND WITH US.
THANOS IS THE KEY! WE KNOW THAT! WHY--
WE MADE A BRAVE BID, HUMAN, BUT IT FAILED. THIS COMES DOWN TO A STRAIGHT FIGHT NOW.

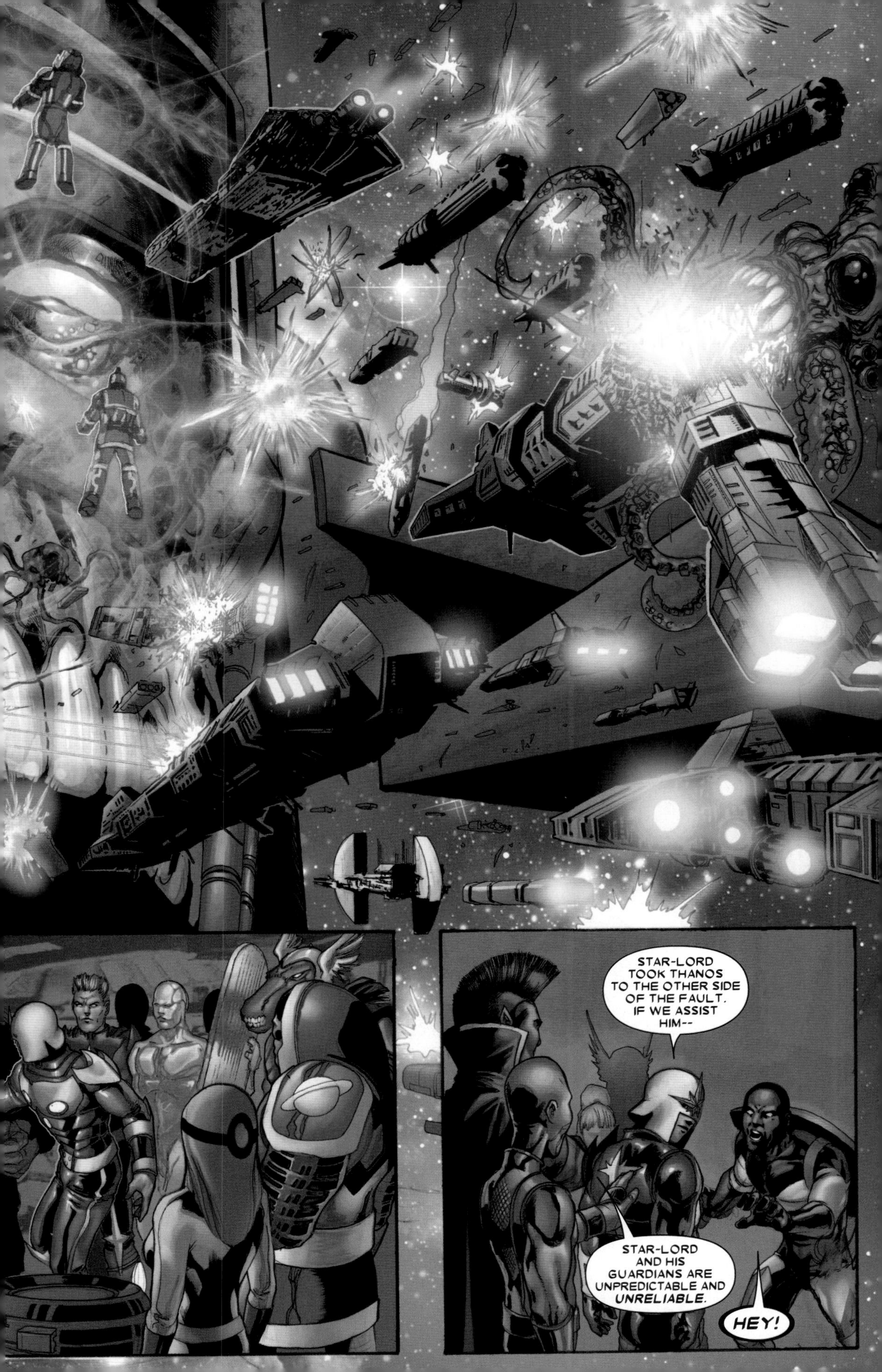
STAR-LORD TOOK THANOS TO THE OTHER SIDE OF THE FAULT. IF WE ASSIST HIM--
STAR-LORD AND HIS GUARDIANS ARE UNPREDICTABLE AND UNRELIABLE.
HEY!

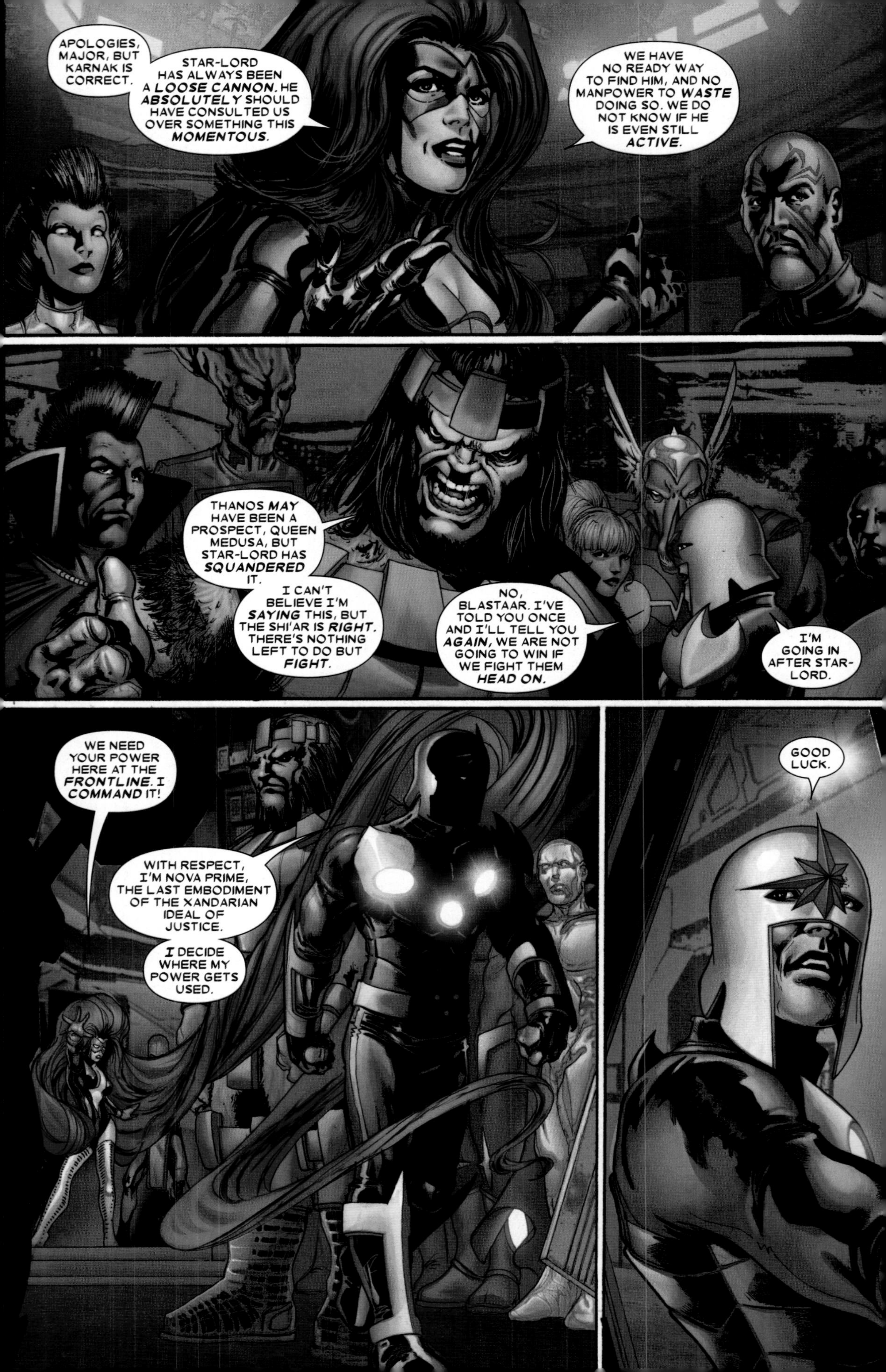
APOLOGIES, MAJOR, BUT KARNAK IS CORRECT.
STAR-LORD HAS ALWAYS BEEN A LOOSE CANNON. HE ABSOLUTELY SHOULD HAVE CONSULTED US OVER SOMETHING THIS MOMENTOUS.
WE HAVE NO READY WAY TO FIND HIM, AND NO MANPOWER TO WASTE DOING SO. WE DO NOT KNOW IF HE IS EVEN STILL ACTIVE.
THANOS MAY HAVE BEEN A PROSPECT, QUEEN MEDUSA, BUT STAR-LORD HAS SQUANDERED IT.
I CAN'T BELIEVE I'M SAYING THIS, BUT THE SHI'AR IS RIGHT. THERE'S NOTHING LEFT TO DO BUT FIGHT.
NO, BLASTAAR. I'VE TOLD YOU ONCE AND I'LL TELL YOU AGAIN, WE ARE NOT GOING TO WIN IF WE FIGHT THEM HEAD ON.
I'M GOING IN AFTER STAR-LORD.
WE NEED YOUR POWER HERE AT THE FRONTLINE. I COMMAND IT!
WITH RESPECT, I'M NOVA PRIME, THE LAST EMBODIMENT OF THE XANDARIAN IDEAL OF JUSTICE.
I DECIDE WHERE MY POWER GETS USED.
GOOD LUCK.

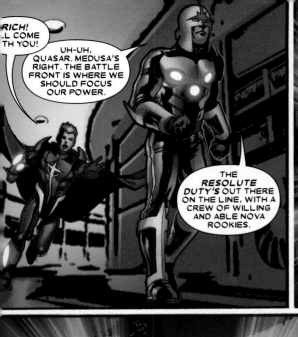

RICH! ..L COME TH YOU!

UH-UH, QUASAR. MEDUSA'S RIGHT. THE BATTLE FRONT IS WHERE WE SHOULD FOCUS OUR POWER.

THE *RESOLUTE DUTY'S* OUT THERE ON THE LINE, WITH A CREW OF WILLING AND ABLE NOVA ROOKIES.

THEY'RE *YOURS* TO COMMAND.

NOT NOW, WORLDMIND.

RIDER! ATTENTION! WHAT ARE YOU DOING?

RICH, WHAT THE HECK?!

YOU LENT ME THE QUANTUM POWER WHEN I NEEDED IT MOST, WENDELL. NOW I'M LOANING YOU SOME *NOVA* FORCE.

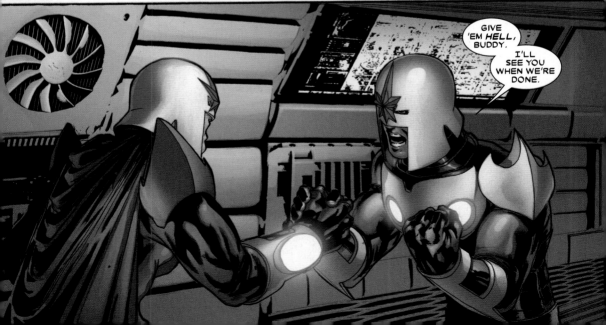

GIVE 'EM *HELL*, BUDDY.

I'LL SEE YOU WHEN WE'RE DONE.

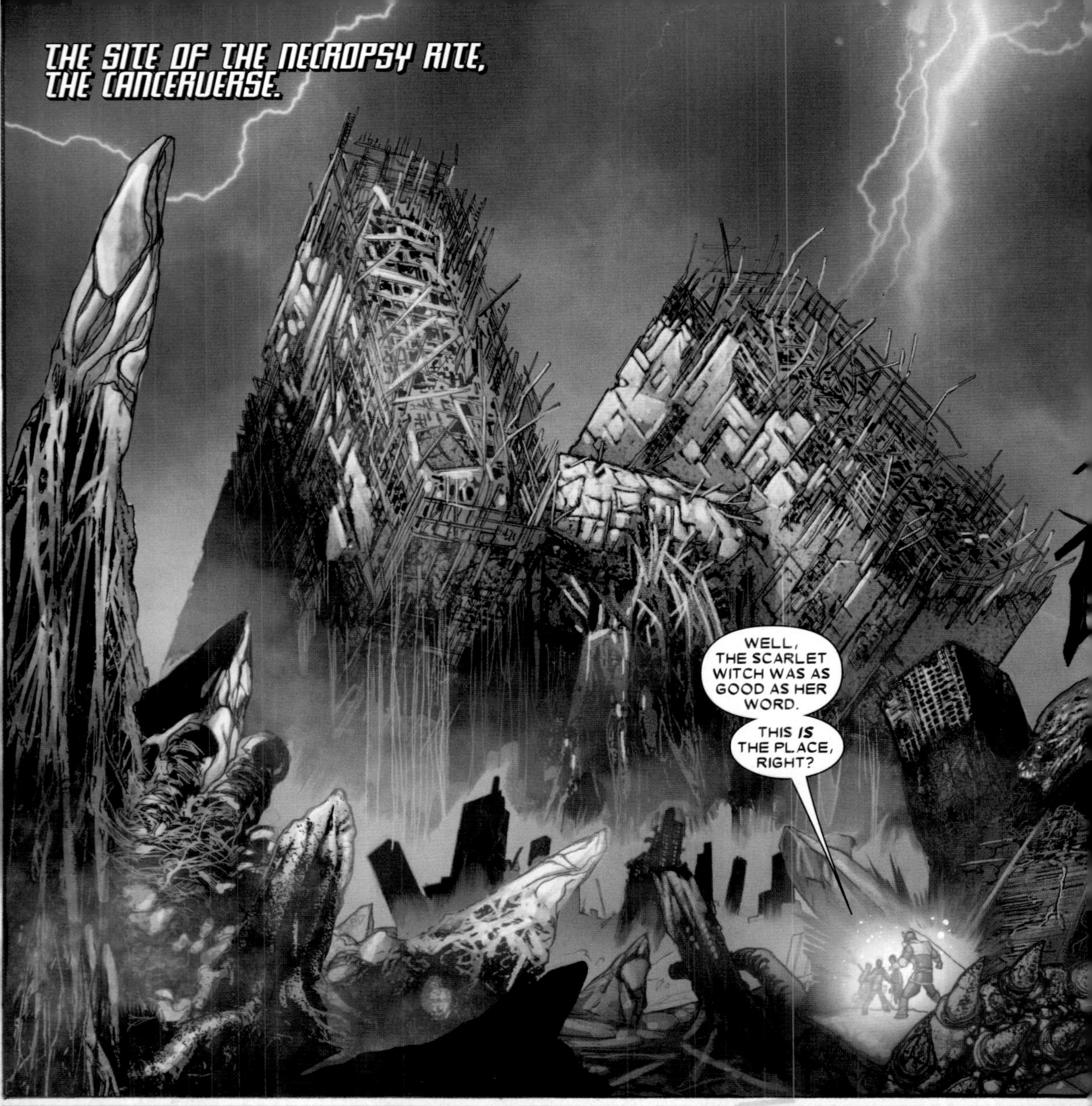
THE SITE OF THE NECROPSY RITE, THE CANCERVERSE.
WELL, THE SCARLET WITCH WAS AS GOOD AS HER WORD.
THIS IS THE PLACE, RIGHT?

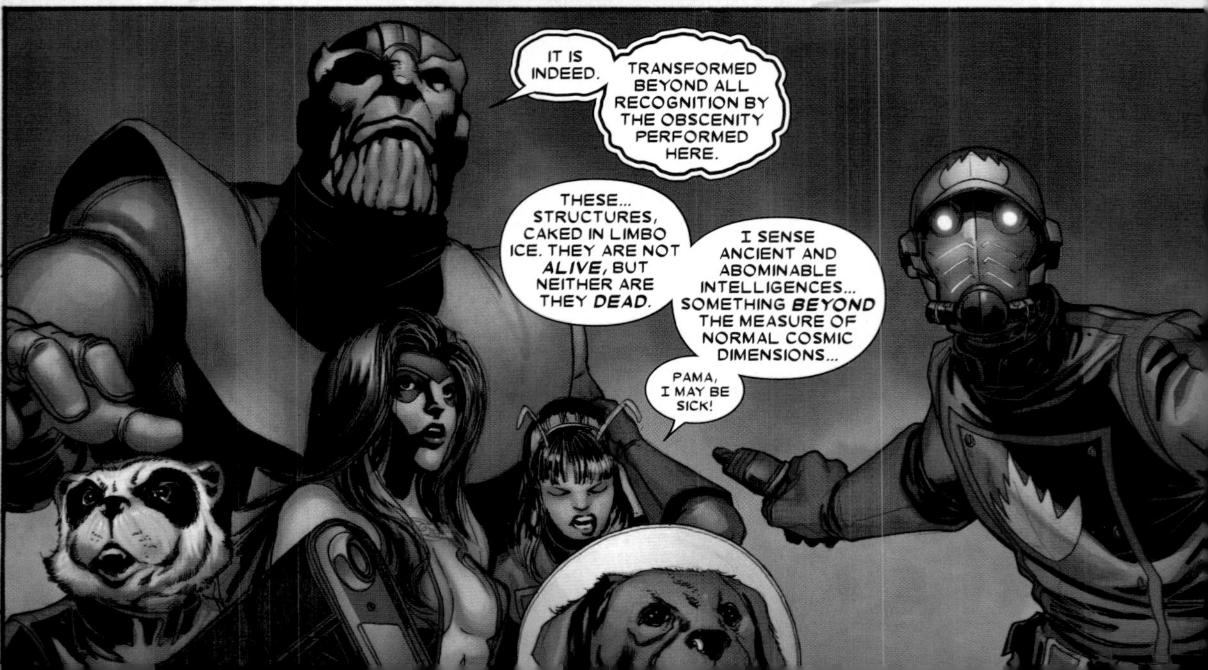
IT IS INDEED.
TRANSFORMED BEYOND ALL RECOGNITION BY THE OBSCENITY PERFORMED HERE.
THESE... STRUCTURES, CAKED IN LIMBO ICE. THEY ARE NOT ALIVE, BUT NEITHER ARE THEY DEAD.
I SENSE ANCIENT AND ABOMINABLE INTELLIGENCES... SOMETHING BEYOND THE MEASURE OF NORMAL COSMIC DIMENSIONS...
PAMA, I MAY BE SICK!

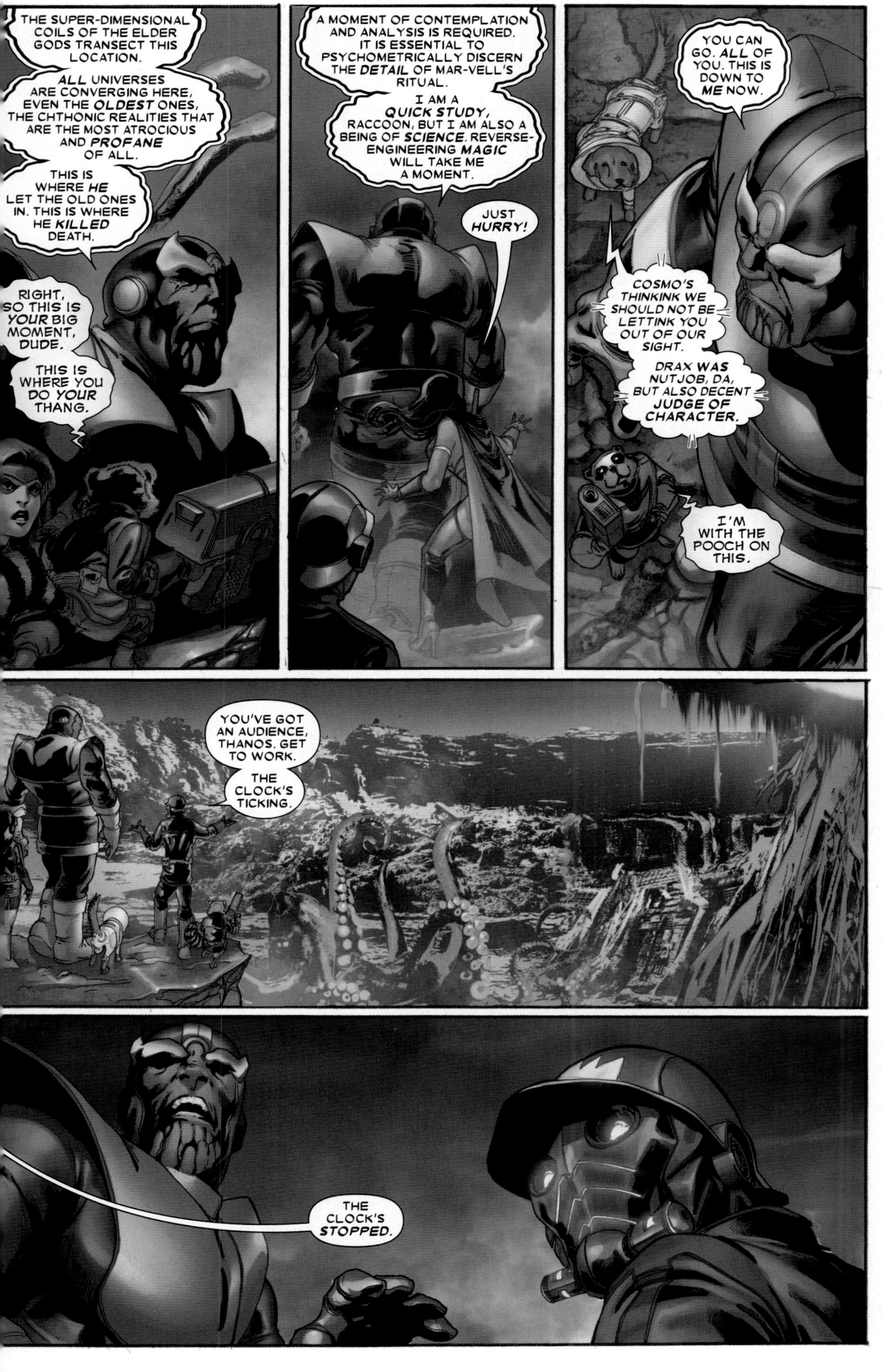
THE SUPER-DIMENSIONAL COILS OF THE ELDER GODS TRANSECT THIS LOCATION.
ALL UNIVERSES ARE CONVERGING HERE, EVEN THE OLDEST ONES, THE CHTHONIC REALITIES THAT ARE THE MOST ATROCIOUS AND PROFANE OF ALL.
THIS IS WHERE HE LET THE OLD ONES IN. THIS IS WHERE HE KILLED DEATH.
RIGHT, SO THIS IS YOUR BIG MOMENT, DUDE.
THIS IS WHERE YOU DO YOUR THANG.
A MOMENT OF CONTEMPLATION AND ANALYSIS IS REQUIRED. IT IS ESSENTIAL TO PSYCHOMETRICALLY DISCERN THE DETAIL OF MAR-VELL'S RITUAL.
I AM A QUICK STUDY, RACCOON, BUT I AM ALSO A BEING OF SCIENCE. REVERSE-ENGINEERING MAGIC WILL TAKE ME A MOMENT.
JUST HURRY!
YOU CAN GO. ALL OF YOU. THIS IS DOWN TO ME NOW.
COSMO'S THINKINK WE SHOULD NOT BE LETTINK YOU OUT OF OUR SIGHT.
DRAX WAS NUTJOB, DA, BUT ALSO DECENT JUDGE OF CHARACTER.
I'M WITH THE POOCH ON THIS.
YOU'VE GOT AN AUDIENCE, THANOS. GET TO WORK.
THE CLOCK'S TICKING.
THE CLOCK'S STOPPED.

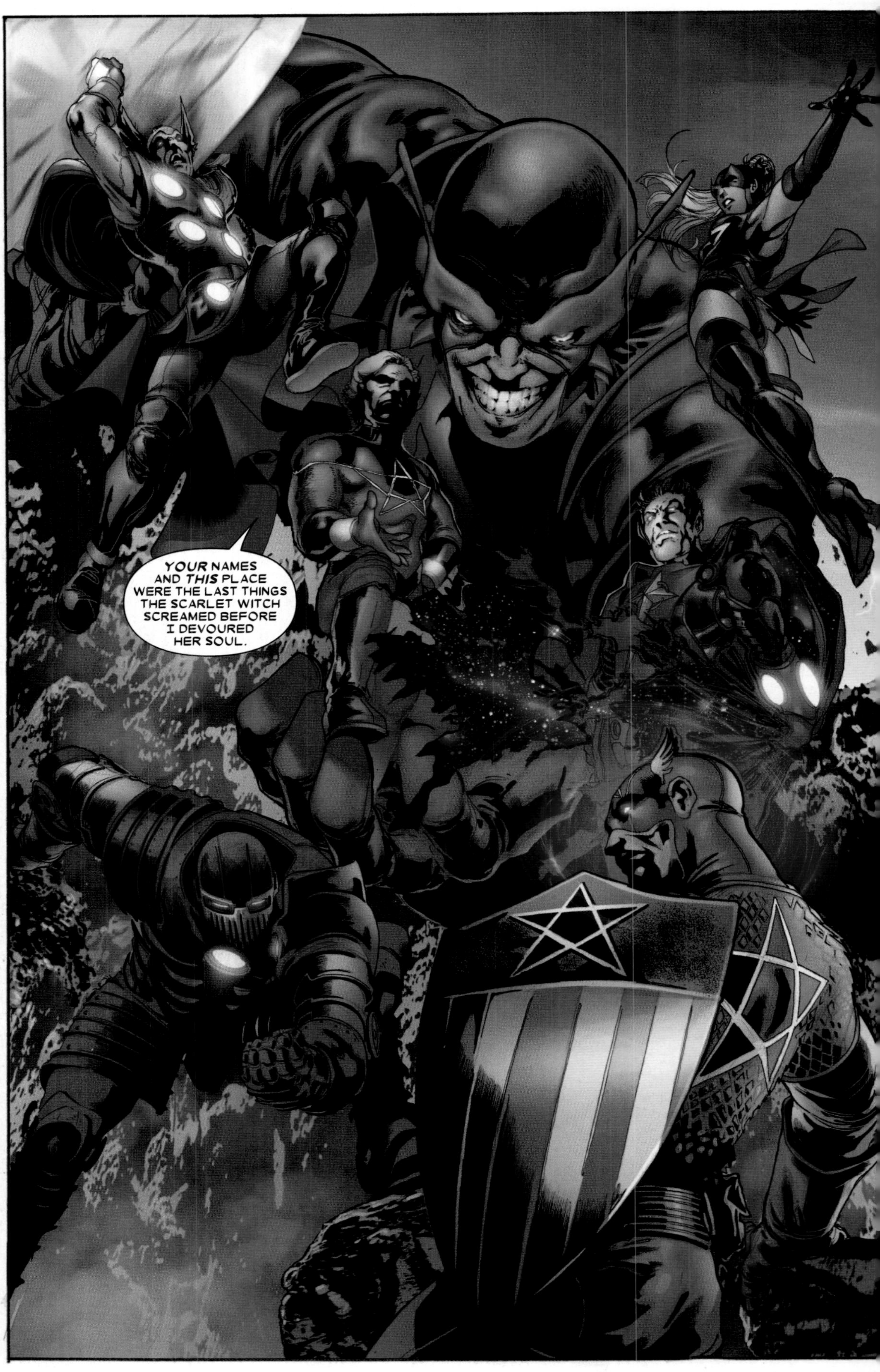
YOUR NAMES AND THIS PLACE WERE THE LAST THINGS THE SCARLET WITCH SCREAMED BEFORE I DEVOURED HER SOUL.

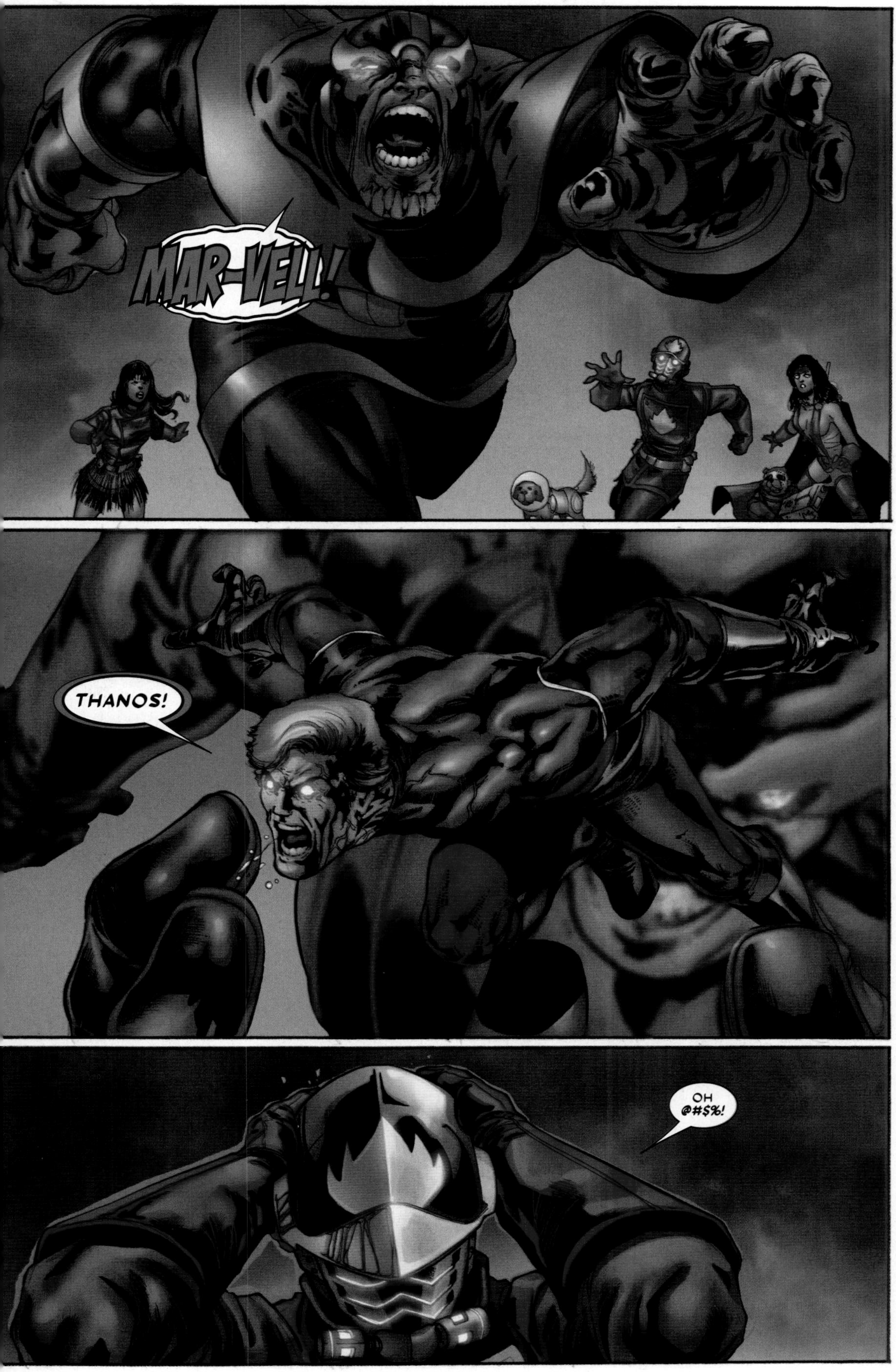
MAR-VELL!
THANOS!
OH @#$%!

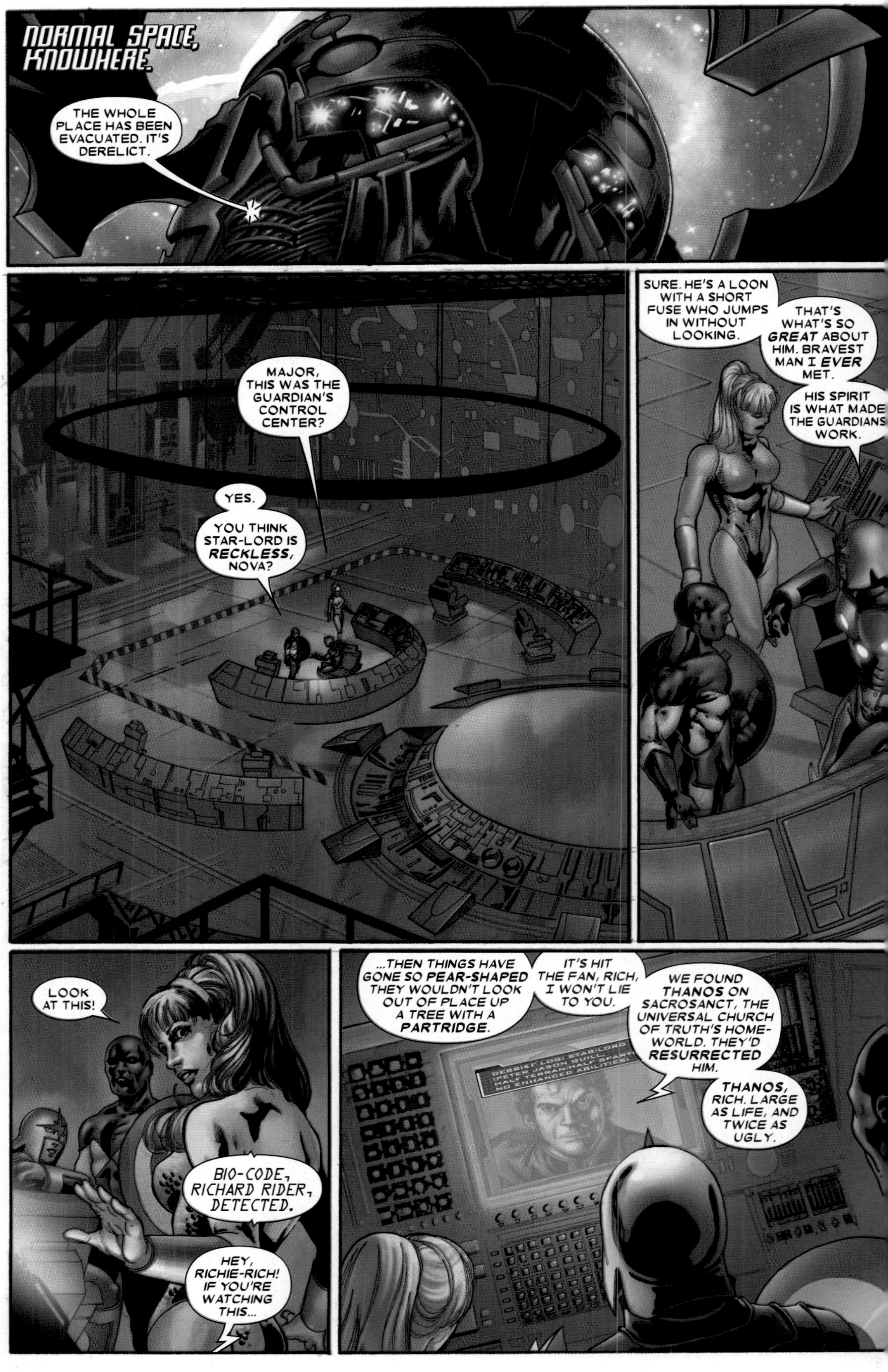

NORMAL SPACE, KNOWHERE.
THE WHOLE PLACE HAS BEEN EVACUATED. IT'S DERELICT.
MAJOR, THIS WAS THE GUARDIAN'S CONTROL CENTER?
YES.
YOU THINK STAR-LORD IS RECKLESS, NOVA?
SURE. HE'S A LOON WITH A SHORT FUSE WHO JUMPS IN WITHOUT LOOKING.
THAT'S WHAT'S SO GREAT ABOUT HIM. BRAVEST MAN I EVER MET.
HIS SPIRIT IS WHAT MADE THE GUARDIANS WORK.
LOOK AT THIS!
BIO-CODE, RICHARD RIDER, DETECTED.
HEY, RICHIE-RICH! IF YOU'RE WATCHING THIS...
...THEN THINGS HAVE GONE SO PEAR-SHAPED THEY WOULDN'T LOOK OUT OF PLACE UP A TREE WITH A PARTRIDGE.
IT'S HIT THE FAN, RICH, I WON'T LIE TO YOU.
DEBRIEF LOG: STAR-LORD
(PETER JASON QUILL.
NO ENHANCED ABILITIES)
WE FOUND THANOS ON SACROSANCT, THE UNIVERSAL CHURCH OF TRUTH'S HOME-WORLD. THEY'D RESURRECTED HIM.
THANOS, RICH. LARGE AS LIFE, AND TWICE AS UGLY.

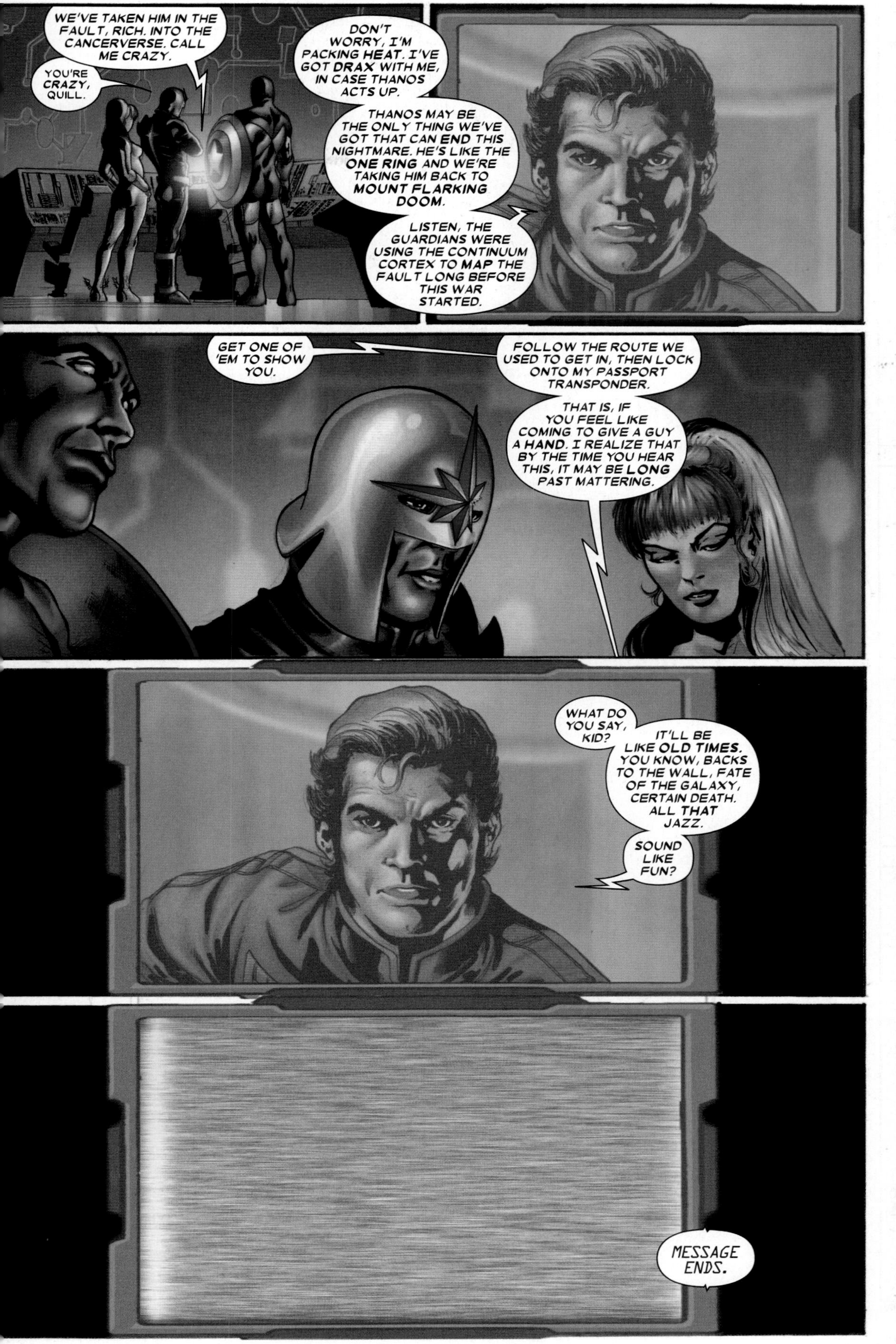
WE'VE TAKEN HIM IN THE FAULT, RICH. INTO THE CANCERVERSE. CALL ME CRAZY.
YOU'RE CRAZY, QUILL.
DON'T WORRY, I'M PACKING HEAT. I'VE GOT DRAX WITH ME, IN CASE THANOS ACTS UP.
THANOS MAY BE THE ONLY THING WE'VE GOT THAT CAN END THIS NIGHTMARE. HE'S LIKE THE ONE RING AND WE'RE TAKING HIM BACK TO MOUNT FLARKING DOOM.
LISTEN, THE GUARDIANS WERE USING THE CONTINUUM CORTEX TO MAP THE FAULT LONG BEFORE THIS WAR STARTED.
GET ONE OF 'EM TO SHOW YOU.
FOLLOW THE ROUTE WE USED TO GET IN, THEN LOCK ONTO MY PASSPORT TRANSPONDER.
THAT IS, IF YOU FEEL LIKE COMING TO GIVE A GUY A HAND. I REALIZE THAT BY THE TIME YOU HEAR THIS, IT MAY BE LONG PAST MATTERING.
WHAT DO YOU SAY, KID?
IT'LL BE LIKE OLD TIMES. YOU KNOW, BACKS TO THE WALL, FATE OF THE GALAXY, CERTAIN DEATH. ALL THAT JAZZ.
SOUND LIKE FUN?
MESSAGE ENDS.

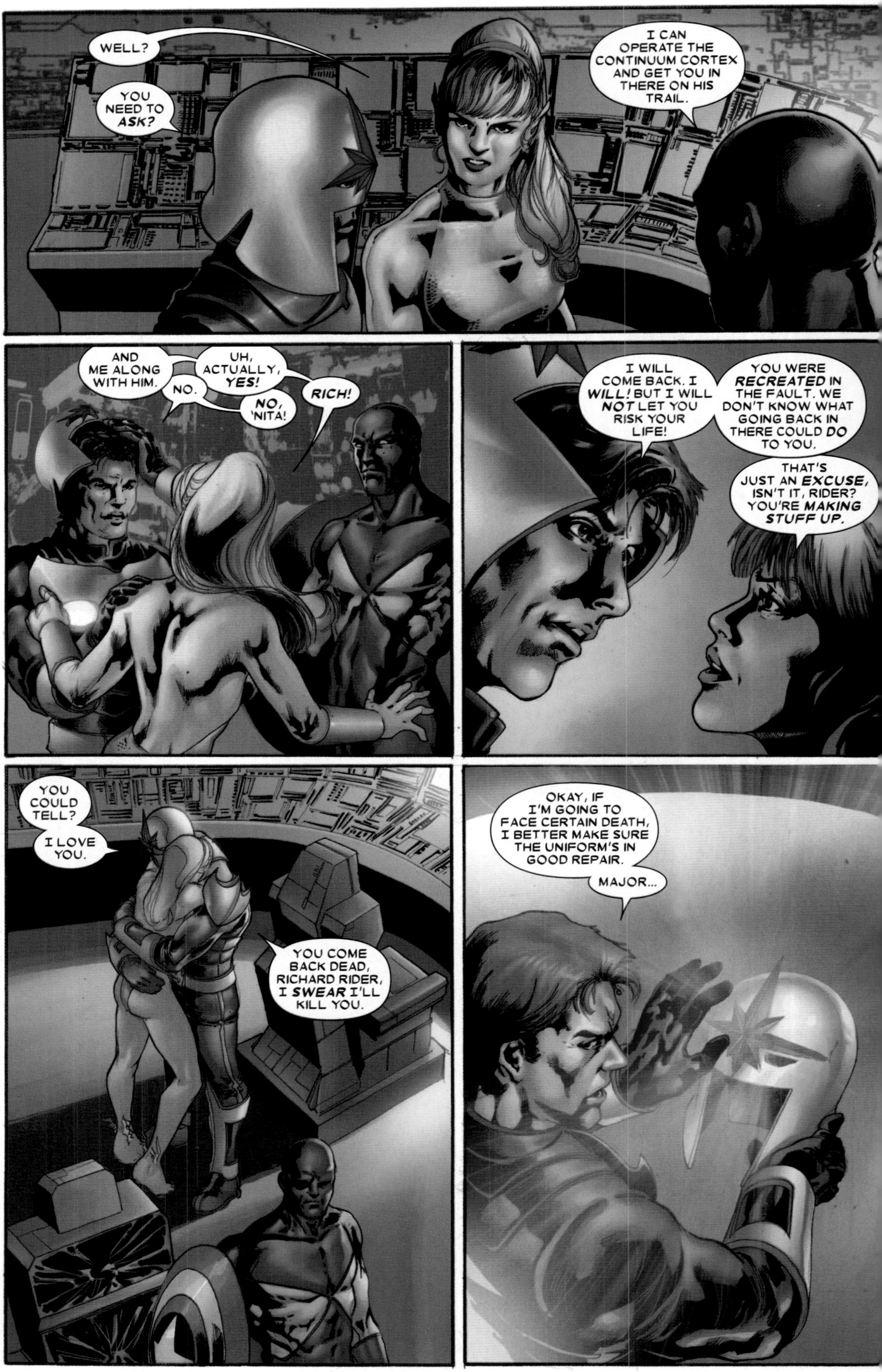
WELL?
YOU NEED TO ASK?
I CAN OPERATE THE CONTINUUM CORTEX AND GET YOU IN THERE ON HIS TRAIL.
AND ME ALONG WITH HIM.
NO.
UH, ACTUALLY, YES!
NO, 'NITA!
RICH!
I WILL COME BACK. I WILL! BUT I WILL NOT LET YOU RISK YOUR LIFE!
YOU WERE RECREATED IN THE FAULT. WE DON'T KNOW WHAT GOING BACK IN THERE COULD DO TO YOU.
THAT'S JUST AN EXCUSE, ISN'T IT, RIDER? YOU'RE MAKING STUFF UP.
YOU COULD TELL?
I LOVE YOU.
YOU COME BACK DEAD, RICHARD RIDER, I SWEAR I'LL KILL YOU.
OKAY, IF I'M GOING TO FACE CERTAIN DEATH, I BETTER MAKE SURE THE UNIFORM'S IN GOOD REPAIR.
MAJOR...

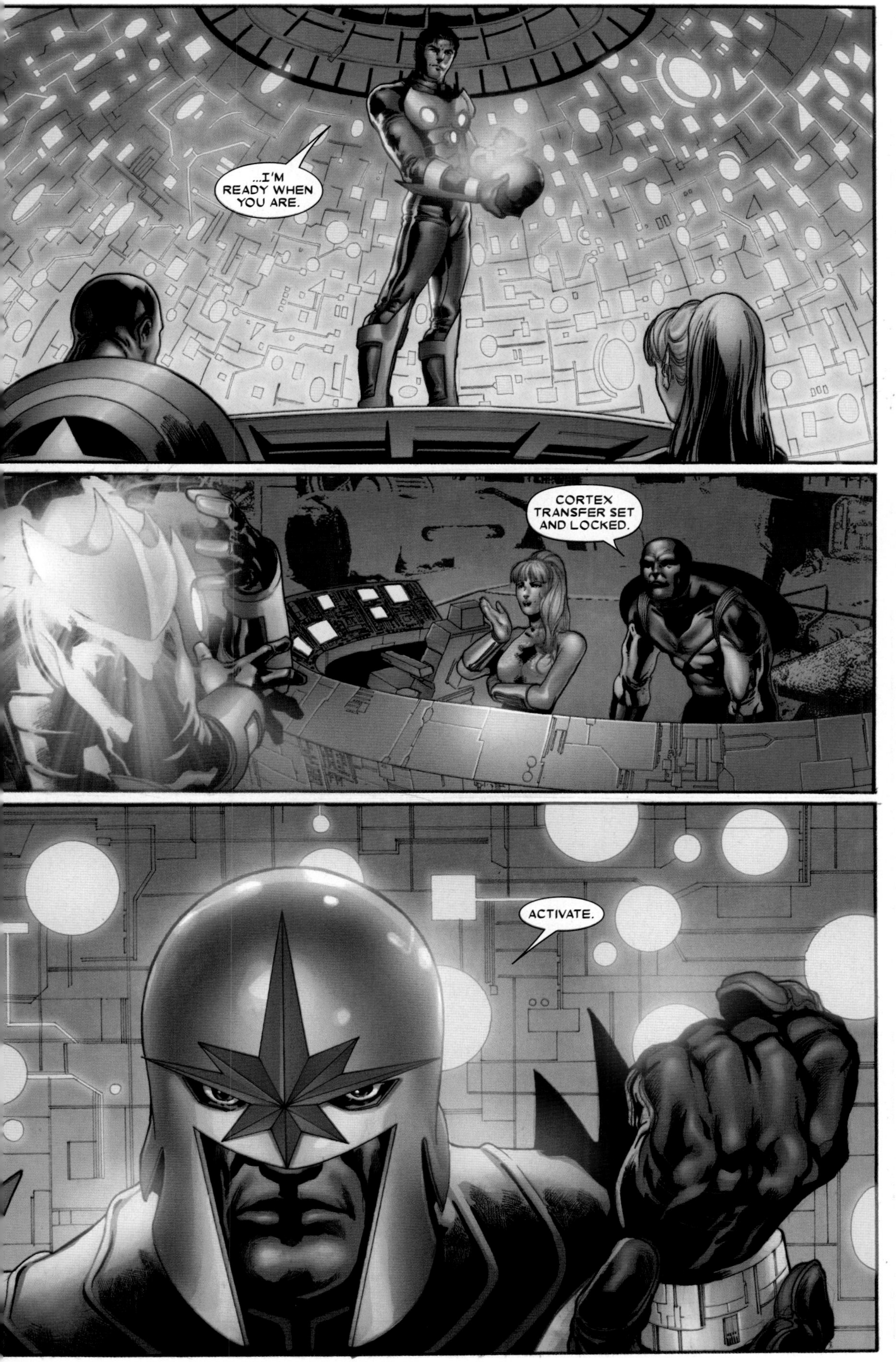
...I'M READY WHEN YOU ARE.
CORTEX TRANSFER SET AND LOCKED.
ACTIVATE.

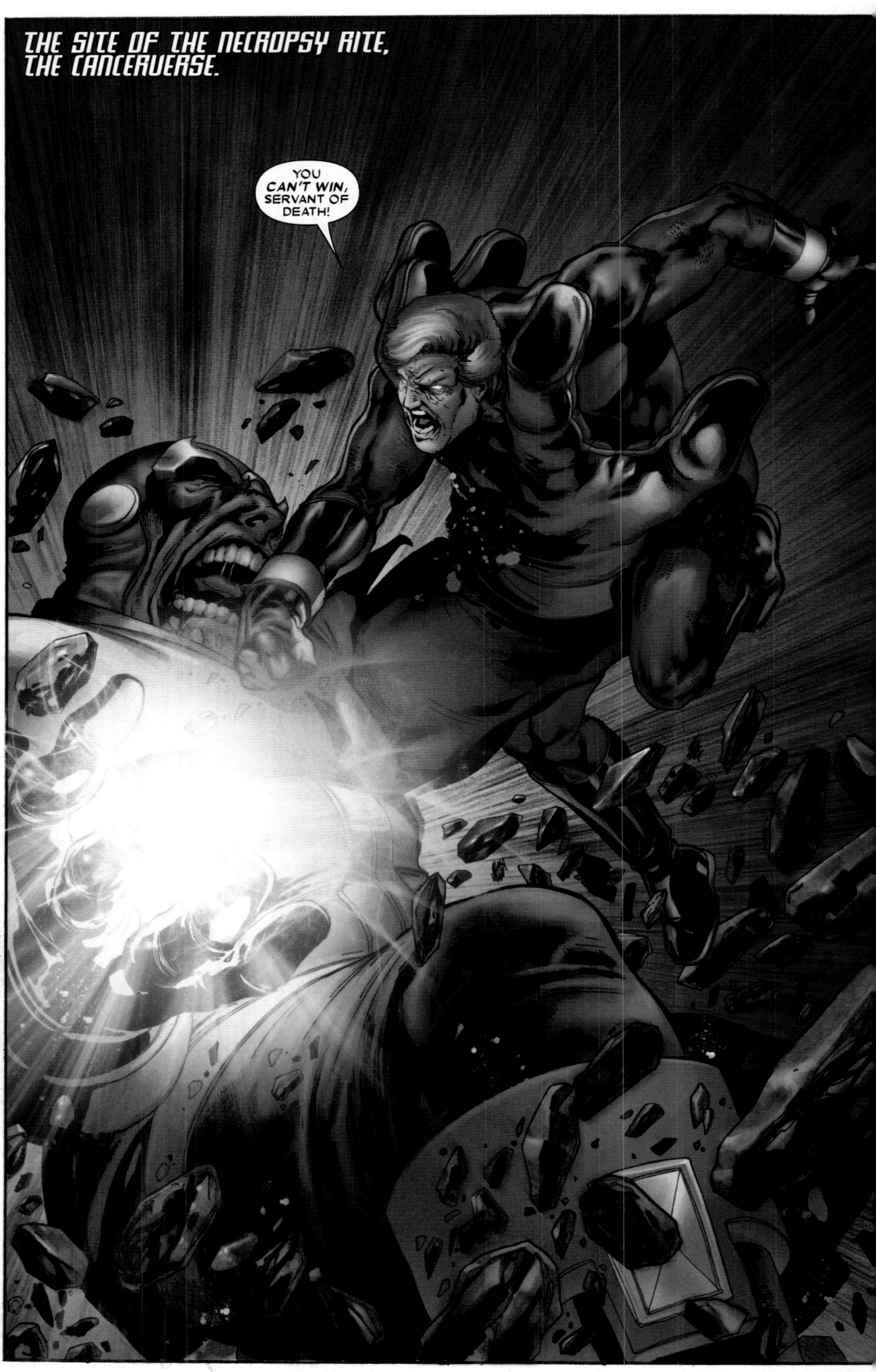
THE SITE OF THE NECROPSY RITE,
THE CANCERVERSE.
YOU CAN'T WIN, SERVANT OF DEATH!

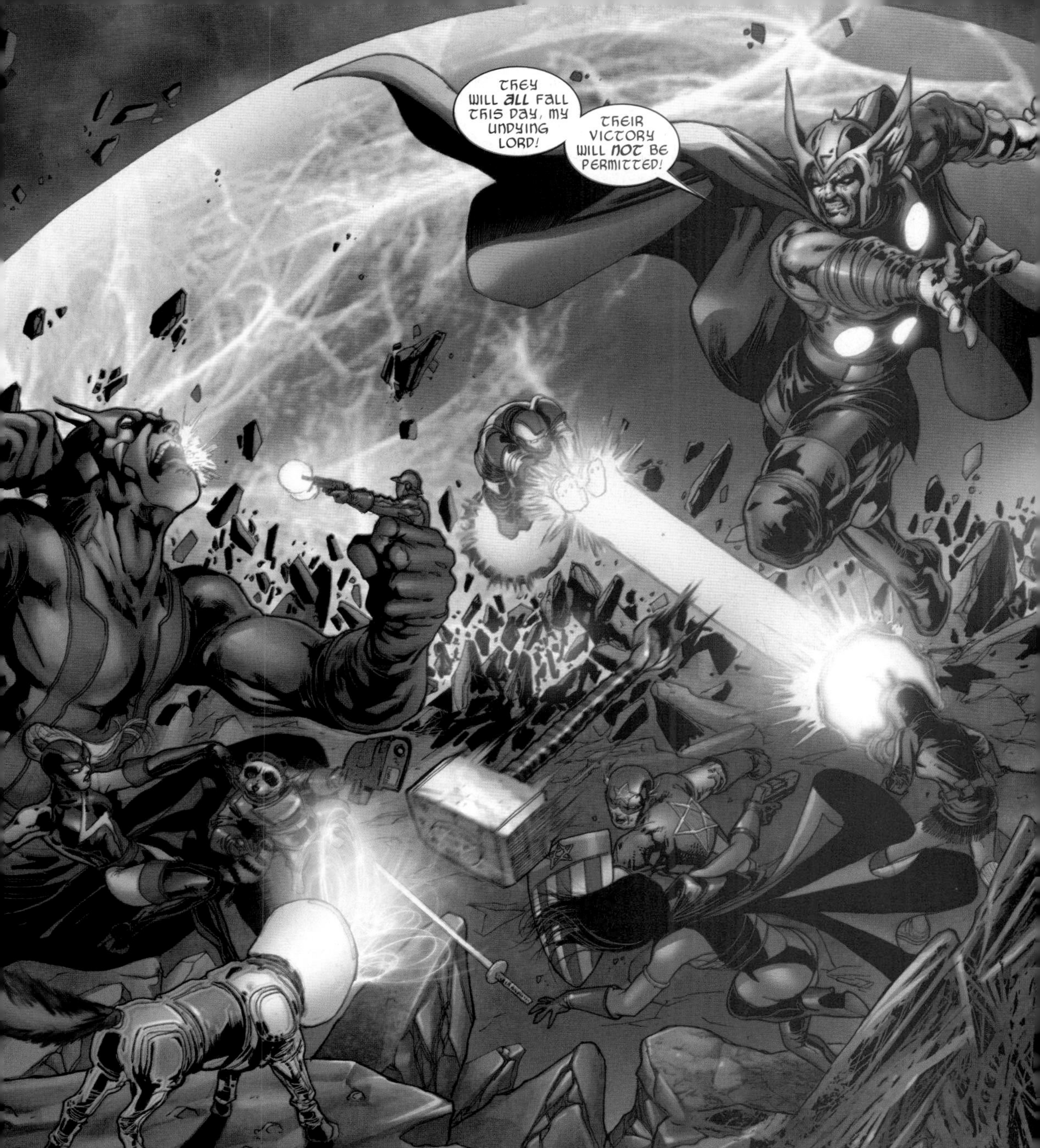
THEY WILL ALL FALL THIS DAY, MY UNDYING LORD!
THEIR VICTORY WILL NOT BE PERMITTED!
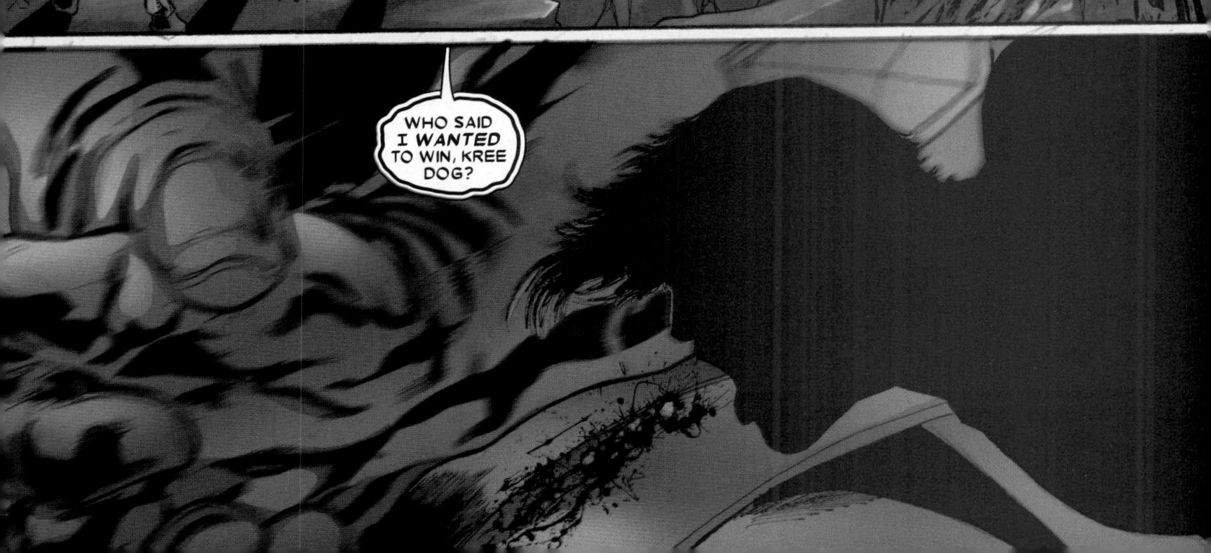
WHO SAID I WANTED TO WIN, KREE DOG?

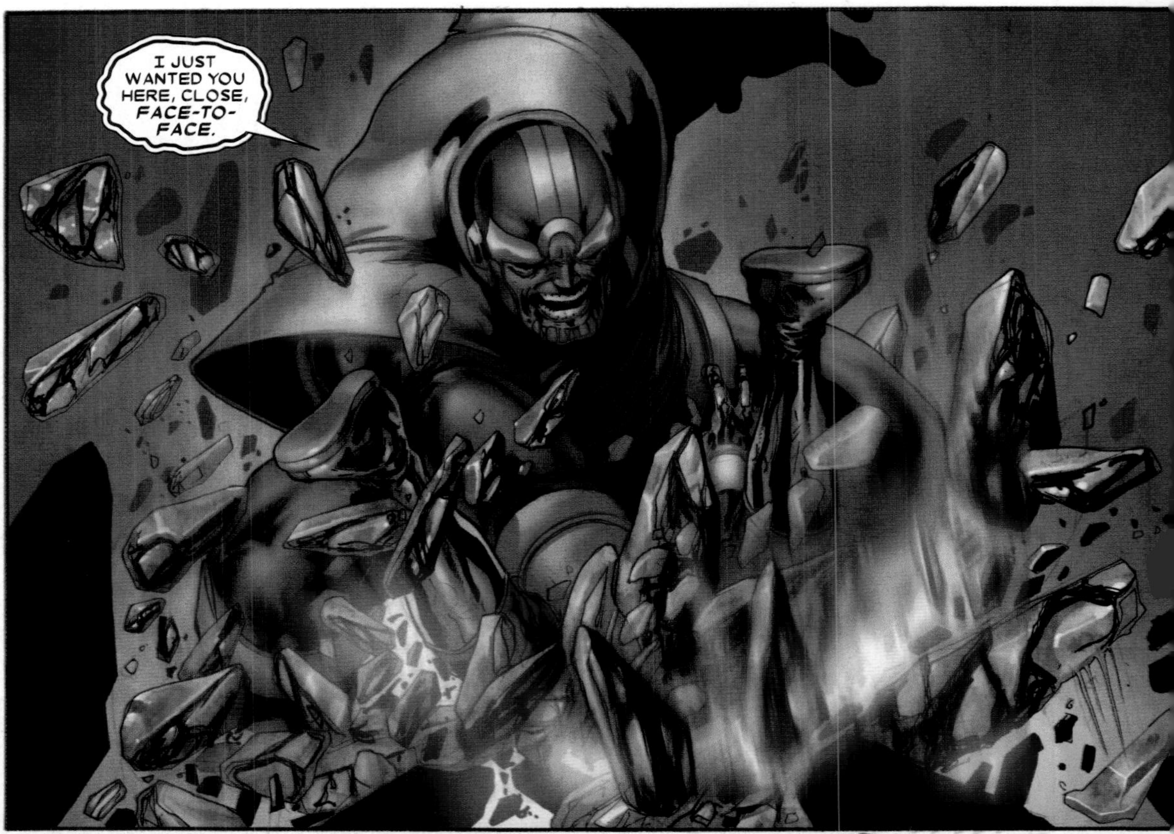
I JUST WANTED YOU HERE, CLOSE, FACE-TO-FACE.

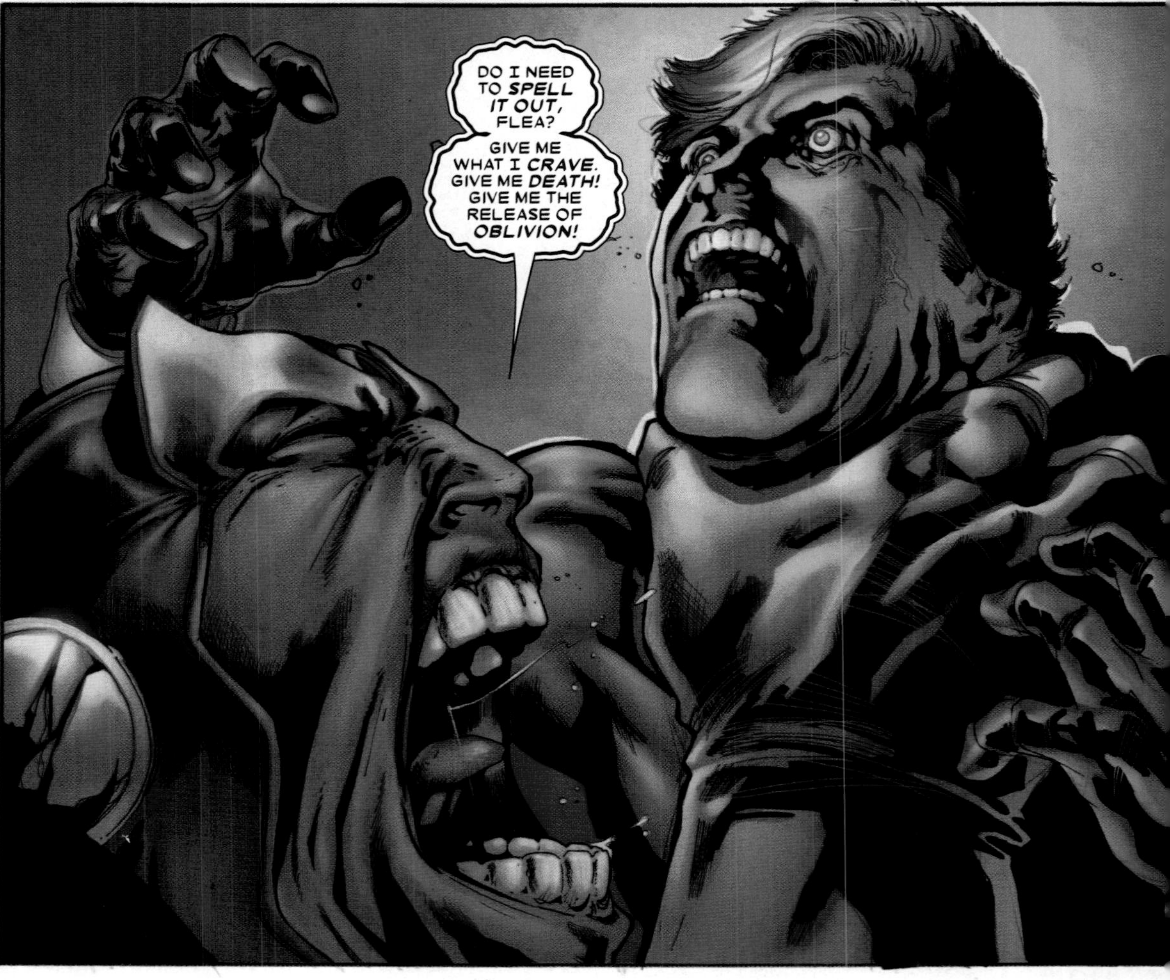
DO I NEED TO SPELL IT OUT, FLEA?
GIVE ME WHAT I CRAVE. GIVE ME DEATH! GIVE ME THE RELEASE OF OBLIVION!

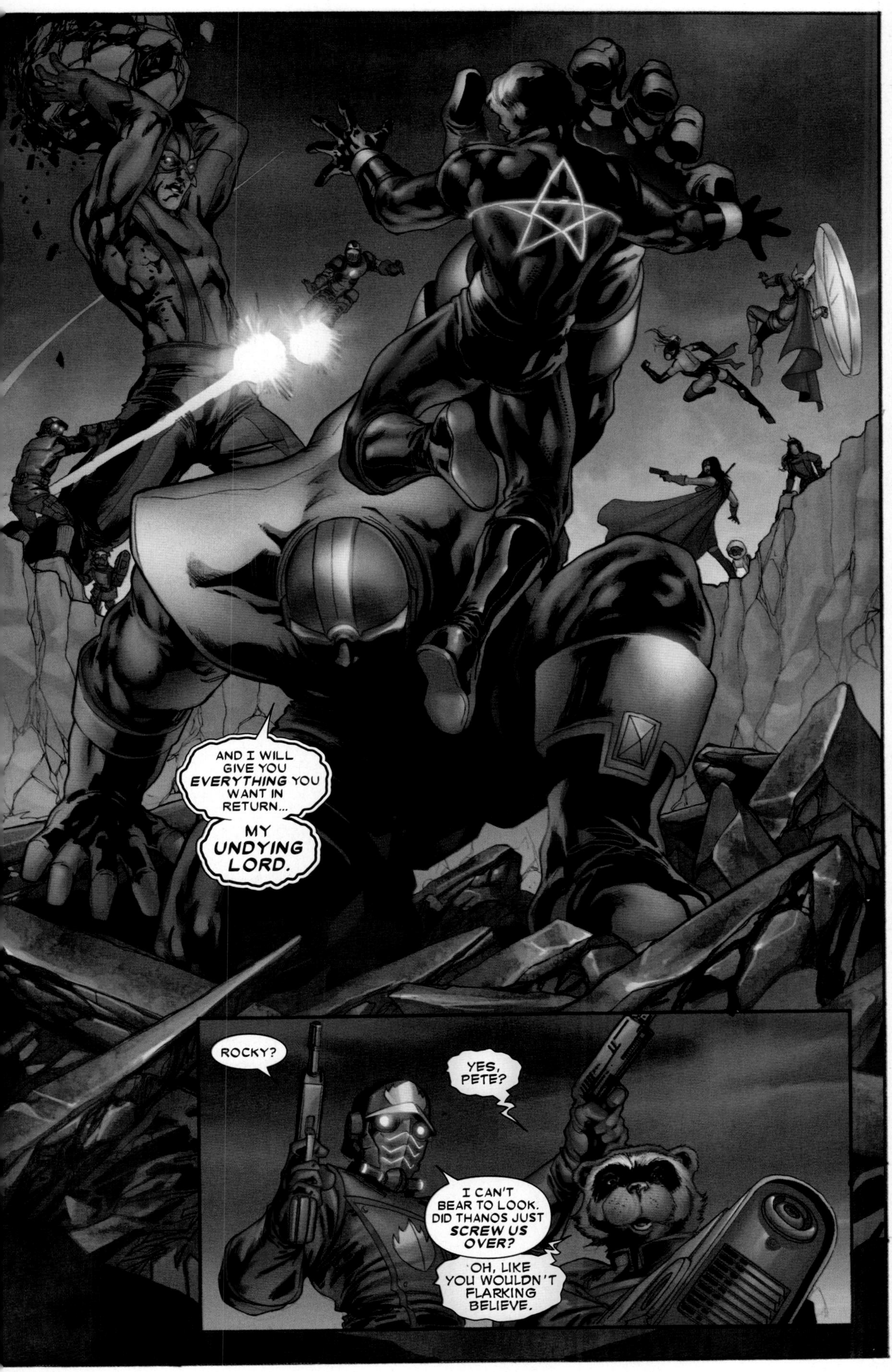
AND I WILL GIVE YOU EVERYTHING YOU WANT IN RETURN...
MY UNDYING LORD.
ROCKY?
YES, PETE?
I CAN'T BEAR TO LOOK. DID THANOS JUST SCREW US OVER?
OH, LIKE YOU WOULDN'T FLARKING BELIEVE.

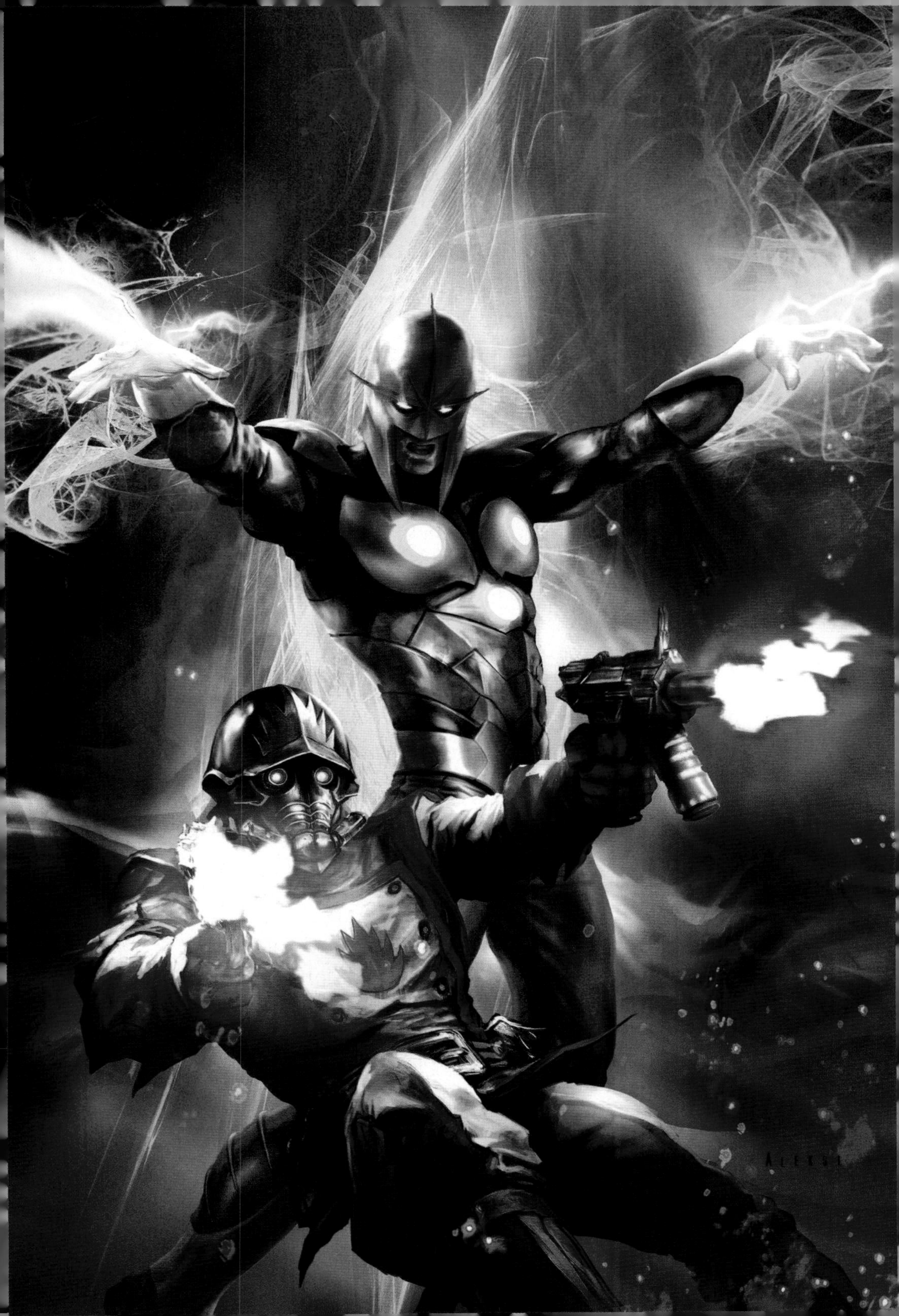
ALEKSI

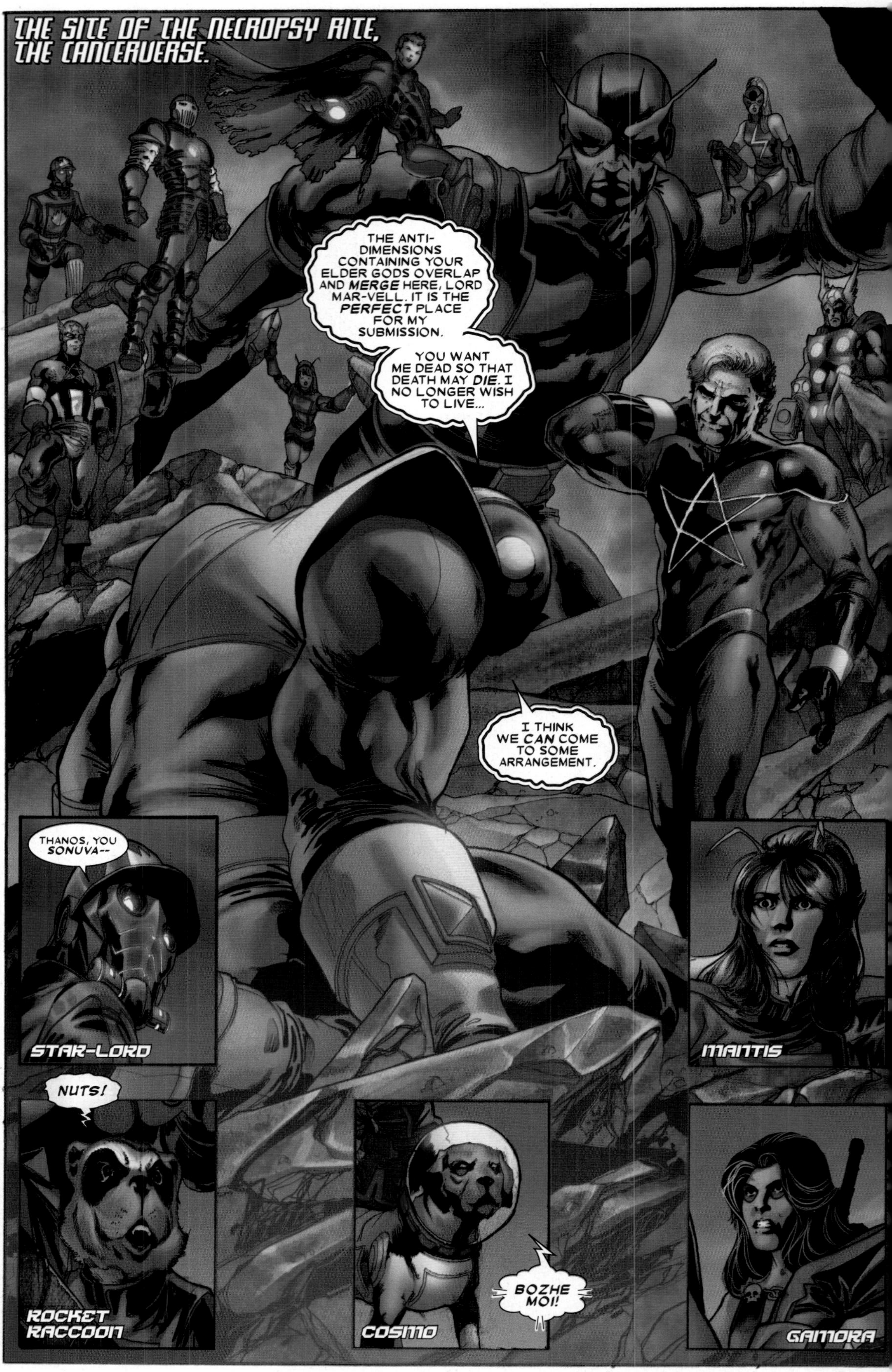

THE SITE OF THE NECROPSY RITE, THE CANCERVERSE.
THE ANTI-DIMENSIONS CONTAINING YOUR ELDER GODS OVERLAP AND MERGE HERE, LORD MAR-VELL. IT IS THE PERFECT PLACE FOR MY SUBMISSION.
YOU WANT ME DEAD SO THAT DEATH MAY DIE. I NO LONGER WISH TO LIVE...
I THINK WE CAN COME TO SOME ARRANGEMENT.
THANOS, YOU SONUVA--
STAR-LORD
MANTIS
NUTS!
ROCKET RACCOON
COSMO
BOZHE MOI!
GAMORA

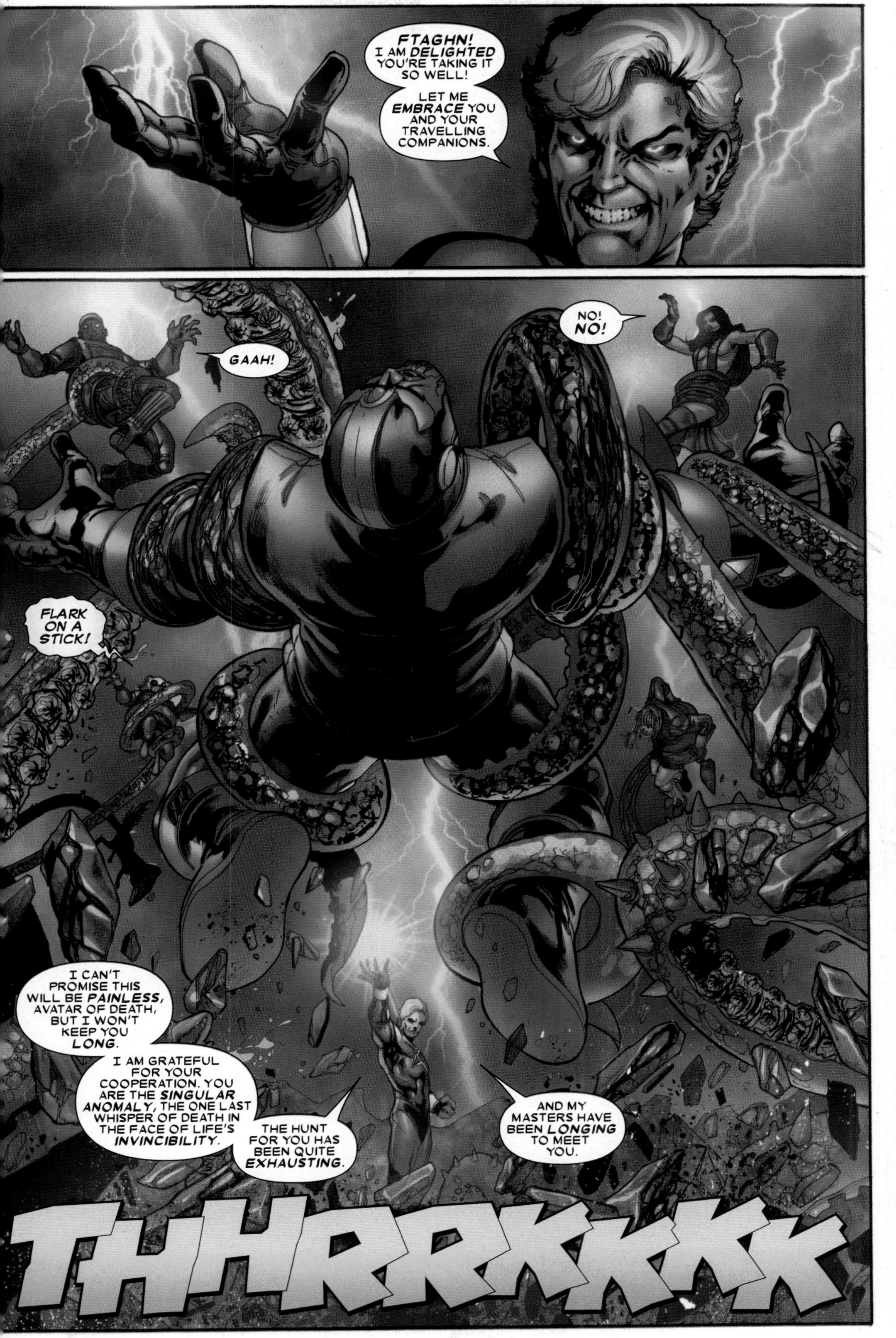
FTAGHN! I AM DELIGHTED YOU'RE TAKING IT SO WELL!
LET ME EMBRACE YOU AND YOUR TRAVELLING COMPANIONS.
NO! NO!
GAAH!
FLARK ON A STICK!
I CAN'T PROMISE THIS WILL BE PAINLESS, AVATAR OF DEATH, BUT I WON'T KEEP YOU LONG.
I AM GRATEFUL FOR YOUR COOPERATION. YOU ARE THE SINGULAR ANOMALY, THE ONE LAST WHISPER OF DEATH IN THE FACE OF LIFE'S INVINCIBILITY.
THE HUNT FOR YOU HAS BEEN QUITE EXHAUSTING.
AND MY MASTERS HAVE BEEN LONGING TO MEET YOU.
THHRRKKKK

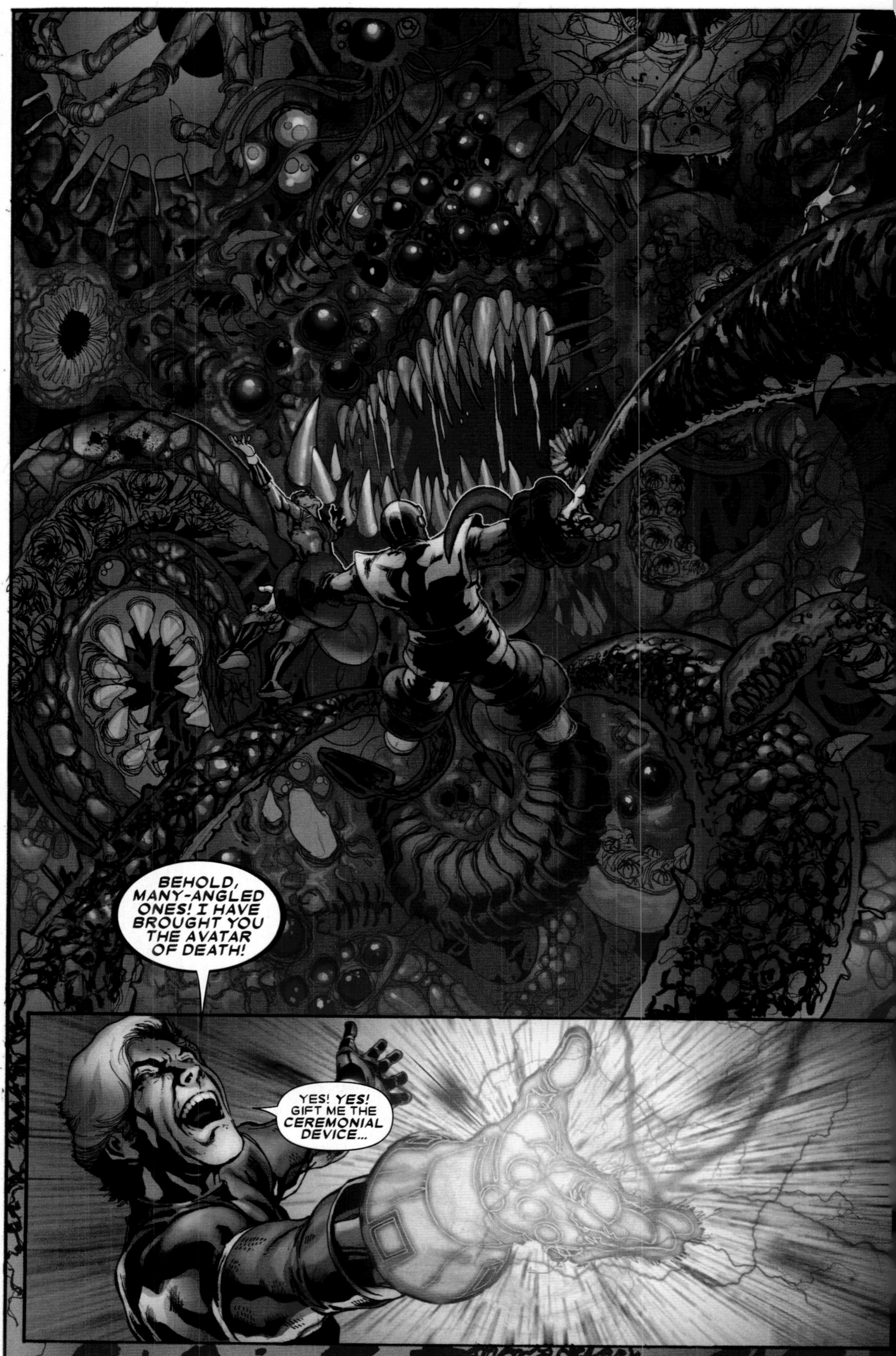
BEHOLD, MANY-ANGLED ONES! I HAVE BROUGHT YOU THE AVATAR OF DEATH!
YES! YES! GIFT ME THE CEREMONIAL DEVICE...

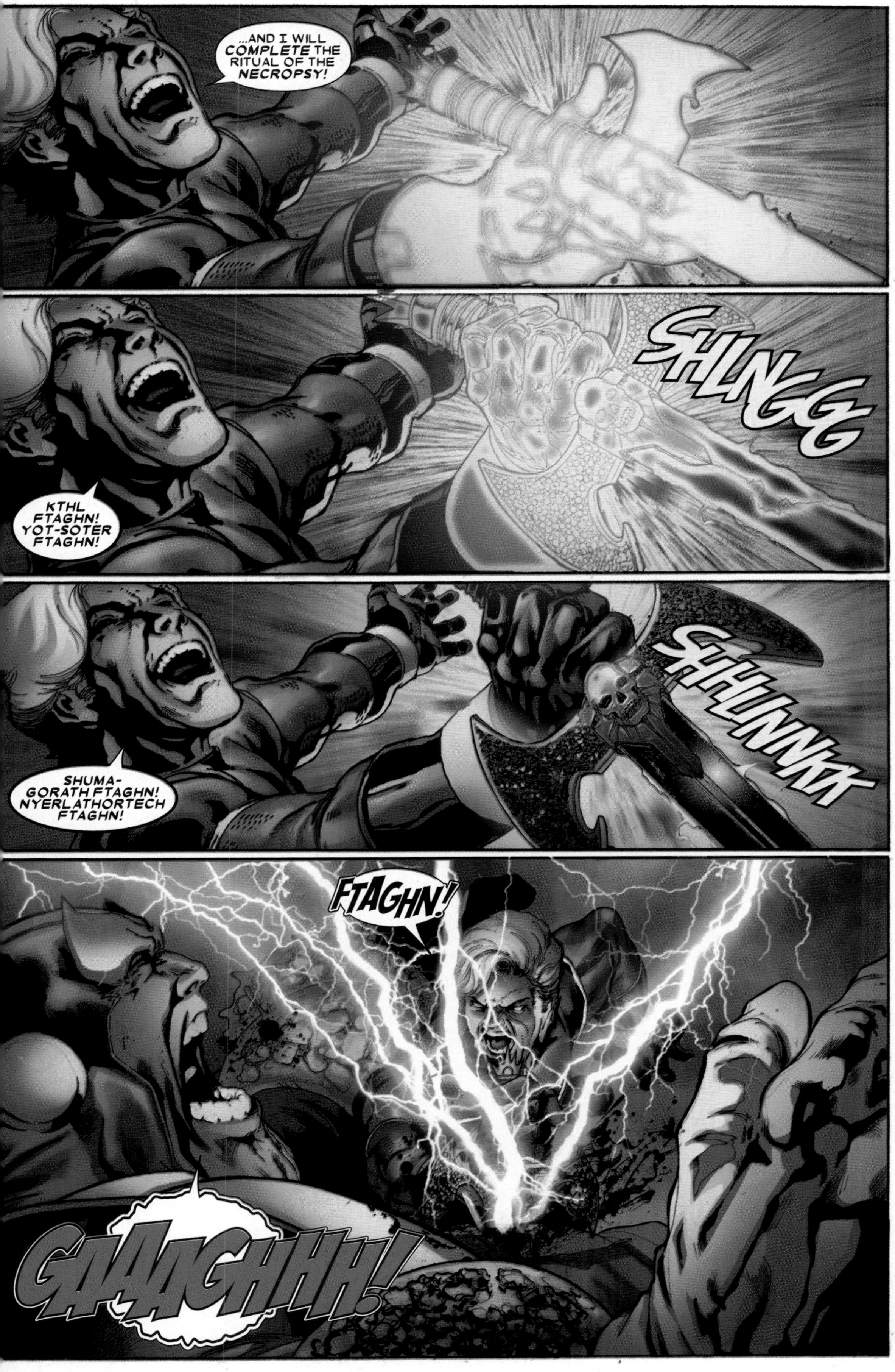
...AND I WILL COMPLETE THE RITUAL OF THE NECROPSY!
SHLNGGG
KTHL FTAGHN! YOT-SOTER FTAGHN!
SHHUNNKK
SHUMA-GORATH FTAGHN! NYERLATHORTECH FTAGHN!
FTAGHN!
GAAAGHHH!

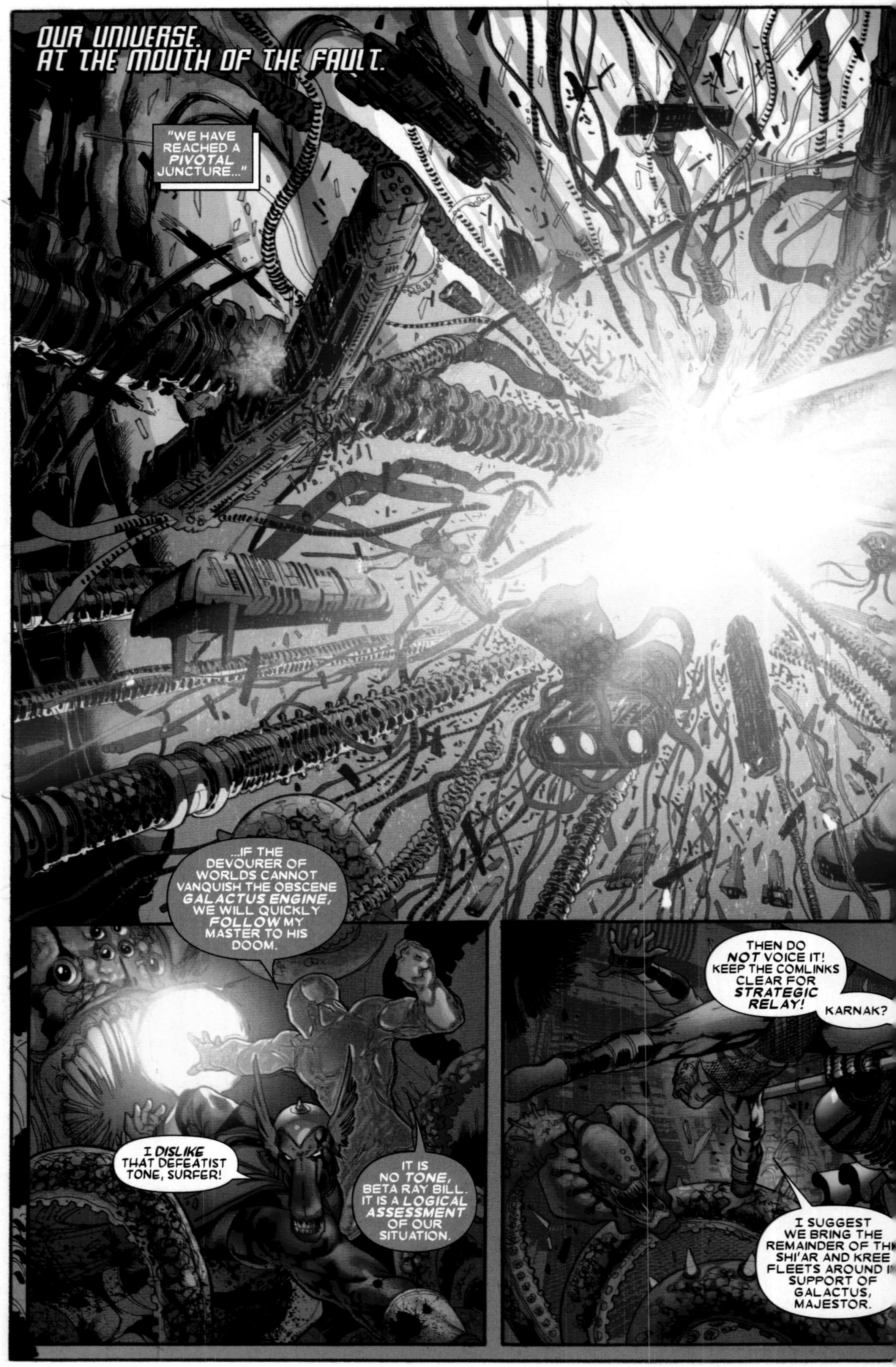
OUR UNIVERSE.
AT THE MOUTH OF THE FAULT.
"WE HAVE REACHED A PIVOTAL JUNCTURE..."
...IF THE DEVOURER OF WORLDS CANNOT VANQUISH THE OBSCENE GALACTUS ENGINE, WE WILL QUICKLY FOLLOW MY MASTER TO HIS DOOM.
I DISLIKE THAT DEFEATIST TONE, SURFER!
IT IS NO TONE, BETA RAY BILL. IT IS A LOGICAL ASSESSMENT OF OUR SITUATION.
THEN DO NOT VOICE IT! KEEP THE COMLINKS CLEAR FOR STRATEGIC RELAY!
KARNAK?
I SUGGEST WE BRING THE REMAINDER OF TH SHI'AR AND KREE FLEETS AROUND I SUPPORT OF GALACTUS, MAJESTOR.

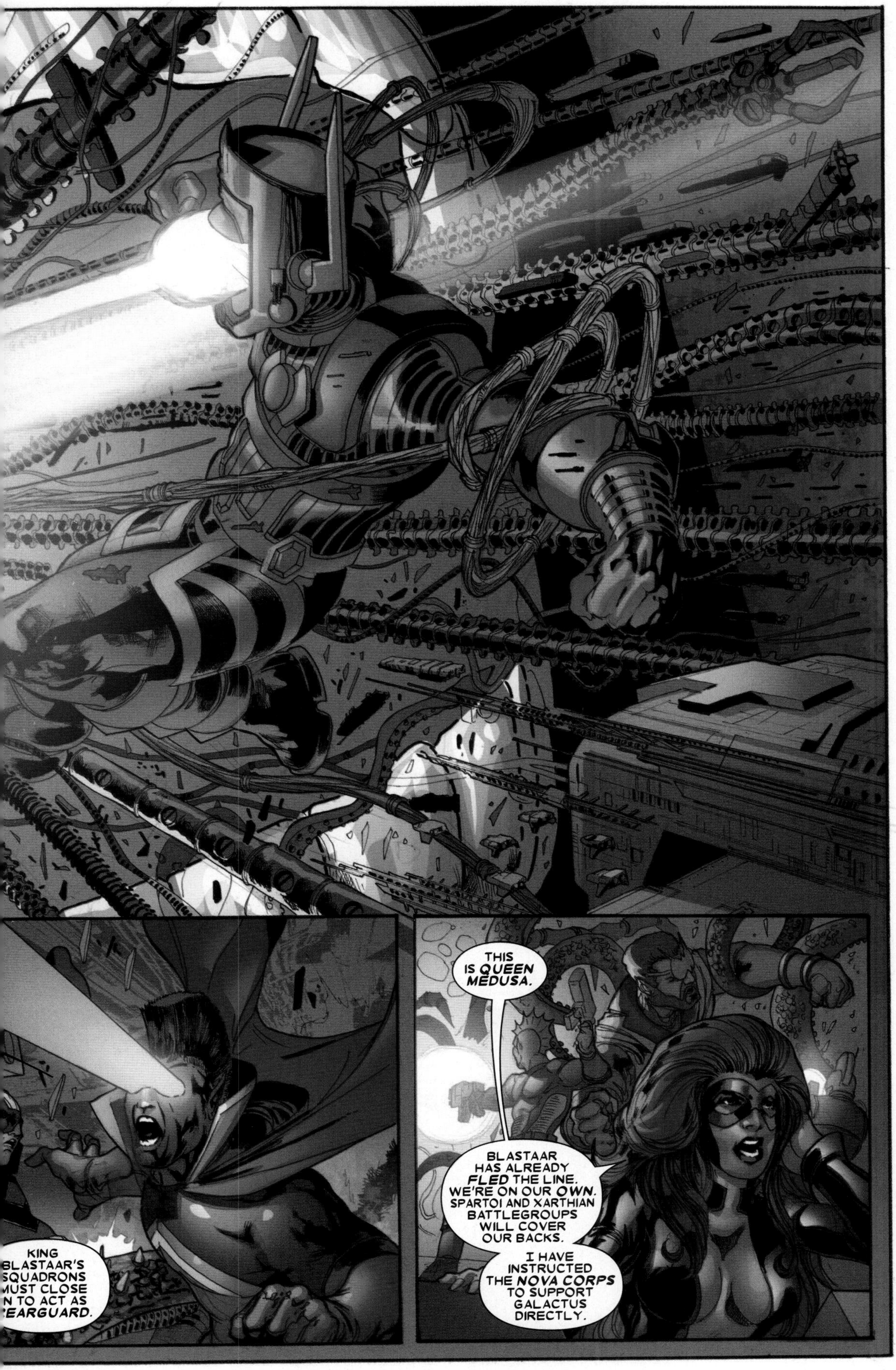
KING BLASTAAR'S SQUADRONS MUST CLOSE N TO ACT AS EARGUARD.
THIS IS QUEEN MEDUSA.
BLASTAAR HAS ALREADY FLED THE LINE. WE'RE ON OUR OWN. SPARTOI AND XARTHIAN BATTLEGROUPS WILL COVER OUR BACKS.
I HAVE INSTRUCTED THE NOVA CORPS TO SUPPORT GALACTUS DIRECTLY.

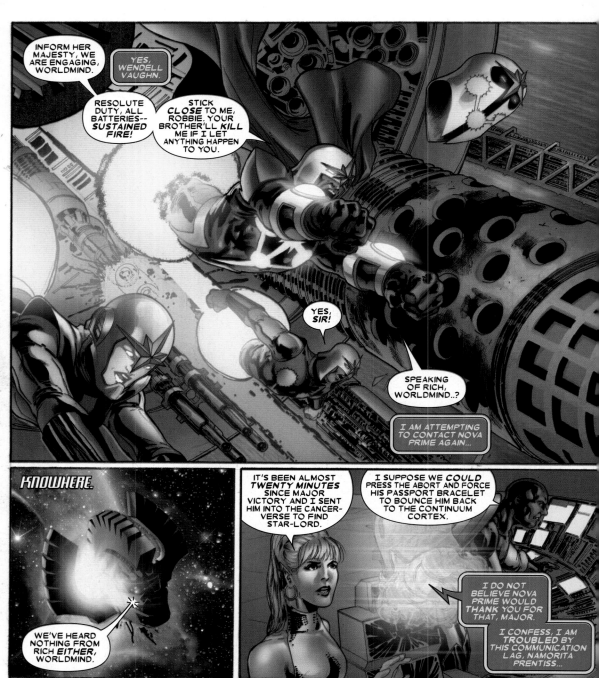

INFORM HER MAJESTY, WE ARE ENGAGING, WORLDMIND.

YES, WENDELL VAUGHN.

RESOLUTE DUTY, ALL BATTERIES-- *SUSTAINED* FIRE!

STICK *CLOSE* TO ME, ROBBIE. YOUR BROTHER'LL *KILL* ME IF I LET ANYTHING HAPPEN TO YOU.

YES, SIR!

SPEAKING OF RICH, WORLDMIND..?

I AM ATTEMPTING TO CONTACT NOVA PRIME AGAIN...

KNOWHERE.

WE'VE HEARD NOTHING FROM RICH *EITHER*, WORLDMIND.

IT'S BEEN ALMOST *TWENTY MINUTES* SINCE MAJOR VICTORY AND I SENT HIM INTO THE CANCER-VERSE TO FIND STAR-LORD.

I SUPPOSE WE *COULD* PRESS THE ABORT AND FORCE HIS PASSPORT BRACELET TO BOUNCE HIM BACK TO THE CONTINUUM CORTEX.

I DO NOT BELIEVE NOVA PRIME WOULD *THANK* YOU FOR THAT, MAJOR.

I CONFESS, I AM TROUBLED BY THIS COMMUNICATION LAG, NAMORITA PRENTISS...

...MY BOND WITH NOVA PRIME HAS ALWAYS BEEN CLOSE.

SO HAS *MINE*, WORLDMIND.

SOMETHING'S HAPPENING.

HELL, SOMETHING'S *REALLY* HAPPENING.

THE CORTEX'S INTERSTITIAL SENSORS HAVE SUDDENLY SPIKED...

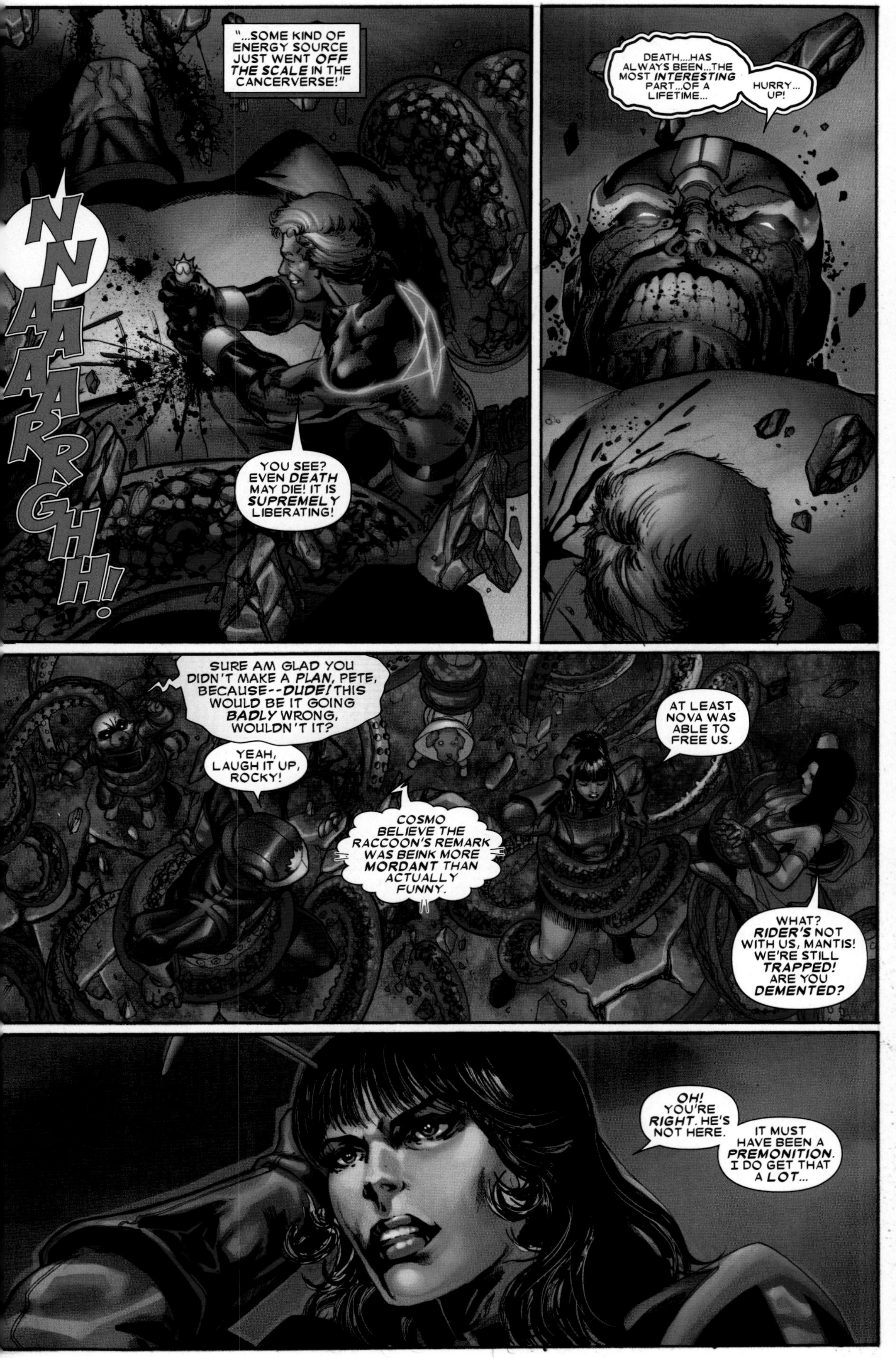
"...SOME KIND OF ENERGY SOURCE JUST WENT OFF THE SCALE IN THE CANCERVERSE!"
NNAAAARRGHH!
YOU SEE? EVEN DEATH MAY DIE! IT IS SUPREMELY LIBERATING!
DEATH...HAS ALWAYS BEEN...THE MOST INTERESTING PART...OF A LIFETIME...
HURRY... UP!
SURE AM GLAD YOU DIDN'T MAKE A PLAN, PETE, BECAUSE--DUDE! THIS WOULD BE IT GOING BADLY WRONG, WOULDN'T IT?
YEAH, LAUGH IT UP, ROCKY!
AT LEAST NOVA WAS ABLE TO FREE US.
COSMO BELIEVE THE RACCOON'S REMARK WAS BEINK MORE MORDANT THAN ACTUALLY FUNNY.
WHAT? RIDER'S NOT WITH US, MANTIS! WE'RE STILL TRAPPED! ARE YOU DEMENTED?
OH! YOU'RE RIGHT. HE'S NOT HERE.
IT MUST HAVE BEEN A PREMONITION. I DO GET THAT A LOT...

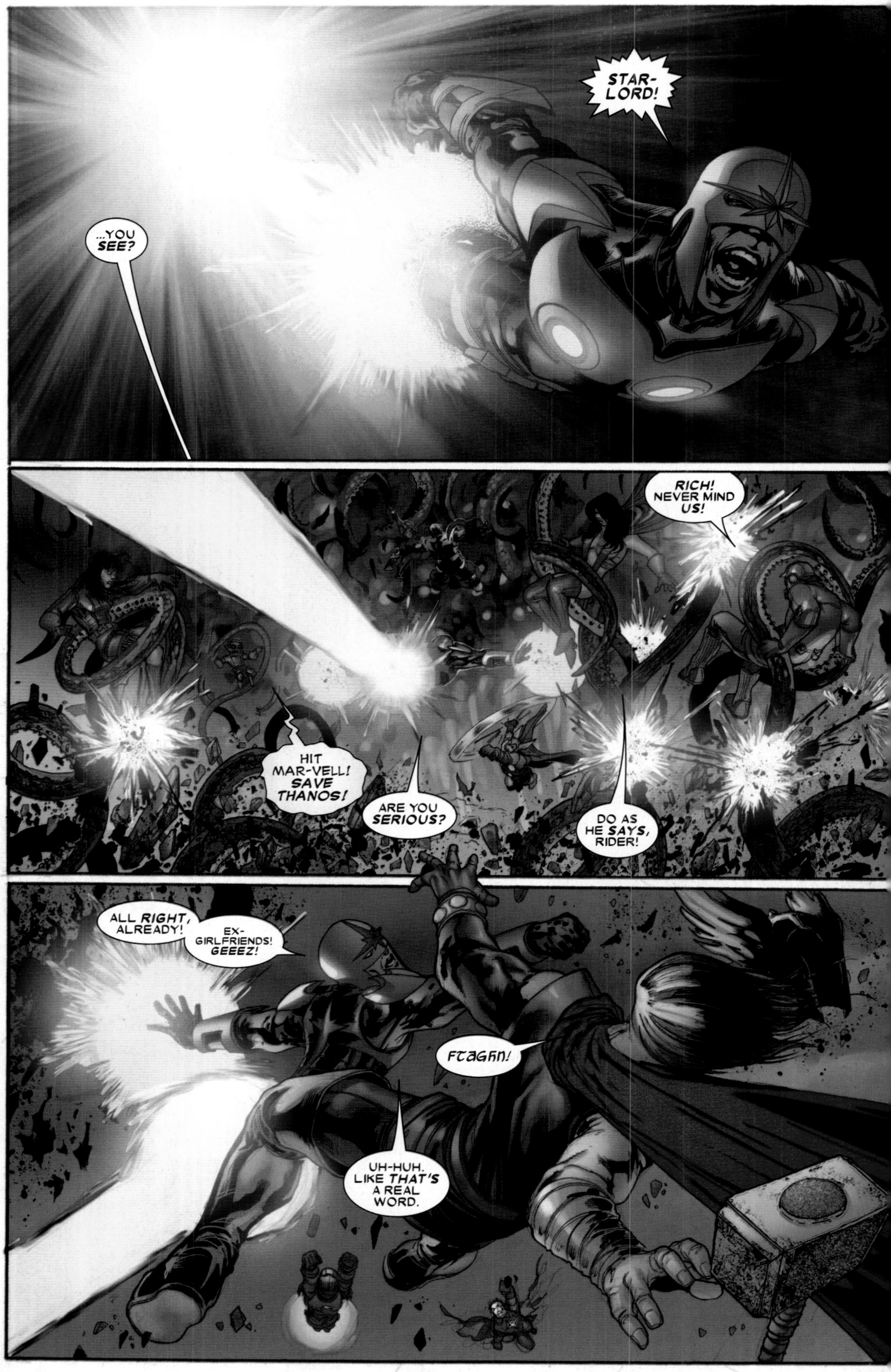
STAR-LORD!
...YOU SEE?
RICH! NEVER MIND US!
HIT MAR-VELL! SAVE THANOS!
ARE YOU SERIOUS?
DO AS HE SAYS, RIDER!
ALL RIGHT, ALREADY!
EX-GIRLFRIENDS! GEEEZ!
FTAGHN!
UH-HUH. LIKE THAT'S A REAL WORD.

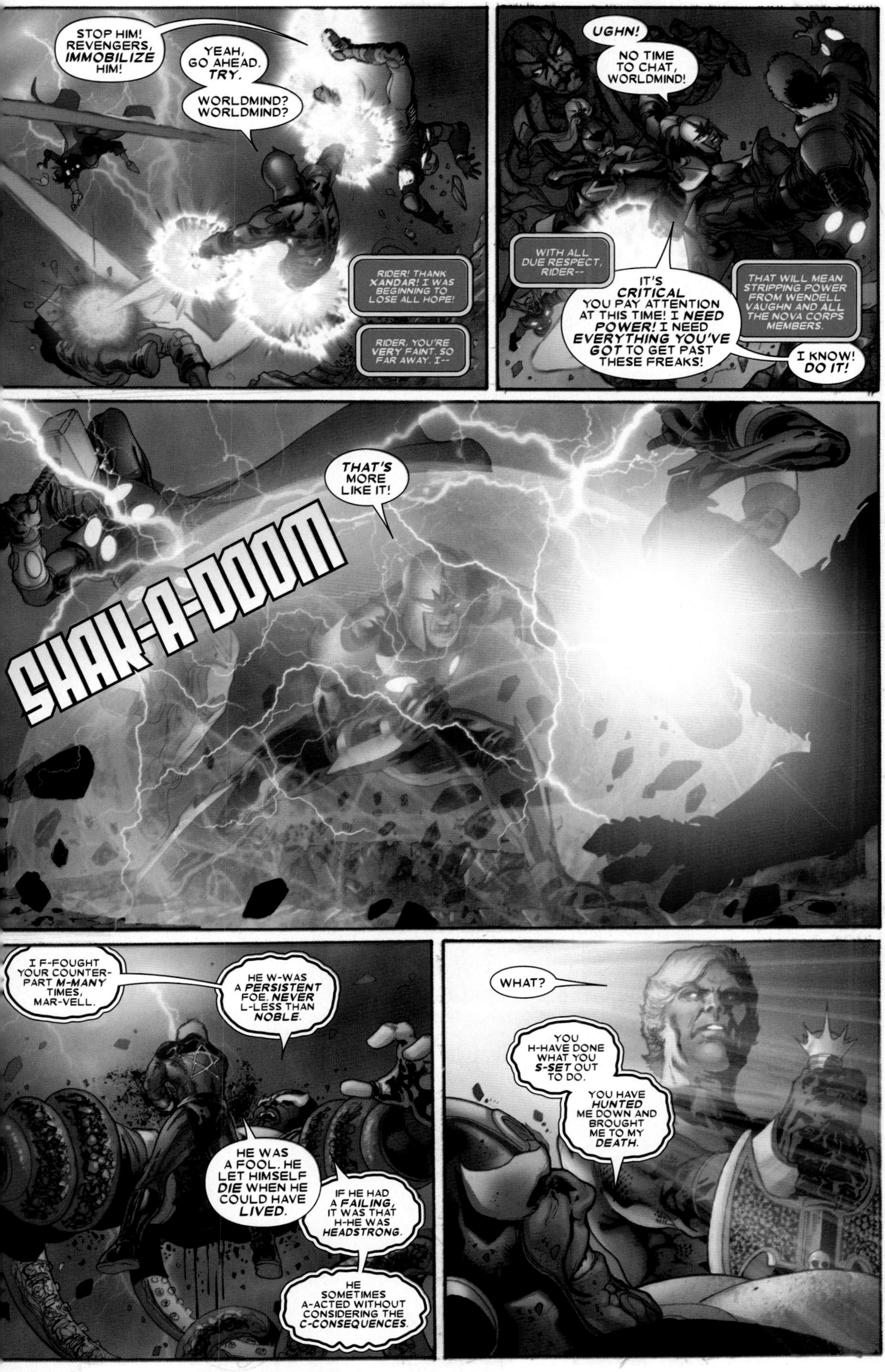
STOP HIM! REVENGERS, IMMOBILIZE HIM!
YEAH, GO AHEAD. TRY.
WORLDMIND? WORLDMIND?
RIDER! THANK XANDAR! I WAS BEGINNING TO LOSE ALL HOPE!
RIDER, YOU'RE VERY FAINT. SO FAR AWAY. I--
UGHN!
NO TIME TO CHAT, WORLDMIND!
WITH ALL DUE RESPECT, RIDER--
IT'S CRITICAL YOU PAY ATTENTION AT THIS TIME! I NEED POWER! I NEED EVERYTHING YOU'VE GOT TO GET PAST THESE FREAKS!
THAT WILL MEAN STRIPPING POWER FROM WENDELL VAUGHN AND ALL THE NOVA CORPS MEMBERS.
I KNOW! DO IT!
THAT'S MORE LIKE IT!
SHAK-A-DOOM
I F-FOUGHT YOUR COUNTER-PART M-MANY TIMES, MAR-VELL.
HE W-WAS A PERSISTENT FOE. NEVER L-LESS THAN NOBLE.
HE WAS A FOOL. HE LET HIMSELF DIE WHEN HE COULD HAVE LIVED.
IF HE HAD A FAILING, IT WAS THAT H-HE WAS HEADSTRONG.
HE SOMETIMES A-ACTED WITHOUT CONSIDERING THE C-CONSEQUENCES.
WHAT?
YOU H-HAVE DONE WHAT YOU S-SET OUT TO DO.
YOU HAVE HUNTED ME DOWN AND BROUGHT ME TO MY DEATH.

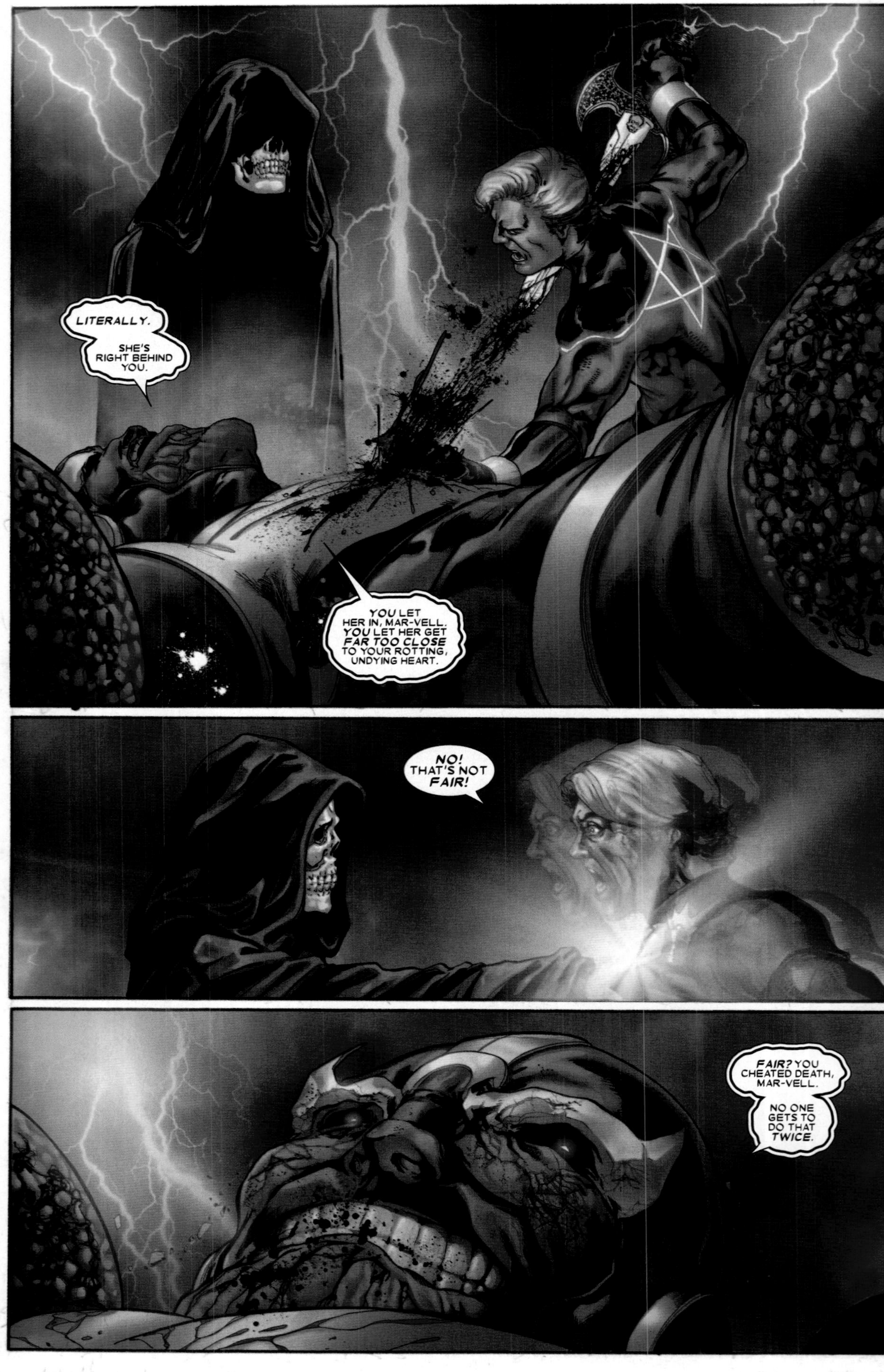
LITERALLY.
SHE'S RIGHT BEHIND YOU.
YOU LET HER IN, MAR-VELL. YOU LET HER GET FAR TOO CLOSE TO YOUR ROTTING, UNDYING HEART.
NO! THAT'S NOT FAIR!
FAIR? YOU CHEATED DEATH, MAR-VELL.
NO ONE GETS TO DO THAT TWICE.

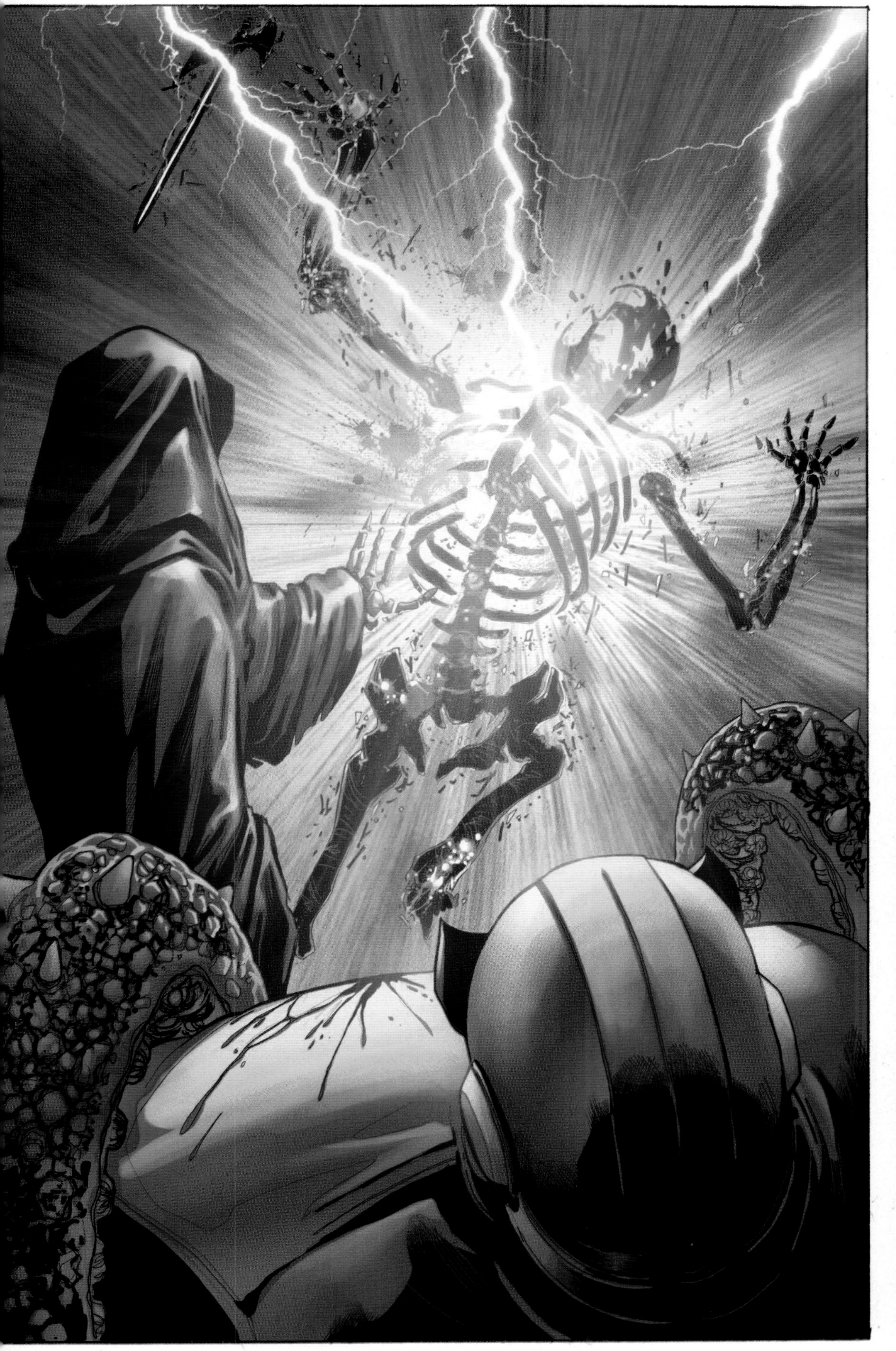

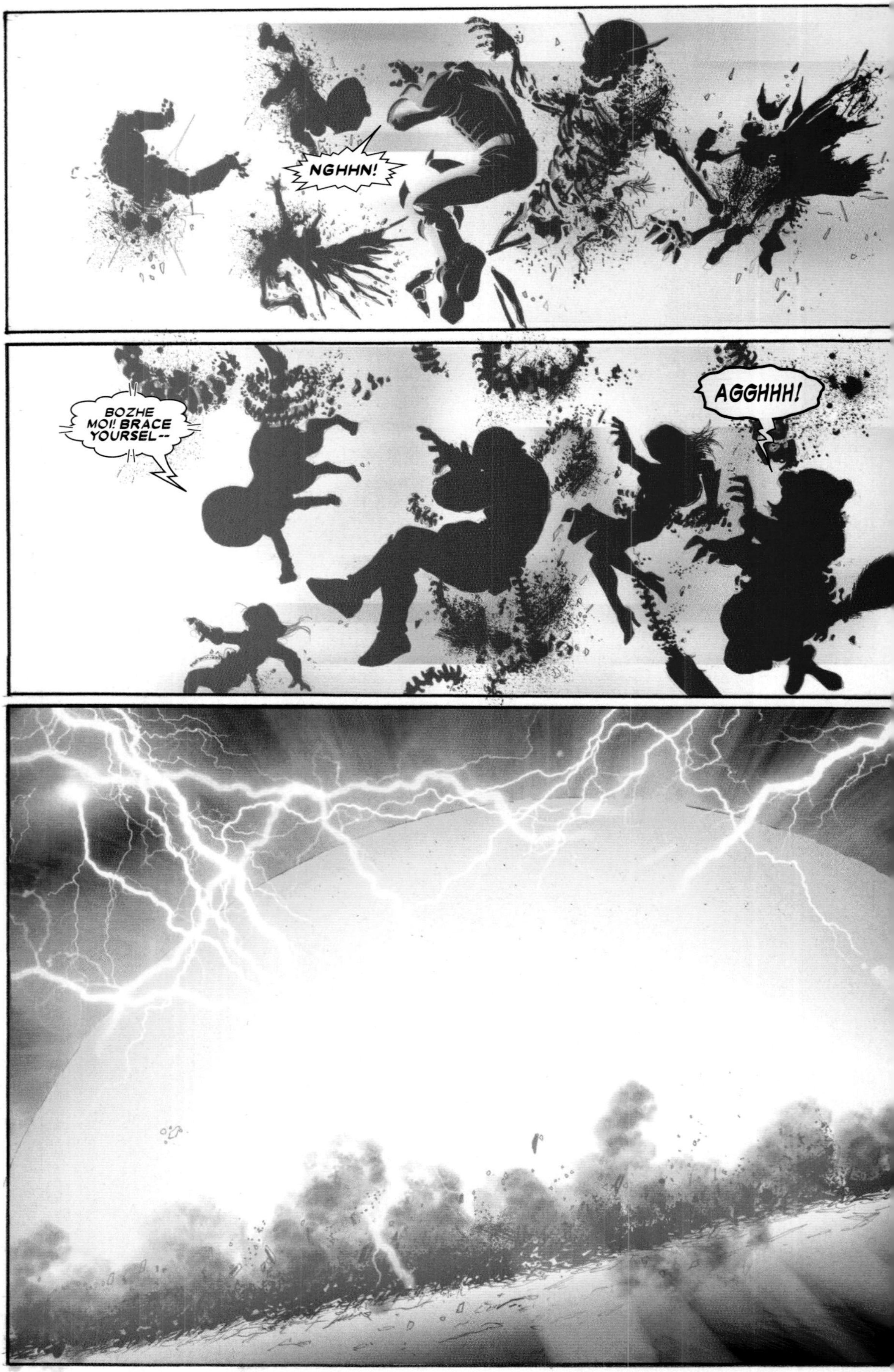
NGHHN!
BOZHE MOI! BRACE YOURSEL--
AGGHHH!

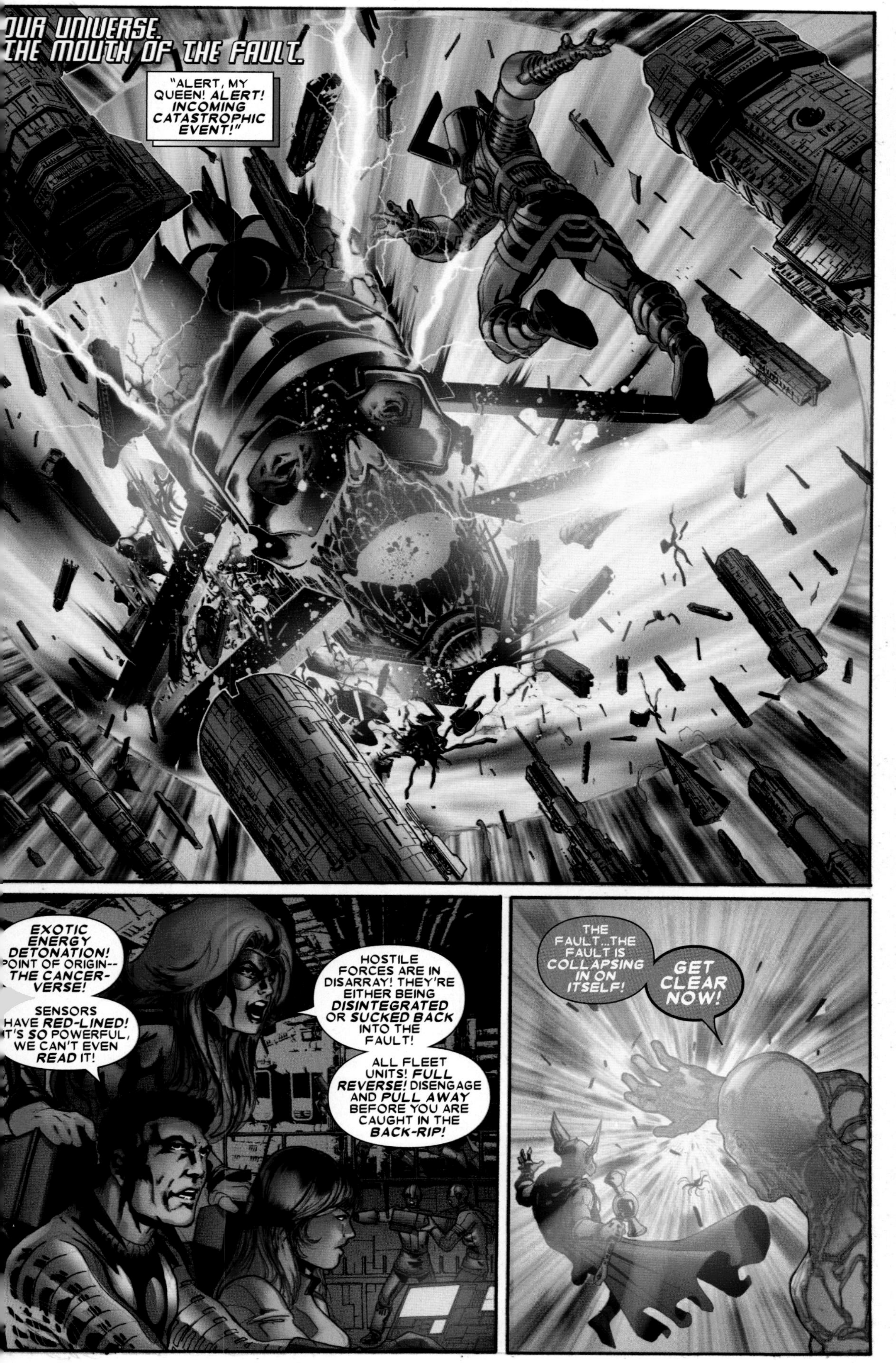
OUR UNIVERSE. THE MOUTH OF THE FAULT.
"ALERT, MY QUEEN! ALERT! INCOMING CATASTROPHIC EVENT!"
EXOTIC ENERGY DETONATION! POINT OF ORIGIN-- THE CANCERVERSE!
SENSORS HAVE RED-LINED! IT'S SO POWERFUL, WE CAN'T EVEN READ IT!
HOSTILE FORCES ARE IN DISARRAY! THEY'RE EITHER BEING DISINTEGRATED OR SUCKED BACK INTO THE FAULT!
ALL FLEET UNITS! FULL REVERSE! DISENGAGE AND PULL AWAY BEFORE YOU ARE CAUGHT IN THE BACK-RIP!
THE FAULT...THE FAULT IS COLLAPSING IN ON ITSELF!
GET CLEAR NOW!

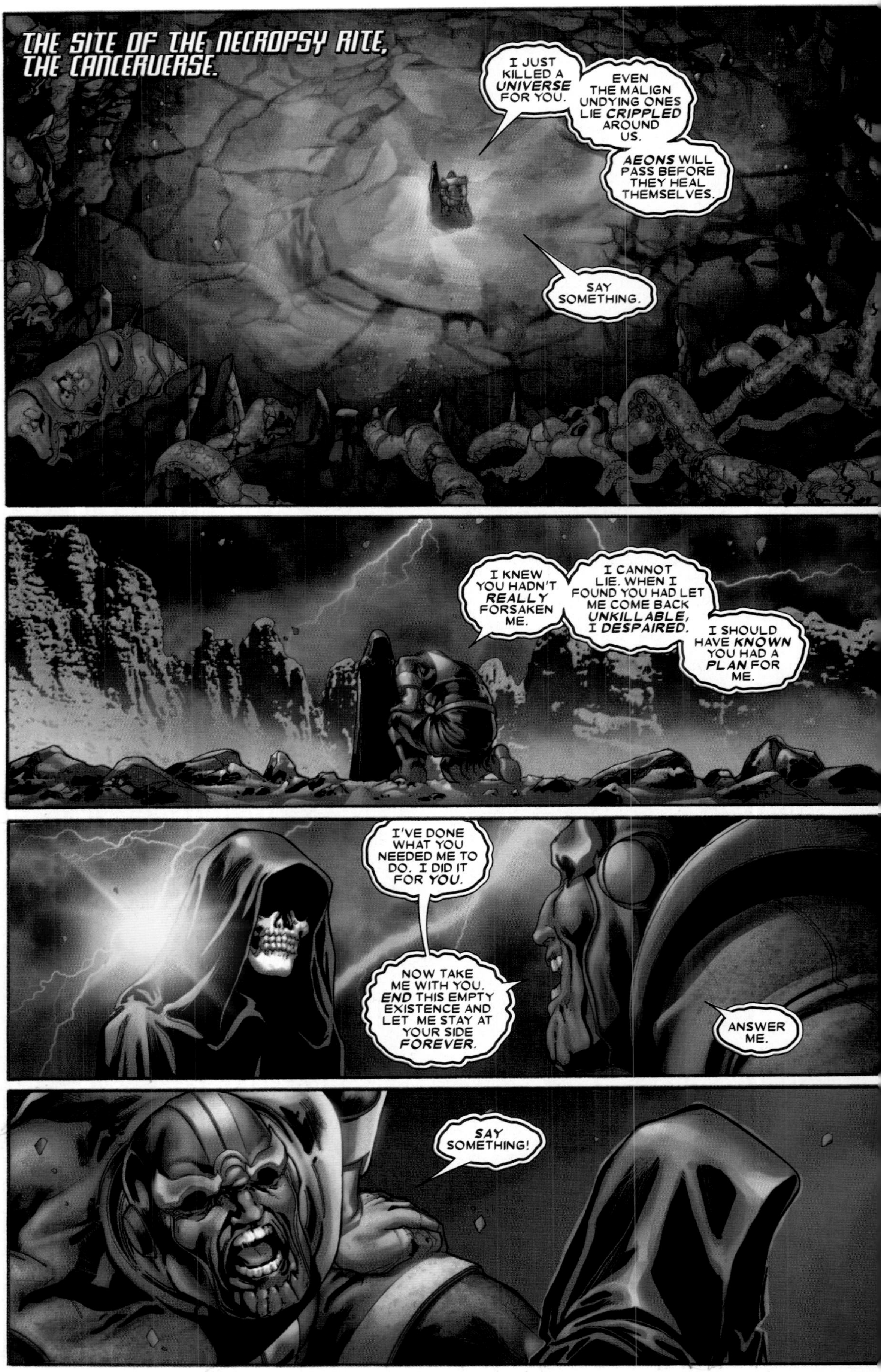
THE SITE OF THE NECROPSY RITE, THE CANCERVERSE.
I JUST KILLED A UNIVERSE FOR YOU.
EVEN THE MALIGN UNDYING ONES LIE CRIPPLED AROUND US.
AEONS WILL PASS BEFORE THEY HEAL THEMSELVES.
SAY SOMETHING.
I KNEW YOU HADN'T REALLY FORSAKEN ME.
I CANNOT LIE. WHEN I FOUND YOU HAD LET ME COME BACK UNKILLABLE, I DESPAIRED.
I SHOULD HAVE KNOWN YOU HAD A PLAN FOR ME.
I'VE DONE WHAT YOU NEEDED ME TO DO. I DID IT FOR YOU.
NOW TAKE ME WITH YOU. END THIS EMPTY EXISTENCE AND LET ME STAY AT YOUR SIDE FOREVER.
ANSWER ME.
SAY SOMETHING!

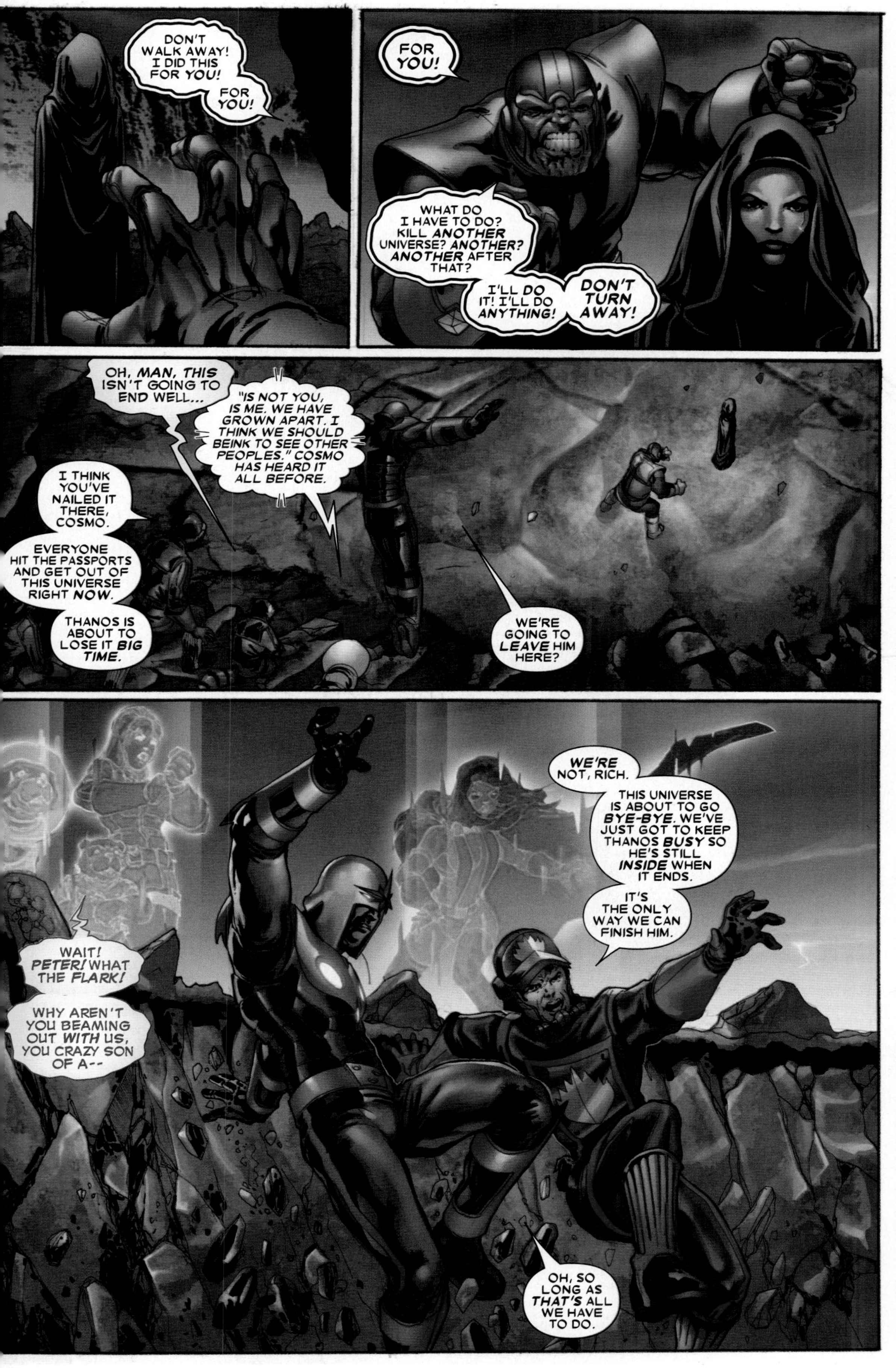
DON'T WALK AWAY! I DID THIS FOR YOU!
FOR YOU!
FOR YOU!
WHAT DO I HAVE TO DO? KILL ANOTHER UNIVERSE? ANOTHER? ANOTHER AFTER THAT?
I'LL DO IT! I'LL DO ANYTHING!
DON'T TURN AWAY!
OH, MAN, THIS ISN'T GOING TO END WELL...
"IS NOT YOU, IS ME. WE HAVE GROWN APART. I THINK WE SHOULD BEINK TO SEE OTHER PEOPLES." COSMO HAS HEARD IT ALL BEFORE.
I THINK YOU'VE NAILED IT THERE, COSMO.
EVERYONE HIT THE PASSPORTS AND GET OUT OF THIS UNIVERSE RIGHT NOW.
THANOS IS ABOUT TO LOSE IT BIG TIME.
WE'RE GOING TO LEAVE HIM HERE?
WE'RE NOT, RICH.
THIS UNIVERSE IS ABOUT TO GO BYE-BYE. WE'VE JUST GOT TO KEEP THANOS BUSY SO HE'S STILL INSIDE WHEN IT ENDS.
IT'S THE ONLY WAY WE CAN FINISH HIM.
WAIT! PETER! WHAT THE FLARK!
WHY AREN'T YOU BEAMING OUT WITH US, YOU CRAZY SON OF A--
OH, SO LONG AS THAT'S ALL WE HAVE TO DO.

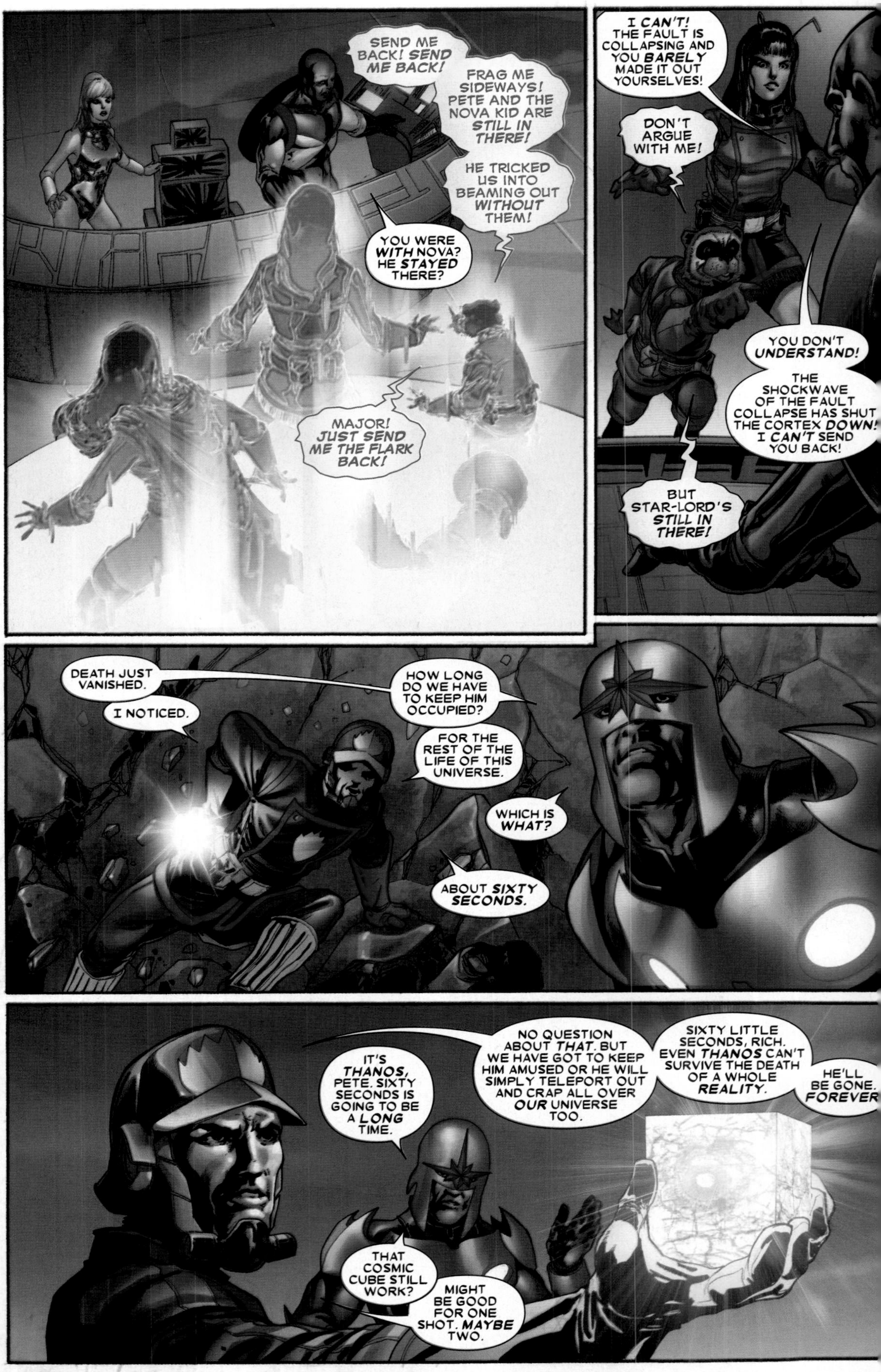

SEND ME BACK! SEND ME BACK!
FRAG ME SIDEWAYS! PETE AND THE NOVA KID ARE STILL IN THERE!
HE TRICKED US INTO BEAMING OUT WITHOUT THEM!
YOU WERE WITH NOVA? HE STAYED THERE?
MAJOR! JUST SEND ME THE FLARK BACK!
I CAN'T! THE FAULT IS COLLAPSING AND YOU BARELY MADE IT OUT YOURSELVES!
DON'T ARGUE WITH ME!
YOU DON'T UNDERSTAND!
THE SHOCKWAVE OF THE FAULT COLLAPSE HAS SHUT THE CORTEX DOWN! I CAN'T SEND YOU BACK!
BUT STAR-LORD'S STILL IN THERE!
DEATH JUST VANISHED.
I NOTICED.
HOW LONG DO WE HAVE TO KEEP HIM OCCUPIED?
FOR THE REST OF THE LIFE OF THIS UNIVERSE.
WHICH IS WHAT?
ABOUT SIXTY SECONDS.
IT'S THANOS, PETE. SIXTY SECONDS IS GOING TO BE A LONG TIME.
NO QUESTION ABOUT THAT. BUT WE HAVE GOT TO KEEP HIM AMUSED OR HE WILL SIMPLY TELEPORT OUT AND CRAP ALL OVER OUR UNIVERSE TOO.
SIXTY LITTLE SECONDS, RICH. EVEN THANOS CAN'T SURVIVE THE DEATH OF A WHOLE REALITY.
HE'LL BE GONE. FOREVER
THAT COSMIC CUBE STILL WORK?
MIGHT BE GOOD FOR ONE SHOT. MAYBE TWO.

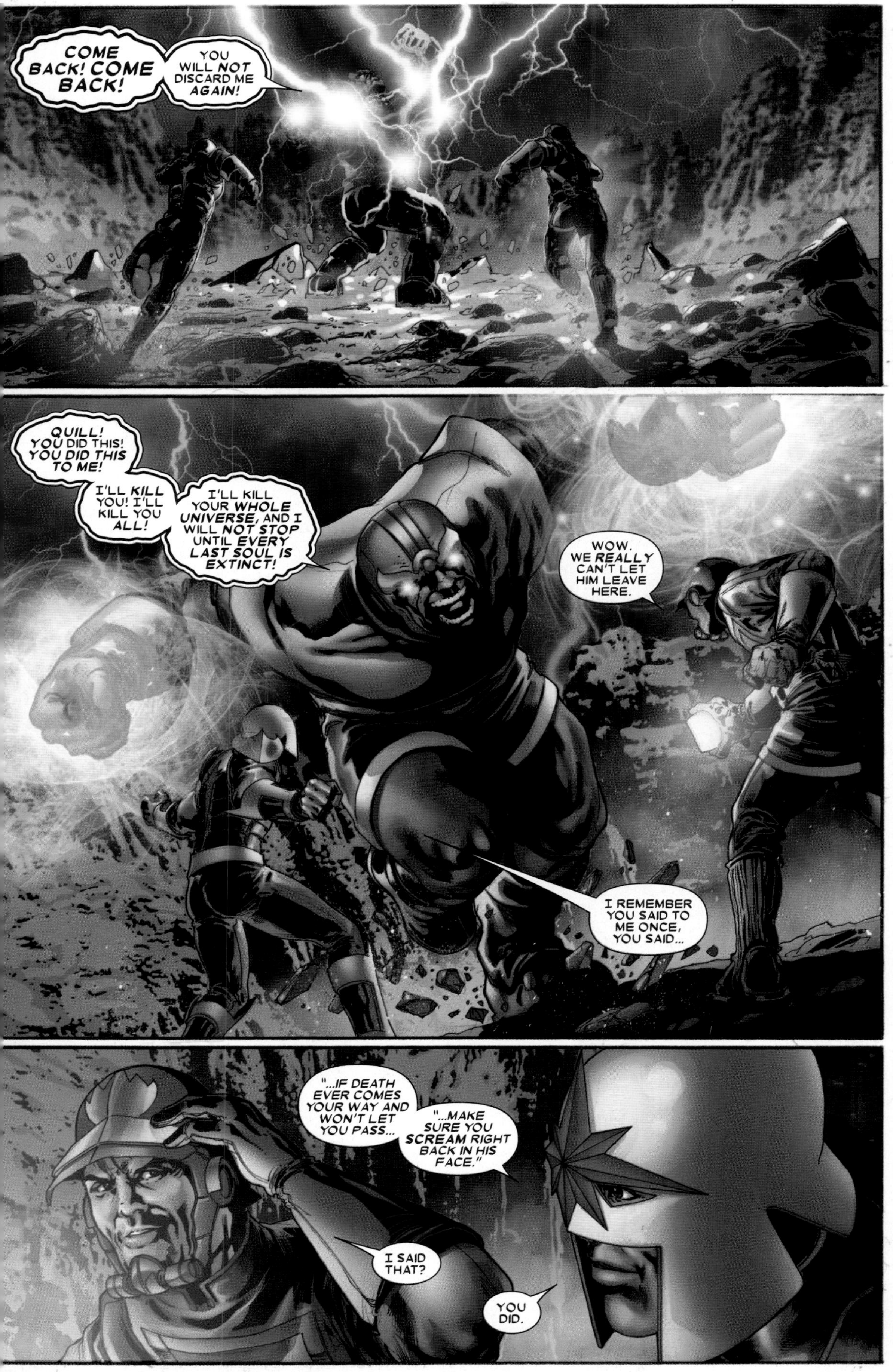
COME BACK! COME BACK!
YOU WILL NOT DISCARD ME AGAIN!
QUILL! YOU DID THIS! YOU DID THIS TO ME!
I'LL KILL YOU! I'LL KILL YOU ALL!
I'LL KILL YOUR WHOLE UNIVERSE, AND I WILL NOT STOP UNTIL EVERY LAST SOUL IS EXTINCT!
WOW. WE REALLY CAN'T LET HIM LEAVE HERE.
I REMEMBER YOU SAID TO ME ONCE, YOU SAID...
"...IF DEATH EVER COMES YOUR WAY AND WON'T LET YOU PASS...
"...MAKE SURE YOU SCREAM RIGHT BACK IN HIS FACE."
I SAID THAT?
YOU DID.

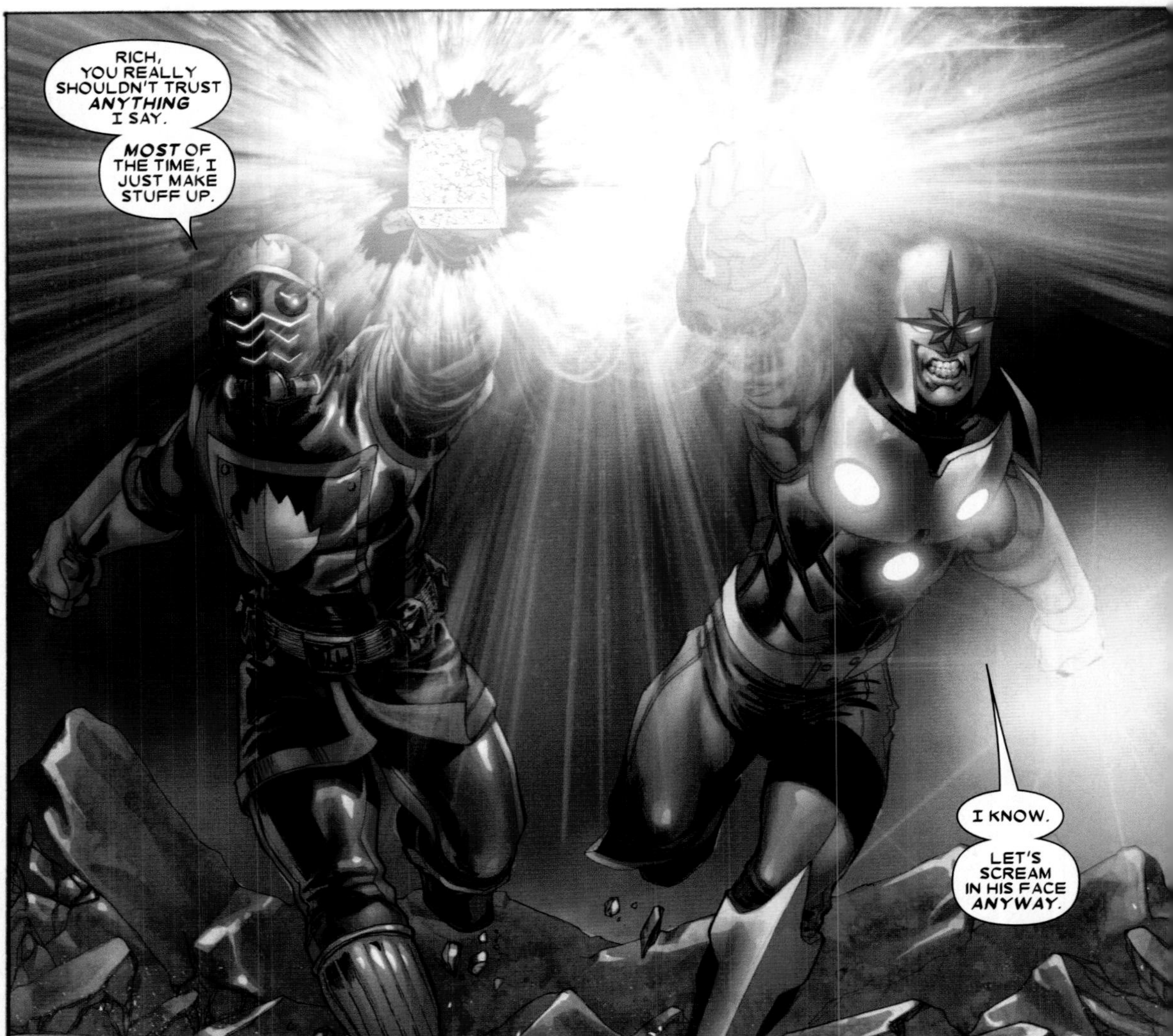
RICH, YOU REALLY SHOULDN'T TRUST ANYTHING I SAY.
MOST OF THE TIME, I JUST MAKE STUFF UP.
I KNOW.
LET'S SCREAM IN HIS FACE ANYWAY.

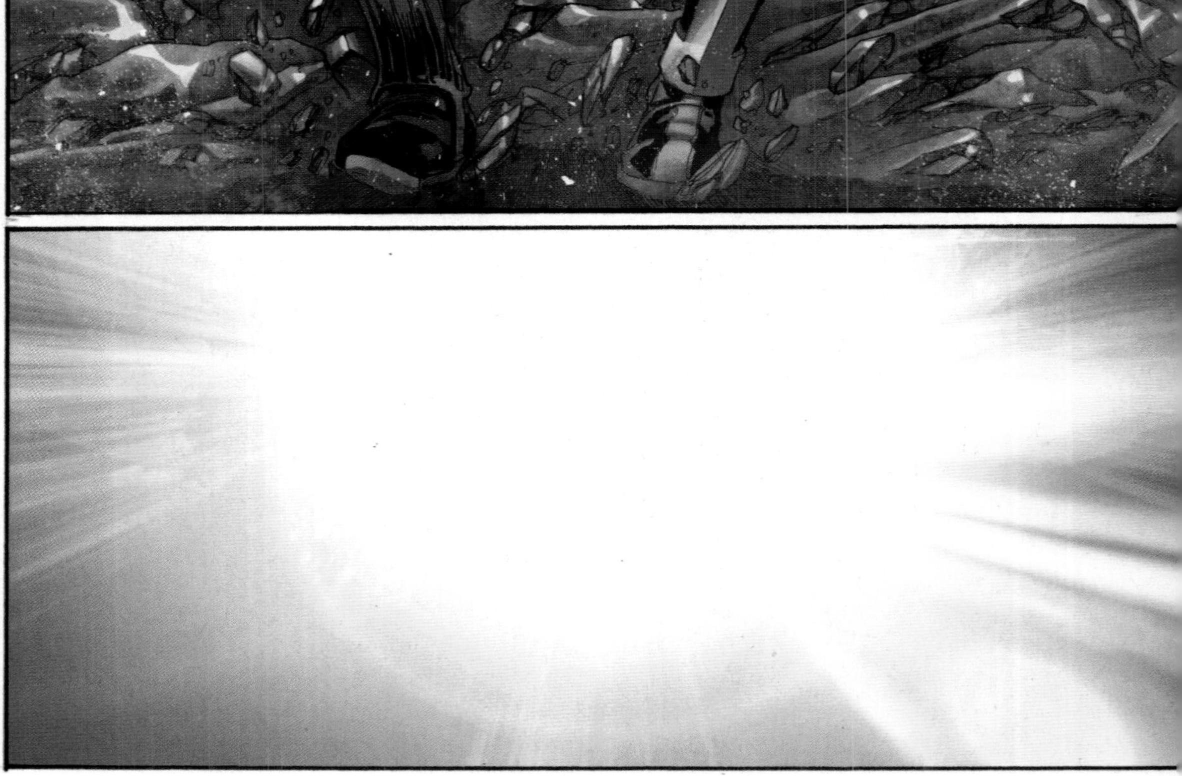

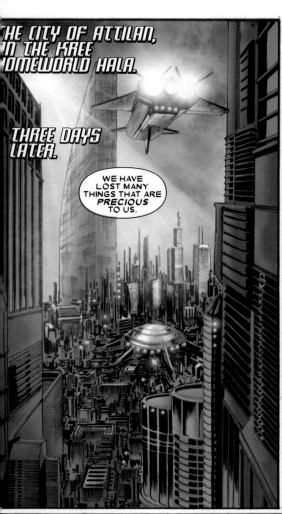

THE CITY OF ATTILAN, IN THE KREE HOMEWORLD HALA.

THREE DAYS LATER.

WE HAVE LOST MANY THINGS THAT ARE *PRECIOUS* TO US.

BUT WE HAVE *PREVAILED*.

THE FAULT HAS COLLAPSED AND SEALED *FOREVER*. THE THREAT OF THE MONSTROUS CANCERVERSE HAS BEEN LIFTED FROM US.

THE CANCERVERSE *ITSELF* HAS, AS FAR AS WE CAN TELL, BEEN *ANNIHILATED*.

ALL THAT REMAINS FOR US TO DO IS REBUILD OUR SHATTERED DOMAINS.

I SAY "*ALL*" LIKE IT WILL BE *SIMPLE*.

TODAY, WE SIMPLY GATHER TO REMEMBER AND *HONOR* THOSE WHO HAVE FALLEN IN THE COURSE OF THIS NIGHTMARISH STRUGGLE.

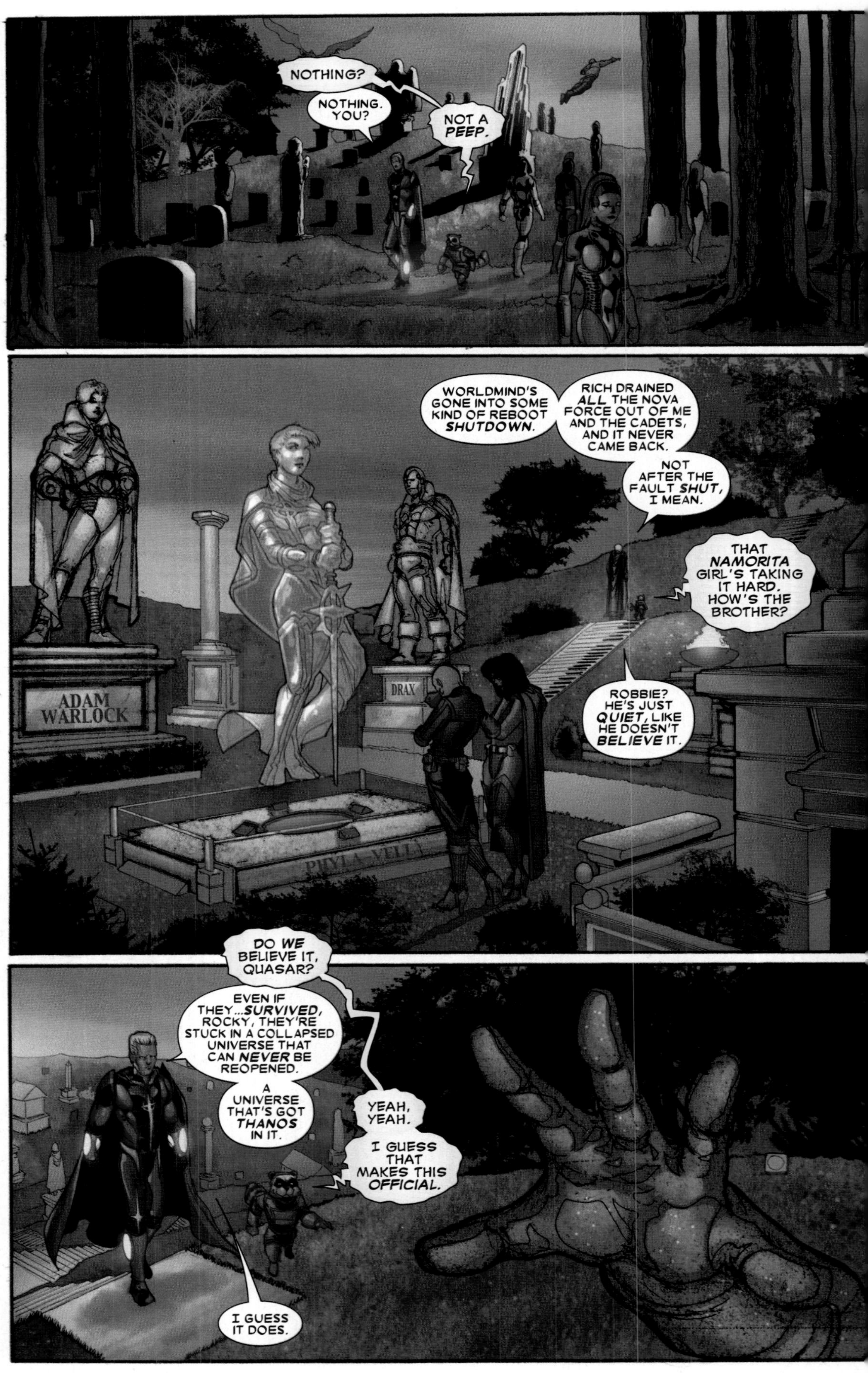
NOTHING?
NOTHING. YOU?
NOT A PEEP.
WORLDMIND'S GONE INTO SOME KIND OF REBOOT SHUTDOWN.
RICH DRAINED ALL THE NOVA FORCE OUT OF ME AND THE CADETS, AND IT NEVER CAME BACK.
NOT AFTER THE FAULT SHUT, I MEAN.
THAT NAMORITA GIRL'S TAKING IT HARD. HOW'S THE BROTHER?
ROBBIE? HE'S JUST QUIET, LIKE HE DOESN'T BELIEVE IT.
ADAM WARLOCK
DRAX
PHYLA-VELL
DO WE BELIEVE IT, QUASAR?
EVEN IF THEY...SURVIVED, ROCKY, THEY'RE STUCK IN A COLLAPSED UNIVERSE THAT CAN NEVER BE REOPENED.
A UNIVERSE THAT'S GOT THANOS IN IT.
YEAH, YEAH.
I GUESS THAT MAKES THIS OFFICIAL.
I GUESS IT DOES.

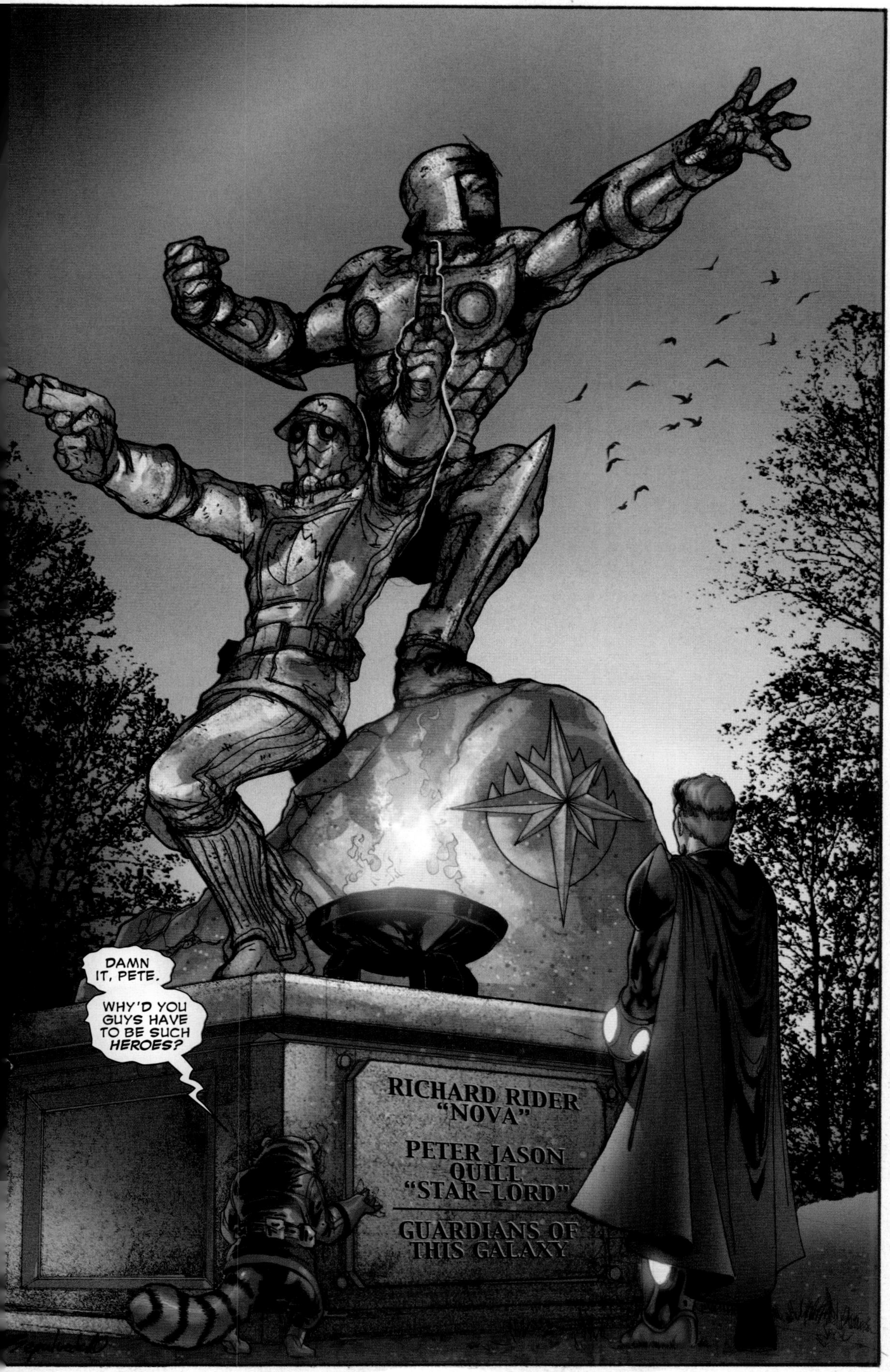
DAMN IT, PETE.
WHY'D YOU GUYS HAVE TO BE SUCH HEROES?
RICHARD RIDER "NOVA"
PETER JASON QUILL "STAR-LORD"
GUARDIANS OF THIS GALAXY

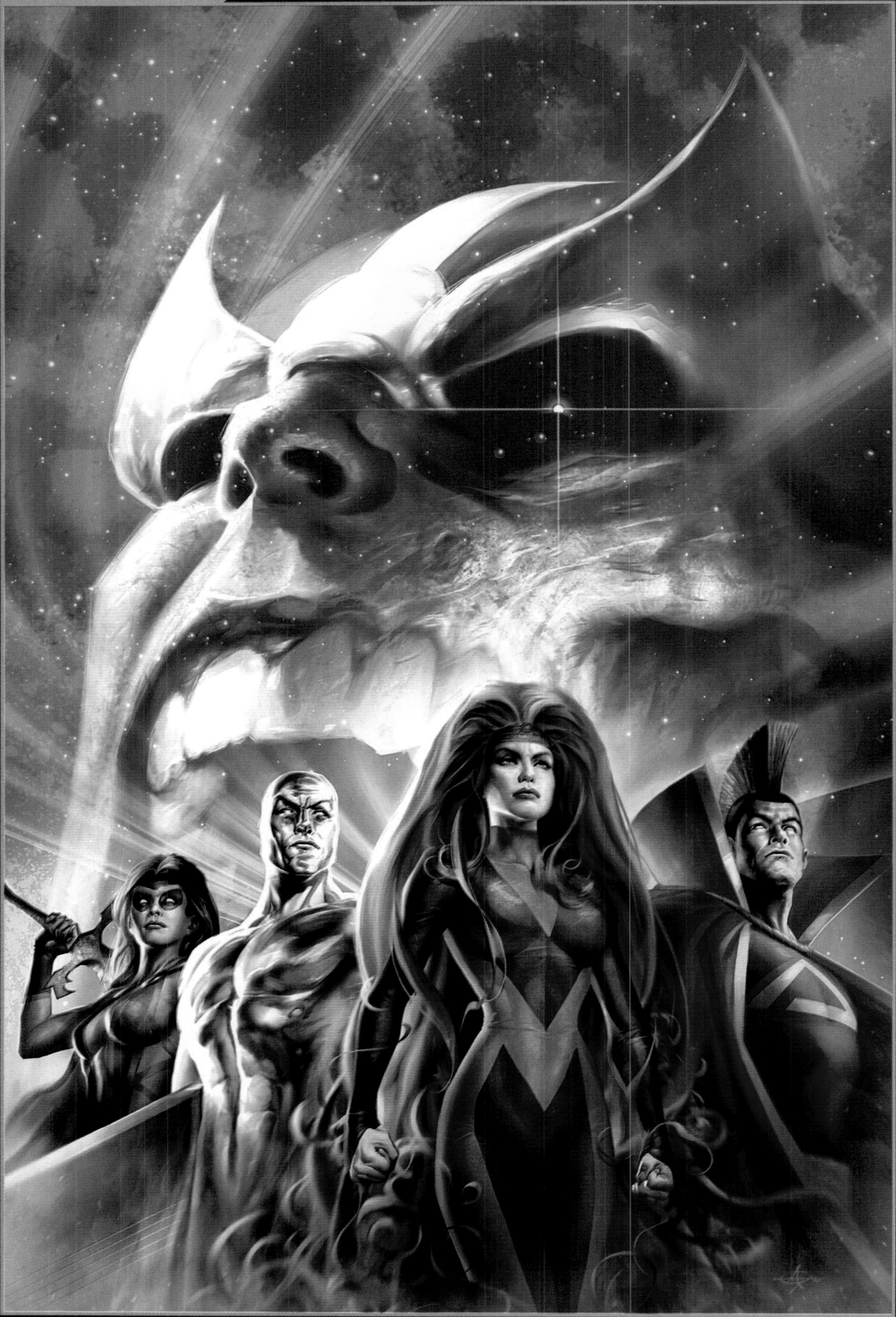

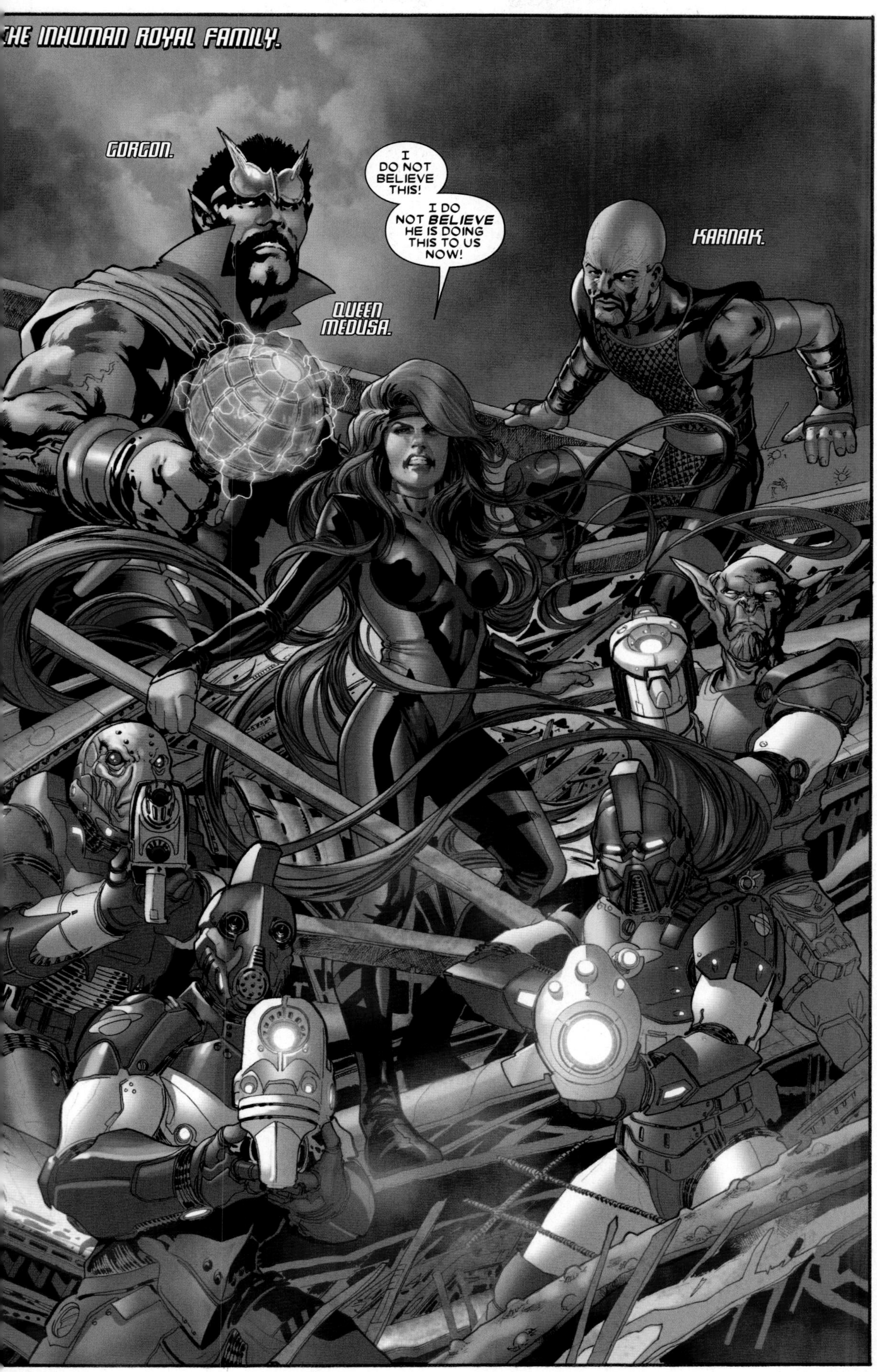
THE INHUMAN ROYAL FAMILY.
GORGON.
I DO NOT BELIEVE THIS!
I DO NOT BELIEVE HE IS DOING THIS TO US NOW!
QUEEN MEDUSA.
KARNAK.

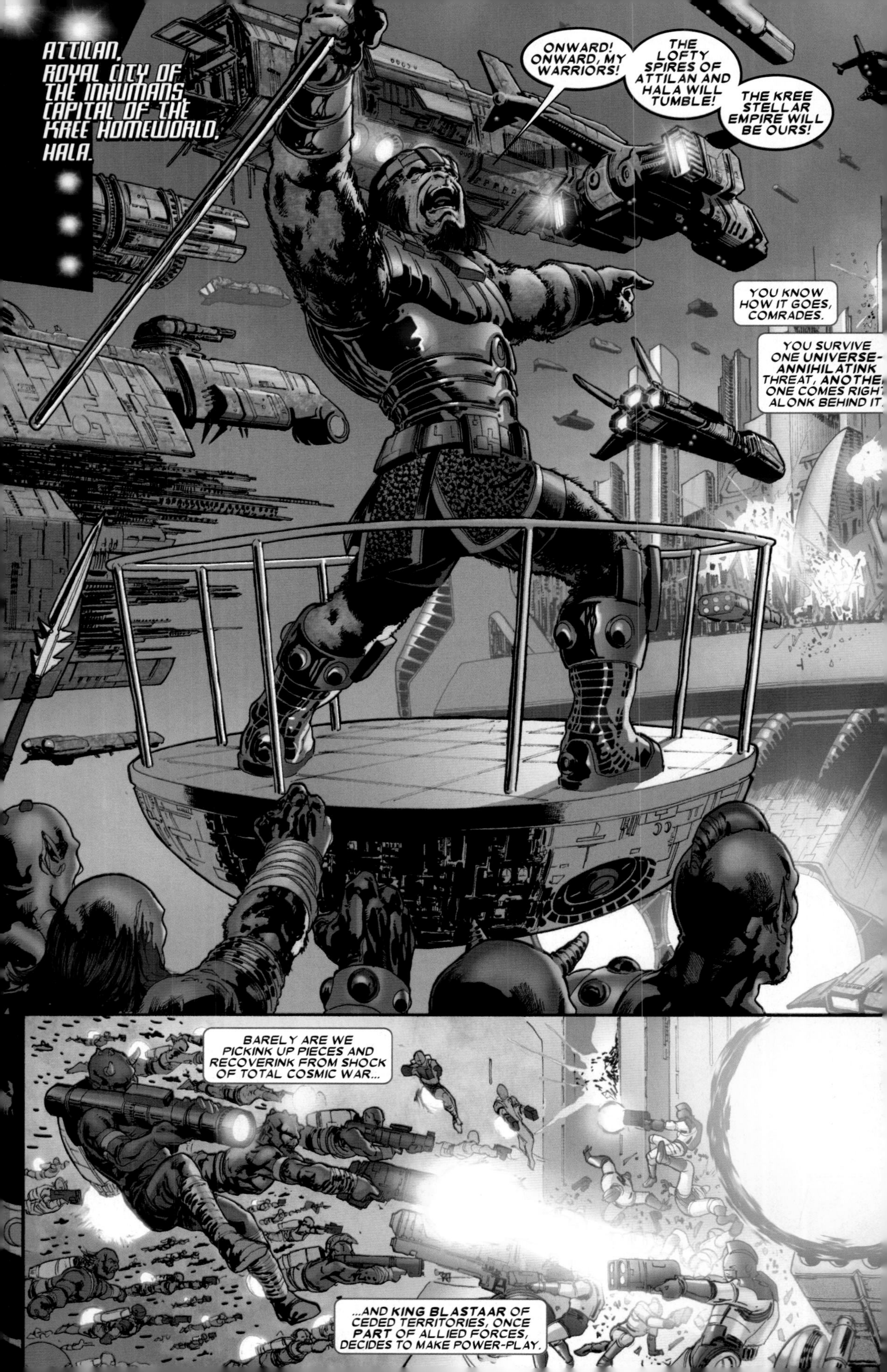
ATTILAN, ROYAL CITY OF THE INHUMANS, CAPITAL OF THE KREE HOMEWORLD, HALA.
ONWARD! ONWARD, MY WARRIORS!
THE LOFTY SPIRES OF ATTILAN AND HALA WILL TUMBLE!
THE KREE STELLAR EMPIRE WILL BE OURS!
YOU KNOW HOW IT GOES, COMRADES.
YOU SURVIVE ONE UNIVERSE-ANNIHILATINK THREAT, ANOTHE ONE COMES RIGHT ALONK BEHIND IT.
BARELY ARE WE PICKINK UP PIECES AND RECOVERINK FROM SHOCK OF TOTAL COSMIC WAR...
...AND KING BLASTAAR OF CEDED TERRITORIES, ONCE PART OF ALLIED FORCES, DECIDES TO MAKE POWER-PLAY.

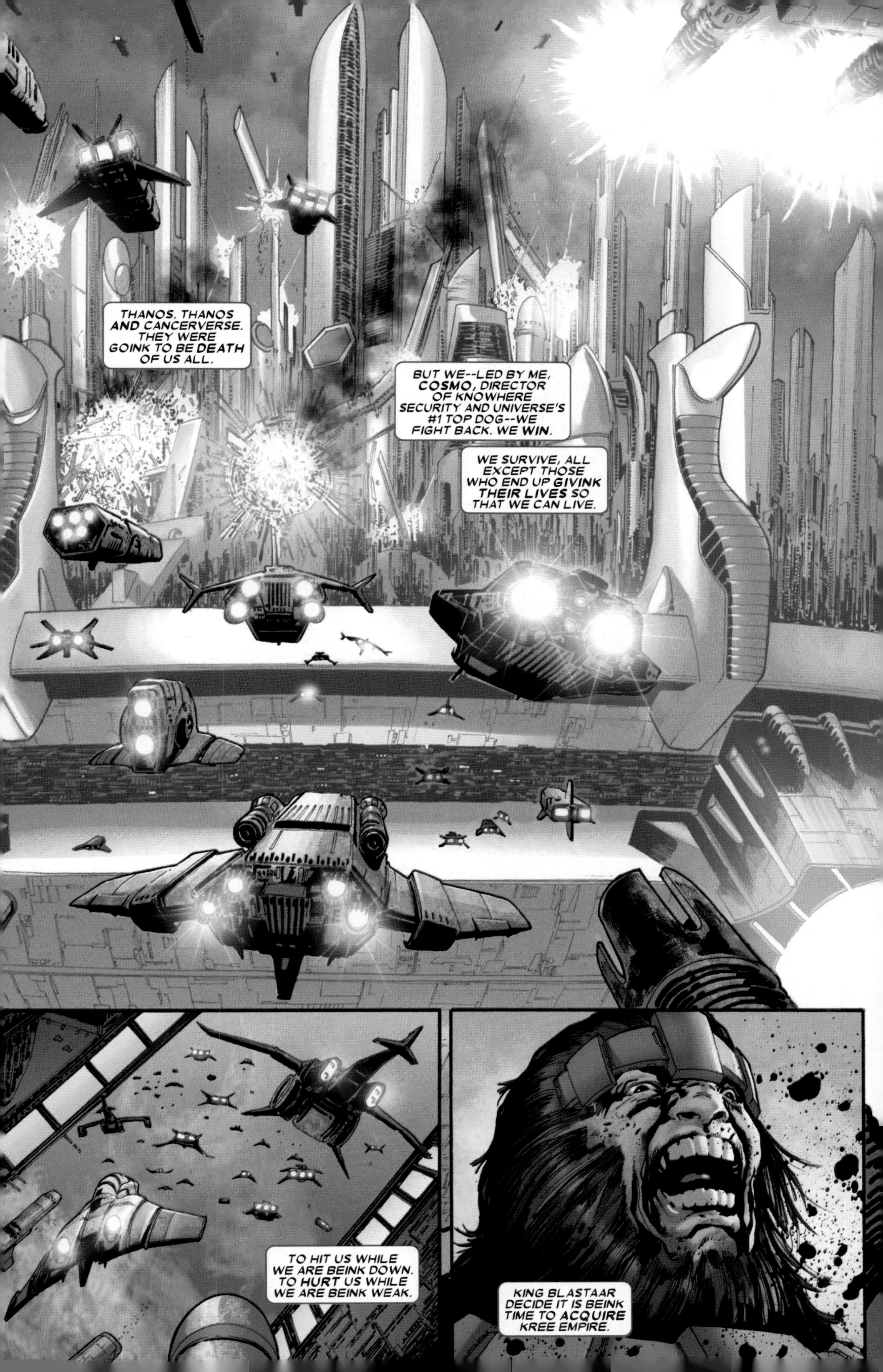
THANOS. THANOS AND CANCERVERSE. THEY WERE GOINK TO BE DEATH OF US ALL.
BUT WE--LED BY ME, COSMO, DIRECTOR OF KNOWHERE SECURITY AND UNIVERSE'S #1 TOP DOG--WE FIGHT BACK. WE WIN.
WE SURVIVE, ALL EXCEPT THOSE WHO END UP GIVINK THEIR LIVES SO THAT WE CAN LIVE.
TO HIT US WHILE WE ARE BEINK DOWN. TO HURT US WHILE WE ARE BEINK WEAK.
KING BLASTAAR DECIDE IT IS BEINK TIME TO ACQUIRE KREE EMPIRE.

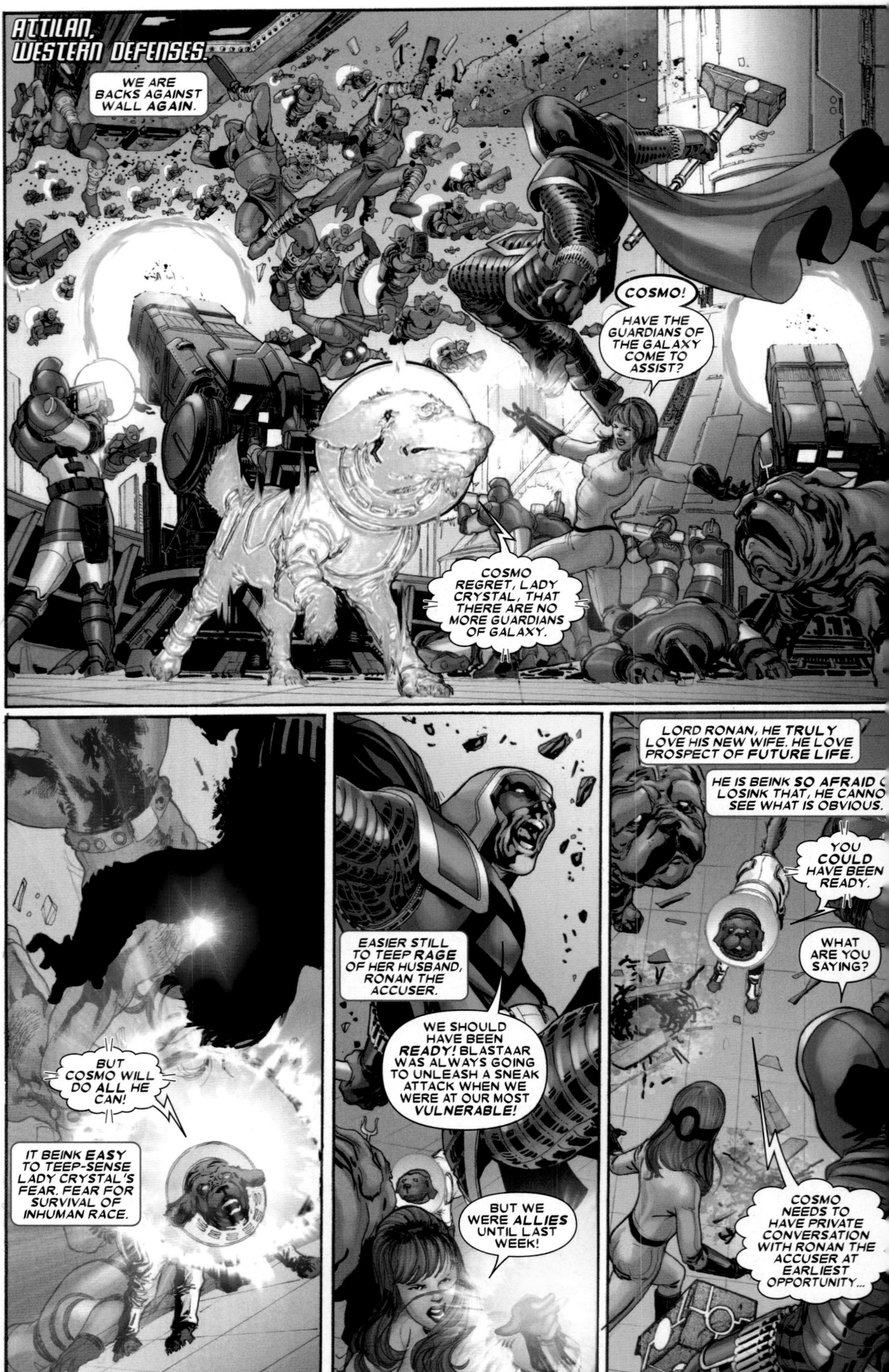
ATTILAN, WESTERN DEFENSES.
WE ARE BACKS AGAINST WALL AGAIN.
COSMO! HAVE THE GUARDIANS OF THE GALAXY COME TO ASSIST?
COSMO REGRET, LADY CRYSTAL, THAT THERE ARE NO MORE GUARDIANS OF GALAXY.
BUT COSMO WILL DO ALL HE CAN!
IT BEINK EASY TO TEEP-SENSE LADY CRYSTAL'S FEAR. FEAR FOR SURVIVAL OF INHUMAN RACE.
EASIER STILL TO TEEP RAGE OF HER HUSBAND, RONAN THE ACCUSER.
WE SHOULD HAVE BEEN READY! BLASTAAR WAS ALWAYS GOING TO UNLEASH A SNEAK ATTACK WHEN WE WERE AT OUR MOST VULNERABLE!
BUT WE WERE ALLIES UNTIL LAST WEEK!
LORD RONAN, HE TRULY LOVE HIS NEW WIFE. HE LOVE PROSPECT OF FUTURE LIFE.
HE IS BEINK SO AFRAID LOSINK THAT, HE CANNO SEE WHAT IS OBVIOUS.
YOU COULD HAVE BEEN READY.
WHAT ARE YOU SAYING?
COSMO NEEDS TO HAVE PRIVATE CONVERSATION WITH RONAN THE ACCUSER AT EARLIEST OPPORTUNITY...

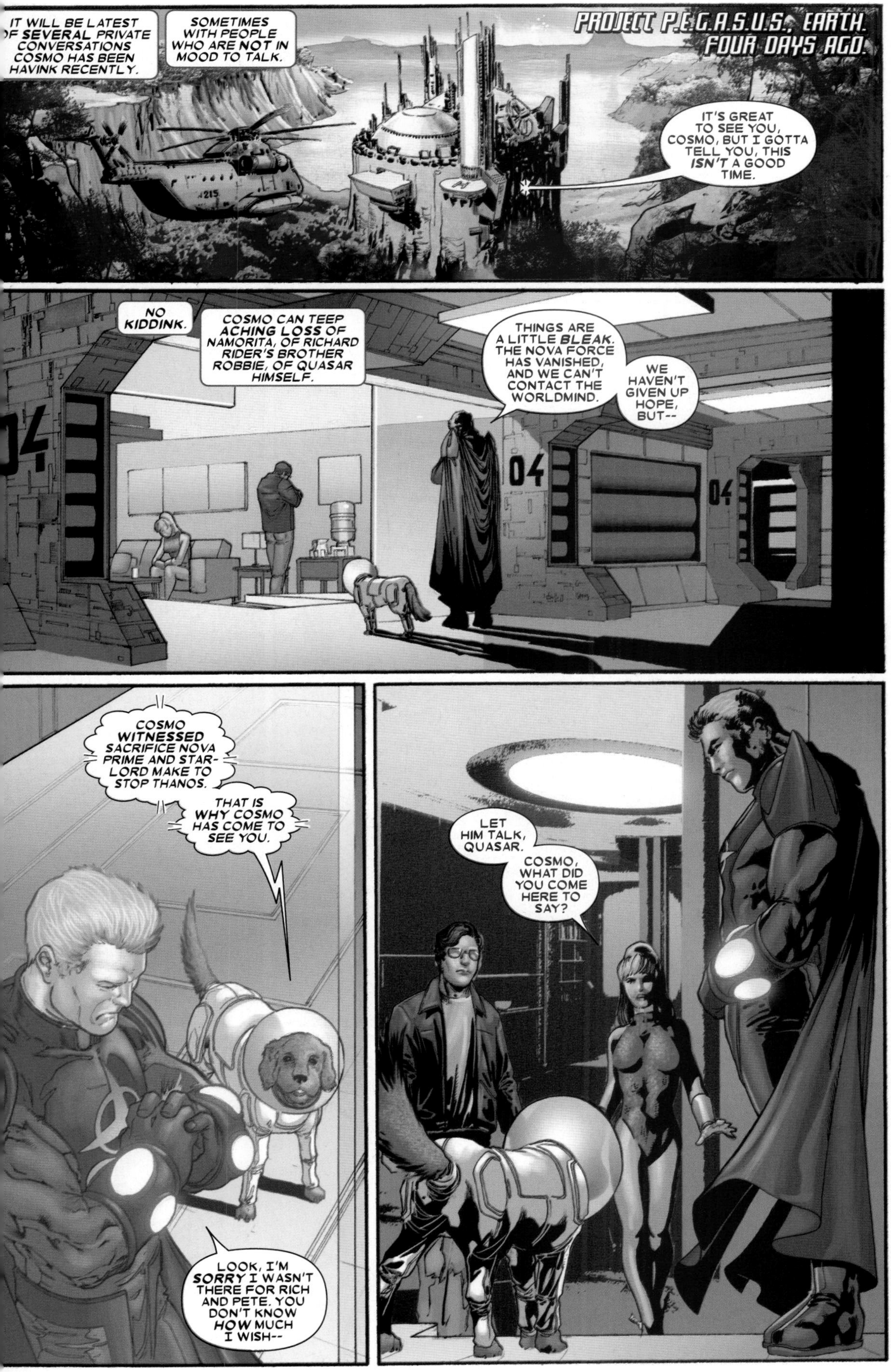
IT WILL BE LATEST OF SEVERAL PRIVATE CONVERSATIONS COSMO HAS BEEN HAVINK RECENTLY.
SOMETIMES WITH PEOPLE WHO ARE NOT IN MOOD TO TALK.
PROJECT P.E.G.A.S.U.S., EARTH. FOUR DAYS AGO.
IT'S GREAT TO SEE YOU, COSMO, BUT I GOTTA TELL YOU, THIS ISN'T A GOOD TIME.
NO KIDDINK.
COSMO CAN TEEP ACHING LOSS OF NAMORITA, OF RICHARD RIDER'S BROTHER ROBBIE, OF QUASAR HIMSELF.
THINGS ARE A LITTLE BLEAK. THE NOVA FORCE HAS VANISHED, AND WE CAN'T CONTACT THE WORLDMIND.
WE HAVEN'T GIVEN UP HOPE, BUT--
COSMO WITNESSED SACRIFICE NOVA PRIME AND STAR-LORD MAKE TO STOP THANOS.
THAT IS WHY COSMO HAS COME TO SEE YOU.
LOOK, I'M SORRY I WASN'T THERE FOR RICH AND PETE. YOU DON'T KNOW HOW MUCH I WISH--
LET HIM TALK, QUASAR.
COSMO, WHAT DID YOU COME HERE TO SAY?

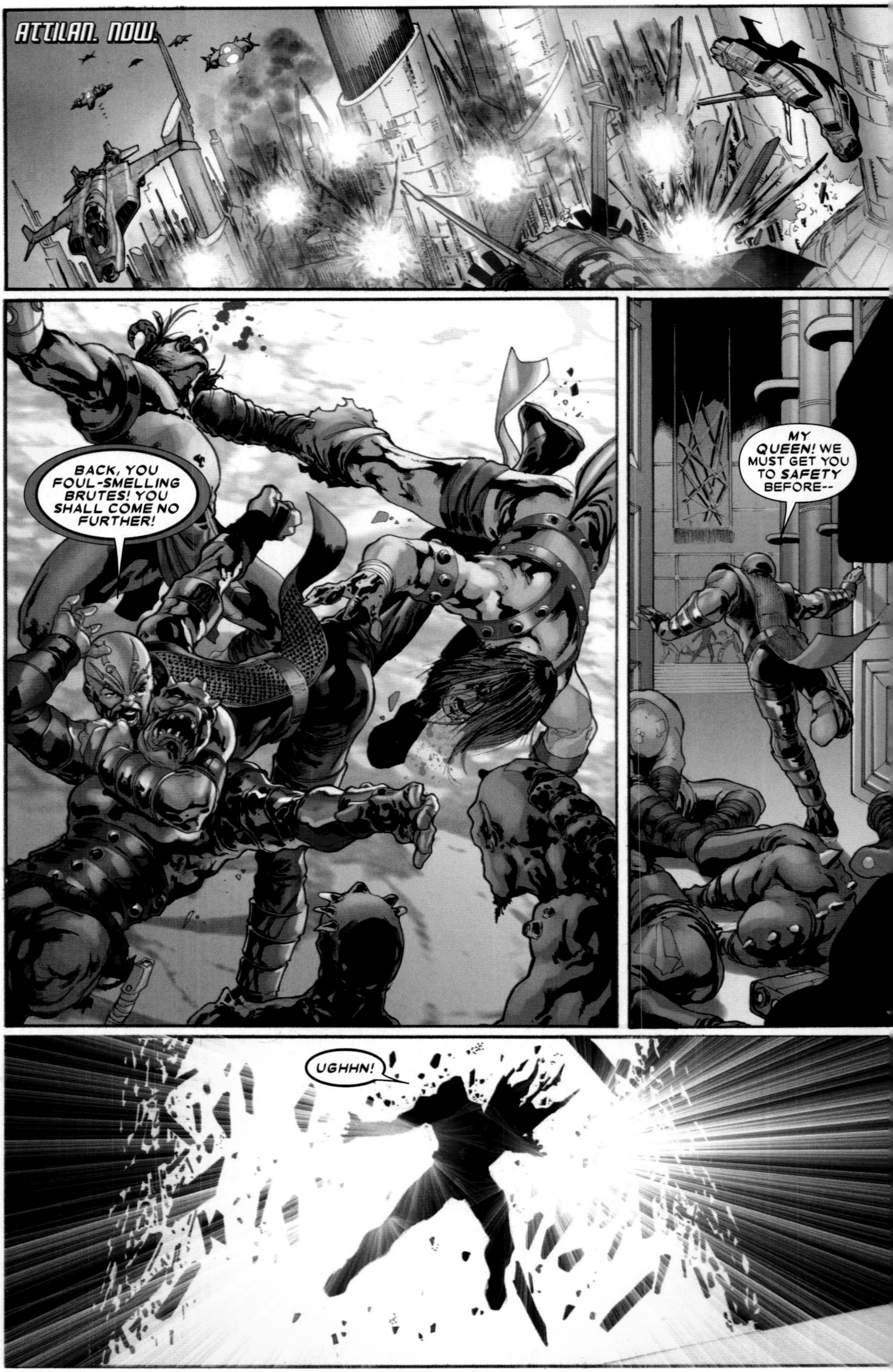
ATTILAN. NOW.
BACK, YOU FOUL-SMELLING BRUTES! YOU SHALL COME NO FURTHER!
MY QUEEN! WE MUST GET YOU TO SAFETY BEFORE--
UGHHN!

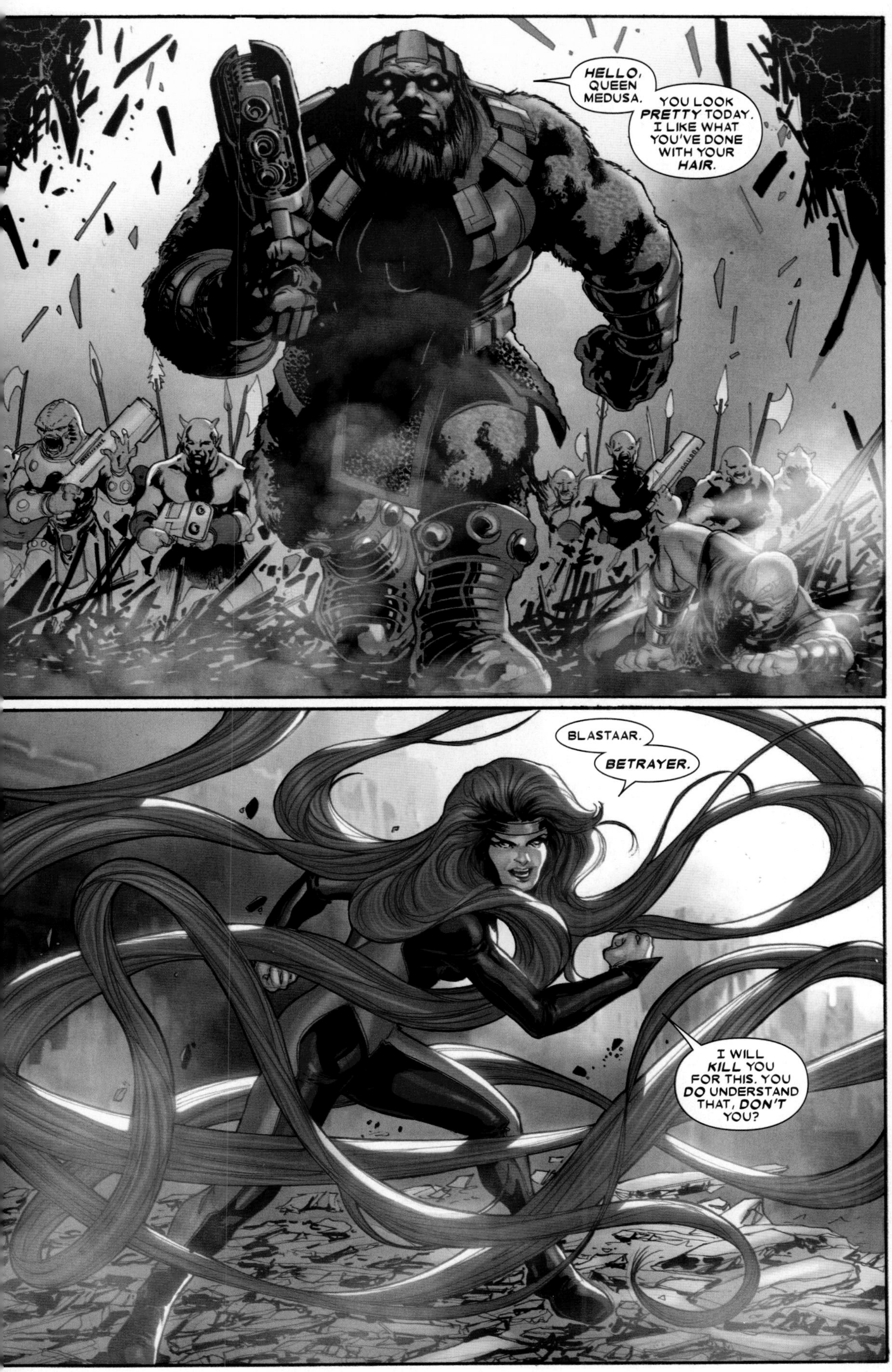
HELLO, QUEEN MEDUSA.
YOU LOOK PRETTY TODAY. I LIKE WHAT YOU'VE DONE WITH YOUR HAIR.
BLASTAAR.
BETRAYER.
I WILL KILL YOU FOR THIS. YOU DO UNDERSTAND THAT, DON'T YOU?

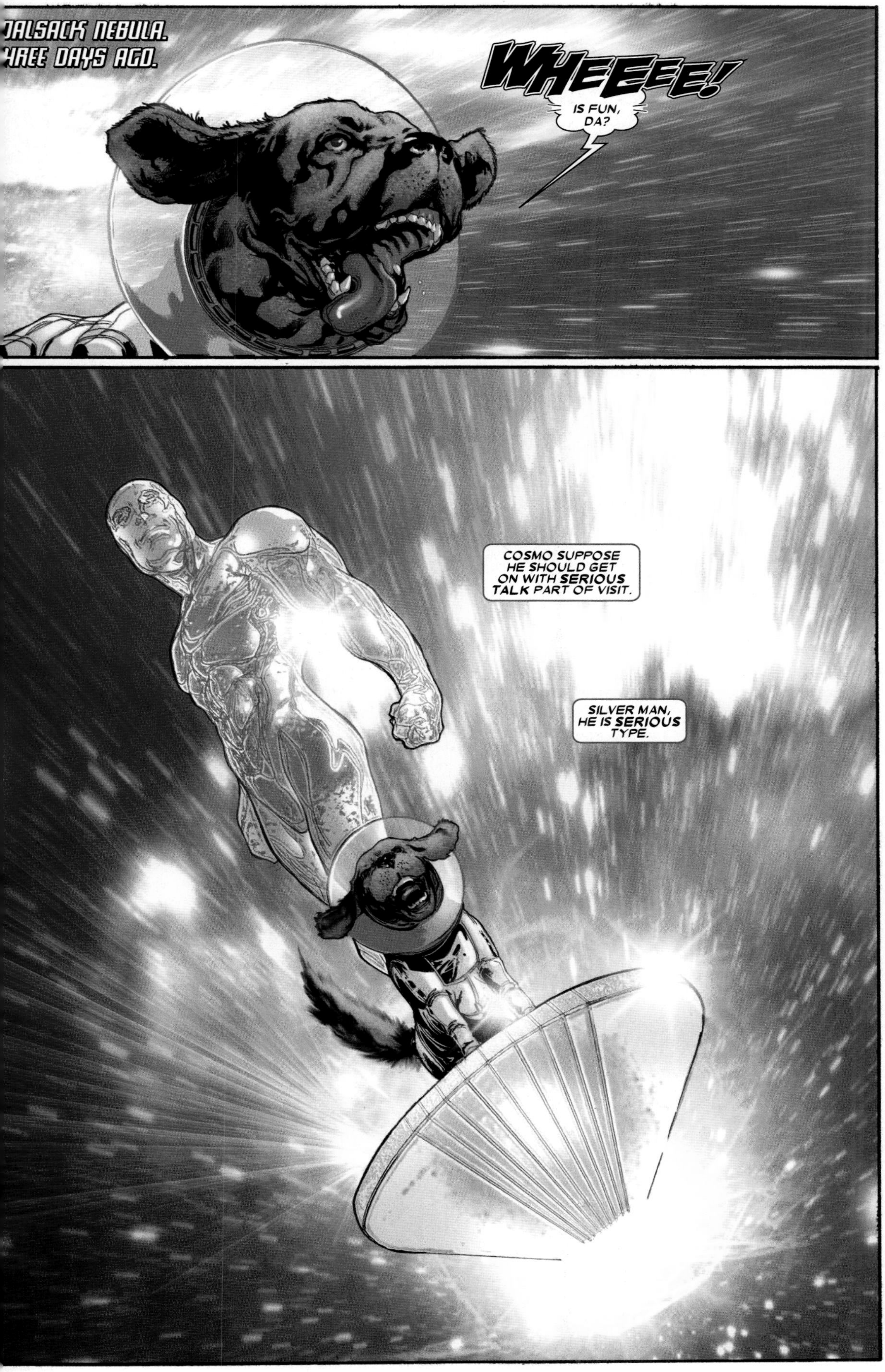
OALSACK NEBULA.
HREE DAYS AGO.
WHEEEEE!
IS FUN, DA?
COSMO SUPPOSE HE SHOULD GET ON WITH SERIOUS TALK PART OF VISIT.
SILVER MAN, HE IS SERIOUS TYPE.

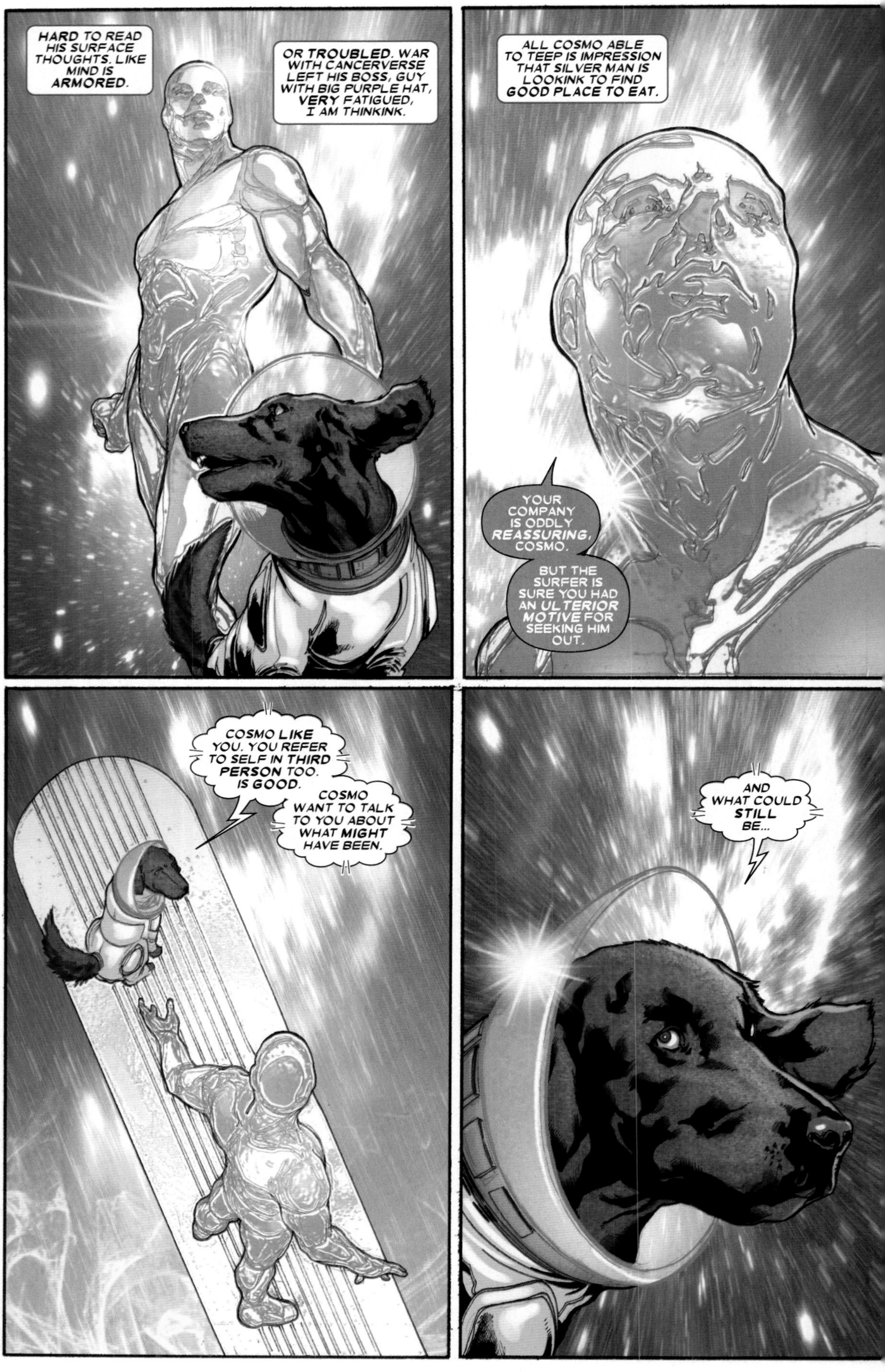
HARD TO READ HIS SURFACE THOUGHTS. LIKE MIND IS ARMORED.
OR TROUBLED. WAR WITH CANCERVERSE LEFT HIS BOSS, GUY WITH BIG PURPLE HAT, VERY FATIGUED, I AM THINKINK.
ALL COSMO ABLE TO TEEP IS IMPRESSION THAT SILVER MAN IS LOOKINK TO FIND GOOD PLACE TO EAT.
YOUR COMPANY IS ODDLY REASSURING, COSMO.
BUT THE SURFER IS SURE YOU HAD AN ULTERIOR MOTIVE FOR SEEKING HIM OUT.
COSMO LIKE YOU. YOU REFER TO SELF IN THIRD PERSON TOO. IS GOOD.
COSMO WANT TO TALK TO YOU ABOUT WHAT MIGHT HAVE BEEN.
AND WHAT COULD STILL BE...

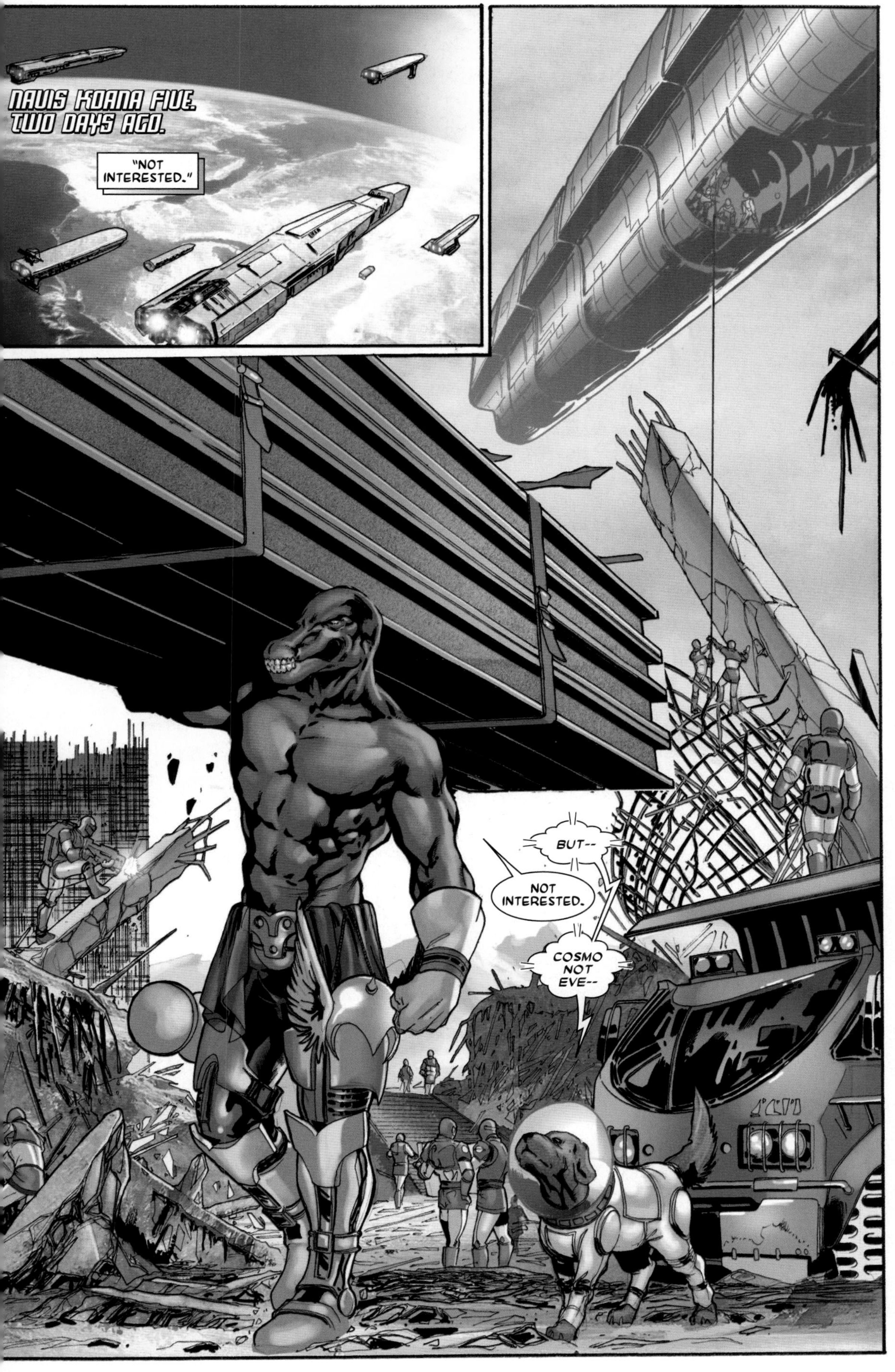
NAVIS KOANA FIVE. TWO DAYS AGO.
"NOT INTERESTED."
BUT--
NOT INTERESTED.
COSMO NOT EVE--

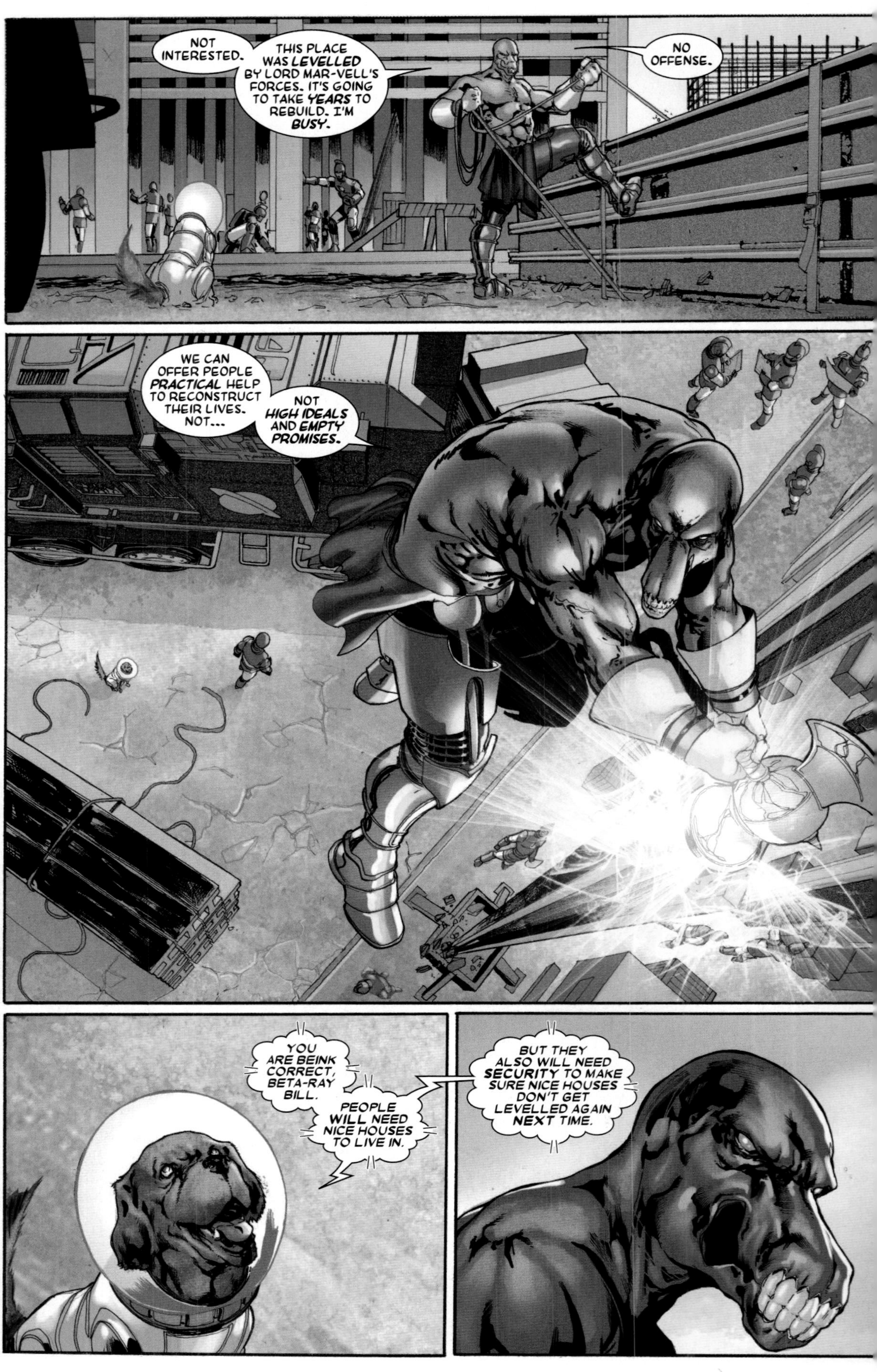
NOT INTERESTED.
THIS PLACE WAS LEVELLED BY LORD MAR-VELL'S FORCES. IT'S GOING TO TAKE YEARS TO REBUILD. I'M BUSY.
NO OFFENSE.
WE CAN OFFER PEOPLE PRACTICAL HELP TO RECONSTRUCT THEIR LIVES. NOT...
NOT HIGH IDEALS AND EMPTY PROMISES.
YOU ARE BEINK CORRECT, BETA-RAY BILL.
PEOPLE WILL NEED NICE HOUSES TO LIVE IN.
BUT THEY ALSO WILL NEED SECURITY TO MAKE SURE NICE HOUSES DON'T GET LEVELLED AGAIN NEXT TIME.

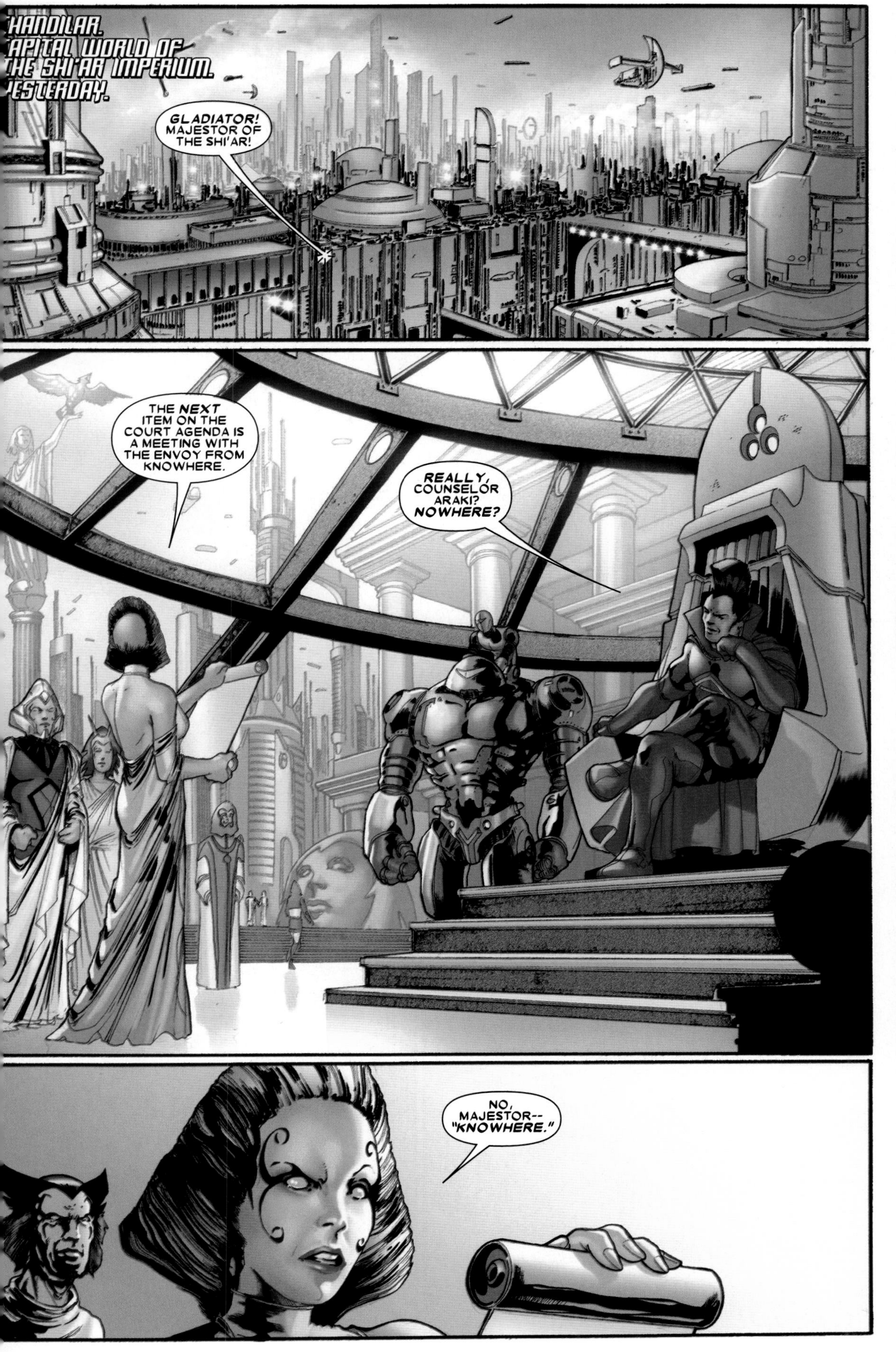
HANDILAR.
APITAL WORLD OF
THE SHI'AR IMPERIUM.
YESTERDAY.
GLADIATOR! MAJESTOR OF THE SHI'AR!
THE NEXT ITEM ON THE COURT AGENDA IS A MEETING WITH THE ENVOY FROM KNOWHERE.
REALLY, COUNSELOR ARAKI? NOWHERE?
NO, MAJESTOR-- "KNOWHERE."

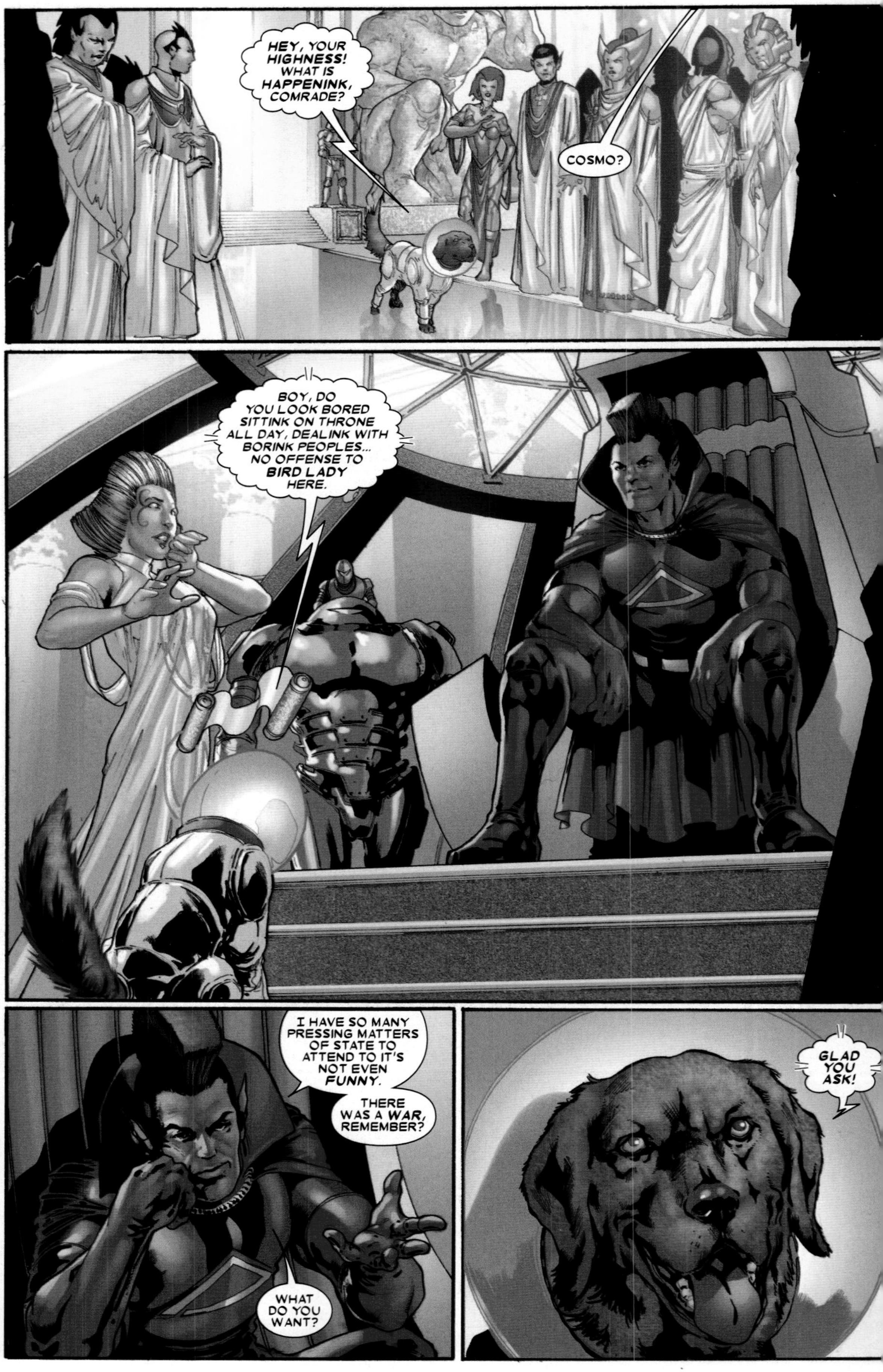
HEY, YOUR HIGHNESS! WHAT IS HAPPENINK, COMRADE?
COSMO?
BOY, DO YOU LOOK BORED SITTINK ON THRONE ALL DAY, DEALINK WITH BORINK PEOPLES... NO OFFENSE TO BIRD LADY HERE.
I HAVE SO MANY PRESSING MATTERS OF STATE TO ATTEND TO IT'S NOT EVEN FUNNY.
THERE WAS A WAR, REMEMBER?
WHAT DO YOU WANT?
GLAD YOU ASK!

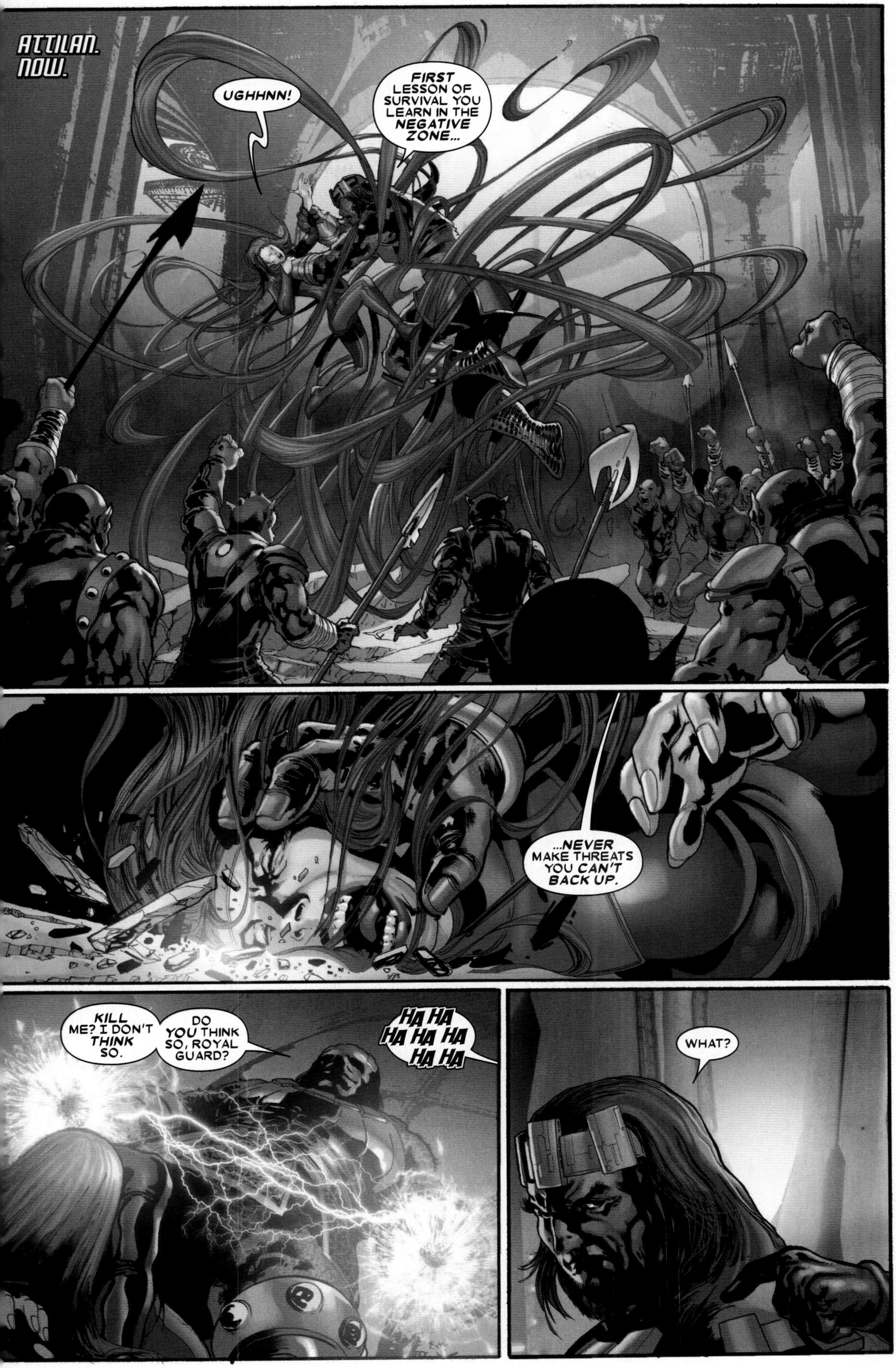
ATTILAN. NOW.
UGHHNN!
FIRST LESSON OF SURVIVAL YOU LEARN IN THE NEGATIVE ZONE...
...NEVER MAKE THREATS YOU CAN'T BACK UP.
KILL ME? I DON'T THINK SO.
DO YOU THINK SO, ROYAL GUARD?
HA HA HA HA HA HA HA
WHAT?

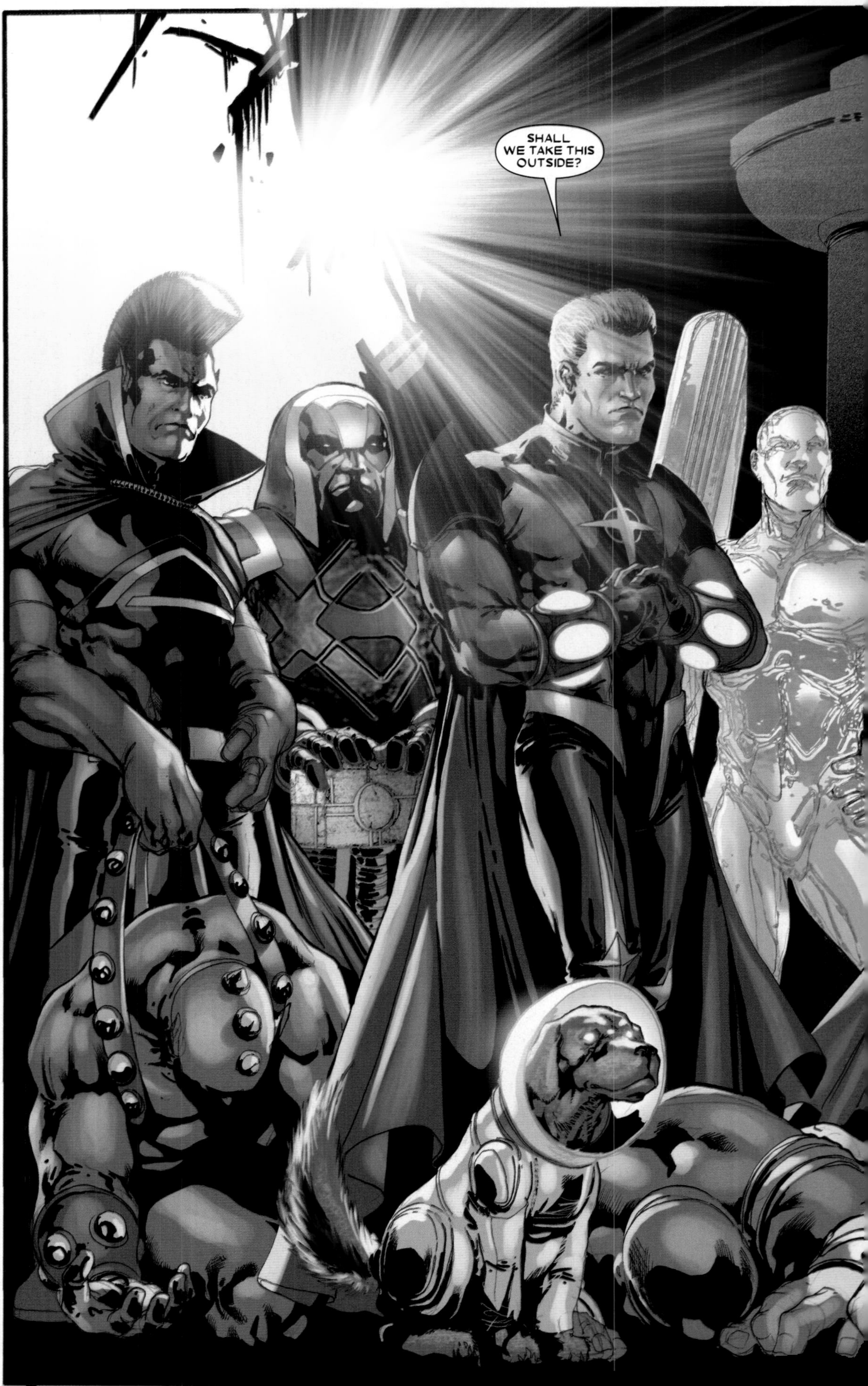
SHALL WE TAKE THIS OUTSIDE?

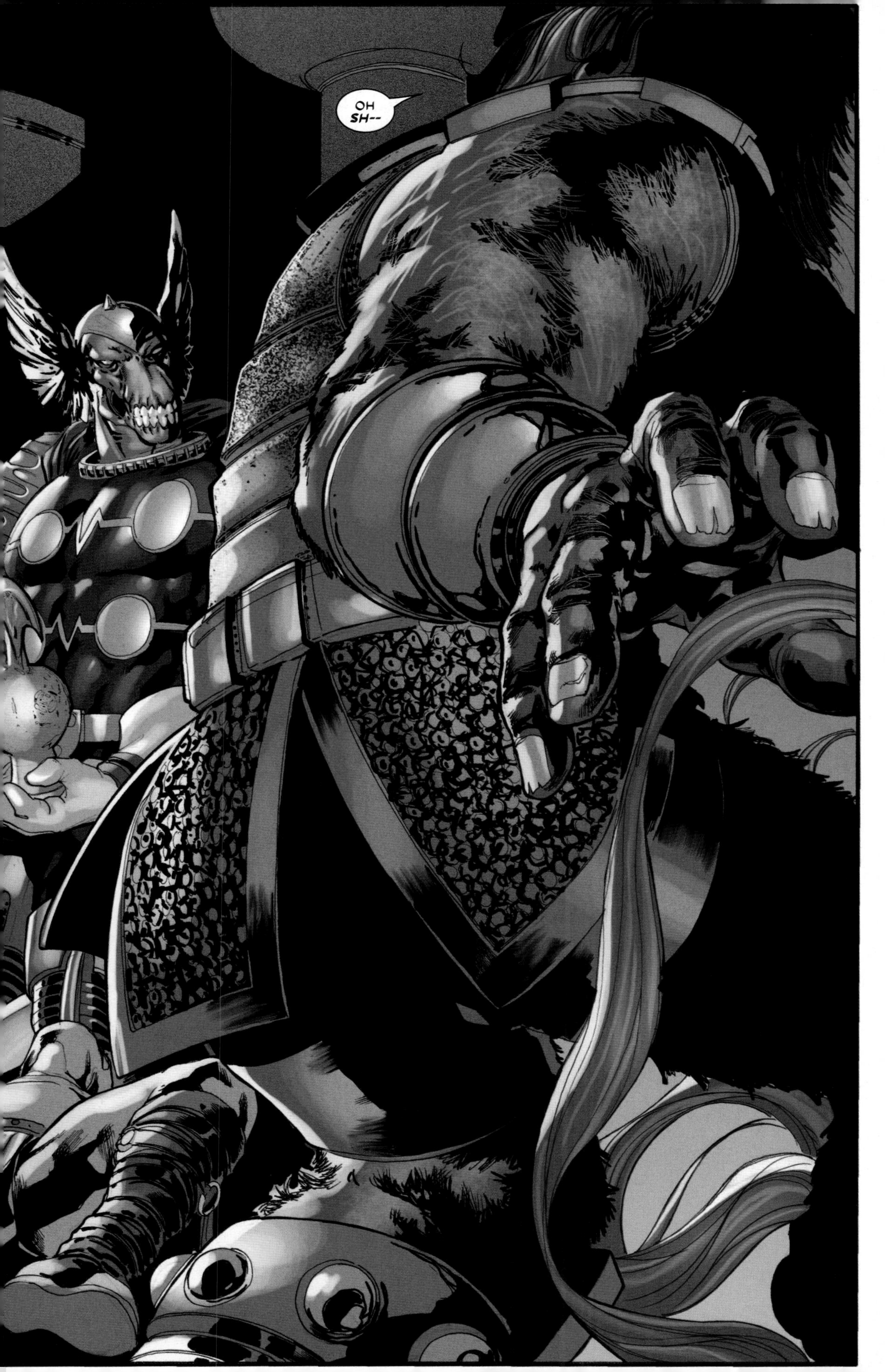
OH SH--

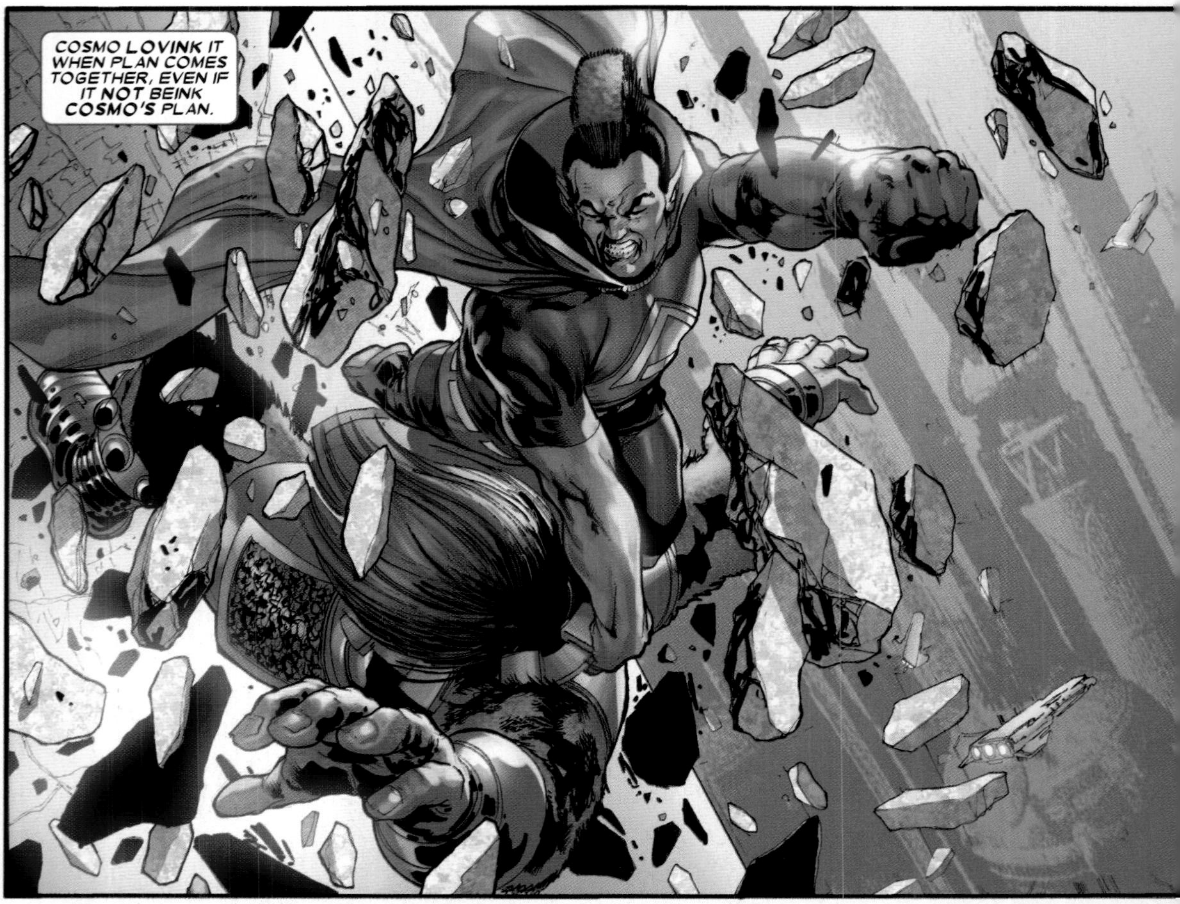
COSMO LOVINK IT WHEN PLAN COMES TOGETHER, EVEN IF IT NOT BEINK COSMO'S PLAN.
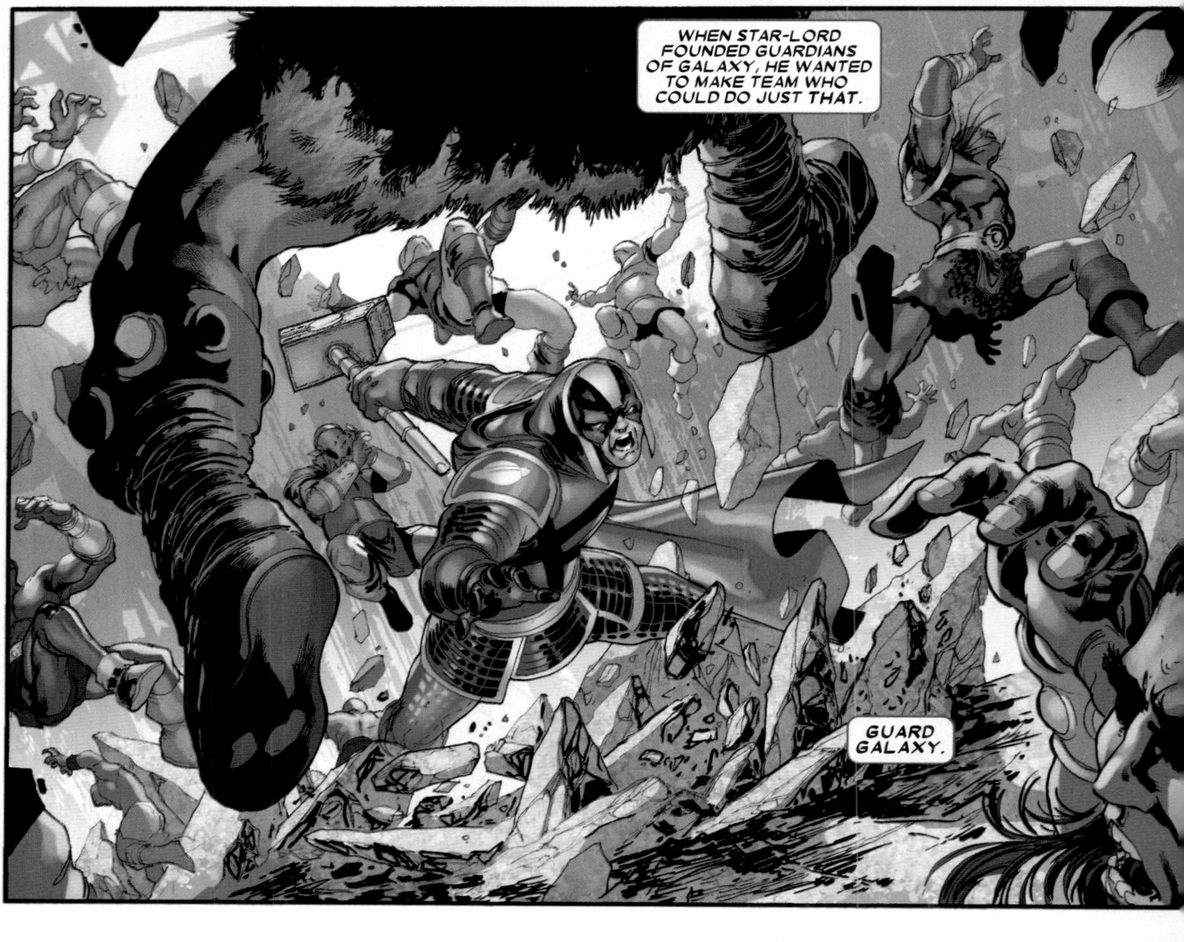
WHEN STAR-LORD FOUNDED GUARDIANS OF GALAXY, HE WANTED TO MAKE TEAM WHO COULD DO JUST THAT.
GUARD GALAXY.

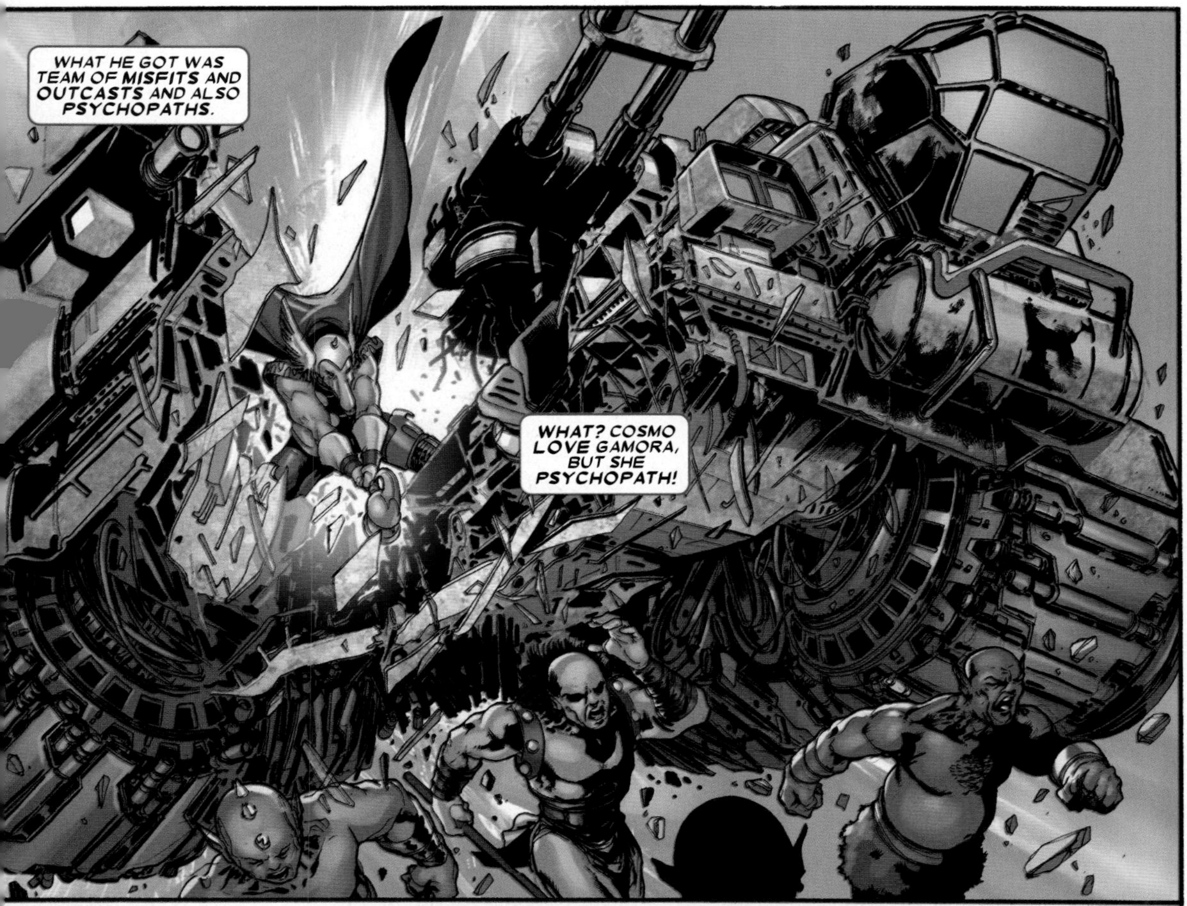
WHAT HE GOT WAS TEAM OF MISFITS AND OUTCASTS AND ALSO PSYCHOPATHS.
WHAT? COSMO LOVE GAMORA, BUT SHE PSYCHOPATH!

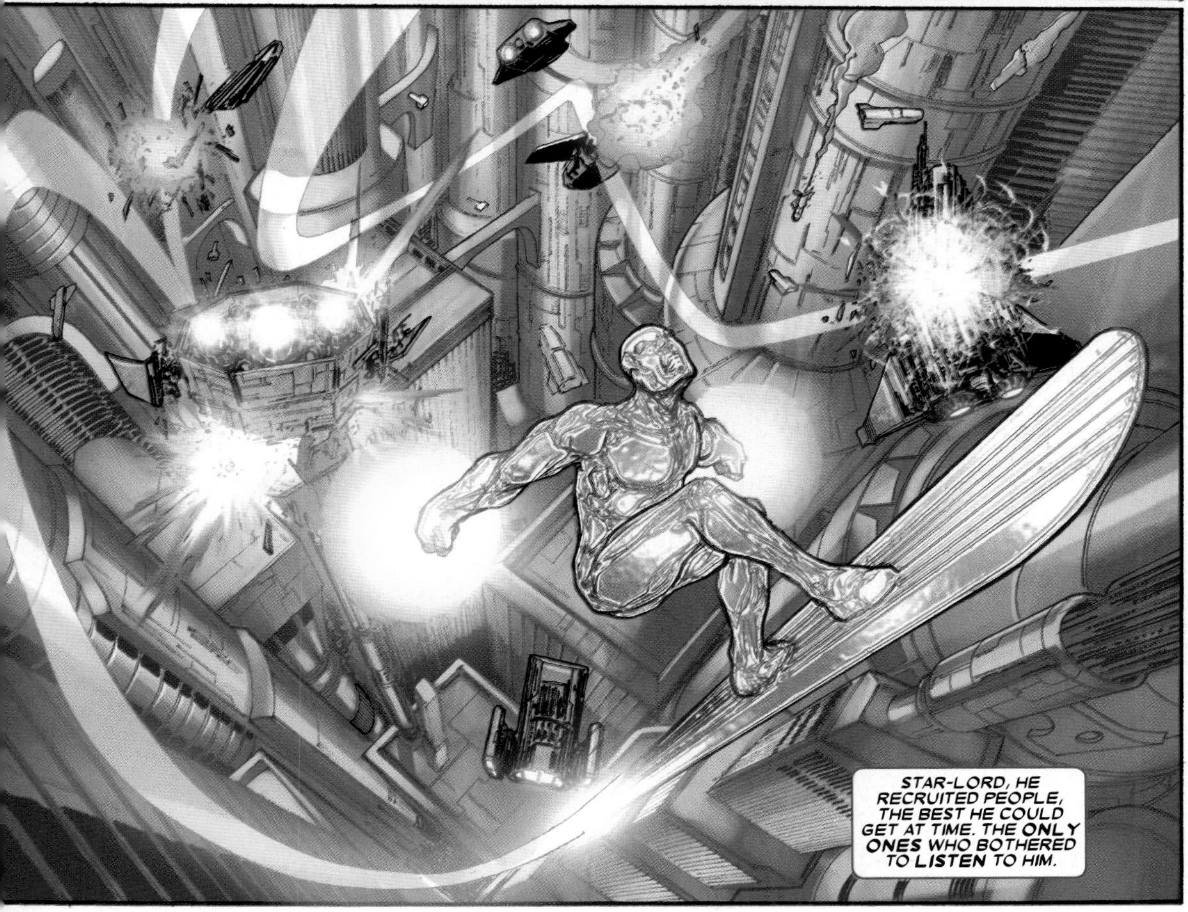
STAR-LORD, HE RECRUITED PEOPLE, THE BEST HE COULD GET AT TIME. THE ONLY ONES WHO BOTHERED TO LISTEN TO HIM.

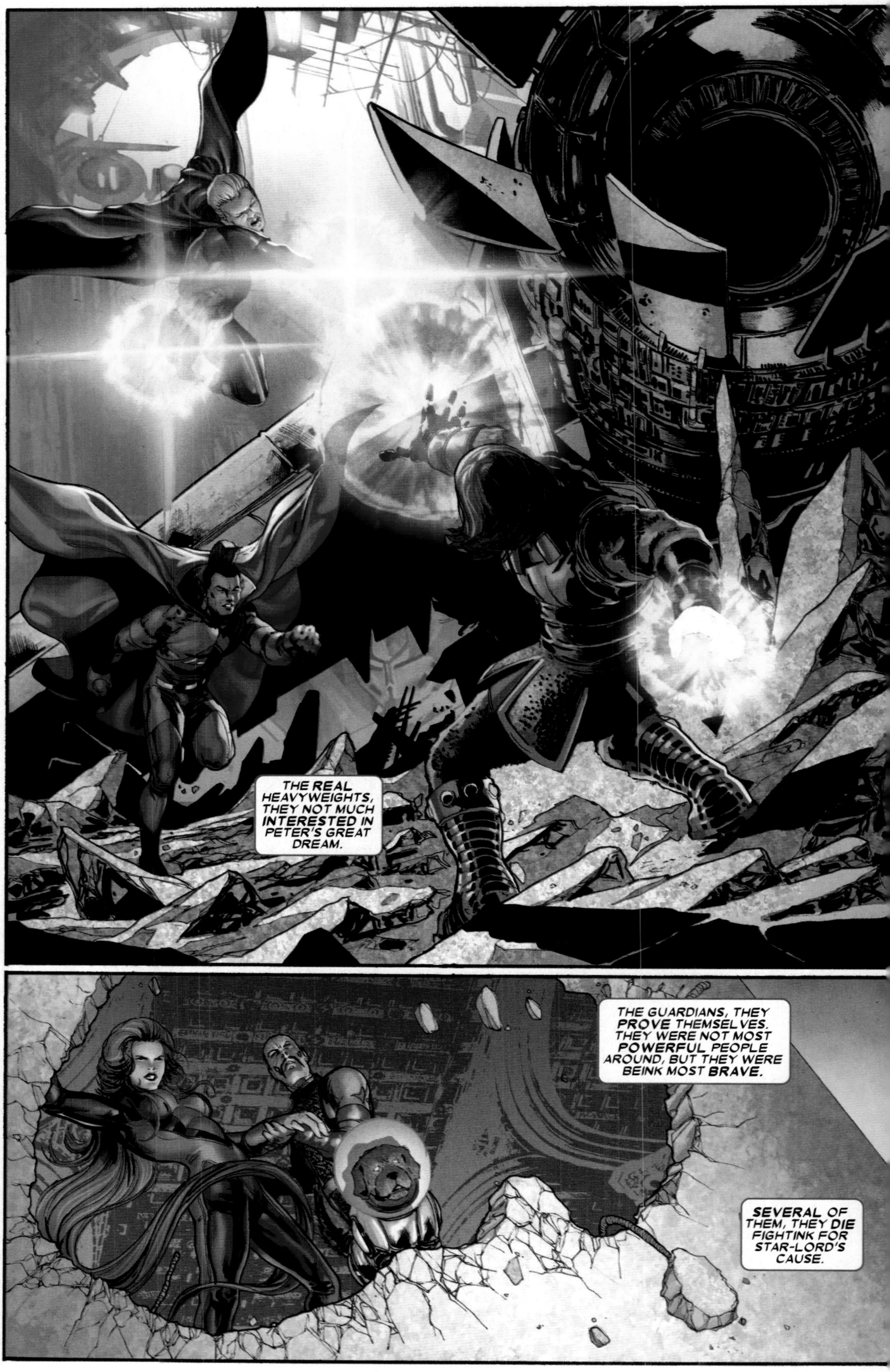
THE REAL HEAVYWEIGHTS, THEY NOT MUCH INTERESTED IN PETER'S GREAT DREAM.
THE GUARDIANS, THEY PROVE THEMSELVES. THEY WERE NOT MOST POWERFUL PEOPLE AROUND, BUT THEY WERE BEINK MOST BRAVE.
SEVERAL OF THEM, THEY DIE FIGHTINK FOR STAR-LORD'S CAUSE.

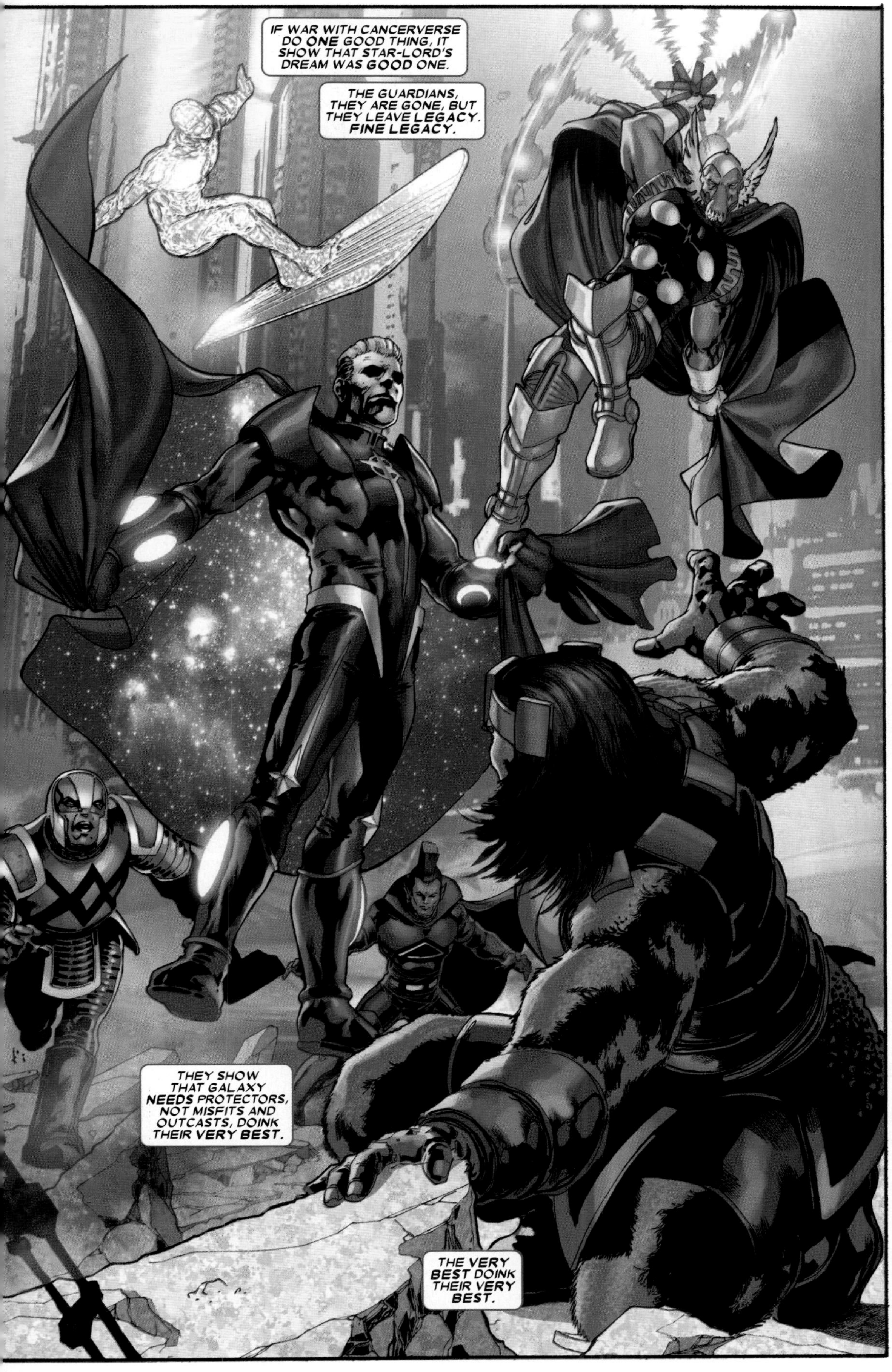
IF WAR WITH CANCERVERSE DO ONE GOOD THING, IT SHOW THAT STAR-LORD'S DREAM WAS GOOD ONE.
THE GUARDIANS, THEY ARE GONE, BUT THEY LEAVE LEGACY. FINE LEGACY.
THEY SHOW THAT GALAXY NEEDS PROTECTORS, NOT MISFITS AND OUTCASTS, DOINK THEIR VERY BEST.
THE VERY BEST DOINK THEIR VERY BEST.

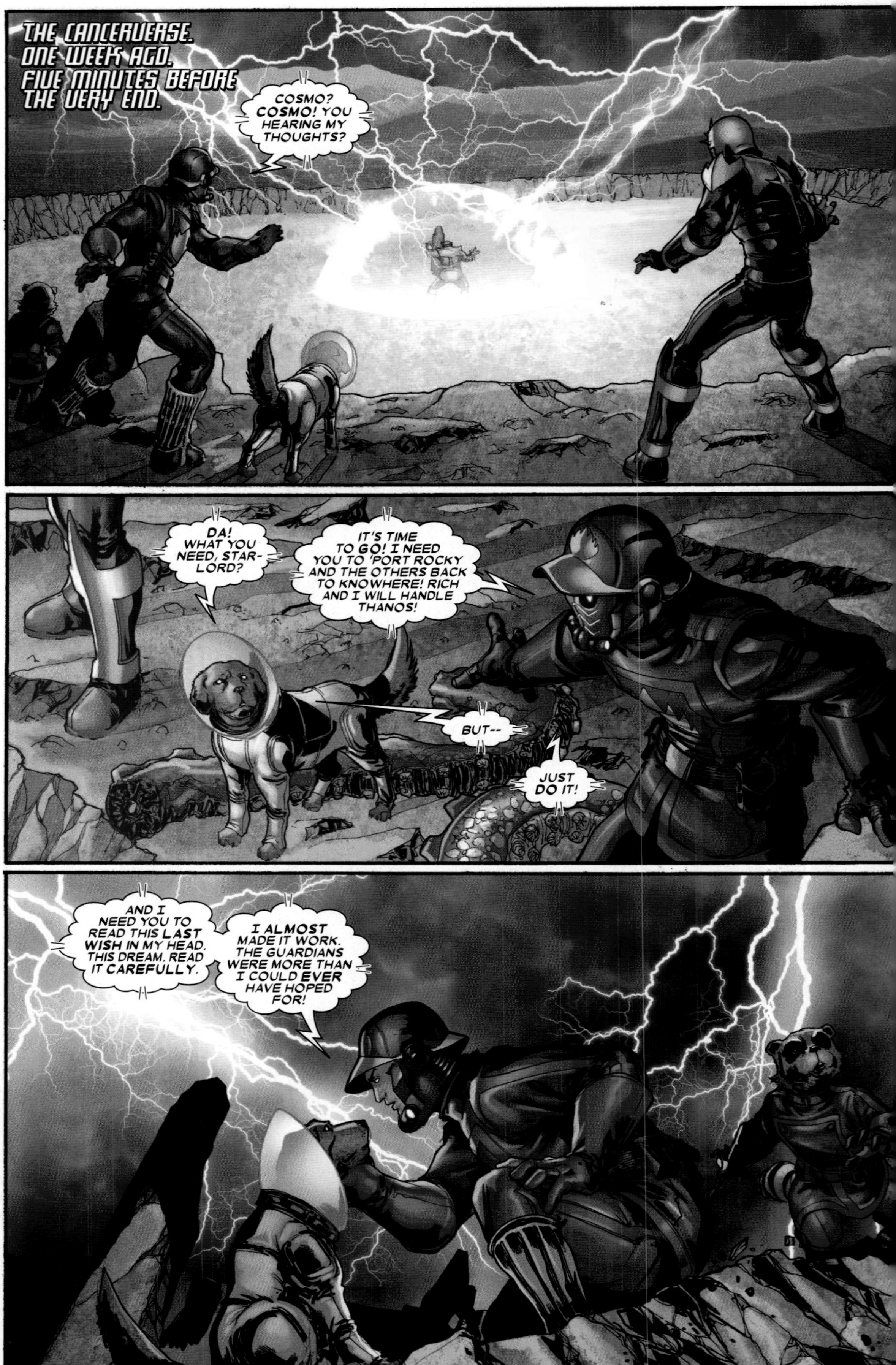
THE CANCERVERSE. ONE WEEK AGO. FIVE MINUTES BEFORE THE VERY END.
COSMO? COSMO! YOU HEARING MY THOUGHTS?
DA! WHAT YOU NEED, STAR-LORD?
IT'S TIME TO GO! I NEED YOU TO 'PORT ROCKY AND THE OTHERS BACK TO KNOWHERE! RICH AND I WILL HANDLE THANOS!
BUT--
JUST DO IT!
AND I NEED YOU TO READ THIS LAST WISH IN MY HEAD. THIS DREAM. READ IT CAREFULLY.
I ALMOST MADE IT WORK. THE GUARDIANS WERE MORE THAN I COULD EVER HAVE HOPED FOR!

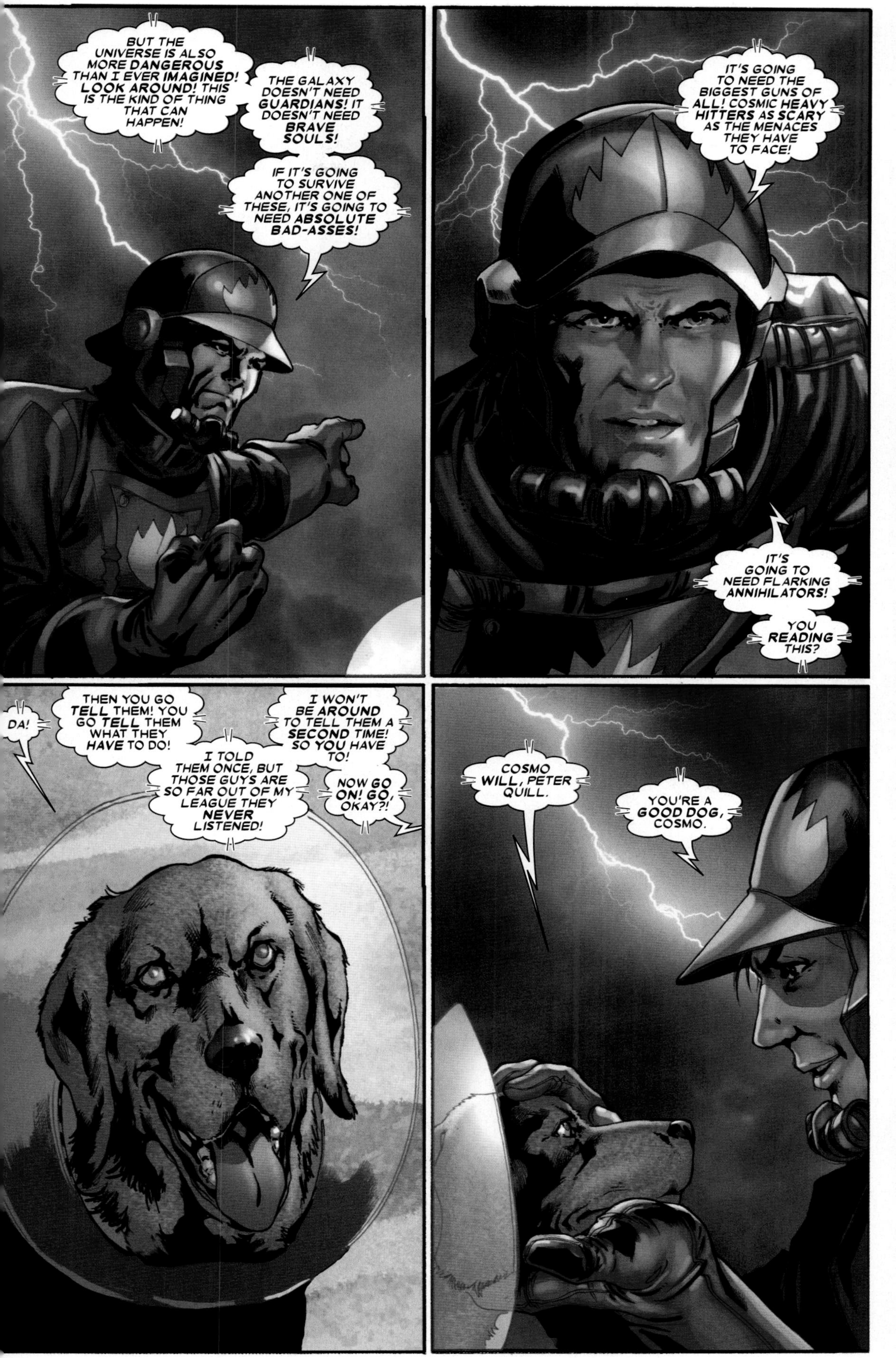
BUT THE UNIVERSE IS ALSO MORE DANGEROUS THAN I EVER IMAGINED! LOOK AROUND! THIS IS THE KIND OF THING THAT CAN HAPPEN!
THE GALAXY DOESN'T NEED GUARDIANS! IT DOESN'T NEED BRAVE SOULS!
IF IT'S GOING TO SURVIVE ANOTHER ONE OF THESE, IT'S GOING TO NEED ABSOLUTE BAD-ASSES!
IT'S GOING TO NEED THE BIGGEST GUNS OF ALL! COSMIC HEAVY HITTERS AS SCARY AS THE MENACES THEY HAVE TO FACE!
IT'S GOING TO NEED FLARKING ANNIHILATORS!
YOU READING THIS?
DA!
THEN YOU GO TELL THEM! YOU GO TELL THEM WHAT THEY HAVE TO DO!
I TOLD THEM ONCE, BUT THOSE GUYS ARE SO FAR OUT OF MY LEAGUE THEY NEVER LISTENED!
I WON'T BE AROUND TO TELL THEM A SECOND TIME! SO YOU HAVE TO!
NOW GO ON! GO, OKAY?!
COSMO WILL, PETER QUILL.
YOU'RE A GOOD DOG, COSMO.

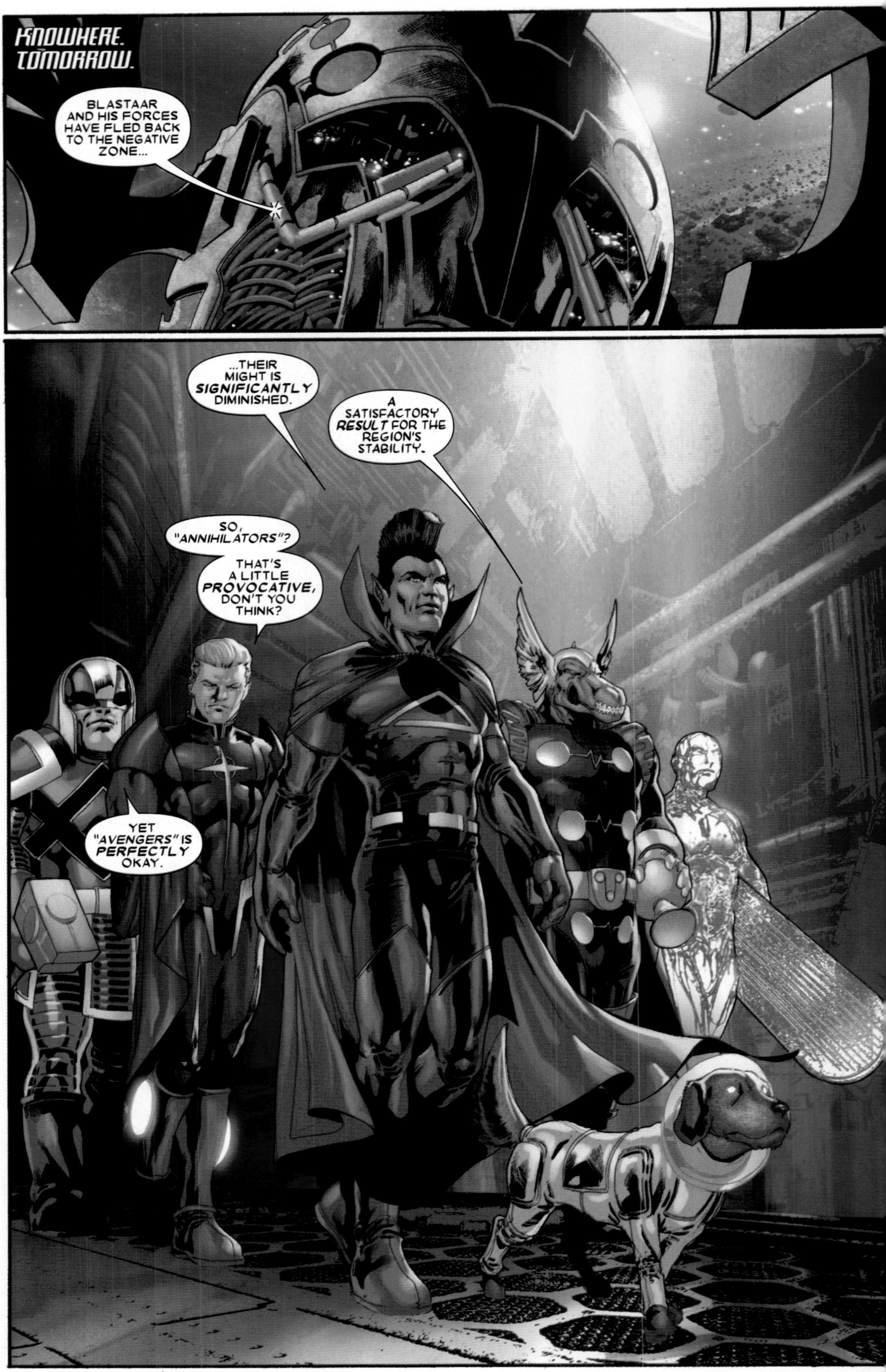
KNOWHERE. TOMORROW.
BLASTAAR AND HIS FORCES HAVE FLED BACK TO THE NEGATIVE ZONE...
...THEIR MIGHT IS SIGNIFICANTLY DIMINISHED.
A SATISFACTORY RESULT FOR THE REGION'S STABILITY.
SO, "ANNIHILATORS"?
THAT'S A LITTLE PROVOCATIVE, DON'T YOU THINK?
YET "AVENGERS" IS PERFECTLY OKAY.

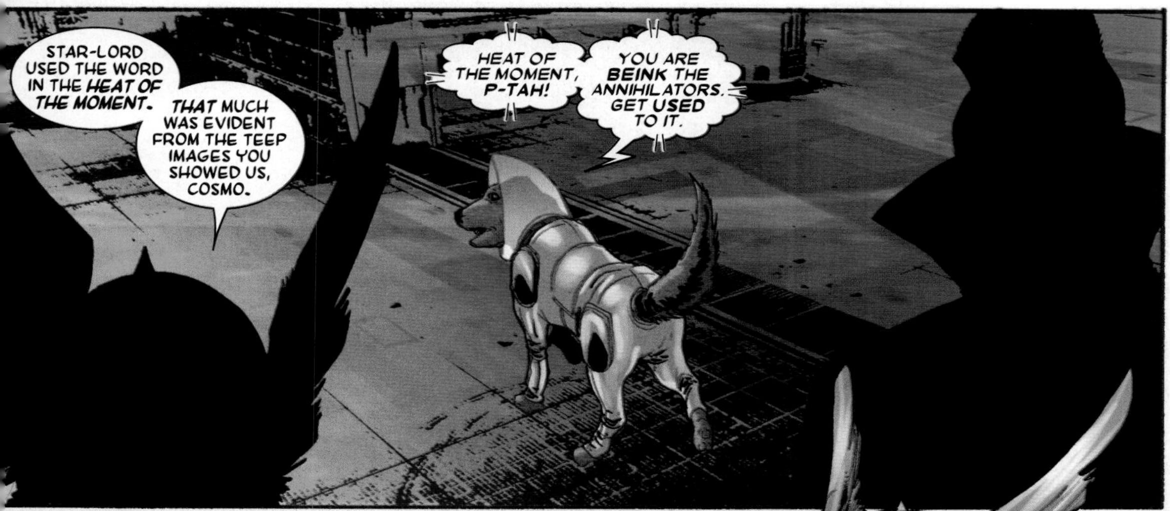
STAR-LORD USED THE WORD IN THE HEAT OF THE MOMENT.
THAT MUCH WAS EVIDENT FROM THE TEEP IMAGES YOU SHOWED US, COSMO.
HEAT OF THE MOMENT, P-TAH!
YOU ARE BEINK THE ANNIHILATORS. GET USED TO IT.

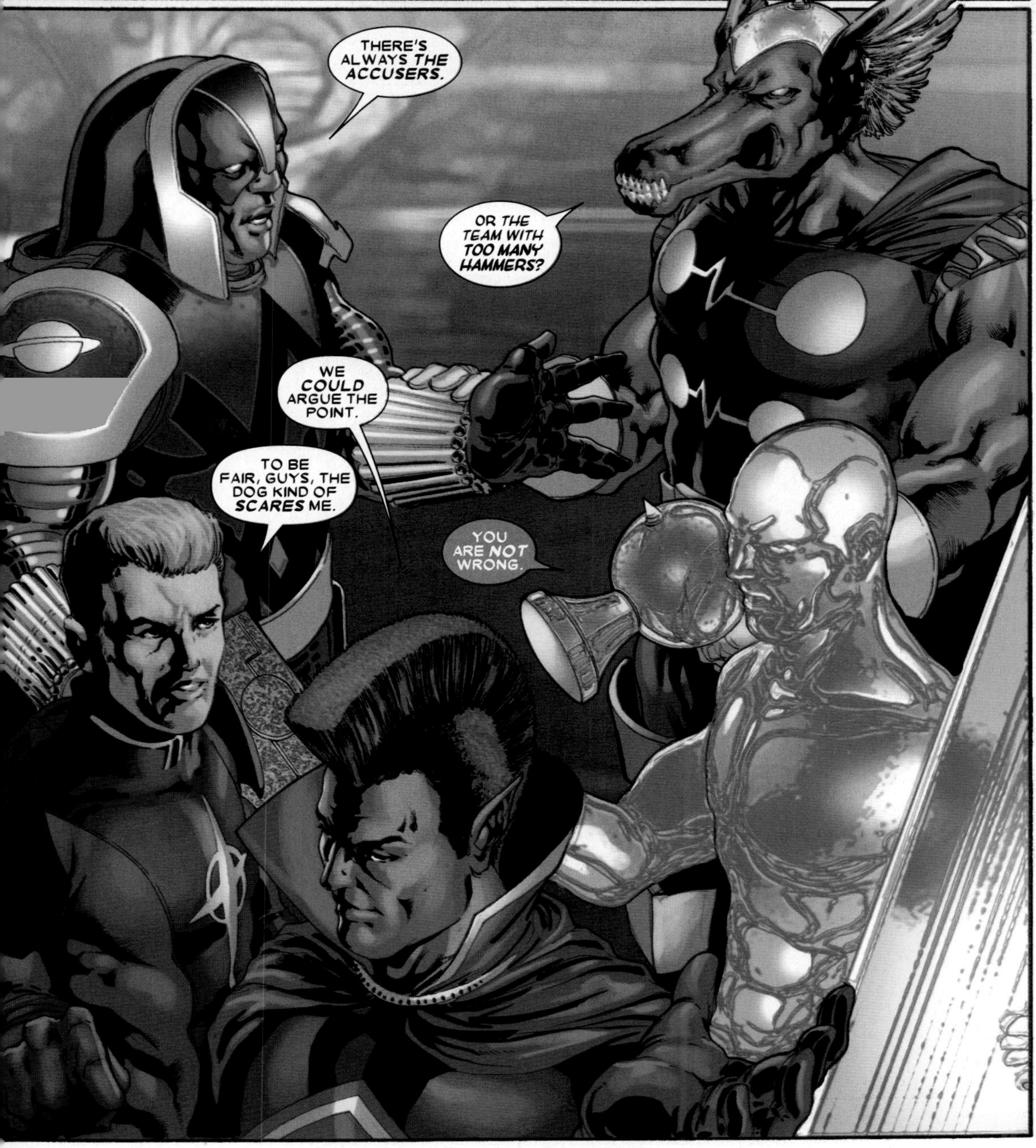
THERE'S ALWAYS THE ACCUSERS.
OR THE TEAM WITH TOO MANY HAMMERS?
WE COULD ARGUE THE POINT.
TO BE FAIR, GUYS, THE DOG KIND OF SCARES ME.
YOU ARE NOT WRONG.

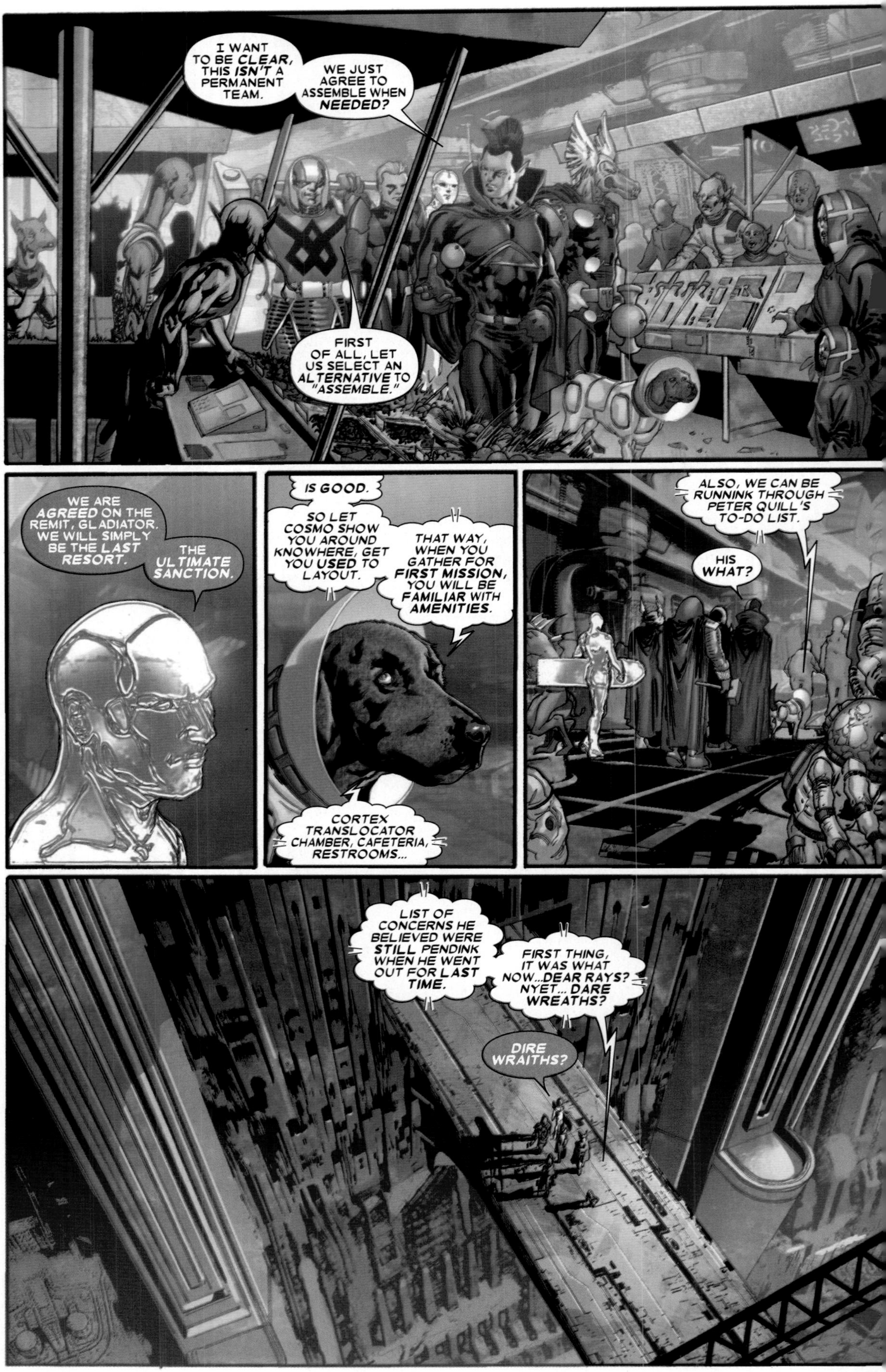
I WANT TO BE CLEAR, THIS ISN'T A PERMANENT TEAM.
WE JUST AGREE TO ASSEMBLE WHEN NEEDED?
FIRST OF ALL, LET US SELECT AN ALTERNATIVE TO "ASSEMBLE."
WE ARE AGREED ON THE REMIT, GLADIATOR. WE WILL SIMPLY BE THE LAST RESORT.
THE ULTIMATE SANCTION.
IS GOOD.
SO LET COSMO SHOW YOU AROUND KNOWHERE, GET YOU USED TO LAYOUT.
THAT WAY, WHEN YOU GATHER FOR FIRST MISSION, YOU WILL BE FAMILIAR WITH AMENITIES.
CORTEX TRANSLOCATOR CHAMBER, CAFETERIA, RESTROOMS...
ALSO, WE CAN BE RUNNINK THROUGH PETER QUILL'S TO-DO LIST.
HIS WHAT?
LIST OF CONCERNS HE BELIEVED WERE STILL PENDINK WHEN HE WENT OUT FOR LAST TIME.
FIRST THING, IT WAS WHAT NOW...DEAR RAYS? NYET... DARE WREATHS?
DIRE WRAITHS?

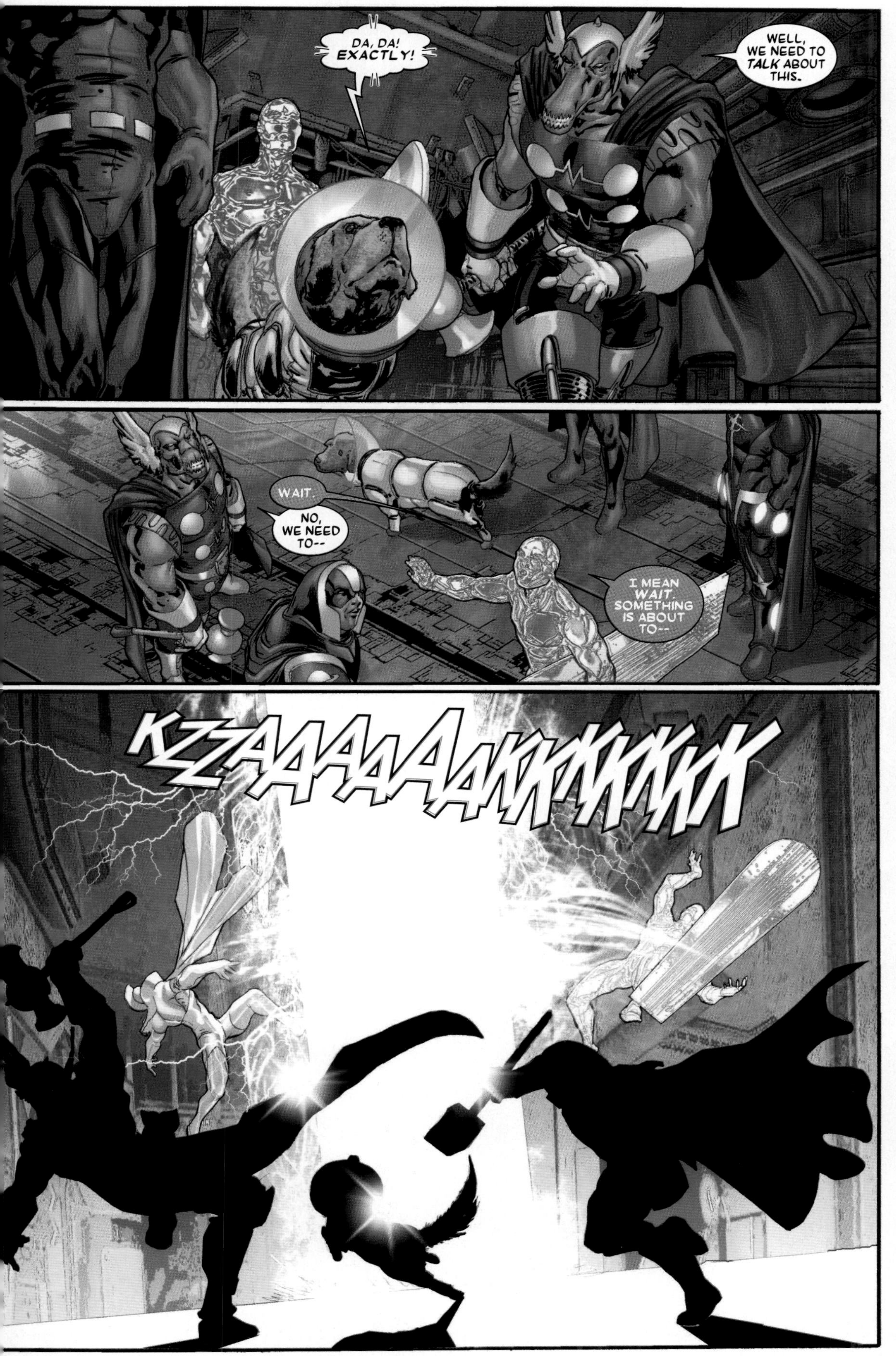
DA, DA! EXACTLY!
WELL, WE NEED TO TALK ABOUT THIS.
WAIT.
NO, WE NEED TO--
I MEAN WAIT. SOMETHING IS ABOUT TO--
KZZAAAAAAKKKKKKK

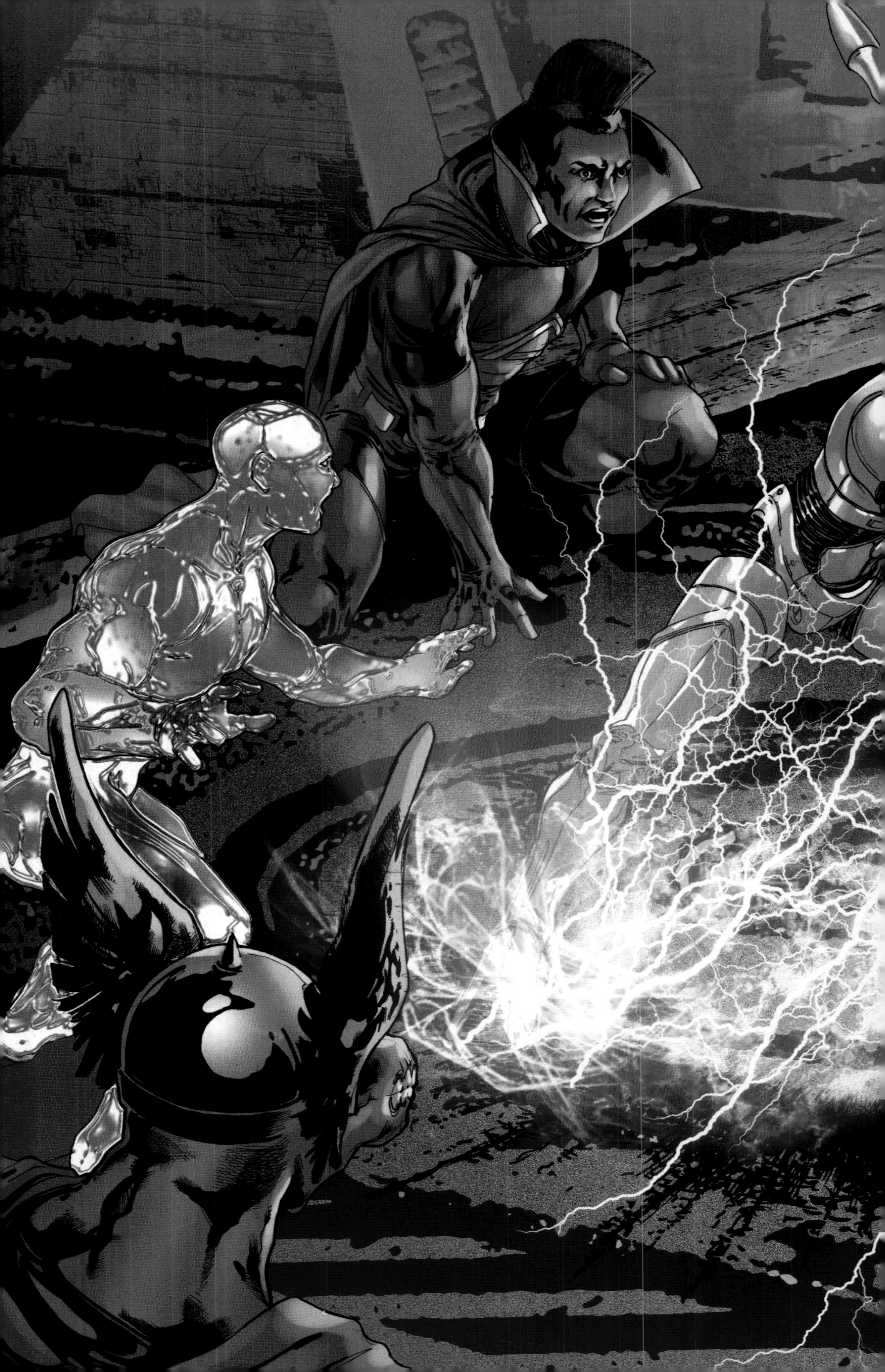

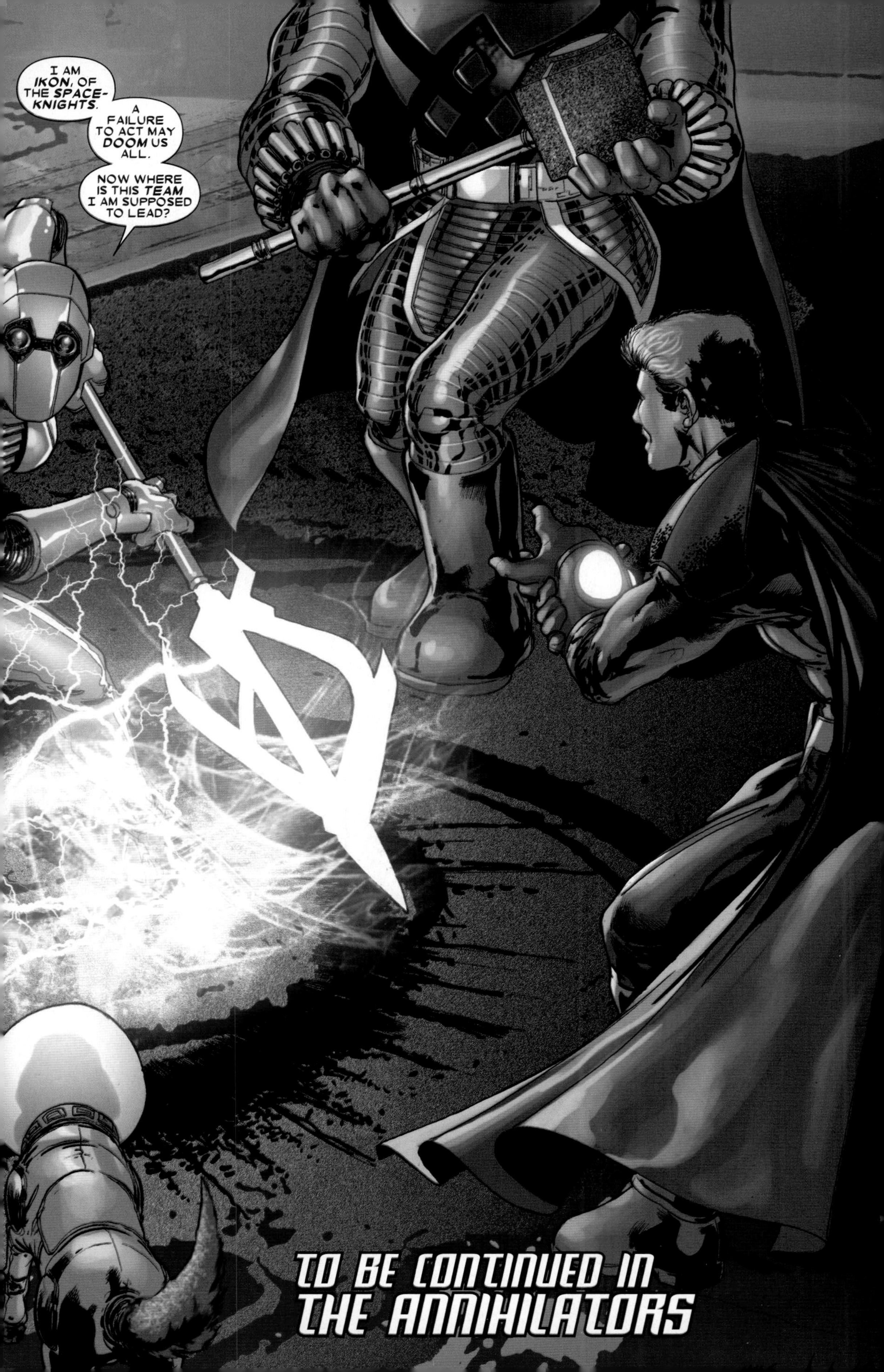
I AM IKON, OF THE SPACE-KNIGHTS.
A FAILURE TO ACT MAY DOOM US ALL.
NOW WHERE IS THIS TEAM I AM SUPPOSED TO LEAD?
TO BE CONTINUED IN THE ANNIHILATORS

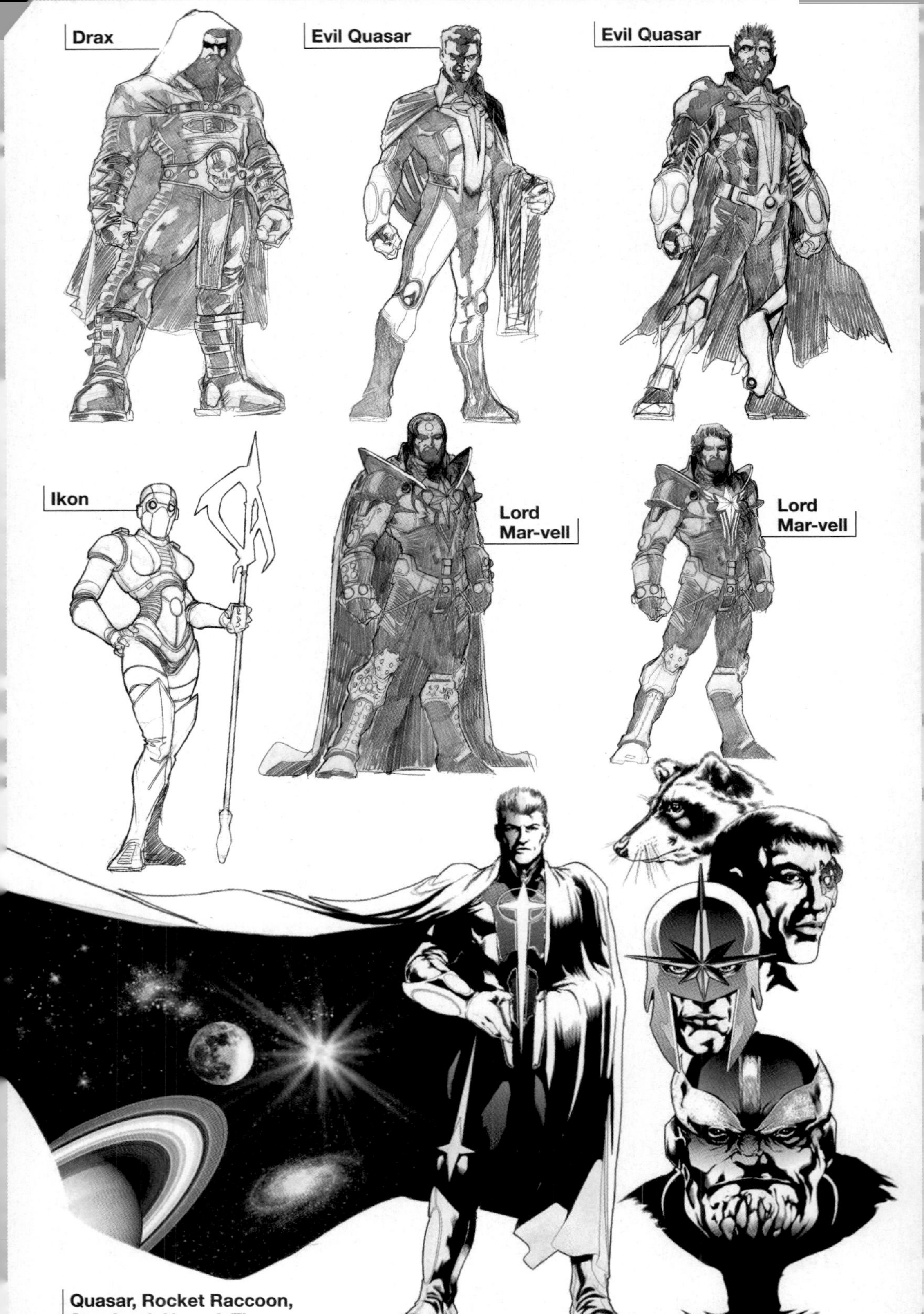
Drax
Evil Quasar
Evil Quasar
Ikon
Lord Mar-vell
Lord Mar-vell
Quasar, Rocket Raccoon, Star-Lord, Nova & Thanos